COMPUTATIONAL MODELLING OF MULTI-SCALE NON-FICKIAN DISPERSION IN POROUS MEDIA - AN APPROACH BASED ON STOCHASTIC CALCULUS

Authored by **Don Kulasiri**

Computational Modelling of Multi-Scale Non-Fickian Dispersion in Porous Media - An Approach Based on Stochastic Calculus
Authored by Don Kulasiri

Published by InTech

Janeza Trdine 9, 51000 Rijeka, Croatia

Publishing Process Manager Jelena Marusic

Technical Editor Teodora Smiljanic

Cover Designer InTech Design Team

Additional hard copies can be obtained from orders@intechopen.com

Computational Modelling of Multi-Scale Non-Fickian Dispersion in Porous Media - An Approach Based on Stochastic Calculus, Authored by Don Kulasiri
p. cm.
ISBN 978-953-307-726-0

For EU product safety concerns:
IN TECH d.o.o., Prolaz Marije Krucifikse Kozulić 3, 51000 Rijeka, Croatia,
info@intechopen.com or visit our website at intechopen.com.

Meet the author

Professor Don Kulasiri obtained B.Sc. (Hons) in Mechanical Engineering (1980) at University of Peradeniya, Sri Lanka, M.S. (1988) and PhD (1990) at Department of Biological Systems Engineering, Virginia Tech, U.S.A. His main research interests are in developing mathematical and computational models of biological and environmental systems to explain the experimental data, and to pursue these interests he has been developing research programmes at Lincoln University, Christchurch, New Zealand since 1991. He was appointed to a personal chair (professorship) in 1999 at Lincoln University, and he has been a visiting professor at the Computation and Mechanics division, Stanford University (6 months in 1998), Department of Mathematics, Princeton University (6 months in 2004) and Mathematical Institute, Oxford University (6 months in 2008 and a month in 2010). He has been a supervisor or co-supervisor of 30 PhD students so far, and co-authored over 100 journal publications and three books. He has been active in Computational Molecular Systems Biology for the last six years.

Contents

Preface

In this research monograph, we explain the development of a mechanistic, stochastic theory of nonfickian solute dispersion in porous media. We have included sufficient amount of background material related to stochastic calculus and the scale dependency of diffusivity in this book so that it could be read independently.

The advection-dispersion equation that is being used to model the solute transport in a porous medium is based on the premise that the fluctuating components of the flow velocity, hence the fluxes, due to a porous matrix can be assumed to obey a relationship similar to Fick's law. This introduces phenomenological coefficients which are dependent on the scale of the experiments. Our approach, based on the theories of stochastic calculus and differential equations, removes this basic premise, which leads to a multiscale theory with scale independent coefficients. We try to illustrate this outcome with available data at different scales, from experimental laboratory scales to regional scales in this monograph. There is a large body of computational experiments we have not discussed here, but their results corroborate with the gist presented here.

In Chapter 1, we introduce the context of the research questions we are seeking answers in the rest of the monograph. We dedicate the first part of Chapter 2 as a primer for Ito stochastic calculus and related integrals. We develop a basic stochastic solute transport model in Chapter 3 and develop a generalised model in one dimension in Chapter 4. In Chapter 5, we attempt to explain the connectivity of the basic premises in our theory with the established theories in fluctuations and dissipation in physics. This is only to highlight the alignment, mostly intuitive, of our approach with the established physics. Then we develop the multiscale stochastic model in Chapter 6, and finally we extend the approach to two dimensions in Chapters 7 and 8. We may not have cited many authors who have published research related to nonfickian dispersion because our intention is to highlight the problem through the literature. We refer to recent books which summarise most of the works and apologise for omissions as this monograph is not intented to be a comprehensive review.

There are many who helped me during the course of this research. I really appreciate Hong Ling's assistance during the last two and half years in writing and testing Mathematica programs. Without her dedication, this monograph would have taken many more months to complete. I am grateful to Amphun Chaiboonchoe for typing of the first six chapters in the first draft, and to Yao He for Matlab programming work for Chapter 6. I also acknowledge my former PhD students, Dr. Channa Rajanayake of Aqualinc Ltd, New Zealand, for the assistance in inverse method computations, and Dr. Zhi Xie of National Institute for Health (NIH), U.S.A., for the assistance in the neural networks computations.

This work is funded by the Foundation for Science and Technology of New Zealand (FoRST) through Lincoln Ventures Ltd. (LVL), Lincoln University. I am grateful to the Chief Scientist of LVL, my colleague, Dr. Ian Woodhead for overseeing the contractual matters to facilitate the work with a sense of humour. I also acknowledge Dr. John Bright of Aqualinc Ltd. for managing the project for many years.

Finally I am grateful to my wife Professor Sandhya Samarasinghe for understanding the value of this work. Her advice on neural networks helped in the computational methods developed in this work. Sandhya's love and patience remained intact during this piece of work. To that love and patience, I dedicate this monograph.

Don Kulasiri
Professor
Centre for Advanced Computational Solutions (C-fACS)
Lincoln University, New Zealand

1

NonFickian Solute Transport

1.1 Models in Solute Transport in Porous Media

This research monograph presents the modelling of solute transport in the saturated porous media using novel stochastic and computational approaches. Our previous book published in the North-Holland series of Applied Mathematics and Mechanics (Kulasiri and Verwoerd, 2002) covers some of our research in an introductory manner; this book can be considered as a sequel to it, but we include most of the basic concepts succinctly here, suitably placed in the main body so that the reader who does not have the access to the previous book is not disadvantaged to follow the material presented.

The motivation of this work has been to explain the dispersion in saturated porous media at different scales in underground aquifers (i.e., subsurface groundwater flow), based on the theories in stochastic calculus. Underground aquifers render unique challenges in determining the nature of solute dispersion within them. Often the structure of porous formations is unknown and they are sometimes notoriously heterogeneous without any recognizable patterns. This element of uncertainty is the over-arching factor which shapes the nature of solute transport in aquifers. Therefore, it is reasonable to review briefly the work already done in that area in the pertinent literature when and where it is necessary. These interludes of previous work should provide us with necessary continuity of thinking in this work.

There is monumental amount of research work done related to the groundwater flow since 1950s. During the last five to six decades major changes to the size and demographics of human populations occurred; as a result, an unprecedented use of the hydrogeological resources of the earth makes contamination of groundwater a scientific, socio-economic and, in many localities, a political issue. What is less obvious in terms of importance is the way a contaminant, a solute, disperses itself within the geological formations of the aquifers. Experimentation with real aquifers is expensive; hence the need for mathematical and computational models of solute transport. People have developed many types of models over the years to understand the dynamics of aquifers, such as physical scale models, analogy models and mathematical models (Wang and Anderson, 1982; Anderson and Woessner, 1992; Fetter, 2001; Batu, 2006). All these types of models serve different purposes.

Physical scale models are helpful to understand the salient features of groundwater flow and measure the variables such as solute concentrations at different locations of an artificial aquifer. A good example of this type of model is the two artificial aquifers at Lincoln University, New Zealand, a brief description of which appears in the monograph by Kulasiri and Verwoerd (2002). Apart from understanding the physical and chemical processes that occur in the aquifers, the measured variables can be used to partially validate the mathematical models. Inadequacy of these physical models is that their flow lengths are fixed (in the case of Lincoln aquifers, flow length is 10 m), and the porous structure cannot be changed, and therefore a study involving multi-scale general behaviour of solute transport in saturated porous media may not be feasible. Analog models, as the name suggests, are used to study analogues of real aquifers by using electrical flow through conductors. While worthwhile insights can be obtained from these models, the development of and experimentation on these models can be expensive, in addition to being cumbersome and time consuming.These factors may have contributed to the popular use of mathematical and computational models in recent decades (Bear, 1979; Spitz and Moreno, 1996; Fetter, 2001).

A mathematical model consists of a set of differential equations that describe the governing principles of the physical processes of groundwater flow and mass transport of solutes. These time-dependent models have been solved analytically as well as numerically (Wang and Anderson, 1982; Anderson and Woessner, 1992; Fetter, 2001). Analytical solutions are often based on simpler formulations of the problems, for example, using the assumptions on homogeneity and isotropy of the medium; however, they are rich in providing the insights into the untested regimes of behaviour. They also reduce the complexity of the problem (Spitz and Moreno, 1996), and in practice, for example, the analytical solutions are commonly used in the parameter estimation problems using the pumping tests (Kruseman and Ridder, 1970). Analytical solutions also find wide applications in describing the one-dimensional and two-dimensional steady state flows in homogeneous flow systems (Walton, 1979). However, in transport problems, the solutions of mathematical models are often intractable; despite this difficulty there are number of models in the literature that could be useful in many situations: Ogata and Banks' (1961) model on one-dimensional longitudinal transport is such a model. A one-dimensional solution for transverse spreading (Harleman and Rumer (1963)) and other related solutions are quite useful (see Bear (1972); Freeze and Cherry (1979)).

Numerical models are widely used when there are complex boundary conditions or where the coefficients are nonlinear within the domain of the model or both situations occur simultaneously (Zheng and Bennett, 1995). Rapid developments in digital computers enable the solutions of complex groundwater problems with numerical models to be efficient and faster. Since numerical models provide the most versatile approach to hydrology problems, they have outclassed all other types of models in many ways; especially in the scale of the problem and heterogeneity. The well-earned popularity of numerical models, however, may lead to over-rating their potential because groundwater systems are complicated beyond our capability to evaluate them in detail. Therefore, a modeller should pay great attention to the implications of simplifying assumptions, which may otherwise become a misrepresentation of the real system (Spitz and Moreno, 1996).

Having discussed the context within which this work is done, we now focus on the core problem, the solute transport in porous media. We are only concerned with the porous media saturated with water, and it is reasonable to assume that the density of the solute in water is similar to that of water. Further we assume that the solute is chemically inert with respect to the porous material. While these can be included in the mathematical developments, they tend to mask the key problem that is being addressed.

There are three distinct processes that contribute to the transport of solute in groundwater: convection, dispersion, and diffusion. Convection or advective transport refers to the dissolved solid transport due to the average bulk flow of the ground water. The quantity of solute being transported, in advection, depends on the concentration and quantity of ground water flowing. Different pore sizes, different flow lengths and friction in pores cause ground water to move at rates that are both greater and lesser than the average linear velocity. Due to these multitude of non-uniform non-parallel flow paths within which water moves at different velocities, mixing occurs in flowing ground water. The mixing that occurs in parallel to the flow direction is called hydrodynamic longitudinal dispersion; the word "hydrodynamic" signifies the momentum transfers among the fluid molecules. Likewise, the hydrodynamic transverse dispersion is the mixing that occurs in directions normal to the direction of flow. Diffusion refers to the spreading of the pollutant due to its concentration gradients, i.e., a solute in water will move from an area of greater concentration towards an area where it is less concentrated. Diffusion, unlike dispersion will occur even when the fluid has a zero mean velocity. Due to the tortuosity of the pores, the rate of diffusion in an aquifer is lower than the rate in water alone, and is usually considered negligible in aquifer flow when compared to convection and dispersion (Fetter, 2001). (Tortuosity is a measure of the effect of the shape of the flow path followed by water molecules in a porous media). The latter two processes are often lumped under the term hydrodynamic dispersion. Each of the three transport processes can dominate under different circumstances, depending on the rate of fluid flow and the nature of the medium (Bear, 1972).

The combination of these three processes can be expressed by the advection - dispersion equation (Bear, 1979; Fetter, 1999; Anderson and Woessner, 1992; Spitz and Moreno, 1996; Fetter, 2001). Other possible phenomenon that can present in solute transport such as adsorption and the occurrence of short circuits are assumed negligible in this case. Derivation of the advection-dispersion equation is given by Ogata (1970), Bear (1972), and Freeze and Cherry (1979). Solutions of the advection-dispersion equation are generally based on a few working assumptions such as: the porous medium is homogeneous, isotropic and saturated with fluid, and flow conditions are such that Darcy's law is valid (Bear, 1972; Fetter, 1999). The two-dimensional deterministic advection - dispersion equation can be written as (Fetter, 1999),

$$\frac{\partial C}{\partial t} = D_L\left(\frac{\partial^2 C}{\partial x^2}\right) + D_T\left(\frac{\partial^2 C}{\partial y^2}\right) - v_x\left(\frac{\partial C}{\partial x}\right), \tag{1.1.1}$$

where C is the solute concentration (M/L^3), t is time (T), D_L is the hydrodynamic dispersion coefficient parallel to the principal direction of flow (longitudinal) (L^2/T), D_T is the hydrodynamic dispersion coefficient perpendicular to the principal direction of flow (transverse) (L^2/T), and v_x is the average linear velocity (L/T) in the direction of flow.

It is usually assumed that the hydrodynamic dispersion coefficients will have Gaussian distributions that is described by the mean and variance; therefore we express them as follows:

Longitudinal hydrodynamic dispersion coefficient,

$$D_L = \frac{\sigma_L^2}{2t} \text{ , and} \tag{1.1.2}$$

transverse hydrodynamic dispersion coefficient,

$$D_T = \frac{\sigma_T^2}{2t} \tag{1.1.3}$$

where σ_L^2 is the variance of the longitudinal spreading of the plume, and σ_T^2 is the variance of the transverse spreading of the plume.

The dispersion coefficients can be thought of having two components: the first measure would reflect the hydrodynamic effects and the other component would indicate the molecular diffusion. For example, for the longitudinal dispersion coefficient,

$$D_L = \alpha_L v_L + D^* , \tag{1.1.4}$$

where α_L is the longitudinal dynamic dispersivity, v_L is the average linear velocity in longitudinal direction, and D^* is the effective diffusion coefficient.

A similar equation can be written for the transverse dispersion as well. Equation (1.1.4) introduces a measure of dispersivity, α_L, which has the length dimension, and it can be considered as the average length a solute disperses when mean velocity of solute is unity. Usually in aquifers, diffusion can be neglected compared to the convective flow. Therefore, if velocity is written as a derivative of travel length with respect to time, the simplified version of equation (1.1.4) ($D_L \approx \alpha_L v_i$) shows a similar relationship as Fick's law in physics.

(Fick's first law expresses that the mass of fluid diffusing is proportional to the concentration gradient. In one dimension, Fick's first law can be expressed as:

$$F = -D_d \frac{dC}{dx},$$

where F is the mass flux of solute per unit area per unit time ($M/L^2/T$), D_d is the diffusion coefficient (L^2/T), C is the solute concentration (M/L^3), and $\frac{dC}{dx}$ is the concentration gradient ($M/L^3/L$).

Fick's second law gives, in one dimension,

$$\frac{dC}{dt} = D_d \frac{\partial^2 C}{\partial x^2} .)$$

In general, dispersivity is considered as a property of a porous medium. Within equation (1.1.1) hydrodynamic dispersion coefficients represent the average dispersion for each direction for the entire domain of flow, and they mainly allude to and help quantifying the fingering effects on dispersing solute due to granular and irregular nature of the porous matrix through which solute flows. To understand how equation (1.1.1), which is a working model of dispersion, came about, it is important to understand its derivation better and the assumptions underpinning the development of the model.

1.2 Deterministic Models of Dispersion

There is much work done in this area using the deterministic description of mass conservation. In the derivation of advection–dispersion equation, also known as continuum transport model, (see Rashidi et al. (1999)), one takes the velocity fluctuations around the mean velocity to calculate the solute flux at a given point using the averaging theorems. The solute flux can be divided into two parts: mean advective flux which stems from the mean velocity and the mean concentration at a given point in space; and the mean dispersive flux which results from the averaging of the product of the fluctuating velocity component and the fluctuating concentration component. These fluctuations are at the scale of the particle sizes, and these fluctuations give rise to hydrodynamic dispersion over time along the porous medium in which solute is dispersed. If we track a single particle with time along one dimensional direction, the velocity fluctuation of the solute particle along that direction is a function of the pressure differential across the medium and the geometrical shapes of the particles, consequently the shapes of the pore spaces. These factors get themselves incorporated into the advection-dispersion equation through the assumptions which are similar to the Fick's law in physics.

To understand where the dispersion terms originate, it is worthwhile to review briefly the continuum model for the advection and dispersion in a porous medium (see Rashidi et al. (1999)). The mass conservation has been applied to a neutral solute assuming that the porosity of the region in which the mass is conserved does not change abruptly, i.e., changes in porosity would be continuous. This essentially means that the fluctuations which exist at the pore scale get smoothened out at the scale in which the continuum model is derived. However, the pore scale fluctuations give rise to hydrodynamic dispersion in the first place, and we can expect that the continuum model is more appropriate for homogeneous media.

Consider the one dimensional problem of advection and dispersion in a porous medium without transverse dispersion. Assuming that the porous matrix is saturated with water of density, ρ, the local flow velocity with respect to pore structure and the local concentration are denoted by $v(x,t)$ and $c(x,t)$ at a given point x, respectively. These variables are interpreted as intrinsic volume average quantities over a representative elementary volume (Thompson and Gray, 1986). Because the solute flux is transient, conservation of solute mass is expressed by the time-dependent equation of continuity, a form of which is given below:

$$\frac{\partial(\varphi\bar{c})}{\partial t}+\overbrace{\frac{\partial(\varphi\bar{v}_x\bar{c})}{\partial x}}^{A0}+\overbrace{\frac{\partial(\varphi J_x)}{\partial x}}^{B0}-\overbrace{\frac{\partial}{\partial x}\left(\varphi D_m(\frac{\partial\bar{c}}{\partial x}+\tau_x)\right)}^{C0}=0, \tag{1.2.1}$$

where $\bar{v}_x$ is the mean velocity in the x- direction, $\bar{c}$ is the intrinsic volume average concentration, φ is the porosity, J_x and τ_x are the macroscopic dispersive flux and diffusive tortuosity, respectively. They are approximated by using constitutive relationships for the medium.

In equation (1.2.1), the rate of change of the intrinsic volume average concentration is balanced by the spatial gradients of ***A0***, ***B0***, and ***C0*** terms, respectively. ***A0*** represents the average volumetric flux of the solute transported by the average flow of fluid in the x-direction at a given point in the porous matrix, x. However, the fluctuating component of the flux due to the velocity fluctuations around the mean velocity is captured through the term $J_x(x,t)$ in ***B0***,

$$J_x(x,t)=\overline{\xi_x c'}\,, \tag{1.2.2}$$

where ξ_x and c' are the "noise" or perturbation terms of the solute velocity and the concentration about their means, respectively. ***C0*** denotes the diffusive flux where D_m is the fundamental solute diffusivity.

The mean advective flux (***A0***) and the mean dispersive flux (***B0***) can be thought of as representations of the masses of solute carried away by the mean velocity and the fluctuating components of velocity. Further, we do not often know the behaviour of the fluctuating velocity component, and the following assumption, which relates the fluctuating component of the flux to the mean velocity and the spatial gradient of the mean concentration, is used to describe the dispersive flux,

$$J_x(x,t)\approx-\alpha_L\overline{v}_x\frac{\partial\overline{c}}{\partial x}. \tag{1.2.3}$$

The plausible reasoning behind this assumption is as follows: dispersive flux is proportional to the mean velocity and also proportional to the spatial gradient of the mean concentration. The proportionality constant, α_L, called the dispersivity, and the subscript L indicates the longitudinal direction. Higher the mean velocity, the pore-scale fluctuations are higher but they are subjected to the effects induced by the geometry of the pore structure. This is also true for the dispersive flux component induced by the concentration gradient. Therefore, the dispersivity can be expected to be a material property but its dependency on the spatial concentration gradient makes it vulnerable to the fluctuations in the concentration as so often seen in the experimental situations. The concentration gradients become weaker as the solute plume disperses through a bed of porous medium, and therefore, the mean dispersivity across the bed could be expected to be dependent on the scale of the experiment. This assumption (equation (1.2.3)) therefore, while making mathematical modelling simpler, adds another dimension to the problem: the scale dependency of the dispersivity; and therefore, the scale dependency of the dispersion coefficient, which is obtained by multiplying dispersivity by the mean velocity.

The dispersion coefficient can be expressed as,

$$D=\alpha_L\overline{v}_x\,. \tag{1.2.4}$$

The diffusive tortuosity is typically approximated by a diffusion model of the form,

$$\tau_x(x,t)\approx-G\frac{\partial\overline{c}}{\partial x}, \tag{1.2.5}$$

where G is a material coefficient bounded by 0 and 1.

By substituting equations (1.2.3), (1.2.4) and (1.2.5) into equation (1.2.1), the working model for solute transport in porous media can be expressed as,

$$\frac{\partial(\varphi \bar{c})}{\partial t}+\frac{\partial(\varphi \bar{v}_x \bar{c})}{\partial x}-\frac{\partial}{\partial x}\left(\varphi D+\varphi D_m(1-G)\frac{\partial \bar{c}}{\partial x}\right)=0. \quad (1.2.6)$$

$$\frac{\partial(\varphi \bar{c})}{\partial t}+\frac{\partial(\varphi \bar{v}_x \bar{c})}{\partial x}-\frac{\partial}{\partial x}\left(\varphi D+\varphi D_m(1-G)\frac{\partial \bar{c}}{\partial x}\right)=0.$$

The sum $D_H=\varphi D+\varphi D_m(1-G)\frac{\partial \bar{c}}{\partial x}$ is called the coefficient of hydrodynamic dispersion. In many cases, $D>>D_m$, therefore, $D_H \approx D$. We simply refer to D as the dispersion coefficient. For a flow with a constant mean velocity through a porous matrix having a constant porosity, we see that equation (1.2.6) becomes equation (1.1.1).

In his pioneering work, Taylor (1953) used an equation analogous to equation (1.2.6) to study the dispersion of a soluble substance in a slow moving fluid in a small diameter tube, and he primarily focused on modelling the molecular diffusion coefficient using concentration profiles along a tube for large time. Following that work, Gill and Sankarasubramanian (1970) developed an exact solution for the local concentration for the fully developed laminar flow in a tube for all time. Their work shows that the time-dependent dimensionless dispersion coefficient approaches an asymptotic value for larger time proving that Taylor's analysis is adequate for steady-state diffusion through tubes. Even though the above analyses are primarily concerned with the diffusive flow in small-diameter tubes, as a porous medium can be modelled as a pack of tubes, we could expect similar insights from the advection-dispersion models derived for porous media flow.

The assumptions described by equations (1.2.3) and (1.2.5) above are similar in form to Fick's first law, and therefore, we refer to equations (1.2.3) and (1.2.5) as Fickian assumptions. In particular, equation (1.2.3) defines the dispersivity and dispersion coefficient, which have become so integral to the modelling of dispersion in the literature. As we have briefly explained, dispersivity can be expected to be dependent on the scale of the experiment. This means that, in equations (1.1.1) and (1.2.6), the dispersion coefficient depends on the total length of the flow; mathematically, dispersion coefficient is not only a function of the distance variable x, but also a function of the total length. To circumvent the problems associated with solving the mathematical problem, the usual practice is to develop statistical relationships of dispersivity as a function of the total flow length. We discuss some of the relevant research related to ground water flow addressing the scale dependency problem in the next section.

1.3 A Short Literature Review of Scale Dependency

The differences between longitudinal dispersion observed in the field experiments and to the those conducted in the laboratory may be a result of the wide distribution of permeabilities and consequently the velocities found within a real aquifer (Theis 1962, 1963). Fried (1972) presented a few longitudinal dispersivity observations for several sites which were within the range of 0.1 to 0.6 m for the local (aquifer stratum) scale, and within 5 to 11 m for the global (aquifer thickness) scale. These values show the differences in magnitude of the dispersivities. Fried (1975) revisited and redefined these scales in terms of 'mean travelled distance' of the tracer or contaminant as local scale (total flow length between 2 and 4 m), global scale 1 (flow length between 4 and 20 m), global scale 2 (flow length between 20 and 100 m), and regional scale (greater than 100 m; usually several kilometres).

When tested for transverse dispersion, Fried (1972) found no scale effect on the transverse dispersivity and thought that its value could be obtained from the laboratory results. However, Klotz et al. (1980) illustrated from a field tracer test that the width of the tracer plume increased linearly with the travel distance. Oakes and Edworthy (1977) conducted the two-well pulse and the radial injection experiments in a sandstone aquifer and showed that the dispersivity readings for the fully penetrated depth to be 2 to 4 times the values for discrete layers. These results are inconclusive about the lateral dispersivity, and it is very much dependent on the flow length as well as the characteristics of porous matrix subjected to the testing.

Pickens and Grisak (1981), by conducting the laboratory column and field tracer tests, reported that the average longitudinal dispersivity, α_L, was 0.035 cm for three laboratory tracer tests with a repacked column of sand when the flow length was 30 cm. For a stratified sand aquifer, by analysing the withdrawal phase concentration histories of a single-well test of an injection withdrawal well, they showed α_L were 3 cm and 9 cm for flow lengths of 3.13 m and 4.99 m, respectively. Further, they obtained 50 cm dispersivity in a two-well recirculating withdrawal-injection tracer test with wells located 8 m apart. All these tests were conducted in the same site. Pickens and Grisak (1981) showed that the scale dependency of α_L for the study site has a relationship of $\alpha_L = 0.1\ L$, where L is the mean travel distance. Lallemand-Barres and Peaudecerf (1978, cited in Fetter, 1999) plotted the field measured α_L against the flow length on a log-log graph which strengthened the finding of Pickens and Grisak (1981) and suggested that α_L could be estimated to be about 0.1 of the flow length. Gelhar (1986) published a similar representation of the scale of dependency α_L using the data from many sites around the world, and according to that study, α_L in the range of 1 to 10 m would be reasonable for a site of dimension in the order of 1 km. However, the relationship of α_L and the flow length is more complex and not as simple as shown by Pickens and Grisak (1981), and Lallemand-Barres and Peaudecerf (1978, cited in Fetter, 1999). Several other studies on the scale dependency of dispersivity can be found in Peaudecef and Sauty (1978), Sudicky and Cherry (1979), Merritt et al. (1979), Chapman (1979), Lee et al. (1980), Huang et al. (1996b), Scheibe and Yabusaki (1998), Klenk and Grathwohl (2002), and Vanderborght and Vereecken (2002). These empirical relationships influenced the way models developed subsequently. For example, Huang et al. (1996a) developed an analytical solution for solute transport in heterogeneous porous media with scale dependent dispersion. In this model, dispersivity was assumed to increase linearly with flow length until some distance and reaches an asymptotic value.

Scale dependency of dispersivity shows that the contracted description of the deterministic model has inherent problems that need to be addressed using other forms of contracted descriptions. The Fickian assumptions, for example, help to develop a description which would absorb the fluctuations into a deterministic formalism. But this does not necessarily mean that this deterministic formalism is adequate to capture the reality of solute transport within, often unknown, porous structures. While the deterministic formalisms provide tractable and useful solutions for practical purposes, they may deviate from the reality they represent, in some situations, to unacceptable levels. One could argue that any contracted description of the behaviour of physical ensemble of moving particles must be mechanistic as well as statistical (Keizer, 1987); this may be one of the plausible reasons why there are many stochastic models of groundwater flow. Other plausible reasons are: formations of real world groundwater aquifers are highly heterogeneous, boundaries of the system are multifaceted, inputs are highly erratic, and other subsidiary conditions can be subject to variation as well. Heterogeneous underground formations pose major challenges of developing contracted descriptions of solute transport within them. This was illustrated by injecting a colour liquid into a body of porous rock material with irregular permeability (Øksendal, 1998). These experiments showed that the resulting highly scattered distributions of the liquid were not diffusing according to the deterministic models.

To address the issue of scale dependence of dispersivity and dispersion coefficient fundamentally, it has been argued that a more realistic approach to modelling is to use stochastic calculus (Holden et al., 1996; Kulasiri and Verwoerd, 1999, 2002). Stochastic calculus deals with the uncertainty in the natural and other phenomena using nondifferentiable functions for which ordinary differentials do not exist (Klebaner, 1998). This well established branch of applied mathematics is based on the premise that the differentials of nondifferential functions can have meaning only through certain types of integrals such as Ito integrals which are rigorously developed in the literature. In addition, mathematically well-defined processes such as Weiner processes aid in formulating mathematical models of complex systems.

Mathematical theories aside, one needs to question the validity of using stochastic calculus in each instance. In modelling the solute transport in porous media, we consider that the fluid velocity is fundamentally a random variable with respect to space and time and continuous but irregular, i.e., nondifferentiable. In many natural porous formations, geometrical structures are irregular and therefore, as fluid particles encounter porous structures, velocity changes are more likely to be irregular than regular. In many situations, we hardly have accurate information about the porous structure, which contributes to greater uncertainties. Hence, stochastic calculus provides a more sophisticated mathematical framework to model the advection-dispersion in porous media found in practical situations, especially involving natural porous formations. By using stochastic partial differential equations, for example, we could incorporate the uncertainty of the dispersion coefficient and hydraulic conductivity that are present in porous structures such as underground aquifers. The incorporation of the dispersivity as a random, irregular coefficient makes the solution of resulting partial differential equations an interesting area of study. However, the scale dependency of the dispersivity can not be addressed in this manner because the dispersivity itself is not a material property but it depends on the scale of the experiment.

1.4 Stochastic Models

The last three decades have seen rapid developments in theoretical research treating groundwater flow and transport problems in a probabilistic framework. The models that are developed under such a theoretical basis are called stochastic models, in which statistical uncertainty of a natural phenomenon, such as solute transport, is expressed within the stochastic governing equations rather than based on deterministic formulations. The probabilistic nature of this outcome is due to the fact that there is a heterogeneous distribution of the underlying aquifer parameters such as hydraulic conductivity and porosity (Freeze, 1975).

The researchers in the field of hydrology have paid more attention to the scale and variability of aquifers over the two past decades. It is apparent that we need to deal with larger scales more than ever to study the groundwater contaminant problems, which are becoming serious environmental concerns. The scale of the aquifer has a direct proportional relationship to the variability. Hence, the potential role of modelling in addressing these challenges is very much dependent on spatial distribution. When working with deterministic models, if we could measure the hydrogeologic parameters at very close spatial intervals (which is prohibitively expensive), the distribution of aquifer properties would have a high degree of detail. Therefore, the solution of the deterministic model would yield results with a high degree of reliability. However, as the knowledge of fine-grained hydrogeologic parameters are limited in practice, the stochastic models are used to understand dynamics of aquifers thus recognising the inherent probabilistic nature of the hydrodynamic dispersion.

Early research on stochastic modelling can be categorised in terms of three possible sources of uncertainties: (i) those caused by measurement errors in the input parameters, (ii) those caused by spatial averaging of input parameters, and (iii) those associated with an inherent stochastic description of heterogeneity porous media (Freeze, 1975). Bibby and Sunada (1971) utilised the Monte Carlo numerical simulation model to investigate the effect on the solution of normally distributed measurement errors in initial head, boundary heads, pumping rate, aquifer thickness, hydraulic conductivity, and storage coefficient of transient flow to a well in a confined aquifer. Sagar and Kisiel (1972) conducted an error propagation study to understand the influence of errors in the initial head, transmissibility, and storage coefficient on the drawdown pattern predicted by the Theis equation. We can find that some aspects of the flow in heterogeneous formations have been investigated even in the early 1960s (Warren and Price, 1961; McMillan, 1966). However, concerted efforts began only in 1975, with the pioneering work of Freeze (1975).

Freeze (1975) showed that all soils and geologic formations, even those that are homogeneous, are non-uniform. Therefore, the most realistic representation of a non-uniform porous medium is a stochastic set of macroscopic elements in which the three basic hydrologic parameters (hydraulic conductivity, compressibility and porosity) are assumed to come from the frequency distributions. Gelhar et al. (1979) discussed the stochastic microdispersion in a stratified aquifer, and Gelhar and Axness (1983) addressed the issue of three-dimensional stochastic macro dispersion in aquifers. Dagan (1984) analysed the solute transport in heterogeneous porous media in a stochastic framework, and Gelgar (1986) demonstrated that the necessity of the use of theoretical knowledge of stochastic subsurface hydrology in real world applications. Other major contributions to stochastic groundwater modelling in the decade of 1980 can be found in Dagan (1986), Dagan (1988) and Neuman et al. (1987).

Welty and Gelhar (1992) studied that the density and fluid viscosity as a function of concentration in heterogeneous aquifers. The spatial and temporal behaviour of the solute front resulting from variable macrodispersion were investigated using analytical results and numerical simulations. The uncertainty in the mass flux for the solute advection in heterogeneous porous media was the research focus of Dagan et al. (1992) and Cvetkovic et al. (1992). Rubin and Dagan (1992) developed a procedure for the characterisation of the head and velocity fields in heterogeneous, statistically anisotropic formations. The velocity field was characterised through a series of spatial covariances as well as the velocity-head and velocity-log conductivity. Other important contributions of stochastic studies in subsurface hydrology can be found in Painter (1996), Yang et al. (1996), Miralles-Wilhelm and Gelhar (1996), Harter and Yeh (1996), Koutsoyiannis (1999), Koutsoyiannis (2000), Zhang and Sun (2000), Foussereau et al. (2000), Leeuwen et al. (2000), Loll and Moldrup (2000), Foussereau et al. (2001) and, Painter and Cvetkovic (2001). In additional to that, Farrell (1999), Farrell (2002a), and Farrell (2002b) made important contributions to the stochastic theory in uncertain flows.

Kulasiri (1997) developed a preliminary stochastic model that describes the solute dispersion in a porous medium saturated with water and considers velocity of the solute as a fundamental stochastic variable. The main feature of this model is it eliminates the use of the hydrodynamic dispersion coefficient, which is subjected to scale effects and based on Fickian assumptions that were discussed in section 1.2. The model drives the mass conservation for solute transport based on the theories of stochastic calculus.

1.5 Inverse Problems of the Models

In the process of developing the differential equations of any model, we introduce the parameters, which we consider the attributes or properties of the system. In the case of groundwater flow, for example, the parameters such as hydraulic conductivity, transmissivity and porosity are constant within the differential equations, and it is often necessary to assign numerical values to these parameters. There are a few generally accepted direct parameter measurement methods such as the pumping tests, the permeameter tests and grain size analysis (details on these tests can be found in Bear et al. (1968) and Bear (1979)). The values of the parameters obtained from the laboratory experiments and/or the field scale experiments, may not represent the often complex patterns across a large geographical area, hence limiting the validity and credibility of a model. The inaccuracies of the laboratory tests are due to the scale differences of the actual aquifer and the laboratory sample. The heterogeneous porous media is, most of the time, laterally smaller than the longitudinal scale of the flow; in laboratory experiments, due to practical limitations, we deal with proportionally larger lateral dimensions. Hence, the parameter values obtained from the laboratory tests are not directly usable in the models, and generally need to be upscaled using often subjective techniques. This difficulty is recognised as a major impediment to wider use of the groundwater models and their full utilisation (Frind and Pinder, 1973). For this reason, Freeze (1972) stated that the estimation of the parameters is the 'Achilles' heel' of groundwater modelling.

Often we are interested in modelling the quantities such as the depth of water table and solute concentration, which are relevant to environmental decision making, and we measure these variables regularly and the measuring techniques tend to be relatively inexpensive. In addition, we can continuously monitor these decision (output) variables in many situations. Therefore, it is reasonable to assume that these observations of the output variables represent the current status of the system and measurement errors. If the dynamics of the system can be reliably modelled using relevant differential equations, we can expect the parameters estimated, based on the observations, may give us more reliable representative values than those obtained from the laboratory tests and literature. The observations often contain noise from two different sources: experimental errors and noisy system dynamics. Noise in the system dynamics may be due to the factors such as heterogeneity of the media, random nature of inputs (rainfall) and variable boundary conditions. Hence, the question of estimating the parameters from the observations should involve the models that consist of plausible representation of "noises".

1.6 Inherent Ill-Posedness

A well-posed mathematical problem derived from a physical system must satisfy the existence, uniqueness and stability conditions, and if any one of these conditions is not satisfied the problem is ill-posed. But in a physical system itself, these conditions do not necessarily have specific meanings because, regardless of their mathematical descriptions, the physical system would respond to any situation. As different combinations of hydrological factors would produce almost similar results, it may be impossible to determine a unique set of parameters for a given set of mathematical equations. So this lack of uniqueness could only be remedied by searching a large enough parameter space to find a set of parameters that would explain the dynamics of the maximum possible number, if not all, of the state variables satisfactorily. However, these parameter searches guarantee neither uniqueness nor stability in the inverse problems associated with the groundwater problems (Yew, 1986; Carrera, 1987; Sun, 1994; Kuiper, 1986; Ginn and Cushman, 1990; Keidser and Rosbjerg, 1991). The general consensus among groundwater modellers is that the inverse problem may at times result in meaningless solutions (Carrera and Neuman, 1986b). There are even those who argue that the inverse problem is hopelessly ill-posed and as such, intrinsically unsolvable (Carrera and Neuman, 1986b). This view aside, it has been established that a well-posed inverse problem can, in practice, yield an acceptable solution (McLaughlin and Townley, 1996). We adopt a positive view point that a mixture of techniques smartly deployed would render us the sets of effective parameters under the regimes of behaviours of the system which we are interested in. Given this stance, we would like to briefly discuss a number of techniques we found useful in the parameter estimation of the models we describe in this monograph. This discussion does not do justice to the methods mentioned and therefore we include the references for further study. We attempt to describe a couple of methods, which we use in this work, inmore detail, but the reader may find the discussion inadequate; therefore, it is essential to follow up the references to understand the techniques thoroughly.

1.7 Methods in Parameter Estimation

The trial and error method is the most simple but laborious for solving the inverse problems to estimate the parameters. In this method, we use a model that represents the aquifer system with some observed data of state variables. It is important, however, to have an expert who is familiar with the system available, i.e., a specific aquifer (Sun, 1994). Candidate parameter values are tried out until satisfactory outputs are obtained. However, if a satisfactory parameter fitting cannot be found, the modification of the model structure should be considered. Even though there are many advantages of this method such as not having to solve an ill-posed inverse problem, this is a rather tedious way of finding parameters when the model is a large one, and subjective judgements of experts may play a role in determining the parameters (Keidser and Rosbjerg, 1991).

The indirect method transfers the inverse problem into an optimisation problem, still using the forward solutions. Steps such as a criterion to decide the better parameters between previous and present values, and also a stopping condition, can be replaced with the computer-aided algorithms (Neuman, 1973; Sun, 1994). One draw back is that this method tends to converge towards local minima rather than global minima of objective functions (Yew, 1986; Kuiper, 1986; Keidser and Rosbjerg, 1991).

The direct method is another optimisation approach to the inverse problem. If the state variables and their spatial and temporal derivatives are known over the entire region, and if the measurement and mass balance errors are negligible, the flow equation becomes a first order partial differential equation in terms of the unknown aquifer parameters. Using numerical methods, the linear partial differential equations can be reduced to a linear system of equations, which can be solved directly for the unknown aquifer parameters, and hence the method is named "direct method" (Neuman, 1973; Sun, 1994).

The above three methods (trial and error, indirect, and direct) are well established and a large number of advanced techniques have been added. The algorithms to use in these methods can be found in any numerical recipes (for example, Press, 1992). Even though we change the parameter estimation problem for an optimisation problem, the ill-posedness of the inverse problems do still exist. The non-uniqueness of the inverse solution strongly displays itself in the indirect method through the existence of many local minima (Keidser and Rosbjerg, 1991). In the direct method the solution is often unstable (Kuiper, 1986). To overcome the ill-posedness, it is necessary to have supplementary information, or as often referred to as prior information, which is independent of the measurement of state variables. This can be designated parameter values at some specific time and space points or reliable information about the system to limit the admissible range of possible parameters to a narrower range or to assume that an unknown parameter is piecewise constant (Sun, 1994).

1.8 Geostatistical Approach to the Inverse Problem

The above described optimisation methods are limited to producing the best estimates and can only assess a residual uncertainty. Usually, output is an estimate of the confidence interval of each parameter after a post-calibration sensitivity study. This approach is deemed insufficient to characterise the uncertainty after calibration (Zimmerman et al., 1998). Moreover, these inverse methods are not suitable enough to provide an accurate representation of larger scales. For that reason, the necessity of having statistically sound methods that are capable of producing reasonable distribution of data (parameters) throughout larger regions was identified. As a result, a large number of geostatistically-based inverse methods have been developed to estimate groundwater parameters (Keidser and Rosbjerg, 1991; Zimmerman et al., 1998). A theoretical underpinning for new geostatistical inverse methods and discussion of geostatistical estimation approach can be found in many publications (Kitanidis and Vomvoris, 1983; Hoeksema and Kitanidis, 1984; Kitanidis, 1985; Carrera, 1988; Gutjahr and Wilson, 1989; Carrera and Glorioso, 1991; Cressie, 1993; Gomez-Hernandez et al., 1997; Kitanidis, 1997).

1.9 Parameter Estimation by Stochastic Partial Differential Equations

The geostatistical approaches mentioned briefly above estimate the distribution of the parameter space based on a few direct measurements and the geological formation of the spatial domain. Therefore, the accuracy of each method is largely dependent on direct measurements that, as mentioned above, are subject to randomness, numerical errors, and the methods of measurements tend to be expensive. Unny (1989) developed an approach based on the theory of stochastic partial differential equations to estimate groundwater parameters of a one-dimensional aquifer fed by rainfall by considering the water table depth as the output variable to identify the current state of the system. The approach inversely estimates the parameters by using stochastic partial differential equations that model the state variables of the system dynamics. Theory of the parameter estimation of stochastic processes can be found in Kutoyants (1984), Lipster and Shirayev (1977), and Basawa and Prakasa Rao (1980). We summarise this approach in some detail as we use this approach to estimate the parameters in our models in this monograph.

Let $V(t)$ denote a stochastic process having many realisations. We define the parameter set $\theta \in \Theta$ of a probability space which is given by a stochastic process $V^{\theta}(t)$, based on a set of realisations $\{ V^{\theta}(t) \; ; \; 0 \le t \le T \}$. Let the evolution of the family of stochastic processes $\{ V^{\theta}(t) \; ; t \in T \; ; \theta \in \Theta \}$ be described by a stochastic partial differential equation (SPDE),

$$\partial V^{\theta}(t) = A V^{\theta} dt + \xi(x,t)\, dt \,, \tag{1.9.1}$$

where A is a partial differential operator in space, and $\xi(x,t)dt$ is the stochastic process to represent a space- and time- correlated noise process.

The stochastic process $V^{\theta}(t)$ forms infinitely many sub event spaces with increasing times. We can describe the stochastic process $\{V^{\theta}(t); t \in T; \theta \in \Theta\}$, and AV^{θ} as a known function of the system,

$$AV^{\theta} = S(t,V,\theta) \,. \tag{1.9.2}$$

Therefore, the stochastic process $V^{\theta}(t)$ can be represented as the solution of the stochastic differential equation (SDE),

$$\partial V^{\theta}(t) = S(t,V,\theta)dt + \xi(x,t)dt, \tag{1.9.3}$$

where $S(.)$ is a given function.

We can transform the noise process by a Hilbert space valued standard Wiener process increments, $\beta(t)$. (A Hilbert space is an inner product space that is complete with respect to the norm defined by the inner product; and a separable Hilbert space should contain a complete orthonormal sequence (Young, 1988).) Therefore,

$$\partial V^{\theta}(t) = S(t,V,\theta)dt + d\beta(t). \tag{1.9.4}$$

The explanation on the transformation of $\xi(x,t)$ to $d\beta(t)$ can be found in Jazwinski (1970), and we develop this approach further in the later chapters. A standard Wiener process (often called a Brownian motion) on the interval $[0,T]$ is a random variable $W(t)$ that depends continuously on $t \in [0,T]$ and satisfies the following:

$$W(0)=0, \tag{1.9.5}$$

For $0 \le s < t \le T$,

$$W(t)-W(s) \approx \sqrt{t-s}\, N(0,1),$$

where $N(0,1)$ is a random variable generated with zero mean and unit variance.

Note that $d\beta(t)$ and $V^{\theta}(t)$ are defined on the same event space. We estimate the parameter θ using the maximum likelihood approach using all the available observations of the groundwater system. The estimate $\hat{\theta}$ of θ maximises the likelihood functions $V^{\theta}(t)$ given by (Basawa and Prakasa Rao, 1980):

$$L(\theta) = \exp\left\{ \int_0^T S(t,\ V,\ \theta)\, dV(t) - \frac{1}{2}\int_0^T S^2(t,\ V,\ \theta) dt \right\}. \tag{1.9.6}$$

The estimate $\hat{\theta}$ can be obtained as the solution to the equation,

$$\frac{\partial L(\theta)}{\partial \theta} = 0\,. \tag{1.9.7}$$

Maximising the likelihood function $L(\theta)$ is equivalent to maximising the log-likelihood function, $l(\theta) = ln\ L(\theta)$; hence, the maximum likelihood estimate can also be obtained as a solution to the equation

$$\frac{\partial l(\theta)}{\partial \theta} = 0\,. \tag{1.9.8}$$

Taking log on both sides of equation (1.9.6) we obtain,

$$l(\theta) = \int_0^T S(t,\ V,\ \theta)\, dV(t) - \frac{1}{2}\int_0^T S^2(t,\ V,\ \theta) dt. \tag{1.9.9}$$

The parameter is estimated as the solution to the equation

$$\int_0^T \frac{\partial}{\partial \theta} S(t,V,\theta)\, dV(t) - \int_0^T S(t,V,\theta) \frac{\partial}{\partial \theta} S(t,V,\theta) dt = 0\,. \tag{1.9.10}$$

The parameters can be estimated from equation (1.9.10), based on a single sample path. Let us now consider the case when M independent sample paths are being observed. The likelihood-function becomes the product of the likelihood functions for M individual sample paths,

$$L(\theta)=L(\theta,V_1)L(\theta,V_2)......L(\theta,V_M). \tag{1.9.11}$$

Taking the log on both sides of equation (1.9.11) we have the log-likelihood function,

$$l(\theta)=l(\theta,V_1)+l(\theta,V_2)+......+l(\theta,V_M). \tag{1.9.12}$$

Using equation (1.9.10) and (1.9.12)

$$l(\theta)=\sum_{i=1}^{M}\int_0^T S(t,\ V_i,\ \theta)\ dV_i(t)-\frac{1}{2}\sum_{i=1}^{M}\int_0^T S^2(t,\ V_i,\ \theta)dt. \tag{1.9.13}$$

Now the parameter estimate is obtained as the solution to

$$\sum_{i=1}^{M}\int_0^T\frac{\partial S(t,\ V_i,\ \theta)}{\partial\theta}\ dV_i(t)-\sum_{i=1}^{M}\int_0^T S(t,\ V_i,\ \theta)\frac{\partial S(t,\ V_i,\ \theta)}{\partial\theta}dt=0. \tag{1.9.14}$$

Lets consider two particular examples in which the drift term $S(t,\ V,\ \theta)$ depends linearly on its parameters θ.

Example 1

We define the problem of estimating a single parameter as follows,

$$S(t,\ V,\ \theta)=a_0(V,t)+\theta_1 a_1(V,t); \qquad \theta_1\in\theta \tag{1.9.15}$$

The log-likelihood function from equation (1.9.13) is

$$l(\theta_1)=\sum_{i=1}^{M}\int_0^T\{a_0(V_i,t)+\theta_1 a_1(V_i,t)\}dV_i(t)-\frac{1}{2}\sum_{i=1}^{M}\int_0^T\{a_0(V_i,t)+\theta_1 a_1(V_i,t)\}\{a_1(V_i,t)\}^2 dt=0. \tag{1.9.16}$$

The estimate $\hat{\theta}$ is obtained as a solution to the equation,

$$\sum_{i=1}^{M}\int_0^T\{a_1(V_i,t)\}dV_i(t)-\sum_{i=1}^{M}\int_0^T\{a_0(V_i,t)+\theta_1 a_1(V_i,t)\}\{a_1(V_i,t)\}dt=0. \tag{1.9.17}$$

Hence the estimate is given by

$$\hat{\theta}=\frac{\sum_{i=1}^{M}\int_0^T\{a_1(V_i,t)\}dV_i(t)-\sum_{i=1}^{M}\int_0^T\{a_0(V_i,t)\}\{a_l(V_i,t)\}dt}{\sum_{i=1}^{M}\int_0^T\{a_l^2(V_i,t)\}dt}. \tag{1.9.18}$$

Example 2

When there are two unknown parameters to be estimated,

$$S(t,\ V,\ \theta)=a_0(V,t)+\theta_1 a_1(V,t)+\theta_2 a_2(V,t); \qquad \theta_1,\theta_2\in\theta. \tag{1.9.19}$$

The log-likelihood function from equation (1.9.13) is,

$$l(\theta_1,\theta_2)=\sum_{i=1}^{M}\int_0^T\{a_0(V_i,t)+\theta_1 a_1(V_i,t)+\theta_2 a_2(V_i,t)\}\,dV_i(t)$$
$$-\frac{1}{2}\sum_{i=1}^{M}\int_0^T\{a_0(V_i,t)+\theta_1 a_1(V_i,t)+\theta_2 a_2(V_i,t)\}^2\,dt. \tag{1.9.20}$$

Differentiating the above two expressions with respect to θ_1 and θ_2, respectively, we can obtain the following two simultaneous equations:

$$\sum_{i=1}^{M}\int_0^T\{a_1(V_i,t)\}\,dV_i(t)-\sum_{i=1}^{M}\int_0^T\{a_0(V_i,t)+\theta_1 a_1(V_i,t)+\theta_2 a_2(V_i,t)\}\{a_1(V_i,t)\}dt=0, \tag{1.9.21}$$

and

$$\sum_{i=1}^{M}\int_0^T\{a_2(V_i,t)\}dV_i(t)-\sum_{i=1}^{M}\int_0^T\{a_0(V_i,t)+\theta_1 a_1(V_i,t)+\theta_2 a_2(V_i,t)\}\{a_2(V_i,t)\}dt=0. \tag{1.9.22}$$

We obtain the values for θ_1 and θ_2 as the solutions to these two equations.

1.10 Use of Artificial Neural Networks in Parameter Estimation

Over the past decades, Artificial Neural Networks (ANN) have become increasingly popular in many disciplines as a problem solving tool in data rich areas (Samarasinghe, 2006). ANN's flexible structure is capable of approximating almost any input-output relationship. Their application areas are almost limitless but fall into categories such as classification, forecasting and data modelling (Maren et al., 1990; Hassoun, 1995).

ANNs are a massively parallel-distributed information processing system that has certain performance characteristics resembling biological neural networks of the human brain (Samarasinghe, 2006, Haykin, 1994). We discuss only a few of main ANN techniques that are used in this work. General detail descriptions of ANN can be found in Samarasinghe (2006), Maren et al. (1990), Hertz et al. (1991), Hegazy et al. (1994), Hassoun (1995), Rojas (1996), and in many other excellent texts.

Back propagation may be the most popular algorithm for training ANN in a multi-layer perceptron (MLP), which is one of many different types of neural networks. MLP comprises a number of active 'neurons' connected together to form a network. The 'strengths' or 'weights' of these links between the neurons are where the functionality of the network resides (NeuralWare, 1998). Its basic structure is shown in Figure 1.1.

Rumelhart et al. (1986) developed the standard back propagation algorithm. Since then it has undergone many modifications to overcome the limitations; and the back propagation is essentially a gradient descent technique that minimises the network error function between the output vector and the target vector. Each input pattern of the training data set is passed through the network from the input layer to the output layer. The network output is compared with the described target output, and an error is computed based on the error function. This error is propagated backward through the network to each node, and correspondingly the connection weights are adjusted.

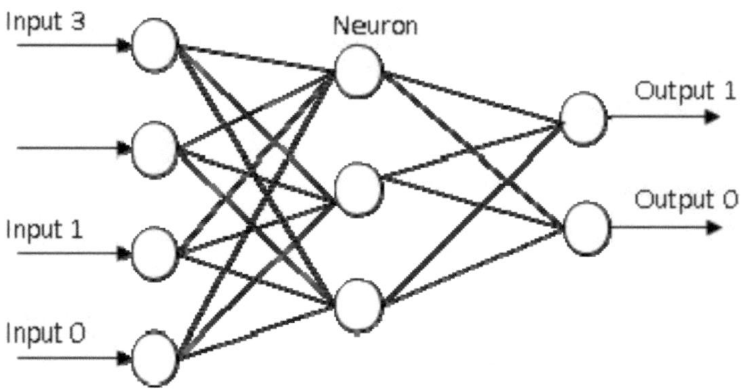

Figure 1.1. Basic structure of a multi-layer perceptron network.

The Self-Organizing Map (SOM) was developed by Kohonen (1982) and arose from the attempts to model the topographically organized maps found in the cortices of the more developed animal brains. The underlying basis behind the development of the SOM was that topologically correct maps can be formed in an n-dimensional array of processing elements that did not have this initial ordering to begin with. In this way, input stimuli, which may have many dimensions, can cluster to be represented by a one or two-dimensional vector which preserves the order of the higher dimensional data (NeuralWare, 1998). The SOM employs a type of learning commonly referred to as competitive, unsupervised or self-organizing, in which adjacent cells within the network are able to interact and adaptively evolved into the detectors of a specific input pattern (Kohonen, 1990). The SOM can be considered to be *"neural"* because the results have indicated that the adaptive processes utilized in the SOM may be similar to the processes at work within the brain (Kohonen, 1990). The SOM has the potential for extending its capability beyond the original purpose of modelling biological phenomena. Sorting items into categories of similar objects is a challenging, yet frequent task. The SOM achieves this task by nonlinearly projecting the data onto a lower dimensional display and by clustering the data (Kohonen, 1990). This attribute has been used in a wide number of applications ranging from engineering (including image and signal processing, image recognition, telecommunication, process monitoring and control, and robotics) to natural sciences, medicine, humanities, economics and mathematics (Kaski et al., 1998).

1.11 ANN Applications in Hydrology

It has been shown that ANN's flexible structure can provide simple and reasonable solutions to various problems in hydrology. Since the beginning of the last decade, ANN have been successfully employed in hydrology research such as rainfall-runoff modelling, stream flow forecasting, precipitation forecasting, groundwater modelling, water quality and management modelling (Morshed and Kaluarachchi, 1998; ASCE Task Committee on Application of ANN in Hydrology, 2000a, b; Maier and Dandy, 2000).

ANN applications in groundwater problems are limited when compared to other disciplines in hydrology. A few of applications relevant to our work are reviewed here. Ranjithan et al. (1993) successfully used ANNs to simulate the pumping index for hydraulic conductivity realisation to remediate groundwater under uncertainty. In the process of designing a reliable groundwater remediation strategy, clear identification of heterogeneous spatial variability of the hydrology parameters is an important issue. The association of hydraulic conductivity patterns and the level of criticalness need to be understood sufficiently for efficient screening. ANNs have been used to recognize and classify the variable patterns (Ranjithan et al., 1993). Similar work has been conducted by Rogers and Dowla (1994) to simulate a regulatory index for multiple pumping realizations at a contaminated site. In this study the supervised learning algorithm of back propagation has been used to train a network. The conjugate gradient method and weight elimination procedures have been employed to speed up the convergence and improve the performance, respectively. After training the networks, the ANN begins a search through various realizations of pumping patterns to determine matching patterns. Rogers et al. (1995) took another step forward to simulate the regulatory index, remedial index and cost index by using ANN for groundwater remediation. This research contributed towards addressing the issue of escalating costs of environmental cleanup.

Zhu (2000) used ANN to develop an approach to populate a soil similarity model that was designed to represent soil landscape as spatial continua for hydrological modelling at watershed of mesoscale size. Coulibaly et al. (2001) modelled the water table depth fluctuations by using three types of functionally different ANN models: Input Delay Neural Network (IDNN), Recurrent Neural Network (RNN) and Radial Basis Function Network (RBFN). This type of study has significant implications for groundwater management in the areas with inadequate groundwater monitoring networks (Maier and Dandy, 2000). Hong and Rosen (2001) demonstrated that the unsupervised self-organising map was an efficient tool for diagnosing the effect of the storm water infiltration on the groundwater quality variables. In addition, they showed that SOM could also be useful in extracting the dependencies between the variables in a given groundwater quality dataset.

Balkhair (2002) presented a method for estimating the aquifer parameters in large diameter wells using ANN. The designed network was trained to learn the underlying complex relationship between input and output patterns of the normalized draw down data generated from an analytical solution and its corresponding transmissivity values. The ANN was trained with a fixed number of input draw down data points obtained from the analytical solution for a pre-specified ranges of aquifer parameter values and time-series data. The trained network was capable of producing aquifer parameter values for any given input pattern of normalized draw down data and well diameter size. The values of aquifer parameters obtained using this approach were in a good agreement with those obtained by other published results. Prior knowledge about the aquifer parameter values has served as a valuable piece of information in this ANN approach.

Rudnitskaya et al. (2001) developed a methodology to monitor groundwater quality using an array of non-specific potentiometric chemical sensors with data processing by ANN. Lischeid (2001) studied the impact of long-lasting non-point emissions on groundwater and stream water in remote watersheds using a neural network approach. Scarlatos (2001) used ANN method to identify the sources, distribution and fate of fecal coliform populations in the North Fork of the New River that flows through the City of Fort Lauderdale, Florida, USA and how the storm water drainage from sewers affects the groundwater. Other ANN applications in water resources can be found in Aly and Peralta (1999), Mukhopadhyay (1999), Freeze and Gorelick (2000), Johnson and Rogers (2000), Hassan and Hamed (2001), Beaudeau et al. (2001), and Lindsay et al. (2002).

2

Stochastic Differential Equations and Related Inverse Problems

2.1 Concepts in Stochastic Calculus

As we have discussed in chapter 1, the deterministic mathematical formulation of solute transport through a porous medium introduces the dispersivity, which is a measure of the distance a solute tracer would travel when the mean velocity is normalized to be one. One would expect such a measure to be a mechanical property of the porous medium under consideration, but the evidence are there to show that dispersivity is dependent on the scale of the experiment for a given porous medium. One of the challenges in modelling the phenomena is to discard the Fickian assumptions, through which dispersivity is defined, and develop a mathematical discription containing the fluctuations associated with the mean velocity of a physical ensemble of solute particles. To this end, we require a sophisticated mathematical framework, and the theory of stochastic processes and differential equations is a natural mathematical setting. In this chapter we review some essential concepts in stochastic processes and stochastic differential equations in order to understand the stochastic calculus in a more applied context.

A deterministic variable expressed as a function of time uniquely determines the value of the variable at a given time. A stochastic variable Y, on the other hand, is one that does not have a unique value; it can have any one out of a set of values. We assign a unique label ω to each possible value of the stochastic variable, and set Ω to denote the set of all such values. When Y represents, for example the outcome of throwing dice, Ω may be a finite set of discrete numbers, and when Y is the instantaneous position of a fluid particle, it may be a continuous range of real numbers. If a particular value y_ω is observed for Y, this is called an event F. In fact, this is only the simplest prototype of an event; other possibilities might be that the value of Y is observed not to be y_ω (the complementary event), or that a value within a certain range of ω values is observed. The set of all possible events is denoted by F. Even though the outcome of a particular observation of Y is unpredictable, the probability of observing y_ω must be determined by a probability function $P(\omega)$. By using the standard methods of probability calculus, this implies that a probability $P(F)$ can also be assigned to compound events F e.g. by appropriate summation or integration over ω values. For this to work, F must satisfy the criteria that for any event F in its complement F^c must also belong to F, and that for any subset of F's the union of these must also belong to F. The explanation above of what it means to call Y a stochastic variable, is encapsulated in formal mathematical language by saying "Y is defined on a probability space (ω, F, P)".

In describing physical systems, deterministic variables usually depend on additional parameters such as time. Similarly, a stochastic variable may depend on an additional parameter t (for example, the probability may change with time, i.e. $P(y_\omega,t)$. The collection of stochastic variables, Y_t, is termed a stochastic process. The word 'process' suggests temporal development and is particularly appropriate when the parameter t has the meaning of time, but mathematically it is equally well used for any other parameter, usually assumed to be a real number in the interval $[0,\infty)$.

The label ω is often explicitly included in writing the notation $Y_t(\omega)$, for an individual value obtained from the set of Y-values at a fixed t. Conversely, we might keep ω fixed, and let t vary; a natural notation would be to write $Y_\omega(t)$. In physical terms, one may think of this as the set of values obtained from a single experiment to observe the time development of the stochastic variable Y. When the experiment is repeated, a different set of observations are obtained; those may be labelled by a different value of ω. Each such sequence of observed Y-values is called a realization (or sometimes a path) of the stochastic process, and from this perspective ω may be considered as labelling the realizations of the process. It is seen that it is somewhat arbitrary which of ω and t is considered to be a label, and which is an independent variable; this is sometimes expressed by writing the stochastic process as $Y(t,\omega)$.

In standard calculus, we deal with differentiable functions which are continuous except perhaps in certain locations of the domain under consideration. To understand the continuity of the functions better we make use of the definitions of the limits. We call a function f, a continuous function at the point $t = t_0$ if $\lim_{t\to t_0} f(t) = f(t_0)$ regardless of the direction t approaches t_0. A right-continuous function at t_0 has a limiting value only when t approaches t_0 from the right direction, i.e. t is larger than t_0 in the vicinity of t_0. We will denote this as

$$f(t+)=\lim_{t\downarrow t_0} f(t)=f(t_0)\ .$$

Similarly a left-continuous function at t_0 can be represented as

$$f(t-)=\lim_{t\uparrow t_0} f(t)=f(t_0)\ .$$

These statements imply that a continuous function is both right-continuous and left-continuous at a given point of t. Often we encounter functions having discontinuities; hence the need for the above definitions. To measure the size of a discontinuity, we define the term "jump" at any point t to be a discontinuity where the both $f(t+)$ and $f(t-)$ exist and the size of the jump be $\Delta f(t)=f(t+)-f(t-)$. The jumps are the discontinuities of the first kind and any other discontinuity is called a discontinuity of the second kind. Obviously a function can only have countable number of jumps in a given range. From the mean value theorem in calculus, it can be shown that we can differentiate a function in a given interval only if the function is either continuous or has a discontinuity of the second kind during the interval. Stochastic calculus is the calculus dealing with often non-differentiable functions having jumps without discontinuities of the second kind. One such example of a function is the Wiener process (Brownian motion). One realization of the standard Wiener process is given in Figure 2.1. These statements imply that a continuous function is both right-continuous and left-continuous at a given point of t. Often we encounter functions having discontinuities; hence the need for the above definitions. To measure the size of a discontinuity, we define the term "jump" at any point t to be a discontinuity where the both $f(t+)$ and $f(t-)$ exist and the size of the jump be $\Delta f(t)=f(t+)-f(t-)$. The jumps are the discontinuities of the first kind and any other discontinuity is called a discontinuity of the second kind. Obviously a function can only have countable number of jumps in a given range. From the mean value theorem in calculus, it can be shown that we can differentiate a function in a given interval only if the function is either continuous or has a discontinuity of the second kind during the interval. Stochastic calculus is the calculus dealing with often non-differentiable functions having jumps without discontinuities of the second kind. One such example of a function is the Wiener process (Brownian motion). One realization of the standard Wiener process is given in Figure 2.1.

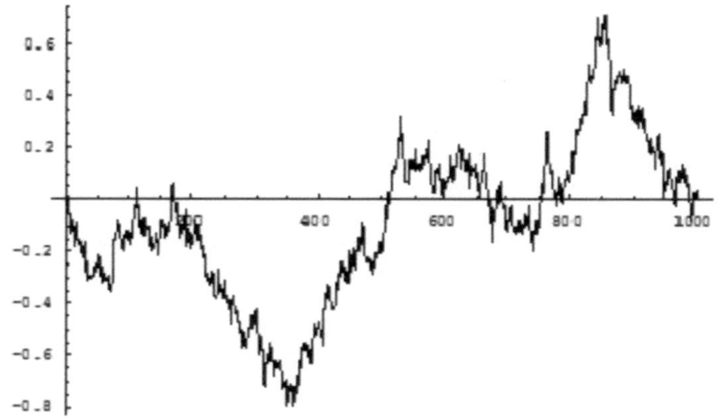

Figure 2.1. A realization of the Wiener process; this is a continuous but non-differentiable function.

The increments of the function shown in Figure 2.1 are irregular and a derivative cannot be defined according to the mean value theorem. This is because of the fact that the function changes erratically within small intervals, however small that interval may be. Therefore we have to devise new mathematical tools that would be useful in dealing with these irregular, non-differentiable functions.

Variation of a function f on $[a,b]$ is defined as

$$V_f([a,b])=\lim_{\delta_n \to 0}\sum_{i=1}^{n}\left|f(t_i^n)-f(t_{i-1}^n)\right| \tag{2.1.1}$$

where $\delta_n=\max_{1\le i\le n}(t_i-t_{i-1})$.

If $V_f([a,b])$ is finite such as in continuous differentiable functions then f is called a function of finite variation on $[a,b]$. Variation of a function is a measure of the total change in the function value within the interval considered. An important result (Theorem 1.7 Klebaner (1998)) is that a function of finite variation can only have a countable number of jumps. Furthermore, if f is a continuous function, f' exists and $\int\left|f'(t)\right|dt<\infty$ then f is a function of finite variation. This implies that a function of finite variation on [*a*,*b*] is differentiable on [*a*,*b*], and a corollary is that a function of infinite variation is non-differentiable. Another mathematical construct that plays a major role in stochastic calculus is the quadratic variation. In stochastic calculus, the quadratic variation of a function *f* over the interval [0,*t*] is given by

$$[f](t)=\lim_{\delta_n\to 0}\sum_{i=1}^{n}(g(t_i^n)-g(t_{i-1}^n))^2 \quad , \tag{2.1.2}$$

where the limit is taken over the partitions:

$$0=t_0^n<t_1^n<...<t_n^n=t \, ,$$

with $\delta_n=\max\limits_{1\le i\le n}(t_i^n-t_{i-1}^n)\to 0.$

It can be proved that the quadratic variation of a continuous function with finite variation is zero. However, the functions having zero quadratic variation may have infinite variation such as zero energy processes (Klebaner, 1998). If a function or process has a finite positive quadratic variation within an interval, then its variation is infinite, and therefore the function is continuous but not differentiable.

Variation and quadratic variation of a function are very important tools in the development of stochastic calculus, even though we do not use quadratic variation in standard calculus.

We also define quadratic covariation of functions f and g on [0,*t*] by extending equation (2.1.2):

$$[f,g](t)=\lim_{\delta_n\to 0}\sum_{i=0}^{n-1}(f(t_{i+1}^n)-f(t_i^n))(g(t_{i+1}^n)-g(t_i^n)) \tag{2.1.3}$$

when the limit is taken over partitions $\{t_i^n\}$ of [0,*t*] with $\delta_n=\max\limits_{1\le i\le n}(t_{i+1}^n-t_i^n)\to 0$. It can be shown that if both the functions are continuous and one is of finite variation, the quadratic covariation is zero.

Quadratic covariation of two functions, *f* and *g*, has the following properties:

1. Polarization identity

Polarization identity expresses the quadratic covariation, $[f,g](t)$, in terms of quadratic variation of individual functions.

$$[f,g](t)=\frac{1}{2}([f+g,f+g](t)-[f,f](t)-[g,g](t)) \tag{2.1.4}$$

2. Symmetry

$$[f,g](\mathrm{t}) = [g,f](\mathrm{t}) \; . \tag{2.1.5}$$

3. Linearity

Using polarization identity and symmetry one can show that covariation is linear for any constants a and b,

$$[af+bg,h](t)=a[f,h](t)+b[g,h](t)\ . \tag{2.1.6}$$

Quadratic variation of a function $[f](t)$ and covariation $[f,g](t)$ are measures of change in the functional values over a given range $[0,t]$.

In many situations where stochastic processes are involved, we would like to know the limiting values of useful random variables, i.e. whether they approach a some sort of a "steady state" or asymptotic behaviour. It is natural to define the steady state of random variable within a probabilistic context. Therefore, in stochastic processes, we define the convergence of random variables using the following four different criteria:

1. Almost sure convergence

Random variables $\{X_n\}$ converges to $\{X\}$ with probability one:

$$P(\{\omega\in\Omega:\lim_{n\to\infty}|X_n(\omega)-X(\omega)|=0\})=1\ .$$

2. Mean-square convergence

$\{X_n\}$ converges to $\{X\}$ such a way that $E(X_n^2)<\infty$ for $n = 1,2,...,n$, $E(X)<\infty$ and

$$\lim_{n\to\infty}E(|X_n-X|^2)=0\ .$$

3. Convergence in probability

$\{X_n\}$ converges to $\{X\}$ with zero probability of having a difference between the two processes:

$$\lim_{n\to\infty}P(\{\omega\in\Omega;|X_n(\omega)-X(\omega)|\geq\varepsilon)=0\ \text{, for all}\ \ \varepsilon>0.$$

Convergence in probability is called stochastic convergence as well.

Note that we adopt the notation of E(,) or E[,] to denote the expected value (mean value) of a stochastic variable. In physical literature, this is denoted by "< , >".

4. Convergence in distribution

Distribution function of $\{X_n\}$ converges to that of $\{X\}$ at any point of continuity of the limiting distribution (i.e. the distribution function of $\{X\}$).

These four criteria add another dimension to our discussion of the asymptotic behaviour of a process. These arguments can be extended in comparing stochastic processes with each other.

Unlike in deterministic variables where any asymptotic behaviour can clearly be identified either graphically or numerically, stochastic variables do require adherence to one of the convergence criteria mentioned above which are called the "criteria for strong convergence". There are weakly converging stochastic processes and we do not discuss the weak convergence criteria as they are not relevant to the development of the material in this book.

In standard calculus we have continuous functions with discontinuities at finitely many points and we integrate them using the definition of Riemann integral of a function $f(t)$ over the interval $[a,b]$:

$$\int_a^b f(t)dt = \lim_{\delta\to 0}\sum_{i=1}^{n} f(\xi_i^n)\,(t_i^n - t_{i-1}^n), \tag{2.1.7}$$

where t_i^n's represents partitions of the interval,

$$a = t_0^n < t_1^n < t_2^n \ldots. < t_n^n = b\,,$$

$$\delta = \max_{1\le i\le n}(t_i^n - t_{i-1}^n), \quad \text{and} \qquad t_{i-1}^n \le \xi_i^n \le t_i^n \quad .$$

Riemann integral is used extensively in standard calculus where continuous functions are the main concern. The integral converges regardless of the chosen ξ_i^n within $[t_{i-1}^n, t_i^n]$.

A generalization of Riemann integral is Stieltjes integral which is defined as the integral of $f(t)$ with respect to a monotone function $g(t)$ over the interval $[a,b]$:

$$\int_a^b f(t)dg(t) = \lim_{\delta\to 0}\sum_{i=1}^{n} f(\xi_i)(g(t_i^n) - g(t_{i-1}^n)) \tag{2.1.8}$$

with the same definitions as above for δ and t_i^n's. It can be shown that for the Stieltjes integral to exist for any continuous function $f(t)$, $g(t)$ must be a function with finite variation on $[a,b]$. This means that if $g(t)$ has infinite variation on $[a,b]$ then for such a function, integration has to be defined differently. This is the case in the integration of the continuous stochastic processes, therefore, can not be integrated using Stieltjes integral. Before we discuss alternative forms of integration that can be applied to the functions of positive quadratic variation, i.e. the functions of infinite variation, we introduce a fundamentally important stochastic process, the Wiener process and its properties.

2.2 Wiener Process

The botanist Robert Brown, first observed that pollen grains suspended in liquid, undergo irregular motion. Centuries later, it was realised that the physical explanation of this is that the pollen grain is continually bombarded by molecules of the liquid travelling with different speeds in different directions. Over a time scale that is large compared with the intervals between molecular impacts, these will average out and no net force is exerted on the grain. However, this will not happen over a small time interval; and if the mass of the grain is small enough to undergo appreciable displacement in the small time interval as the result of molecular impacts, an observable erratic motion results. The crucial point to notice in the present context is that while the impacts and therefore the individual displacements suffered by the grain can be considered independent at different times, the actual position of the grain can only change continuously.

In the physical Brownian motion, there are small but nevertheless finite intervals between the impulses of molecules colliding with the pollen grain. Consequently, the path that the grain follows, consists of a sequence of straight segments forming an irregular but continuous line - a so-called random walk. Each straight segment can be considered an increment of the momentary position of the grain.

The mathematical idealisation of the Brownian motion let the interval between increments approach zero. The resulting process - called the Wiener process due to N. Wiener - is difficult to conceptualise: for example, consideration shows that the resulting position is everywhere continuous, but nowhere differentiable. This means that while the particle has a position at any moment, and since this position is changing it is moving, yet no velocity can be defined. Nevertheless as discussed by Stroock and Varadhan (1979) a consistent mathematical description is obtained by defining the position as a stochastic process $B(t,\omega)$ with the following properties that are suggested as a mathematical model for the Brownian motion- a Wiener process:

P1: $B(0,\omega) = 0$, i.e. choose the position of the particle at the arbitrarily chosen initial time $t = 0$ as the coordinate origin;

P2: $B(t,\omega)$ has independent increments, i.e. $B(t_1,\omega)$, $\{B(t_2,\omega) - B(t_1,\omega)\}$,…, $\{B(t_k,\omega) - B(t_{k-1},\omega)\}$ are independent for all $0 \le t_1 < t_2 \ldots < t_k$;

P3: $\{B(t_{i+1},\omega) - B(t_i,\omega)\}$ is normally distributed with mean 0 and variance $(t_{i+1} - t_i)$;

P4: The stochastic variation of $B(t,\omega)$ at fixed time t is determined by a Gaussian probability;

P5: The Gaussian has a zero mean, $E[B(t,\omega)] = 0$ for all values of t;

P6: $B(t,\omega)$ are continuous functions of t for $t \ge 0$;

P7: The covariance of Brownian motion is determined by a correlation between the values of $B(t,\omega)$ at times t_i and t_j (for fixed ω), given by

$$E\left[B(t_i,\omega)\ B(t_j,\omega)\right] = \min(t_i,t_j). \tag{2.2.1}$$

When applied to $t_i = t_j = t$, P7 reduces to the statement that

$$Var\left[B(t,w)\right] = t, \tag{2.2.2}$$

where '*Var*' means statistical variance. For the Brownian motion this can be interpreted as the statement that the radius within which the particle can be found increases proportional to time.

Because the Wiener process is defined by the independence of its increments, it is for some purposes convenient to reformulate the variance of a Wiener process in terms of the variance of the increments:

From P3, for $t_i < t_j$:

$$Var[B(t_j,\omega) - B(t_i,\omega)] = t_j - t_i \tag{2.2.3}$$

Bearing in mind that the statistical definition of the variance of a quantity X reduces to the expectation value expression $Var[X]=E[X^2]-(E[X])^2$ and that the expectation value or mean of a Wiener process is zero, we can rewrite this as,

$$E[\{B(t_2,\omega) - B(t_1,\omega)\}^2] = Var[B(t_2,\omega) - B(t_1,\omega)], \quad \text{i.e.} \quad E[\Delta B \cdot \Delta B] = \Delta t\,, \tag{2.2.4}$$

where Δt is defined to mean the time increment for a fixed realization ω.

The connection between the two formulations is established by similarly rewriting equation (2.2.3) and then applying equation (2.2.1):

$$\begin{aligned} Var[B(t_1,\omega) - B(t_2,\omega)] &= E[\{B(t_1,\omega) - B(t_2,\omega)\}^2] \\ &= E[B^2(t_1,\omega) + B^2(t_1,\omega) - 2B(t_1,\omega)B(t_2,\omega)] \\ &= t_1 + t_2 - 2\min(t_1,t_2) \\ &= t_1 - t_2 \text{ for } t_1 > t_2\,. \end{aligned}$$

2.3 Further Properties of Wiener Process and their Relationships

Consider a stochastic process $X(t,\omega)$ having a stationary joint probability distribution and $E(X(t,\omega)) = 0$, i.e. the mean value of the process is zero. The Fourier transform of $Var(X(t,\omega))$ can be written as,

$$S(\lambda,\omega) = \frac{1}{2\pi}\int_{-\infty}^{\infty} Var(X(\tau,\omega)\, e^{-i\lambda\tau} d\tau \quad . \tag{2.3.1}$$

$S(\lambda,\omega)$ is called the spectral density of the process $X(t,\omega)$ and is also a function of angular frequency λ. The inverse of the Fourier transform is given by

$$Var(X(\tau,\omega)) = \int_{-\infty}^{\infty} S(\lambda,\omega)\, e^{i\lambda\tau} d\lambda\,. \tag{2.3.2}$$

Therefore variance of $X(0,\omega)$ is the area under a graph of spectral density $S(\lambda,\omega)$ against λ :

$$Var(X(0,\omega)) = E(X^2(0,\omega)) \quad \text{because} \quad E(X(t,\omega)){=}0\,.$$

Spectral density $S(\lambda,\omega)$ is considered as the "average power" per unit frequency at λ which gives rise to the variance of $X(t,\omega)$ at $\tau = 0$. If the average power is a constant, the power is distributed uniformly across the frequency spectrum, such as the case for white light, then $X(t,\omega)$ is called white noise. White noise is often used to model independent random disturbances in engineering systems, and the increments of Wiener process have the same characteristics as white noise. Therefore white noise $(\zeta(t))$ is defined as

$$\zeta(t) = \frac{dB(t)}{dt} \quad , \quad \text{and} \quad dB(t) = \zeta(t)dt \, . \tag{2.3.3}$$

We will use this relationship to formulate stochastic differential equations.

As shown before, the relationships among the properties mentioned above can be derived starting from P1 to P7. For example, let us evaluate the covariance of Wiener processes, $B(t_i,\omega)$ and $B(t_j,\omega)$:

$$Cov(B(t_i,\omega)B(t_j,\omega)) = E(B(t_i,\omega)\,B(t_j,\omega)) \, . \tag{2.3.4}$$

Assuming $t_i < t_j$, we can express:

$$B(t_j,\omega) = B(t_i,\omega) + B(t_j,\omega) - B(t_i,\omega) \, . \tag{2.3.5}$$

Therefore,

$$\begin{aligned} E(B(t_i,\omega)\,B(t_j,\omega)) &= E(B(t_i,\omega)(B(t_i,\omega) + B(t_j,\omega) - B(t_i,\omega)) \\ &= E(B^2(t_i,\omega) + B(t_i,\omega)B(t_j,\omega) - B^2(t_i,\omega)) \\ &= E(B^2(t_i,\omega) + B(t_j,\omega)(B(t_i,\omega) - B(t_j,\omega))) \\ &= E(B^2(t_i,\omega)) + E(B(t_j,\omega)(B(t_i,\omega) - B(t_j,\omega))) \end{aligned} \tag{2.3.6}$$

From P2, $B(t_j,\omega)$ and $(B(t_i,\omega) - B(t_j,\omega))$ are independent processes and therefore we can write ,

$$E(B(t_j,\omega)(B(t_i,\omega) - B(t_j,\omega))) = E(B(t_i,\omega))E(B(t_i,\omega) - B(t_j,\omega)) \quad . \tag{2.3.7}$$

According to P3 and P5, $E(B(t_j,\omega)) = 0$ and $E(B(t_i,\omega) - B(t_j,\omega)) = 0$.

Therefore, from equation (2.3.7)

$$E(B(t_j,\omega)B(t_i,\omega) - B(t_j,\omega))) = 0 \, .$$

This leads equation (2.3.6) to $E(B(t_i,\omega)B(t_j,\omega)) = E(B^2(t_i,\omega))$,

$$\text{And} \quad E(B^2(t_i,\omega)) = E((B(t_i,\omega)) - 0)^2) \, . \tag{2.3.8}$$

From P3, $\{B(t_i,\omega) - B(0,\omega)\}$ is normally distributed with a variance $(t_i - 0)$, and equation (2.3.8) becomes, $E(B^2(t_i,\omega)) = t_i$, and , therefore, $Cov(B(t_i,\omega)B(t_j,\omega)) = t_i$.

Using a similar approach it can be shown that if $t_i > t_j$,

$$Cov(B(t_i,\omega)B(t_j,\omega)) = t_j \, . \tag{2.3.9}$$

This leads to P7: $E(B(t_i,\omega)B(t_j,\omega)) = \min(t_i,t_j)$.

The above derivations show the relatedness of the variance of an independent increment, $Var\{B(t_1,\omega) - B(t_2,\omega)\}$ to the properties of Wiener process given by P1 to P7. The fact that

$\{B(t_{i+1},\omega)-B(t_i,\omega)\}$ is a Gaussian random variable with zero mean and $\{t_{i+1}-t_i\}$ variance can be used to construct Wiener process paths on computer. If we divide the time interval $[0,t]$ into n equidistant parts having length Δt, and at the end of each segment we can randomly generate a Brownian increment using the Normal distribution with mean 0 and variance Δt. This increment is simply added to the value of Wiener process at the point considered and move on to the next point. When we repeat this procedure starting from $t=\Delta t$ to $t=t$ and taking the fact that $B(0,\omega)=0$ into account, we can generate a realization of Wiener process. We can expect these Wiener process realizations to have properties quite distinct from other continuous functions of t. We will briefly discuss some important characteristics of Wiener process realizations next as these results enable us to utilise this very useful stochastic process effectively.

Some useful characteristics of Wiener process realizations $B(t,\omega)$ are

1. $B(t,\omega)$ is a continuous , nondifferentiable function of t.

2. The quadratic variation of $B(t,\omega)$, $[B(t,\omega),B(t,\omega)](t)$ over $[0,t]$ is t.

Using the definition of covariation of functions,

$$\begin{aligned}[B(t,\omega),B(t,\omega)](t) &= [B(t,\omega),B(t,\omega)]([0,t]) \\ &= \lim_{\delta_n\to 0}\sum_{i=1}^{n}[B(t_i^n)-B(t_{i-1}^n)]^2\end{aligned} \quad (2.3.10)$$

where $\delta_n=\max(t_{i+1}^n-t_i^n)$ and $\{t_i^n\}_{i=1}^n$ is a partition of $[0,t]$, as $n\to\infty,\delta_n\to o$.

Taking the expectation of the summation,

$$E(\sum(B(t_i^n)-B(t_{i-1}^n))^2)=\sum(E((B(t_i^n)-B(t_{i-1}^n))^2)). \quad (2.3.11)$$

$E((B(t_i^n)-B(t_{i-1}^n))^2)$ is the variance of an independent increment $\{B(t_i^n)-B(t_{i-1}^n)\}$.

As seen before, $Var[B(t_i^n)-B(t_{i-1}^n)]=(t_i^n-t_{i-1}^n)$.

Therefore,

$$\begin{aligned}E\left(\sum(B(t_i^n)-(B(t_{i-1}^n))^2\right) &= \sum Var[B(t_i^n)-B(t_{i-1}^n)] \\ &= \sum_{i=1}^{n}(t_i^n-t_{i-1}^n)=t-0=t.\end{aligned} \quad (2.3.12)$$

Let us take the variance of $\sum(B(t_i^n)-B(t_{i-1}^n))^2$:

$$Var\left(\sum(B(t_i^n)-B(t_{i-1}^n))^2\right)=\sum 3(t_i^n-t_{i-1}^n)^2\le 3\ \max(t_i^n-t_{i-1}^n)\,t=3t\delta_n, \text{ and}$$

as $n\to\infty,\delta_n\to 0,\sum Var(B(t_i^n)-B(t_{i-1}^n))^2\to 0$.

Summarizing the results,

$$E(\sum(B(t_i^n)-B(t_{i-1}^n))^2)=t,$$

and

$$Var(\sum(B(t_i^n)-B(t_{i-1}^n))^2)\to 0 \text{ as } n\to\infty .$$

This implies that, according to the monotone convergence theories that $\sum(B(t_i^n)-B(t_{i-1}^n))^2\to t$ almost surely as $n\to\infty$.

Therefore, the quadratic variation of Brownian motion $B(t,\omega)$ is *t*:

$$[B(t,\omega),B(t,\omega)](t)=t . \tag{2.3.13}$$

Omitting *t* and ω, $[B,B](t)=t$.

3. Wiener process $(B(t,\omega))$ is a martingale.

A stochastic process, $\{X(t)\}$ is a martingale, when the future expected value of $\{X(t)\}$ is equal to {X (*t*)}. In mathematical notation, $E(X(t+s)|F_t)=X(t)$ with converging almost surely, F_t *is* the information about {*X*(*t*)} up to time *t*. We do not give the proof of these martingale characteristics of Brownian motion here but it is easy to show that $E(B(t+s)\,|\,F_t)=B(t)$.

It can also be shown that $\{B(t,\omega)^2-t\}$ and $\{\exp(\alpha B(t,\omega)-\frac{\alpha^2}{2}t)\}$ are also martingales. These martingales can be used to characterize the Wiener process as well and more details can be found in Klebaner (1998).

4. Wiener process has Markov property

Markov property simply states that the future of a process depends only on the present state. In other words, a stochastic process having Markov property does not "remember" the past and the present state contains all the information required to drive the process into the future states.

This can be expressed as

$$P(X(t+s)\le y\,|\,F_t)=P(X(t+s)\le y\,|\,X(t)), \tag{2.3.14}$$

Converging almost surely.

From the very definition of increments of the Wiener process for the discretized intervals of [0,t], $\{B(t_{i+1}^n)-B(t_i^n)\}$, the Wiener process increment behaves independently to its immediate predecessor $\{B(t_i^n)-B(t_{i-1}^n)\}$.

In other words $\{B(t_{i+1}^n)-B(t_i^n)\}$ does not remember the behaviour of $\{B(t_i^n)-B(t_{i-1}^n)\}$ and only element common to both increments is $B(t_i^n)$.

One can now see intuitively why Wiener process should behave as a Markov process. This can be expressed as

$$P(B(t_i+s)\le x_i \mid \{B(t_i), B(t_{i-1})...0)\}) = P(B(t_i+s)\le x_i \mid B(t_i)), \tag{2.3.15}$$

which is another way of expressing the previous equation (2.3.14).

5. Generalized form of Wiener process

The Wiener process as defined above is sometimes called the standard Wiener process, to distinguish it from that obtained by the following generalization:

$$E[\ B(t_i,\omega)\ B(t_j,\omega)\ ] \ = \int_0^{\min(t_i,t_j)} q(\tau)\,d\tau\ .$$

The integral kernel $q(\tau)$ is called the correlation function and determines the correlation between stochastic process values at different times. The standard Wiener process is the simple case that $q(\tau)$=1 , i.e. full correlation over any time interval; the generalised Wiener process includes, for example, the case that q decreases, and there is progressively less correlation between the values in a given realization as the time interval between them increases.

2.4 Stochastic Integration

At this point of our discussion, we need to define the integration of stochastic process with respect to the Wiener process $(B(t,\omega))$ so that we understand the conditions under which this integral exists and what kind of processes can be integrated using this integral. The Stieltjes integral can not used to integrate the functions of infinite variation, and therefore, there is a need to define the integrals for the stochastic process such as the Wiener process. There are two choices available: Ito definition of integration and Stratanovich integration. These two definitions produce entirely different integral stochastic process.

The Ito definition is popular among mathematicians and physicists tend to use the Stratanovich integral. The Ito integral has the martingale property among many other useful technical properties (Keizw, 1987), and in addition, the Stratanovich integrals can be reduced to Ito integrals (Klebaner, 1998). In this monograph, we confine ourselves to Ito definition of integration:

$$I[X](\omega) = \int_S^T X(t,\omega)\,dB(t,\omega)\,.$$

$I[X](\omega)$ implies that the integration of $X(t,\omega)$ is along a realization ω and with respect to the Wiener process (a.k.a Brownian motion) which is a function of t. $I[X](\omega)$ is also a stochastic process in its own right and have properties originating from the definition of the integral. It is natural to expect $I[X](\omega)$ to be equal to $c(B(t,\omega)-B(s,\omega))$ when $X(t,\omega)$ is a constant c. If $X(t)$ is a deterministic process, which can be expressed as a sequence of constants over small intervals, we can define Ito integral as follows:

$$\begin{aligned} I[X] &= \int_S^T X(t)\,dB(t) \\ &= \sum_{i=0}^{n-1} c_i((B(t_{i+1}) - B(t_i))) \end{aligned}, \tag{2.4.1}$$

where $X(t) = \begin{cases} c_0, & t=S \\ c_i, & t_i < t \le t_{i+1} \end{cases} \quad i = 0, \cdots, n-1$.

The time interval $[S,T]$ has been discretized into n intervals : $S = t_0 < t_1 < \cdots < t_n = T$.

Using the property of independent increments of Brownian motion, we can show that the mean of $I[X](\omega)$ is zero and,

$$Variance = Var(I[X]) = \sum_{i=0}^{n-1} c_i^2 (t_{i+1} - t_i) . \tag{2.4.2}$$

It turns out that if $X(t,\omega)$ is a continuous stochastic process and its future values are solely dependent on the information of this process only up to t, Ito integral $I[X](\omega)$ exists. The future states on a stochastic process, $X(t,\omega)$, is only dependent on F_t then it is called an adapted process. A left-continuous adapted process $X(t,\omega)$ is defined as a predictable process and it satisfies the following condition: $\int_0^T X^2(t,\omega)\,dt < \infty$ with almost surely convergence.

As we are only concerned about continuous processes driven by the past events, we limit our discussion of predictable processes. Reader may want to refer to Øksendal (1998) and Klebaner (1998) for more rigorous discussion of these concepts.

We can now define Ito integral $I[X](\omega)$ similarly to equation (2.4.1) if $X(t,\omega)$ is a continuous and adapted process then $I[X](\omega)$ can be defined as

$$\sum_{i=0}^{n-1} X(t_i^n,\omega)(B(t_{i+1}^n,\omega) - B(t_i^n,\omega)) , \tag{2.4.3}$$

and this sum converges in probability.

Dropping ω for convenience and adhering to the same discretization of interval $[S, T]$ as in equation (2.4.1),

$$I[X] = \int_S^T X(t)dB(t) = \sum_{i=0}^{n-1} X(t_i^n)(B(t_{i+1}^n) - B(t_i^n)) . \tag{2.4.4}$$

Equation (2.4.4) expresses an approximation of $\int_S^T X(t)dB(t)$ based on the convergence in probability. We take equation (2.4.3) as the definition of Ito integral for the purpose of this book. As stated earlier $I[X](\omega)$ is a stochastic process and it has the following properties (see, for example, Øksendal (1998) for more details):

1. Linearity

If $X(t)$ and $Y(t)$ are predictable processes and α and β as some constants, then

$$I[\alpha X+\beta\, Y](\omega)=\alpha\; I[X](\omega)+\beta\; I[Y](\omega)\,. \tag{2.4.5}$$

2. Zero mean Property

$$E(I[X](\omega))=0\,. \tag{2.4.6}$$

3. Isometry Property

$$E[(\int_S^T X(t)\,dB(t))^2]=\int_S^T E(X^2(t))\,dt\,. \tag{2.4.7}$$

The isometry property says that the expected value of the square of Ito integral is the integral with respect to t of the expectation of the square of the process X (t).

Since $E[(\int_S^T X(t)\,dB(t))]=0$ from zero mean property, we can express the left hand side of equation (2.4.7) as

$$\begin{aligned}&E((\int_S^T X(t)dB(t))^2-E(\int_S^T X(t)dB(t)))\\&=E[\int_S^T X(t)dB(t)-E(\int_S^T X(t)dB(t))]^2=Var\Big(\int_S^T X(t)dB(t)\Big)\end{aligned}\,. \tag{2.4.8}$$

Therefore the variance of Ito integral process is $\int_S^T E(X^2(t))dt$ and this result will be useful to us in understanding the behaviour of Ito integral process. We say that Ito integral is square integrable. According to Fubuni's Theorem, which states that, for a stochastic process $X(t)$, with continuous realizations,

$$E(\int_S^T X(t)dt)=\int_S^T E(X(t))dt\,, \tag{2.4.9}$$

and

$$E(\int_S^T X^2(t)dt)=\int_S^T E(X^2(t))dt\,. \tag{2.4.10}$$

4. Ito integral is a martingale

It can be shown that $E(I[X(t)]\,|\,F_t)=I[X(t)]$. Strictly speaking $X(t)$ should satisfy $\int_S^T X^2(t)dt<\infty$ and $\int_S^T E(X^2(t))dt<\infty$ for martingale property to be true. Therefore, Ito integrals are square integrable martingales.

5. Ito integral of a deterministic function $X(t)$ is a Guassian process with zero mean and covariance function,

$$Cov(I[X(t)], I[X(t+t_0)]) = \int_0^t X^2(s)ds\,,\ t_0 \geq 0. \tag{2.4.11}$$

$I[X(t)]$ is a square integrable martingale.

6. Quadratic variation of Ito integral,

$$[I[X], I[X]](t) = \int_0^T X^2(t)dt\,. \tag{2.4.12}$$

We see that Ito integral has a positive quadratic variation making it a process with infinite variation i.e., it is a nondifferentiable continuous function of t.

7. Quadratic covariation of Ito integral with respect to processes $X_1(t)$ and $X_2(t)$ is given by

$$[I[X_1], I[X_2]](t) = \int_0^T X_1(t)X_2(t)dt\,. \tag{2.4.13}$$

Armed with these properties we can proceed to discuss the machinery of stochastic calculus such as stochastic chain rule, which is also known as Ito formula.

2.5 Stochastic Chain Rule (Ito Formula)

As we have seen previously, the quadratic variations of Brownian motion, $[B(t,\omega), B(t,\omega)](t)$, is the limit in probability over the interval $[0,t]$:

$$[B(t,\omega), B(t,\omega)](t) = \lim_{\delta_n \to 0} \sum_{i=0}^{n-1} (B(t_{i+1}^n) - B(t_i^n))^2\,, \tag{2.5.1}$$

$\delta_n = \max(t_{i+1}^n - t_i^n) \to 0$. Using the differential notation, $\Delta B = B(t_{i+1}^n) - B(t_i^n)$, and summation as an integral ,

$$[B(t,\omega), B(t,\omega)](t) = \int_0^t (dB(s))^2\,. \tag{2.5.2}$$

We have shown that $[B,B](t) = t$, and therefore, $\int_0^t (dB(s))^2 = t$.

For our convenience and also to make the notation similar to the one in standard differential calculus, we denote

$$\int_0^t (dB(s))^2 = t \tag{2.5.3}$$

$$\text{as} \qquad (dB(t))^2 = dt\,. \tag{2.5.4}$$

This equation does not have a meaning outside the integral equation (2.5.3) and should not be interpreted in any other way.

Similarly for any other continuous function $g(t)$,

$$g(t)(dB(t))^2 = g(B(t))dt \, , \qquad (2.5.5)$$

which means,

$$g(t)(dB(t))^2 = g(B(t))dt \, . \qquad (2.5.6)$$

This equation is an expression of the approximation, converging in probability, of

$$\lim_{\delta_n \to 0} \sum_{i=0}^{n-1} g(t_i^n)(B(t_{i+1}^n) - B(t_i^n))^2 = \int_0^t g(B(s))ds \, . \qquad (2.5.7)$$

As the quadratic variation of a continuous and differentiable function is zero,

$$[t,t]\,(t) = 0. \qquad (2.5.8)$$

This equation in integral notation,

$$\int_0^t (dt)^2 = 0 \, ,$$

and in differential notation,

$$(dt)^2 = 0 \, . \qquad (2.5.9)$$

Similarly, quadratic covariation of t (a continuous and differentiable function) and Brownian notion,

$$[t,B](t) = 0 \, . \qquad (2.5.10)$$

This relationship can be proved by expressing quadratic covariation as

$$[t,B](t) = \lim_{\delta_n \to o} \sum_{i=0}^{n-1} (t_{i+1}^n - t_i^n)(B(t_{i+1}^n) - B(t_i^n))$$

$$\delta_n = \max(t_{i+1}^n - t_i^n) \, ,$$

$$\begin{aligned} [t,B](t) &\leq \delta_n \sum_{i=0}^{n-1} (B(t_{i+1}^n) - B(t_i^n)) \\ &\leq \delta_n B(t) \end{aligned} \, .$$

Therefore as $n \to \infty$, $\delta_n \to 0$ (because t is a function of finite variation),

$$[t,B](t) \to 0 \quad \text{as} \quad n \to \infty \, .$$

Hence, $[t,B](t) = 0$ and in integral notation, $\int_0^t dt\, dB = 0$.

This can be written in differential notation,

$$dt.dB = 0 \, . \qquad (2.5.11)$$

Therefore, we can summarize the following rules in differential notation as follows,

$$dt.dt = 0\,;\quad dt.dB = 0\,;\quad dB.dt = 0, \quad \text{and} \quad dB.dB = dt\,. \tag{2.5.12}$$

In order to come to grips with the interpretation of the differential properties of dB_t, it is useful to consider the chain rule of differentiation. This will also lead us to formulas that are often more useful in calculating Ito integrals than the basic definition as the limit of a sum. Consider first the case in ordinary calculus of a function $g(x,t)$, where x is also a function of t. We can write the change in g as t changes, as follows:

$$\Delta g = \frac{\partial g(t,x)}{\partial t}\Delta t + \frac{\partial g(t,x)}{\partial x}\Delta x + \tfrac{1}{2}\frac{\partial^2 g(t,x)}{\partial x^2}(\Delta x)^2 + \ldots$$

From this, an expression for dg/dt is obtained by taking the limit $\Delta t \to 0$ of the ratio $(\Delta g/\Delta t)$.

Since $\Delta x = (dx/dt)\ \Delta t$, when $\Delta t \to 0$ the 2nd derivative term shown is of order $(\Delta t)^2$ and falls away together with all higher derivatives, and the well-known chain rule formula for the total derivative (dg/dt) is obtained. However, if , instead of x , we have a Wiener process B_t , we get

$$\Delta g = \frac{\partial g(t,B_t)}{\partial t}\Delta t + \frac{\partial g(t,B_t)}{\partial x}\Delta B_t + \tfrac{1}{2}\frac{\partial^2 g(t,B_t)}{\partial x^2}(\Delta B_t \cdot \Delta B_t) + \ldots$$

If the expectation value of this expression over all realizations is taken, the above shows that the second derivative term is now only of order Δt and cannot be ignored. Since this holds for the expectation value, for consistency we also cannot neglect the term if the limit $\Delta t \to 0$ is taken without considering the expectation value. Unlike the case of ordinary calculus where all expressions containing products of differentials higher than 1 is neglected, in Ito calculus we therefore have different rules.

Recall that in standard calculus chain rule is applied to composite functions.

For example, if $Y=f(t)$ then $g(Y)$ is a function of Y.

Then $\dfrac{dg}{dt} = \dfrac{dg}{dY}.\dfrac{dY}{dt}$

In differential notation,

$$dg = \frac{dg}{dY}.df\,.$$

By integrating

$$g(f(t)) = g(0) + \int_0^t g'(f(t))df\,.$$

Suppose say $f(t) = B(t)$ (Brownian motion) and $g(x)$ is twice continuously differentiable function. Then by using stochastic Taylor series expansion,

$$g(B(t)) = g(0) + \int_0^t g'(B(s))dB(s) + \frac{1}{2}\int_0^t g''(B(s))ds\,. \tag{2.5.13}$$

Comparing equation (2.5.13) and the corresponding stochastic chain rule, we can see that the second derivative term of the Taylor series plays a significant role in changing the chain rule in the standard calculus to the stochastic one.

For example, let $g(x) = e^x$

$$\text{Therefore,}\quad e^{B(t)} = e^{(0)} + \int_0^t e^{B(s)} dB(s) + \frac{1}{2}\int_0^t e^{B(s)} ds . \tag{2.5.14}$$

In differential notation (which is only a convention),

$$d(e^{B(t)}) = e^{B(t)} dB(t) + \frac{1}{2} e^{B(t)} dt . \tag{2.5.15}$$

As an another example, let $g(x) = x^2$.

Therefore, from the chain rule

$$(B(t))^2 = (B(0))^2 + 2\int_s^t B(s)dB(s) + \frac{1}{2}\int_0^t 2ds ,$$

$$\int_0^t B(s)dB(s) = \frac{1}{2}(B(t))^2 - \frac{1}{2}t . \tag{2.5.16}$$

This is quite a different result from the standard integration. In differential convention,

$$B(t)\, dB(t) = \frac{1}{2} d((B(t))^2) - \frac{1}{2} dt . \tag{2.5.17}$$

In other words, the stochastic process $\int_0^t B(s)dB(s)$ can be calculated by evaluating $\{\frac{1}{2}(B(t))^2 - \frac{1}{2}t\}$. We will show how this process behaves using computer simulations in section 2.6.

We can write Ito integral as

$$Y(t) = \int_0^t \sigma(s) dB(s) . \tag{2.5.18}$$

Then we can add a "drift term" to the "diffusion term" given by equation (2.5.18):

$$Y(t) = Y(0) + \int_0^t \mu(s)ds + \int_0^t \sigma(s)dB(s) . \tag{2.5.19}$$

We recall that $\sigma(s)$ should be a predictable process and is subjected to the condition $\int_0^T \sigma^2(t)dt < \infty$ converging almost surely. $\mu(t)$ is, on the other hand, an adapted continuous process of finite variation. In equation (2.5.19) $\int_0^t \sigma(s)dB(s)$ represents the diffusion part of the process and $\int_0^t \mu(s)ds$ does not contain the noise; therefore it represents the drifting of the process. $Y(t)$ is called an Ito process and in differential notation we can write,

$$dY(t) = \mu(t)dt + \sigma(t)dB(t) . \tag{2.5.20}$$

Equation (2.5.20) can be quite useful in practical applications where the main driving force is perturbed by an irregular noise. A particle moving through a porous medium is such an example. In this case, advection gives rise to the drift term and hydrodynamic dispersion and microdiffusion give rise to the "diffusive" term. In the population dynamics, the diffusive term is a direct result of noise in the proportionality constant. Therefore it is important to study Ito process further in order to apply it in modeling situations. $\mu(t)$ is called the drift coefficient and $\sigma(t)$ the diffusion coefficient and they can depend on $Y(t)$ and/or $B(t)$. For example, we can write in pervious result (equation (2.5.17)),

$$d(B(t)^2) = dt + 2B(t)dB(t) . \tag{2.5.21}$$

This is an Ito process with the drift coefficient of 1 and the diffusion coefficient of $2B(t)$. Quadratic variation of Ito process on $[0,T]$

$$Y(t) = Y(0) + \int_0^t \mu(s)ds + \int_0^t \sigma(s)dB(s). \tag{2.5.22}$$

is given by

$$[Y,Y](t) = \int_0^t \sigma^2(s)ds \quad . \tag{2.5.23}$$

This can be deduced from the fact that $\int_0^t \mu(s)ds$ is a continuous function with finite variation and using quadratic variation of Ito integral. In differential notation,

$$\begin{aligned}(dY(t))^2 &= dY(t).dY(dt),\\ &= \mu^2(t)(dt)^2 + 2\mu\, \sigma dtdB + \sigma^2(dB)^2,\\ &= \sigma^2(t)dt.\end{aligned} \tag{2.5.24}$$

The chain rule given in equation (2.5.12) gives us a way to compute the behaviour of a function of Brownian motion. It is also useful to know the chain rule to compute a function of a given Ito process. Suppose an Ito process is given by a general form,

$$dX(t) = \mu dt + \sigma dB(t) , \tag{2.5.25}$$

where μ is the drift coefficient and σ is the diffusion coefficient and let $g(t, x)$ is a twice differentiable continuous function. Let $Y(t) = g(t, X(t))$. Here $Y(t)$ is a function of t and Ito process $X(t)$, and is also a stochastic process. $Y(t)$ can also be expressed as an Ito process. Then Ito formula states,

$$dY(t) = \frac{dg}{dt}(t,X(t))dt + \frac{\partial g}{\partial x}(t,X(t))dX(t) + \frac{1}{2}\frac{\partial^2 g}{\partial x^2}(t,X(t)).(dX(t))^2. \tag{2.5.26}$$

$$\text{where, } (dX(t))^2 = d(X(t)).d(X(t)) , \tag{2.5.27}$$

and is evaluated according to the rules given by equation (2.5.12).

As an example, consider the Ito process

$$dX(t) = dt + 2B(t)dB(t) \tag{2.5.28}$$

where $\mu = 1$ and $\sigma = 2B(t)$.

Assume $g(t,x) = x^2$, therefore,

$$\frac{\partial g}{\partial t} = 0\,; \; \frac{\partial g}{\partial x} = 2x \;\; ; \; \frac{\partial^2 g}{\partial^2 x} = 2\,. \tag{2.5.29}$$

Substituting to Ito formula above ,

$$\begin{aligned} dg &= 2X(t)dX(t) + dX(t).dX(t), \\ &= 2(dt + 2B(t)dB(t))B(t) + 4B^2(t)dt. \end{aligned} \tag{2.5.30}$$

$$dX^2(t) = (2X(t) + 4B^2(t))dt + \; 4X(t)B(t)dB(t). \tag{2.5.31}$$

As seen above $dX^2(t)$ is also an Ito process with $u = 2X(t) + 4B^2(t)$ (drift coefficient), a function of $X(t)$ and $B(t)$, and $v = 4X(t)B(t)$ (diffusion coefficient) , also a function of $X(t)$ and $B(t)$.

Substituting $X(t) = B^2(t)$ to equation (2.5.31),

$$\begin{aligned} d(B^4(t)) \; &= 2(B^2(t) + 2B^2(t)dt + 4(B^2(t))B(t)dB(t) \\ &= 6B^2(t)dt + 4B^3(t)dB(t) \end{aligned} \;. \tag{2.5.32}$$

We can derive this from chain rule for a function of B(t) as well.

Let $g(x) = x^4$, and from Ito formula:

$$\begin{aligned} dg &= g'(B(t))dB(t) + \frac{1}{2}g''(t)dt \\ &= 4B^3(t)dB(t) + \frac{1}{2}4.3.B^2(t)dt, \end{aligned} \tag{2.5.33}$$

$$d(B^4(t)) = 6B^2(t)dt + 4B^3(t)dB(t)\;. \tag{2.5.34}$$

This is the same Ito process as in equation (2.5.32). Let us consider another example which will be useful. Consider the function $g(x) = \ln x$ and the Ito process

$$dX(t) = \frac{1}{2}X(t) + X(t)dB(t)\,. \tag{2.5.35}$$

For this Ito process $\mu = \frac{1}{2}X(t)$ and $\sigma = X(t)$.

From the Ito formula (equation (2.5.26)),

$$\begin{aligned} d(\ln X(t)) &= \frac{1}{X(t)}dX(t) + \frac{1}{2}\left(-\frac{1}{X^2(t)}\right)(X^2(t)dt), \\ &= \frac{1}{X(t)}\left(\frac{1}{2}X(t)dt + X(t)dB(t)\right) - \frac{1}{2}dt, \\ &= \frac{1}{2}dt + dB(t) - \frac{1}{2}dt, \\ &= dB(t). \end{aligned} \tag{2.5.36}$$

By convention, the above stochastic differential is given by the following integral equation:

$$\ln X(t) = \ln X(0) + \int_0^t dB(t), \tag{2.5.37}$$

$$\ln\left[\frac{X(t)}{X(0)}\right] = B(t) \ , \tag{2.5.38}$$

$$X(t) = X(0)e^{B(t)}.$$

We can show that $X(t) = X(0)e^{B(t)}$ satisfies $dX(t) = \frac{1}{2}X(t)dt + X(t)dB(t)$. In other words $X(t) = X(0)e^{B(t)}$ is a "solution" to the stochastic differential $dX(t) = \frac{1}{2}X(t)dt + X(t)dB(t)$.

This idea of having a solution to a stochastic differential is similar to having a solution to differential equations in standard calculus.

Suppose $X_1(t)$ and $X_2(t)$ are Ito processes given by the following differentials:

$$dX_1(t) = \mu_1(t)dt + \sigma_1(t)dB(t) \ , \tag{2.5.39}$$

$$dX_2(t) = \mu_2(t)dt + \sigma_2(t)dB(t) \ . \tag{2.5.40}$$

Quadratic covariation is given by

$$\begin{aligned} d[X_1, X_2] &= dX_1(t).dX_2(t), \\ &= \mu_1\mu_2(dt)^2 + \mu_1\ \sigma_2 dt.dB(t) + \mu_2\ \sigma_1 dt.dB(t) + \sigma_1\sigma_2(dB(t))^2. \end{aligned}$$

And $(dt)^2 = dt.dB(t) = 0$.

$$\begin{aligned} d[X_1, X_2] &= \sigma_1(t)\sigma_2(t)(dB(t))^2 \\ &= \sigma_1(t)\sigma_2(t)dt \end{aligned}. \tag{2.5.41}$$

The stochastic product rule is given by,

$$\begin{aligned} & X_1(t)X_2(t) - X_1(0)X_2(0) \\ &= \int_0^t X_1(s)dX_2(s) + \int_0^t X_2(s)dX_1(s) + [X_1, X_2](t) \end{aligned}. \tag{2.5.42}$$

If at least one of X_1 and X_2 is a continuous function with finite variation, then $[X_1, X_2](t) = 0$ and equation (2.5.42) reduces to the integration by parts formula in the standard calculus.

Stochastic product rule can be expressed in differential form:

$$\begin{aligned} &d(X_1(t)X_2(t)) \\ &= X_1(t)dX_2(t) + X_2(t)dX_1(t) + \sigma_1(t)\sigma_2(t)dt. \end{aligned} \tag{2.5.43}$$

As an example, consider $Y(t) = t\,B(t)$,

$$Y(t) = X_1(t)X_2(t),$$

where $X_1(t) = t$, a continuous function with finite variation and $\sigma_1 = 0$, and $X_2(t) = B(t)$, Brownian motion with infinite variation and $\sigma_2 = 1$.

From the product rule,

$$d(Y(t)) = tdB(t) + B(t)dt + (0)(1)dt,$$

$$d(tB(t)) = tdB(t) + B(t)dt \tag{2.5.44}$$

This is the same result we obtain if we use the standard product rule. The reason for this is that quadratic covariation of a continuous function and a function with infinite variation is zero as we have mentioned previously.

Suppose $dX_1(t) = tdB(t) + B(t)dt$, and

$dX_2(t) = \frac{1}{2}X_2(t)dt + X_2(t)dB(t)$, where

$\mu_1(t) = B(t)$; $\sigma_1(t) = t$; $\sigma_2(t) = X_2(t)$; and $\mu_2(t) = \frac{1}{2}X_2$.

From the product rule,

$$\begin{aligned} d(X_1(t)X_2(t)) &= X_1(t)dX_2(t) + X_2(t)dX_1(t) + \sigma_1\sigma_2 dt, \\ &= X_1(t)dX_2(t) + X_2(t)dX_1(t) + tX_2(t)dt. \end{aligned} \tag{2.5.45}$$

By substitution,

$$\begin{aligned} &d(X_1(t)X_2(t)) = X_1(t)(\frac{1}{2}X_2dt + X_2(t)dB(t)) + X_2(t)(tdB(t) + B(t)dt) + tX_2(t)dt, \\ &= \left(\frac{1}{2}X_1(t)X_2(t) + X_2(t)B(t) + tX_2(t)\right)dt + (X_1(t)X_2(t) + tX_2(t))dB(t). \end{aligned} \tag{2.5.46}$$

This is again an Ito process.

$$d(X_1(t)X_2(t)) = \left(\frac{1}{2}X_1(t)X_2(t) + tX_2(t) + X_2(t)B(t)\right)dt + \left(X_1(t)+t)\right)X_2(t)dB(t),$$
$$= X_2(t)\left(\frac{1}{2}X_1(t) + t + B(t)\right)dt + X_2(t)\left(X_1(t)+t\right)dB(t)). \tag{2.5.47}$$

As an integral equation,

$$X_1(t)X_2(t) - X_1(0)X_2(0) = \int_0^t X_2(t)(\frac{1}{2}X_1(t) + t + B(t))dt + \int_0^t X_2(t)(X_1(t)+t)dB(t).$$

If $g(x_1, x_2)$ is a continuous and twice differentiable function of x_1 and x_2, and we are given Ito processes of the forms, $dX_1(t) = \mu_1 dt + \sigma_1\, dB(t)$ and $dX_2(t) = \mu_2 dt + \sigma_2 dB(t)$.

Then $g(X_1(t), X_2(t))$ is also an Ito process and given by the following differential form:

$$dg(X_1(t), X_2(t)) = \frac{\partial g(X_1)}{\partial x_1}dX_1(t) + \frac{\partial g(X_2)}{\partial x_2}dX_2(t) + \frac{1}{2}\frac{\partial^2 g(X_1)}{\partial^2 x_1}(dX_1(t))^2$$
$$+\frac{1}{2}\frac{\partial^2 g(X_2)}{\partial^2 x_2}(dX_2(t))^2 + \frac{\partial^2 g(X_1X_2)}{\partial x_1 x_2}dX_1(t).dX_2(t). \tag{2.5.48}$$

Using quadratic variation and covariation of Ito processes,

$$(dX_1(t))^2 = dX_1(t)\,.\,dX_1(t) = \sigma_1^2 dt\,,$$

$$(dX_2(t))^2 = dX_2(t)\,.\,dX_2(t) = \sigma_2^2 dt\,, \text{ and}$$

$$dX_1(t)\,.\,dX_2(t) = \sigma_1\sigma_2 dt\,.$$

These can be considered as a generalization of the rules on differentials given by equation (2.5.12). We use this generalized Ito formula for a function of two Ito processes in the following example.

We will express the stochastic process $X(t) = 2 + t + e^{B(t)}$ as an Ito process having the standard form, $dX(t) = \mu dt + \sigma dB(t)$.

We can consider

$$X(t) = g(t, B(t)) = 2 + t + e^{B(t)}. \tag{2.5.49}$$

Therefore, $g(t,y) = 2 + t + e^y$, where

$$X_1(t) = t\,,$$

$$X_2(t) = y = B(t)\,.$$

These equations give, $dX_1 = dt$ and $dX_2 = dB(t)$, where $\mu_1 = 1$; $\sigma_1 = 0$; $\mu_2 = 0$; and $\sigma_2 = 1$.

Using equation (2.5.48),

$$dg = (1)dt + e^{B(t)}dB(t) + \frac{1}{2}(0)(dB(t))^2 + \frac{1}{2}e^{B(t)}(dB(t))^2 + (0)dt.dB(t)$$

$$= dt + e^{B(t)}dB(t) + \frac{1}{2}e^{B(t)}dt.$$

Using $(dB(t))^2 = dt$,

$$dg = dX(t) = \left(1 + \frac{1}{2}e^{B(t)}\right)dt + e^{B(t)}dB(t).$$

From a previous example, $d(e^{B(t)}) = e^{B(t)}dB(t) + \frac{1}{2}e^{B(t)}dt$.

Therefore $dX(t) = dt + (\frac{1}{2}e^{B(t)}dt + e^{B(t)}dB(t)) = dt + d(e^{B(t)})$.

From the integral notation,

$$X(t) = X(0) + \int_0^t dt + \int_0^t d(e^{B(t)}),$$

$$X(t) = (0) + t + e^{B(t)} - 1,$$

$$X(t) = (X(0) - 1) + t + e^{B(t)}.$$

Comparing with

$$X(t) = 2 + t + e^{B(t)},$$

$$X(0) - 1 = 2,$$
$$X(0) = 3.$$

X(t)= constant + t + $e^{B(t)}$ can be considered as a solution process to the stochastic differential,

$$dX(t) = (1 + \frac{1}{2}e^{B(t)})dt + e^{B(t)}dB(t).$$

As we can see in the above solution, the solution process contains the characteristics of both the drift and diffusion phenomena. In this case, diffusion phenomenon dominates as t increases because of the expected value of the exponential of Brownian motion increases at a faster rate in general. If we examine the drift term of the stochastic differential above, we see that the drift term is also affected by the Brownian motion, so the final solution is always a result of complex interactions between the drift term and the diffusion term.

We now to discuss a population dynamics example equipped with the knowledge of Ito process and formula:

$$\frac{dx(t)}{dt} = \alpha(t)x(t) . \quad (2.5.50)$$

If the coefficient α (f) is "noisy", we can express if as follows:

$$\alpha(t) = r(t) + \sigma(t)W_t ,$$

where W_t = white noise, then

$$dX(t) = (r(t)dt + \sigma(t)dB(t)) . X(t) ,$$

and Brownian motion increments $dB(t) = W_t dt$.

Therefore ,

$$dX(t) = \left(r(t)dt + \sigma(t)W_t dB(t)\right)X(t) ,$$

$$dX(t) = r(t)X(t)dt + \sigma(t)X(t)d(t) . \quad (2.5.51)$$

As seen from the above equation (2.5.51), $X(t)$ is an Ito process.

Consider the case with $r(t)= r$, a constant and $\sigma(t) = \sigma$, a constant then the process $X_1(t)$ can be written in the differential form:

$$dX(t) = rX(t)dt + \sigma X(t)dB(t) .$$

Assume $g(x)=ln\ x$,

Then using the Ito formula,

$$dg(x(t)) = \frac{\partial(\ln x)}{\partial x}dX(t) + \frac{1}{2}\frac{\partial^2 g}{\partial x^2}(dX(t))^2 ,$$

$$\begin{aligned} d(\ln(X(t)) &= \frac{dX(t)}{X(t)} + \frac{1}{2}\left(\frac{-1}{X(t)^2}\right)(\sigma^2), \\ &= \frac{dX(t)}{X(t)} - \frac{\sigma^2}{2}dt, \\ &= \frac{1}{X(t)}(rX(t)dt + \sigma X(t)dB(t)) - \frac{\sigma^2}{2}dt. \end{aligned}$$

$$\begin{aligned} d(\ln(X(t)) &= rdt + \sigma dB(t) - \frac{\sigma^2}{2}dt, \\ &= \left(r - \frac{\sigma^2}{2}\right)dt + \sigma dB(t). \end{aligned}$$

Converting back to the integral form,

$$\ln(X(t)) = \ln(X(0)) + \int_0^t \left(r - \frac{\sigma^2}{2}\right)dt + \int_0^t \sigma dB(t),$$

$$\ln\left(\frac{X(t)}{X(0)}\right) = \left(r - \frac{\sigma^2}{2}\right)t + \sigma B(t),$$

$$X(t) = X(0)\exp(\sigma B(t))\exp\left((r - \frac{\sigma^2}{2})t\right). \quad (2.5.52)$$

$X(t)$ process, therefore, satisfies the Ito process,

$$dX(t) = rX(t)dt + \sigma X(t)dB(t),$$

and equation (2.5.52) can be considered as a solution to the stochastic differential equation. As discussed earlier, this solution significantly different from its deterministic counterpart.

This section we have reviewed the essentials of stochastic calculus and presented the results which could be useful in developing models and solving stochastic differential equations. While analytical expressions are quite helpful to understand stochastic processes, computer simulation provides us with an intuitive "feel" for the simulated phenomena. Sometimes it is revealing to simulate a number of realizations of a process and visualize them on computers to understand the behaviours of the process.

2.6 Computer Simulation of Brownian Motion and Ito Processes

In the previous section, we have introduced Brownian motion (the Wiener process) as a stationary, continuous stochastic process with independent increments. This process is a unique one to model the irregular noise such as Gaussian white noise in systems, and once such a process is incorporated in differential equations, the process of obtaining solutions involve stochastic calculus. Only a limited number of stochastic differential equations have analytical solutions and some of these equations are given by Kloeden and Platen (1992). In many instances we have to resort to numerical methods. We illustrate the behaviour of the Wiener process and Ito processes through computer simulations so that reader can appreciate the variable nature of individual realizations.

For the numerical implementation, it is most convenient to use the variance specification of the Wiener process $B(t)$. The time span of the simulation, [0,1] is discretised into small equal time increments *delt*, and the corresponding independent Wiener increments selected randomly from a normal distribution with zero mean and variance, *delt*.

Figure 2.2 shows the Wiener process increments as a single stochastic process. Since Gaussian white noise is the derivative of Wiener process and the time interval is a constant, Figure 2.2 depicts a realization of an approximation of white noise process.

The Wiener process is very irregular (Figure 2.1), and the only discernible pattern is that as time progresses, the position tends to wander away from the starting position at the origin. In other words, if the statistical variance over realisations for a fixed time is evaluated, this increases gradually - a property referred to as time varying variance. The use of the Wiener process in a modelling situation to represent the noise in the system should be carefully thought through. If the noise can be represented as white noise, then Wiener process enters into the equation because of the relationship between the white noise and the Wiener process. It is also important to realize that the Ito integral is a stochastic process dependent on the Wiener process. This is analogous to integration in standard calculus because an indefinite integral is a function of the independent, deterministic variable.

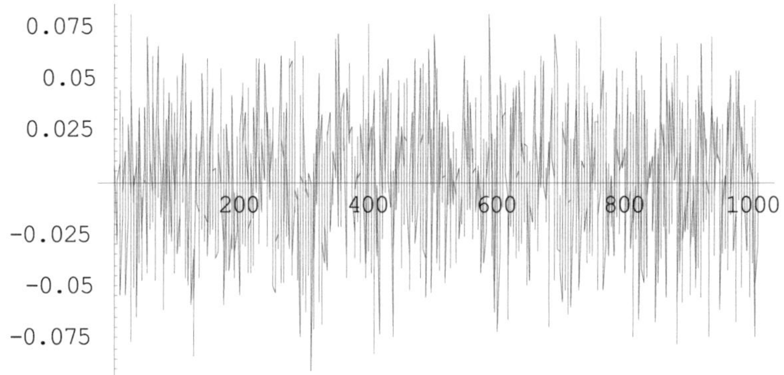

Figure 2.2. A realization of the Wiener process increment.

Given the Wiener process realization depicted in Figure 2.1, we compute the Ito integral of Wiener process, $\int_0^t B(t,\omega)dB$.

As we have previously seen, this integral can be evaluated by using the following stochastic relationship converging in probability; and it is shown in Figure 2.4.

$$\int_0^t B(s,\omega)dB(s,\omega) = \frac{1}{2}B^2(t,\omega) - \frac{1}{2}t .$$

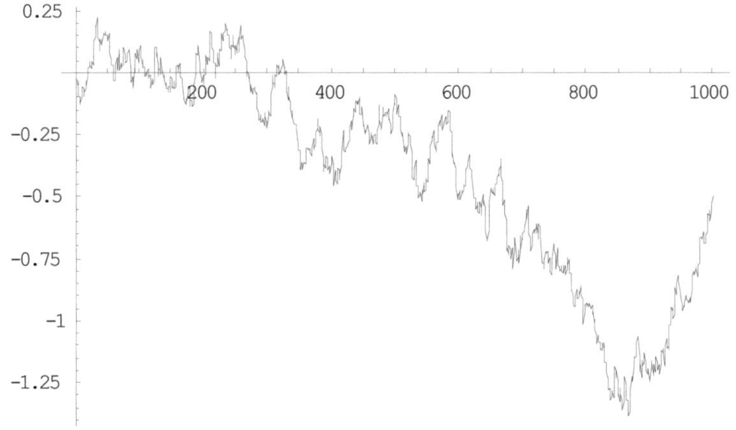

Figure 2.3. The realization of the Wiener process used in the calculation of the Ito Integral shown in Figure 2.4.

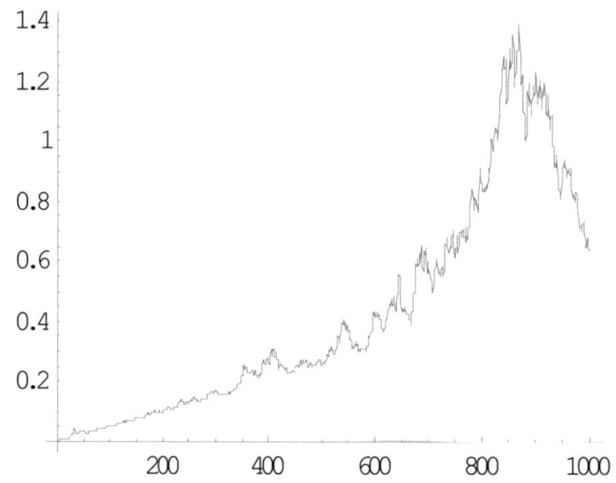

Figure 2.4. A realization of $\int_0^t B(t,\omega)dB$.

Let us consider the following Ito process which we have derived in section 2.5. In differential notation,

$$d(B^4(t))=6B^2(t)dt+4B^3(t)dB(t),$$

which means,

$$B^4(t)=B^4(0)+\int_0^t 6B^2(t)dt+\int_0^t 4B^3(t)dB(t), \text{ and}$$

$$B^4(t)=\int_0^t 6B^2(t)dt+\int_0^t 4B^3(t)dB(t). \qquad (2.6.1)$$

The Ito process given in equation (2.6.1) is simulated in Figure 2.6 for the Wiener realization depicted in Figure 2.5.

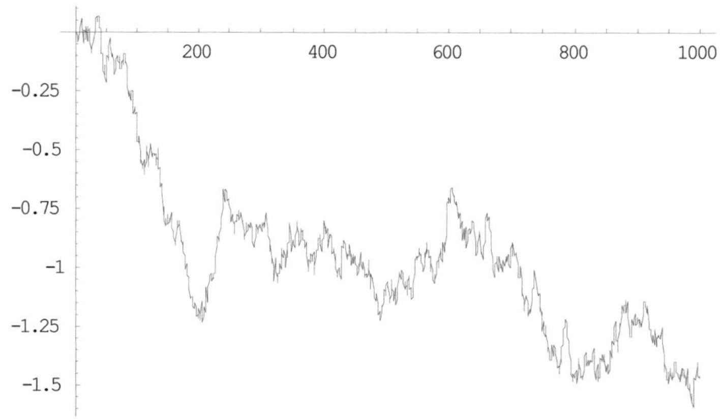

Figure 2.5. Wiener realization used in evaluating the Ito process $B^4(t)$.

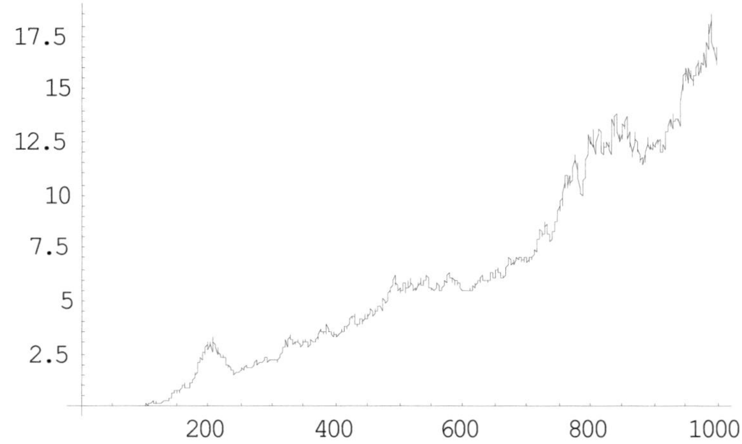

Figure 2.6. Ito process $B^4(t) = \int_0^t 6B^2(t)dt + \int_0^t 4B^3(t)dB(t)$.

Even for a decreasing and erratic Wiener process, the Ito process $\left\{\int_0^t 6B^2(t)dt + \int_0^t 4B^3(t)dB(t)\right\}$ in general has a smoother realization which has an overall growth in positive direction. The effect of Ito integration tends to smoothen the erratic behaviour of Wiener process. We have evaluated the above Ito process for 3 different realizations of the standard Wiener process, and they are shown in Figure 2.7.

As seen in Figure 2.7, individual realizations of the Ito process $\left\{\int_0^t 6B^2(t)dt + \int_0^t 4B^3(t)dB(t)\right\}$ are distinct from each other; and they show the complexity in stochastic integration as opposed to integration in standard calculus.

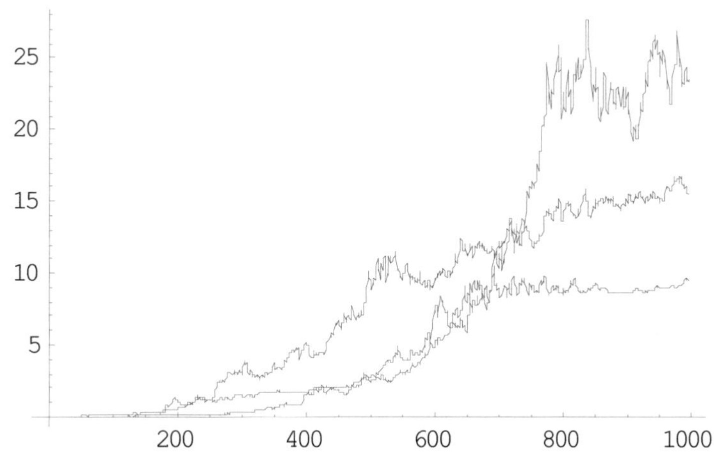

Figure 2.7. Three realizations of $\left\{\int_0^t 6B^2(t)dt + \int_0^t 4B^3(t)dB(t)\right\}$.

2.7 Solving Stochastic Differential Equation

Let us consider an ordinary differential equation which relates the derivative of the dependent variable ($y(t)$) to the independent variable (t) through a function, $\phi(y(t),t)$, with the initial condition $y(0) = y_0$:

$$\frac{dy}{dt} = \phi(y,t), \tag{2.7.1}$$

$$\text{and } dy = \phi(y,t)dt. \tag{2.7.2}$$

In many natural systems, this rate of change can be influenced by random noise caused by a combination of factors, which could be difficult to model. As a model of this random fluctuations, white noise $(\xi(t))$ is a suitable candidate. Therefore we can write, in general, the increments of the noise process as $\sigma(y,t)\,\xi(t)$ where σ is an amplitude function modifying the white noise.

Hence,

$$\frac{dy}{dt} = \phi(y,t) + \sigma(y,t)\,\xi(t). \tag{2.7.3}$$

As we have seen before (equation (2.3.3)),

$$\sigma(y,t)\,\xi(t) = \sigma(y,t)\frac{dB}{dt} \tag{2.7.4}$$

where, $B(t)$ = the standard Wiener process.

Therefore,

$$\frac{dy}{dt} = \phi(y,t) + \sigma(y,t)\frac{dB}{dt}, \tag{2.7.5}$$

$$dy = \phi(y,t)d\phi + \sigma(y,t)dB. \tag{2.7.6}$$

In general, $\phi(y,t)$ and $\sigma(y,t)$, could be stochastic processes. This equation is called a stochastic differential equation (SDE) driven by Wiener process. Once the Wiener process enters into equation (2.7.4), y becomes a stochastic process, $Y(t,\omega)$, and in the differential notation SDE is written as

$$dY(t) = \phi(Y(t),t)dt + \sigma(Y(t),t)\,dB(t). \tag{2.7.7}$$

This actually means,

$$Y(t) = Y(0) + \int_o^t \phi(Y(t),t)\,dt + \int_o^t \sigma(Y(t),t)\,dB(t). \tag{2.7.8}$$

If we can find a function of Wiener process in the form of an Ito process that satisfies the above integral equation (2.7.8), we call that function a strong solution of SDE.

Strong solutions do not depend on individual realizations of Brownian motion. In other words, all possible realizations of an Ito process, which is a strong solution of a SDE, satisfy the SDE under consideration. Not all the SDEs have strong solutions. Other class of solutions is called weak solutions where solution to each individual realization is different from each other. In this section we will focus only on strong solutions. In many situations, finding analytical solutions to SDEs is impossible and therefore we will review a minimum number of SDEs and their solutions in order to facilitate the discussion in the subsequent chapters.

If $X(t)$ is a stochastic process and another stochastic process $Y(t)$ is related to $X(t)$ through the stochastic differential,

$$dY(t) = Y(t)\, dX(t) \quad , \tag{2.7.9}$$

with $Y(0) = 1$.

Thus $Y(t)$ is called the stochastic exponential of $X(t)$. If $X(t)$ is a stochastic process of finite variation thus the solution to equation (2.7.9) is,

$$Y(t) = e^{X(t)}, \tag{2.7.10}$$

and, for any process $X(t)$,

$Y(t) = e^{\xi(t)}$ satisfies the stochastic differential given above when

$$\xi(t) = X(t) - X(0) - \frac{1}{2}[X, X](t). \tag{2.7.11}$$

$[X, X](t)$ is quadratic variation of $X(t)$ and for a continuous function with finite variation $[X,X](t) = 0$.

For example, consider the following stochastic differential equation in differential form,

$$dX(t) = X(t)\, dB(t). \tag{2.7.12}$$

This SDE does not have a drift term and the diffusion term is an Ito integral.

We know, $[B, B](t) = t$.

Therefore from the above result,

$$\begin{aligned} \xi(t) &= B(t) - B(0) - \frac{1}{2}t, \\ &= B(t) - \frac{1}{2}(t). \end{aligned} \tag{2.7.13}$$

Then the solution to the SDE is

$$X(t) = e^{B(t) - \frac{1}{2}t}. \tag{2.7.14}$$

Now let us consider a similar SDE with a drift term:

$$dX(t) = \alpha\, X(t)\, dt + \beta\, X(t)\, dB(t)\,, \tag{2.7.15}$$

where α and β are constants.

Dividing it by $X(t)$,

$$\frac{dX(t)}{X(t)} = \alpha\ dt + \beta\ dB(t)\,. \tag{2.7.16}$$

This differential represents,

$$\begin{aligned}\int_0^t \frac{dX}{X(t)} &= \int_0^t \alpha\, dt + \int_0^t \beta\, dB(t), \\ &= \alpha\, t + \beta(B(t) - B(0)), \\ &= \alpha\, t + \beta\, B(t).\end{aligned} \tag{2.7.17}$$

The second term on the right hand side comes from Ito integration.

Now let us assume

$$\phi\,(t) = \alpha\, t + \beta\, B(t)\,. \tag{2.7.18}$$

Then the SDE becomes,

$$\int_0^t \frac{dX(t)}{X(t)} = \phi\,(t),$$

and

$$\xi(t) = \phi(t) - \phi(0) - \frac{1}{2}[\phi,\phi](t)\,.$$

$$\begin{aligned}[\phi,\phi](t) &= [(\alpha t + \beta\, B(t)),(\alpha t + \beta\, B(t))](t), \\ &= [\alpha t,\alpha t](t) + 2\alpha\, \beta\, [t, B(t)](t) + \beta^{\,2}\, [B,B](t), \\ &= 0 + 0 + \beta^2\, t.\end{aligned}$$

Therefore $\xi(t) = \alpha t + \beta B(t) - 0 - \frac{1}{2}\beta^{\,2} t\,.$

Then the solution to the SDE is

$$X(t) = \exp((\alpha - \frac{1}{2}\beta^{\,2})t + \beta\, B(t))\,.$$

Let us examine whether the stochastic process

$$X(t) = \exp((\alpha - \frac{1}{2}\beta^2)t + \beta\, B(t)). \tag{2.7.19}$$

is a strong solution to the differential equation

$$dX(t) = \alpha X(t)dt + \beta\, X(t)\, dB(t)\,.$$

We will define a function,

$$f(x,t) = \exp((\alpha - \frac{1}{2}\beta^2)t + \beta\, X).$$

$$\begin{aligned} X(t) &= f(B(t),t), \\ &= \exp((\alpha - \frac{1}{2}\beta^2)t + \beta\, B(t)). \end{aligned}$$

We need to apply Ito formula for the two Ito processes $X_1(t)$ and $X_2(t)$.

$X_1(t) = B(t)$; $X_2(t) = t$ (a continuous function with finite variation);

$$dX_1.dX_2(t) = d[X_1, X_2] = 0\,; \quad (dX_1)^2 = dt\,; \quad (dX_2)^2 = 0\,.$$

$$\frac{\partial f}{\partial x} = \beta \exp((\alpha - \frac{1}{2}\beta^2)t + \beta x) \quad ,$$

$$\frac{\partial^2 f}{\partial x^2} = \beta^2 \exp((\alpha - \frac{1}{2}\beta^2)t + \beta x) \quad ,$$

$$\begin{aligned} \frac{\partial f}{\partial t} &= (\alpha - \frac{1}{2}\beta^2)\exp((\alpha - \frac{1}{2}\beta^2)t + \beta x) \\ &= (\alpha - \frac{1}{2}\beta^2)\exp((\alpha - \frac{1}{2}\beta^2)t + \beta x) \end{aligned}.$$

From Ito formula,

$$\begin{aligned} &d(f(X_1, X_2)) \\ &= \frac{\partial f}{\partial x} dB(t) + \frac{\partial f}{\partial t} dt + \frac{1}{2}\frac{\partial^2 f}{\partial x^2} dt + \frac{1}{2}\frac{\partial^2 f}{\partial t^2}(0) + \frac{1}{2}\frac{\partial^2 f}{\partial x\, \partial t}(0), \\ &= \beta \exp((\alpha - \frac{1}{2}\beta^2)t + \beta\, B(t)) + (\alpha - \frac{1}{2}\beta^2)\exp(\alpha - \frac{1}{2}\beta^2)dt + \frac{1}{2}\beta^2 \exp(\alpha - \frac{1}{2}\beta^2)dt. \end{aligned}$$

$$\begin{aligned} d(X(t)) &= d(f(B(t),t)) \\ &= \alpha \exp((\alpha - \frac{1}{2}\beta^2)t + \beta\, B(t))dt + \beta \exp((\alpha - \frac{1}{2}\beta^2)t + \beta\, B(t)dB(t), \\ &= \alpha X(t)dt + \beta X(t)\, dB(t). \end{aligned}$$

This proves that $X(t) = f(B(t),t)$ is a strong solution of the SDE given by equation (2.7.19).

We can see that if we can find a function $f(x,t)$, and for a given Wiener process $B(t)$, $X(t) = f(B(t),t)$ is a solution to the SDE of the form

$$dX(t) = \mu\,(X(t),t)dt + \sigma\,(X(t),t)\, dB(t)\,. \tag{2.7.20}$$

$X(t)$ should also satisfy,

$$X(t) = X(0) + \int_0^t \mu(X(s),s) + \int_0^t \sigma \, dB(s) \,,$$

provided that $\int_o^t \mu \; ds$ and $\int_o^t \sigma \, ds(s)$ exist.

Solution to the general linear SDE of the form,

$$dX(t) = (\alpha(t) + \beta(t)X(t))dt + (\gamma\,(t) + \delta(t)X(t))\, dB(t). \tag{2.7.21}$$

where α, β, γ and δ are given adapted processes and continuous functions of t, can be quite useful in applications.

The solution can be expresses as a product of two Ito processes (Klebaner, 1998)

$$X(t) = u(t)\, v(t) \text{, where ,}$$

$$du(t) = \beta\, u(t)dt + \delta u(t)\, dB(t) \text{ , and}$$

$$dv(t) = a\; dt + b\; dB(t) \,.$$

$u(t)$ can be solved by using a stochastic exponential as shown above and once we have a solution, we can obtain $a(t)$, $b(t)$ by solving the following two equations:

$$b(t)\, u(t) = \gamma(t) \text{ , and}$$

$$a(t)\, u(t) = \alpha(t) - \delta(t)\, \gamma(t) \,.$$

Then the solution to the general linear SDE is given by (Klebaner, 1998) :

$$X(t) = u(t)\left(X(0) + \int_0^t \frac{\alpha(s) - \delta(s)\, \gamma(s)}{u(s)} ds + \int_0^t \frac{\gamma(s)}{u(s)} dB(s) \right) \tag{2.7.22}$$

As an example let us solve the following linear SDE:

$$dx(t) = a\; X(t)\; dt + dB(t) \,, \tag{2.7.23}$$

where a is a constant.

Here $\beta(t) = a,\; \gamma(t) = 1,\; \alpha(t) = 0$, and $\delta(t) = 0$.

Using the general solution with

$$\begin{aligned} du(t) &= a\; u(t)\; dt + (0)\; dB(t), \\ &= a(t)\; u(t)\; dt. \end{aligned}$$

From stochastic exponential,

$$u(t) = \exp(a\, t) \quad .$$

Therefore,

$$X(t) = \exp(at)(X(o) + \int_{o}^{t} \exp(-as)\ dB(s)).$$

This is also the solution of the SDE given by equation (2.7.23).

The integral in the solution given above is an Ito integral and should be calculated according Ito integration. For non-linear stochastic differential equations, appropriate substitutions may be found to reduce them to linear ones.

2.8 The Estimation of Parameters for Stochastic Differential Equations Using Neural Networks

Stochastic differential equations (SDEs) offer an attractive way of modelling the random system dynamics, but the estimation of the drift and diffusion coefficients remains a challenging problem in many situations. There are various statistical methods that are used to estimate the parameters in differential equations driven by Wiener processes. In this section we offer an alternative approach based on artificial neural networks to estimate the parameters in a SDE. Readers who are familiar with neural networks may skip this section. Artificial Neural Networks (ANNs) as discussed in chapter 1 are universal function approximators that can map any nonlinear function, and they have been used in a variety of fields, such as prediction, pattern recognition, classification and forecasting. ANNs are less sensitive to error term assumptions and they can tolerate noise and chaotic behaviour better than most other methods. Other advantages include greater fault tolerance, robustness and adaptability due to ANNs' large number of interconnected processing elements that can be trained to learn new patterns (Bishop, 1995). The Multilayer Perceptron (MLP) network is among the most common ANN architecture in use. It is one type of feed forward networks wherein the connections are only allowed from the nodes in layer i to the nodes in layer i+1. There are other more complex neural network architectures available, such as recurrent networks and stochastic networks; however MLP networks are always sufficient for dealing with most of the recognition and classification problems if enough hidden layers and hidden neurons are used (Samarasinghe, 2006). We show how to use the output values from the SDE solutions of the equations to train neural networks, and use the trained networks to estimate the SDE parameters for given output data. MLP networks will be used to solve this type of mapping problem.

The general form of SDE can be expressed by

$$dy(t)=\mu(y,t,\theta)dt+\sigma(y,t,\theta)dw(t) \tag{2.8.1}$$

where $y(t)$ = the state variable of interest, θ = a set of parameters (known and unknown), and $w(t)$ = a standard Wiener process. In practice, to determine the parameter θ, the system output variable y is usually observed at discrete time intervals, t, where $0 \le t \le T$, at M independent points: $y = \{y_1, y_2, ..., y_M\}$. Observed data are recorded in discrete time intervals, regardless whether the model is described best by a continuous or discrete intervals.

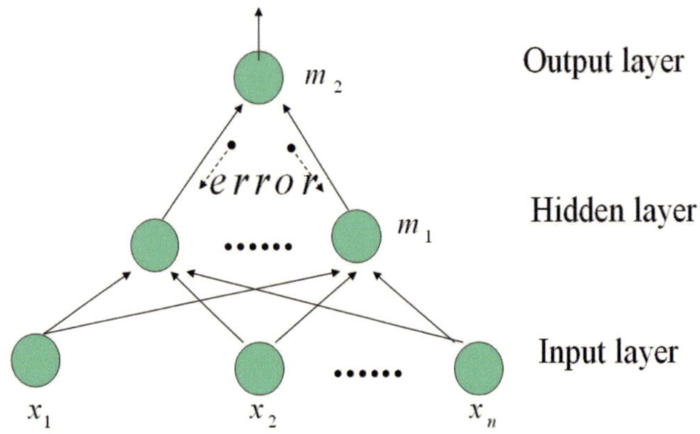

Figure 2.8. Basic structure of a MLP with backpropagation algorithm.

A MLP shown in Figure 2.8 has one hidden layer (m_1) and one output layer (m_2), and all the layers are fully connected to their subsequent layer. Connections are only allowed from the input layer to the hidden layer, and then, from the hidden layer to the output layer.

Rumelhart (1986) developed the backpropagation learning algorithm and it is commonly used to train ANNs due to its advanced ability to generalize wider variety of problems. A typical backpropagation learning algorithm is based on an architecture that contains a layer of input neurons, output neurons, and one or more hidden layers; these neurons are all interconnected with different weights. In the backpropagation training algorithm, the error information is passed backward from the output layer to the input layer (Figure 2.8). Weights are adjusted with the gradient descent method.

The ANN is trained by first setting up the network with all its units and connections, and then initialising with arbitrary weights. Then the network is trained by presenting examples. During the training phase the weights on connections change enabling the network to learn. When the network performs well on all training examples it should be validated on some other examples that it has not seen before. If the network can produce reasonable output values which are similar to validation targets and contain only small errors, it is then considered to be ready to use for problem solving.

Both linear and nonlinear SDEs are examined in this section. The linear SDE (Eq. (2.8.2)) is expressed by a one-dimensional diffusion equation. Its drift term has a linear relationship to the output variable of the model, and the diffusion term represents the noise in the model. Eq. (2.8.3) is arbitrarily chosen as a representative nonlinear SDE:

$$dX(t) = \alpha X(t)dt + \gamma X(t)dw(t)\text{, and} \tag{2.8.2}$$

$$dX(t) = \alpha X(t)dt + \beta X^2(t)dt + \gamma dw(t)\text{,} \tag{2.8.3}$$

where a, β = constant coefficients to be estimated as parameters, and γ = a constant coefficient to adjust the noise level (amplitude).

For each particular parameter a or the combination of parameters a and β, we can generate one realisation of SDE output through Eq. (2.8.2) or (2.8.3). The range of α and β used in the experiments is assumed to be [1, 2]. In addition, γ is used to adjust the proportion of the contribution of diffusion term, and the range of γ is [0.01, 0.1] in the linear case and [0.5, 3] in the nonlinear case.

The discrete observations $X(t)$ of these two equations are obtained at the sampling instants. Suppose the number of samples to be t_n, we consider the first t_n time steps starting from $X_0 = 1$ and the size of sampling interval Δt = 0.001. All the values come from the solution of SDEs. It has been shown that using Ito formula, Eq. (2.8.2) has an analytical solution (section 2.7),

$$X(t) = X_0 \exp\left[(\alpha - \frac{\gamma^2}{2})t + \gamma w(t) \right]. \tag{2.8.4}$$

For Eq. (2.8.4), we use the Euler method for the numerical solution. The numerical solution of $\gamma = 0$ has been compared with the analytical solution of the equation.

Before we describe the neural networks data sets, we clarify the terminology about "training", "validation" and "test" data sets. In the literature of machine learning and neural networks communities, different meaning of the words "validation" and "test" are employed. We restrict ourselves to the definitions given by Ripley (1996): a training set is used for learning, a validation set is used to tune the network parameters and a test set is used only to assess the performance of the network.

We generate a number of SDE realisations for a specified range of parameters with some patterns of Wiener processes to train the ANN. These data sets are called training data sets and validation sets are randomly chosen from the training sets. In order to test the prediction capability of the ANN, test data sets are generated with different patterns of Wiener processes within the same range of parameters as the training data sets.

Obviously if the test data sets were generated from SDEs which contain only a single Wiener process, the result would be biased if this Wiener process was coincidently similar to the one used to generate the training data sets. To fairly assess the performance of networks, five different patterns of Wiener processes are used to generate the test data sets.

To determine the value of time step t_n, we have taken different t_n values, where $t_n^{\min}$ = 10 to $t_n^{\max}$ = 200 and Δt_n = 10, to generate the training and test data sets. We found that 50 values were sufficient to represent the pattern of SDEs in order to train neural networks. Further increase in t_n did not increase the neural networks performance in parameter estimation. Therefore 50 time steps are used in our computational experiments.

All the experiments are carried out on a personal computer running the Microsoft Windows XP operating system. We use a commercial ANN software, namely NeuroShell2, for the neural network computations. It is recommended for academic users only, or those users who are concerned with classic neural network paradigms like backpropagation. Users interested in solving real problems should consider the NeuroShell Predictor, NeuroShell Classifier, or the NeuroShell Trader (Group, W.S., 2005).

Among all the parameters in MLP, the numbers of input and output neurons are the easiest parameters to be determined because each independent variable is represented by its own input neuron. The number of inputs is determined by the number of sampling instants in the SDE's solution, and the number of outputs is determined by the number of parameters which need to be predicted. In terms of the number of hidden layers and hidden layer neurons, we try a network that started with one layer and a few neurons, and then test different hidden layers and neurons to achieve the best ANN performance. In the following experiments, (X – Y – Z) is used to denote to the networks, where X is the number of input nodes, Y is the number of hidden nodes and Z is the number of output nodes.

We found that the logistic function was always superior to other five transfer functions used in NeuroShell2, logistic, linear, hyperbolic tangent function, Sine and Gaussian, as input, output and hidden layer functions because of its nonlinear and continuously differentiable properties, which are desirable for learning complex problems. In addition to the logistic function, we use the default values of 0.1 in NeuroShell2 for both learning rate and momentum as we found that it was always appropriate.

The number of training epochs plays an important role in determining the performance of the ANN. An epoch is the presentation of the entire training going through the network. ANNs need sufficient training epochs to learn complex input-output relationships. However excessive training epochs require unnecessarily long training time and cause over fitting problems where the network performs during the training very well but fails in testing (Caruana, 2001). To monitor the over fitting problem, we set up 20% of the training sets as validation sets and and the ANN monitors errors on the validation sets during training. The profile of the error plot for the training and validation sets during the training procedure indicates whether further training epoch is needed. We can stop training when the error of the training set plot keeps decreasing but that of the validation set plot has an increasing or flat line at the end.

In order to test the robustness of neural networks, we need to measure the level of noise in the diffusion term of a SDE with respect to its drift term. Thus the diffusion parameter γ is used to adjust the noise level. The higher γ value indicates greater noise and increases the influence of the contribution of the diffusion term to the entire solution. As one can assume, the increased noise levels raises the difficulty of estimation. To measure it, we define P_γ for linear equation (2.8.2) as

$$P_\gamma \equiv \frac{1}{n}\sum_{i=1}^{n}\left|\frac{\gamma\, dw(i)}{\alpha\, dt}\right|,$$

and for nonlinear equation (2.8.3),

$$P_\gamma \equiv \frac{1}{n}\sum_{i=1}^{n}\left|\frac{\gamma\, dw(i)}{\alpha\, dt\, x(i) + \beta\, dt\, x(i)^2}\right|, \tag{2.8.5}$$

where n = the number of time steps, and dt = time differential.

There are two parameters, α and β, in the drift term of the nonlinear SDE. We define P_a to determine the strength of the linear term (i.e. $\alpha\, dt\, x(t)$). Similarly, P_β indicates the measurement of strength of nonlinear term. They can be defined as

$$P_\alpha \equiv \frac{1}{n}\sum_{i=1}^{n}\left|\frac{\alpha\, dt}{\alpha\, dt + \beta\, dt\, x(i)}\right|, \tag{2.8.6}$$

and

$$P_\beta \equiv \frac{1}{n}\sum_{i=1}^{n}\left|\frac{\beta\, dt\, x(i)}{\alpha\, dt + \beta\, dt\, x(i)}\right|. \tag{2.8.7}$$

R^2 (coefficient of multiple determinations) is a statistical indication of data sets which is determined by multiple regression analysis, and it is an important indicator of the ANN performance used in NeuroShell2 (Triola, 2004). R^2 compares the results predicted by ANN with actual values, and it is defined by

$$R^2 = 1 - \frac{\sum_{i=1}^{m}(y_i - \hat{y}_i)^2}{\sum_{i=1}^{m}(y_i - \overline{y})^2}, \tag{2.8.8}$$

where y = actual value, $\hat{y}$ = predicted value of y, $\overline{y}$ = mean of y, and m = number of data patterns. In the case of parameter estimation for the linear SDE, one R^2 value is obtained for determining the accuracy of the predicted parameter a. For the nonlinear SDE, two R^2 values are calculated for determining the accuracy of the predicted parameters a and β. If the ANN predicts all the values correctly as the actual values, a perfect fit would result in an R^2 value of 1. In a very poor fit, the R^2 value would be close to 0. If ANN predictions are worse than the mean of samples, the R^2 value will be less than 0.

In addition to R^2, the Average Absolute Percentage Error (*AAPE*) is also used for evaluating the prediction performance where needed (Triola, 2004). The *AAPE* can be defined as,

$$AAPE = \frac{1}{m}\sum_{i=1}^{m}\frac{|y_i - \hat{y}_i|}{y_i}100 \tag{2.8.9}$$

where y = target value, $\hat{y}$ = predicted value of y, and m = number of data patterns.

The performance of ANN is evaluated by assessing the accuracy of the estimated parameters. Different ANN architectures including various combinations of hidden layers, neurons, and training epochs are used to obtain the optimum neural network. Further, a range of diffusion term is used to evaluate the effect of different level of stochasticity on the performance of ANN.

We do not have *a priori* knowledge of the optimal ANN architecture at first; therefore we choose the default parameters in NeuroShell2 for one hidden layer MLP network, which has

68 hidden neurons and the logistic transfer function for the hidden layers and output layer. In addition, α = [1, 2], $\Delta\alpha$ = 0.01 and γ = 0.03 are used for the parameters of SDE.

The experiments show that when training data set is developed using only one Wiener process, over fitting problem is obvious. The average error in the training set continues to decrease during training process. Because of the powerful mapping capability of neural networks, the average error between the target and network outputs approaches zero as the training continues. During the first four epochs, the average error in the test set drops significantly. It reaches the lowest at the epoch 8. After that, the validation set error starts rising although the training set error is getting smaller. The reason for this increasingly poor generalization is that the neural network tends to track every individual point in the training set created by a particular pattern of Wiener process, rather than seeing the whole character of the equation.

When the training data set is produced by more than one Wiener process, over fitting significantly decreases. The average error in the validation set continues to drop and remains stable after certain epochs. We examine the relationship between the number of Wiener processes and ANN prediction ability.

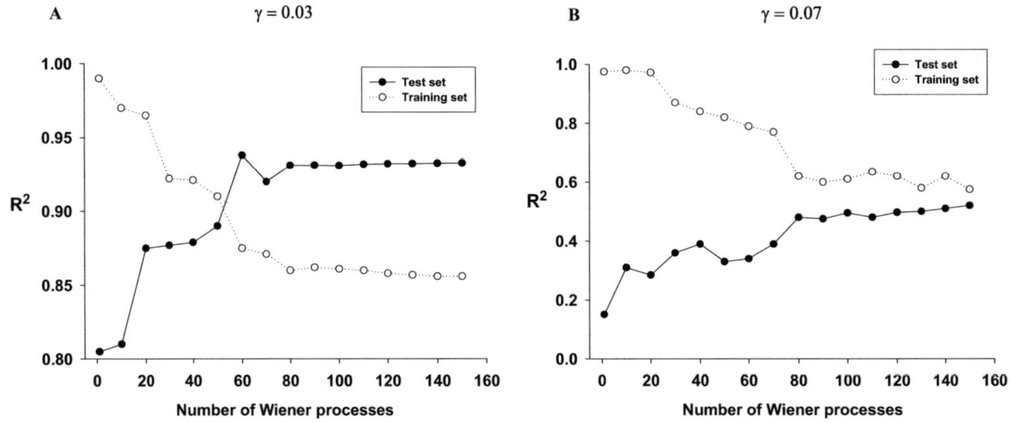

Figure 2.9. R^2 on the training and test sets against the number of Wiener Processes used to produce the training sets in the case of γ = 0.03 (A) and γ = 0.07 (B).

The same ANN architecture and SDE parameters as the previous section are used here. Additionally we test a set of noisier data with γ = 0.07. The results are obtained with the same numbers of training epochs. Figure 2.9 shows the influence of the number of Wiener processes that are used to produce training data sets. It indicates that as the number of Wiener Processes in the training sets increases, the network produces higher R^2 values for the test sets. It should be noted that the size of training data set expands as more Wiener processes are employed, and consequently the expansion causes slower training. Therefore, although there is a marginal improvement on R^2 value when more than 80 Wiener processes are used, we limit the number of Wiener Processes to 100 in further investigations.

We use the same SDE parameters except γ = 0.07 to create training and test data sets, and 100 Wiener processes are used to produce the training data sets. All the R^2 values are obtained by using early stopping. The results in Table 2.1 suggest that when there is only one hidden layer and the number of neurons in the hidden layer is very small, the performance of the network is poor because the network does not have enough "power" to learn the input-output relationship. When the number of neurons in the hidden layer is close to the half number of input neurons, the performance reaches a higher accuracy. Further increase in the number of hidden layers and neurons does not improve the performance.

The ANN performance is investigated for different combinations of drift and diffusion terms. We use three different MLP architectures, 50-30-1, 50-15-15-1, and 50-10-10-10-1, to train and test the data sets, and record the best performance.

The ANN performance is investigated for different combinations of drift and diffusion terms. We use three different MLP architectures, 50-30-1, 50-15-15-1, and 50-10-10-10-1, to train and test the data sets, and record the best performance.

1 hidden layer	Test set R^2	2 hidden layers	Test set R^2	3 hidden layer	Test set R^2
50-3-1	0.2728	50-3-3-1	0.5103	50-3-3-3-1	0.4920
50-10-1	0.5222	50-5-5-1	0.4916	50-5-5-5-1	0.4576
50-30-1	0.5392	50-15-15-1	0.5125	50-10-10-10-1	0.5075
50-50-1	0.5151	50-25-25-1	0.4986	50-20-20-20-1	0.4987
50-100-1	0.4980	50-50-50-1	0.4936	50-30-30-30-1	0.5072
50-200-1	0.4969	50-100-100-1	0.4669	50-100-100-100-1	0.4892

Table 2.1. R^2 variation on test set with different hidden neurons and hidden layers.

Figure 2.10A demonstrates that the ANN performance decreases as the magnitude of the diffusion term increases and Figure 2.10B shows that the target and network output in the test sets are in good agreement when γ = 0.01. Because the test set is created by 5 Wiener processes, it should be noticed that there are five repetitive sub-data sets and each of them represents a range of α values, which is from 1 to 2, with one pattern of Wiener process. By observing the sub-data sets separately, we can gain a better understanding on how noise influences the estimation of the parameter. As the γ value reaches 0.05 (Figure 2.10C) and the ratio of diffusion term and drift term reaches 0.67 (shown in Figure 2.10A), the 2nd, 3rd and 5th sub-data sets show more accurate predictions than the 1st and 4th sets. Figure 2.10D demonstrates that the network-generated outputs just tend to use the average of targets in most of the sub-data sets when γ = 0.10 where the weight of diffusion term is more than that of the drift term (P_γ = 1.39 as shown in Figure 2.10A).

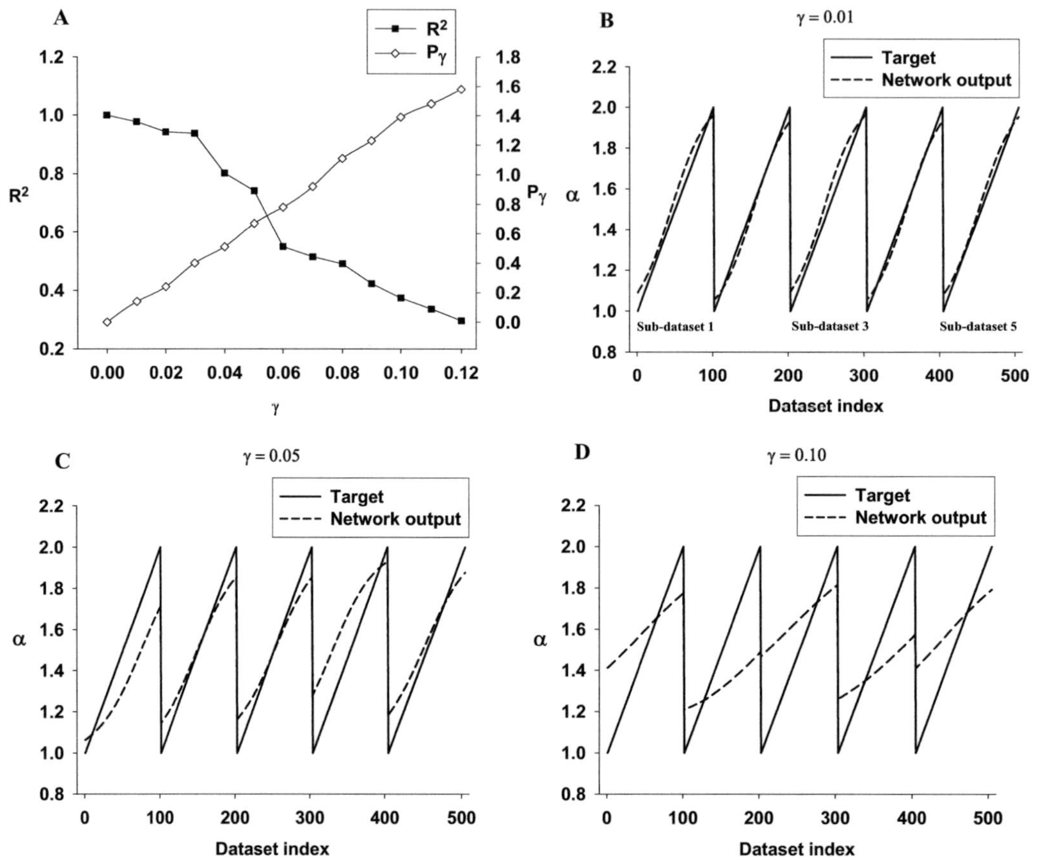

Figure 2.10. A: The neural network performance decreases as the diffusion term in SDEs increases. B, C and D: Target values and network outputs when γ= 0.01, 0.05 and 0.10; x-axis represents the index in testing datasets where five Wiener processes were used.

We investigate nonlinear SDE as well. Moreover, because the nonlinear SDE contains two parameters, we investigate how the accuracy of estimation varies for different combination of parameters. The parameter values and ranges of the SDE are as follows: α = [1, 2], $\Delta\alpha$ = 0.05, β = [1, 2], $\Delta\beta$ = 0.05 and γ= 0.5. We use early stopping to find out the best results. From Table 2.2, the different network architectures result in a very similar performance. The R^2 values for α are very close to zero while the R^2 values for β are all more than 0.9. According to the statistical meaning of R^2 given previously, we consider that the neural networks fail to predict a and succeed in predicting β. We explore the reason for the difference between a and β later.

Network architecture	$R^2(\alpha)$	$R^2(\beta)$	Network architecture	$R^2(\alpha)$	$R^2(\beta)$
50-10-2	0.0256	0.9161	50-10-10-2	-0.0135	0.9209
50-30-2	0.0349	0.9453	50-20-20-2	-0.0183	0.9299
50-60-2	0.0395	0.9406	50-50-50-2	0.0134	0.9310
50-100-2	0.0296	0.9209	50-10-10-10-2	0.0128	0.9198
50-200-2	0.0354	0.9299	50-50-50-50-2	-0.0164	0.9257

Table 2.2. Network performance in the nonlinear SDE as network architecture changes.

We use three network architectures, 50-30-2, 50-60-2 and 50-50-50-2, to estimate parameters for different SDEs and recorded the best results. The results in Table 2.3 indicate that the accuracy of network performance decreases as the strength of diffusion terms in SDEs increases, which is similar to the linear equation. Figure 2.11 shows that comparing with the results in the linear case (Figure 2.10A), the prediction capability of networks for the nonlinear case is poorer due to the complexity of input-output relationship in the nonlinear SDEs.

Range of a	Range of β	γ	P_α	P_β	P_γ	$R^2(a)$	AAPE (α)	$R^2(\beta)$	AAPE (β)
[1,2]	[1,2]	0.5	0.12	0.88	0.10	0.0349	17.79	0.9453	4.02
[1,2]	[1,2]	2	0.11	0.89	0.40	0.0006	18	0.6833	9.92
[1,2]	[1,2]	3	0.11	0.89	0.60	-0.012	17.59	0.3687	12.96

Table 2.3. Network performance in the nonlinear SDE as diffusion term increases.

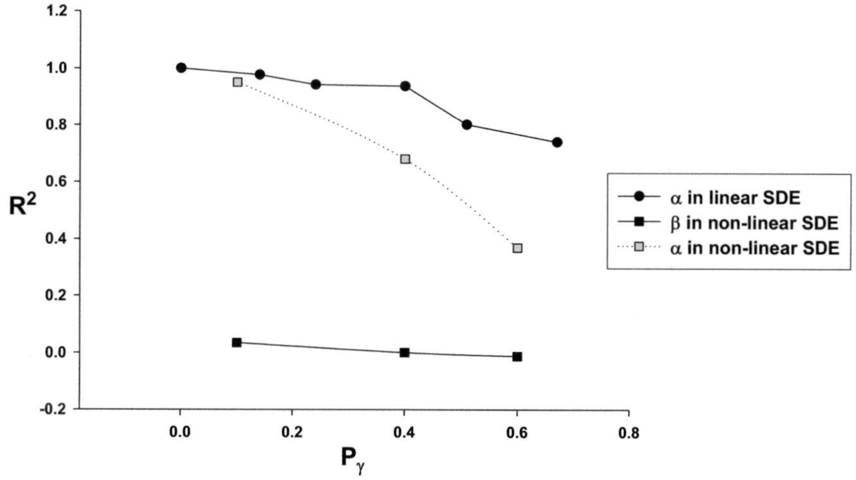

Figure 2.11. The scattered graph of R^2 values for the parameters in the linear and the nonlinear equations against their corresponding P_γ values.

Range of a	Range of β	γ	P_α	P_β	P_γ	$R^2(\alpha)$	AAPE (α)	$R^2(\beta)$	AAPE (β)
[1,2]	[0.2,0.4]	0.35	0.47	0.53	0.39	0.2932	13.91	0.3891	12.98
[1,2]	[1,2]	2	0.11	0.89	0.40	0.0006	18	0.6833	9.92
[0.8,1.6]	[0.02,0.04]	0.15	0.89	0.11	0.42	0.7735	8.46	0.0108	17.94

Table 2.4. Network performance for different parameters in the nonlinear SDE

To investigate the reason for largest differences in R^2 values for a and β, we change the magnitudes of α term and β term in SDEs by altering parameters α and β values while keeping diffusion level an approximate constant. Table 2.4 shows that the bigger the contribution of a term containing a particular parameter (P_a or P_β), the smaller the error (*AAPE*) and better the prediction (R^2) for that parameter. Therefore, we conclude that the accuracy of a parameter in a nonlinear SDE is dependent on its term that contributes *pro rata* to the drift term.

In the data preparation stage, we use different time steps to solve SDEs and found 50 data points are sufficient to represent the realisation of SDEs. In addition, we emphasise the effect of the number of Wiener processes used to create training data sets. Increasing the number of Wiener processes boosts the performance of networks considerably and eliminates the over fitting problem. When over fitting occurs, the resulting network is accurate on the training set but perform poorly on the test set. When the number of Wiener processes used to generate training data sets is increased, the learning procedure finds common features amongst the training sets that enable the network to correctly estimate the parameter(s) in test data sets.

In the ANN training procedure, we use early stopping to obtain the optimum test results. We also employ different MLP architectures, transfer functions, learning rates and momentums. However we find that these factors do not increase the performance of ANNs significantly.

The diffusion level in a SDE has a significant impact on the network performance. In the linear SDE, when the ratio of diffusion term and drift term is below 0.40, the network can estimate the parameter accurately (R^2>0.93). When the ratio reaches 0.67, the network estimates the parameter accurately only when Wiener processes in test sets and in training sets are similar. If the diffusion term is larger than the drift term, the network cannot predict the parameter(s) and only tends to give an average value of the parameters used for training datasets. For nonlinear SDEs, the estimation ability of a network is generally poorer than that for the linear SDEs. Furthermore, the accuracy of a parameter in a nonlinear SDE is dependent on its term that contributes *pro rata* to the drift term.

We can conclude that the classical neural networks method (MLP with backpropagation algorithm) provides a simple but robust parameter estimation approach for the SDEs that are under certain noisy conditions, but this estimation capability is limited for the SDEs having a high diffusion level. When the diffusion level is high (>10%-20%), the statistical methods also fail to estimate parameters accurately.

3

A Stochastic Model for Hydrodynamic Dispersion

3.1 Introduction

We have seen in chapter 1 that, in the derivation of advection–dispersion equation, also known as continuum transport model (Rashidi et al. ,1999), the velocity fluctuations around the mean velocity enter into the calculation of solute flux at a given point through averaging theorems. The mean advective flux and the mean dispersive flux are then related to the concentration gradients through Fickian–type assumptions. These assumptions are instrumental in defining dispersivity as a measure of solute dispersion. Dispersivity is proven to be scale dependant.

To address the issue of scale dependence of dispersive fundamentally, it has been argued that a more realistic mathematical framework for modelling is to use stochastic calculus (Holden et al., 1996; Kulasiri and Verwoerd, 1999, 2002). Stochastic calculus deals with the uncertainty in the natural and other phenomena using nondifferentiable functions for which ordinary differentials do not exist (Klebaner, 1998). Stochastic calculus is based on the premise that the differentials of nondifferential functions can have meaning only through certain types of integrals such as Ito integrals which are rigorously developed in the literature. In addition, mathematically well-defined processes such as the Weiner process aid in formulating mathematical models of complex systems. Mathematical theories aside, one needs to question the validity of using stochastic calculus in each instance. In modelling the solute transport in porous media, we consider that the fluid velocity is fundamentally a random variable with respect to space and time and continuous but irregular, i.e., nondifferentiable. In many natural porous formations, geometrical structures are irregular and therefore, as fluid particles encounter porous structures, velocity changes are more likely to be irregular than regular. In many situations, we hardly have accurate information about the porous structure, which contributes to greater uncertainties. Hence, stochastic calculus provides a more sophisticated mathematical framework to model the advection-dispersion in porous media found in practical situations, especially involving natural porous formations. By using stochastic partial differential equations, for example, we could incorporate the uncertainty of the dispersion coefficient and hydraulic conductivity that are present in porous structures such as underground aquifers. The incorporation of the dispersivity as a random, irregular coefficient makes the solution of resulting partial differential equations an interesting area of study. However, the scale dependency of the dispersivity can not be addressed in this manner because the dispersivity itself is not a material property but a constant that depends on the scale of the experiment.

In this chapter we develop one dimensional model without resorting to Fickian assumptions and discuss the methods of estimating the parameters. As of many contracted description of a natural phenomena the model presented in this chapter has its weaknesses. But we model the fluctuation of the solute velocity due to porous structure and incorporate the fluctuation in the mass conservation of solute. Then we need to characterise the fluctuations so that we can relate them to the porous structure

3.2 The Model Development

The basic assumption on the formulation of this model is that the velocity of solute particles is fundamentally a stochastic variable with irregular but continuous realisations.

Let us consider an infinite cylindrical volume having a cross sectional area, A, within a one-dimensional porous medium with the solute concentration of $C(x, t)$ (Figure 3.1). Within the context of solute transport in heterogeneous groundwater systems, the velocity, $V(x, t)$, the contaminant flux, $J(x, t)$, and $C(x,t)$ are stochastic functions of space and time, having irregular (may be highly irregular) and continuous realisations. Therefore, when formulating the mass conservation model for the solute transport, it is important to use higher order terms in the Taylor expansion.

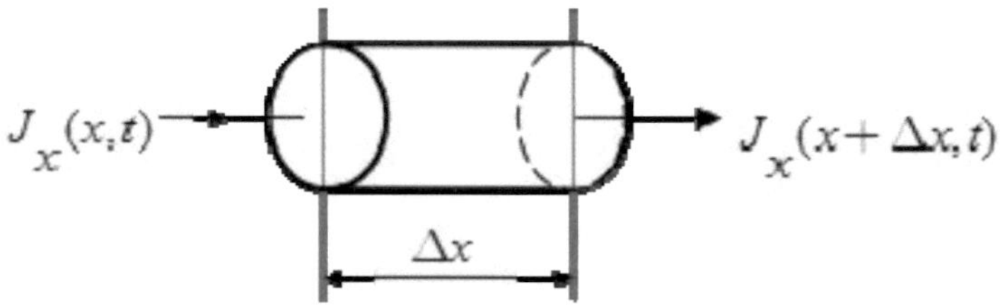

Figure 3.1. An infinitesimal cylindrical volume within a one-dimensional porous medium.

The mass balance for change of solute of the infinitesimal cylindrical volume for a small time interval, Δt, could be written as,

$$\Delta C(x,t) n_e A \Delta x = (J_x(x,t) - J_x(x+\Delta x,t) n_e A \Delta t \ ,$$

$$\left(\frac{\Delta C}{\Delta t}\right)_{x,t} = \frac{(J_x(x,t) - J_x(x+\Delta x,t))}{\Delta x}, \qquad (3.2.1)$$

where n_e is the effective porosity of the material, $\Delta C(x,t)$ and Δt are infinitesimal changes of solute concentration, $C(x,t)$, and time, respectively.

For the convenience, let us indicate $J_x(x,t)$ as J_x and $J_x(x+\Delta x,t)$ as $J_{x+\Delta x}$.

The Taylor series expansion can be shown as

$$J_{x+\Delta x} - J_x = \frac{1}{1!}\frac{\partial J_x}{\partial x}\Delta x + \frac{1}{2!}\frac{\partial^2 J_x}{\partial x^2}(\Delta x)^2 + \frac{1}{3!}\frac{\partial^3 J_x}{\partial x^3}(\Delta x)^3 + R(\varepsilon) \ ,$$

where $R(\varepsilon)$ is the remainder of the series.

Let us assume that the terms up to second order would be sufficient to adequately represent the irregular behaviour of the flow, thus, the higher order derivatives of the flux greater than three of the flux are negligible. Therefore, equation (3.2.1) can be written as,

$$\frac{\partial C}{\partial t}=-\frac{\partial J_x}{\partial x}-\frac{1}{2}\frac{\partial^2 J_x}{\partial x^2}dx+R_c(x,t), \tag{3.2.2}$$

where $R_c(x,t)=-\frac{1}{6}\frac{\partial^3 J_x}{\partial x^3}(dx)^2-\frac{1}{24}\frac{\partial^4 J_x}{\partial x^4}(dx)^3-R(\varepsilon)$.

Substituting $dx=h_x$, we can write equation (3.2.2),

$$\frac{\partial C}{\partial t}=-\frac{\partial J_x}{\partial x}-\frac{h_x}{2}\frac{\partial^2 J_x}{\partial x^2}+R_c(x,t). \tag{3.2.3}$$

Multiplying the both sides of equation (3.2.3) by *dt*, we obtain,

$$dC=-\left(\frac{\partial J_x}{\partial x}+\frac{h_x}{2}\frac{\partial^2 J_x}{\partial x^2}\right)dt+R_c(x,t)\,dt. \tag{3.2.4}$$

Equation (3.2.4) represents the mass conversation of the solute within the infinitesimal cylindrical volume shown in Figure 3.1. $C(x,t)$ describes the average solute concentration over the cylindrical volume and the smallest possible Δx would increase the accuracy of the stochastic model. However, if Δx is in the same order of magnitude of a typical grain size of the porous media, $C(x,t)$ would lose its meaning. Therefore, it is important to use a realistic Δx value for the scale under consideration for the computational solutions.

Compared to the first term on the right hand side of equation (3.2.4), it is assumed that $R_c(x,t)\,dt\approx 0$. (However, this assumption needs to be tested for any given situation, especially when porous media is extremely heterogeneous.) Under this assumption,

$$dC=-\left(\frac{\partial J_x}{\partial x}+\frac{h_x}{2}\frac{\partial^2 J_x}{\partial x^2}\right)dt. \tag{3.2.5}$$

The contaminant flux can be expressed in terms of the velocity in the *x* direction and the concentration of the contaminant is expressed as,

$$J(x,t)=V(x,t)\,C(x,t). \tag{3.2.6}$$

The velocity is modelled as,

$$V(x,t)=\bar{V}(x,t)+\xi(x,t), \tag{3.2.7}$$

where $\bar{V}(x,t)$ is the mean velocity of the flow that may be described by Darcy's law,

$$\bar{V}(x,t)=-\frac{K(x)}{n_e(x)}\frac{\partial p}{\partial x},$$

$K(x)$ = an average value of the hydraulic conductivity of the region,
$n_e(x)$ = porosity of the material,

p = pressure head, and

$\xi(x,t)$ = stochastic perturbation of the fluid velocity described by noise correlated in space and δ - correlated in time such that,

$$E[\xi(x,t)]=0, \tag{3.2.8}$$

$$E[\xi(x_1,t_1)\xi(x_2,t_2)]=q(x_1,x_2)\delta(t_1-t_2), \tag{3.2.9}$$

where $q(x_1,x_2)$ is the velocity covariance kernel in space, and $\delta(t_1-t_2)$ is the Dirac's delta function.

Since, $\Delta t=t_2-t_1$, we can rewrite equation (3.2.9) as,

$$E[\xi(x_1,t_1)\,\xi(x_2,t_1+\Delta t)]=q(x_1,x_2)\delta(\Delta t)\,. \tag{3.2.10}$$

In equation (3.2.6) the velocity, $V(x,t)$, is modelled as a stochastic process with the fluctuating component ($\xi(x,t)$) superimposed on the expectation of velocity (mean velocity). The expected value of the velocity $\bar{V}(x,t)$ can be obtained from other considerations without involving Darcy's law. The use of Darcy's law is only one way of prescribing $\bar{V}(x,t)$ within a given region of the porous medium. The fluctuating velocity ($\xi(x,t)$) is assumed to be a zero-mean stochastic process as given by equation (3.2.7), and the two-time correlation function is expressed as a product of a function of space ($q(x_1,x_2)$) and a function of time ($\delta(t_1-t_2)$) in equation (3.2.9) and (3.2.10). (As $\xi(x,t)$ is a zero-mean process, the two-time correlation function and the covariance are the same). The spatial function, $q(x_1,x_2)$, reflects the contribution of the porous structure to the fluctuations and helps characterise the structural influence on the flow. The Dirac's delta function makes the stochastic process behave as a white noise process along the time line. For low velocity situations, such as in aquifers, this is not an unreasonable assumption, but the alternative approach of assembling a time correlation function along the time line would complicate the mathematics a fair deal, and unless the flow is turbulent, there is no justification to take that approach.

Substituting equations (3.2.5) and (3.2.6) into equation (3.2.4), we can obtain,

$$\begin{aligned} dC &= -\frac{\partial}{\partial x}\left[\bar{V}(x,t)C(x,t)+C(x,t)\xi(x,t)\right]dt-\frac{h_x}{2}\frac{\partial^2}{\partial x^2}\left[\bar{V}(x,t)C(x,t)+C(x,t)\xi(x,t)\right]dt, \\ &= -\left(\frac{\partial}{\partial x}+\frac{h_x}{2}\frac{\partial^2}{\partial x^2}\right)\left[\bar{V}(x,t)C(x,t)+C(x,t)\xi(x,t)\right]dt. \end{aligned} \tag{3.2.11}$$

An operator in space can be defined such that,

$$S=-\left(\frac{\partial}{\partial x}+\frac{h_x}{2}\frac{\partial^2}{\partial x^2}\right) \tag{3.2.12}$$

for a given h_x.

Therefore, we can write equation (3.2.11) as,

$$dC = S\left(\overline{V}(x,t)C(x,t)\right)dt + S\left(C(x,t)\xi(x,t)\right)dt. \tag{3.2.13}$$

Equation (3.2.13) is a stochastic (partial) differential equation and both terms on the right hand side need to be integrated as Ito integrals to obtain the concentration. $\xi(x,t)dt$ can be transformed by $d\beta(t)$ which is a Wiener process increments in Hilbert space for a given x. The explanation on the transformation of $\xi(x,t)dt$ to $d\beta(t)$ can be found in Jazwinski (1970).

The transformation of $\xi(x,t)dt$ to $d\beta(t)$ can be understood if we interpret $\xi(x,t)dt$ to be fluctuating component of the travel length of a solute particle during of time interval dt. As we see later this fluctuating travel length component can be expressed as a random vector field ($d\beta(t)$) in an orthonormal set of co-ordinate space (Hilber space). The co-ordinates depend on the covariance kernel $q(x_1,x_2)$, and these are called basis functions in Hilbert space (Hernandez, 1995).

Equation (3.2.13) can be written as,

$$dC = S\left(\overline{V}(x,t)C(x,t)\right)dt + S\left(C(x,t)d\beta(t)\right), \tag{3.2.14}$$

And

$$C(x,t) = \int_0^t S\left(\overline{V}(x,t)C(x,t)\right)dt + \int_0^t S\left(C(x,t)d\beta(t)\right). \tag{3.2.15}$$

We call equation (3.2.15) a stochastic solute transport model (SSTM) in which $C(x,t)$ is stochastic solute concentration at a given point in space and time; $\overline{V}(x,t)$ is the expected value of stochastic velocity; h_x approximates the spatial discretization interval, dx; and $d\beta(t)$ can be considered as a "noise" term which models the velocity fluctuations.

In this model, instead of the Fickian assumption (equation (1.2.3)), a covariance kernel for the velocity fluctuations $q(x_1,x_2)$ is assumed. The emphasis on modelling of the velocity fluctuation as a random field of second order has its own strengths and weaknesses. The expectation is that by directly incorporating the velocity fluctuation in the solute mass conservation, we expect to reduce the scale dependency because the assumed covariance kernel is a function of the pore structure. The major weakness is that we usually do not have velocity data to construct the kernel for velocity fluctuations. On the other hand, different velocity kernels can be assumed based on plausible reasoning. In this chapter, for the illustration purposes, we assume that the covariance kernel to be exponentially decaying function, $\sigma^2 e^{-\frac{|x_1 - x_2|}{b}}$, where σ^2 is the variance and b is the correlation length.

In SSTM, the first term on the right hand side of equation (3.2.15) can be considered as the drift term of the stochastic partial differential equations (SPDE). The velocity, $\overline{V}(x,t)$, can be considered as the mean velocity of a local region but for the simplicity, we can assume that $\overline{V}(x,t)$ is a constant in this chapter. This assumption is reasonable in practice as we often calculate the Darcian velocity over a region. As $C(x,t)$ is a stochastic variable, at a given point in space, the integral can be evaluated as an Ito integral to simplify the numerical solution. This argument can also be applied to the dispersion term, the second integral of the right hand side of equation (3.2.15), but $d\beta(t)$ term has to be evaluated. (We use the term "dispersion" instead of "diffusion" to denote the second integral of the right hand side of equation (3.2.15) to allude to the physical nature that is being represented by the term. But in the mathematical literature, the term "diffusion" is used to denote the stochastic (Ito or Stratonovich) integral of analogous stochastic differential equations because it is a diffusion process in mathematical sense.) It should also be noted that $\overline{V}(x,t)$ could also vary from location to location at a higher scale, and we can assume that we can identify regions of sufficiently large magnitudes within which $\overline{V}(x,t)$ can be treated as a smoothly varying function if not a constant. However, this assumption is not necessary if we know the mean velocity profiles based on more aggregate properties. $\xi(x,t)$, on the other hand, relaxes the assumption expressed by equation (1.2.3) and allows us to include a much more realistic assumption as to how the noise behaves. There is some experimental evidence to suggest that the normalised longitudinal velocity covariances for different flow rates had similar exponential behaviour with respect to time in a homogenous porous media (Moroni and Cushman, 2001). However, there is no experimental evidence to date as to how the covariance of velocity fluctuation around the mean velocity, $\xi(x,t)$, behaves with respect to space, but the exponential decay in this situation is quite plausible.

3.3 Construction of $d\beta(t)$ Random Fields Using Spectral Expansion

We summarise the pertinent theoretical background here to explain the assumptions in our model of velocity fluctuations. Let K be a compact set in R^d, over which we define a second order random field, having a covariance function, $q(x,y)$ which is assumed to be square integrable over $K \times K$ (see Hernandez,1995):

$$\iint_{K\times K} |q(x,y)|^2 dx\,dy < +\infty .$$

Let $A: L_2(K) \rightarrow L_2(K)$ be the integral operator

$$A\,\phi(x) = \int_K q(x,y)\,\phi(y)\,dy \tag{3.3.1}$$

with the set of eigen values $\{\lambda_i : i = 1, 2, 3.....\}$ and the set of orthonormal eigenfunctions $\{\psi_i : i = 1, 2, 3 ...\}$. This means

$$A\psi_i = \lambda_i \psi_i, \quad i = 1,2,3...,\tag{3.3.2}$$

$$\text{and } \langle \psi_i, \psi_j \rangle = \delta_{ij} \quad i,j = 1,2,3.....,\tag{3.3.3}$$

$$\text{where } \langle \psi_i, \psi_j \rangle = \int_K \psi_i(x)\,\overline{\psi_j(x)}\,dx .\tag{3.3.4}$$

If $q(x,y)$ is continuous then $\langle A\psi_i, \psi_i \rangle \geq 0$ for $\psi_i \in L_2(K)$.

Now we can make use of Mercer's theorem (Hernandez, 1995) to express $q(x,y)$ in terms of eigenfunctions (ψ_i) and the corresponding eigenvalues (λ_i) ,

$$q(x,y)=\sum_{k=1}^{\infty}\lambda_k\psi_k(x)\overline{\psi_k(y)}, \tag{3.3.5}$$

and convergence is uniform and absolute over $K \times K$. Now let us define a set of (complex) random variables $\{Z_i : i=1, 2, 3...\}$ with the following moments:

$$EZ_n=0, \quad n=1,2,... \text{ , and}$$

$$EZ_n\overline{Z_m}=\lambda_n\delta_{nm}, \quad n=1,2,......$$

Then the Karhunen-Loeve theorem states that random field $\gamma(x)$ can be expressed as a series expansion of Zi s,

$$\gamma(x):=\sum_{n=1}^{\infty}\psi_n(x)Z_n, \tag{3.3.6}$$

which converges in quadratic mean for any x in K. In addition, the following conditions hold,

$$E\gamma(x)\overline{Z_n}=\lambda_n\psi_n(x), \quad n=1,2,..... \text{ and,}$$

$$\lim_{x\to x^0}E\left|\gamma(x)-\gamma(x^0)\right|^2=0 \quad \text{for any } x^0 \text{ in } K.$$

What Karhunen-Loeve (KL) expansion does is to model a random field by using two separate mathematical objects: continuous functions, which stem as the solutions of an integral equation (equation (3.3.1)) and random variables. If we assume the random variables (Z_i) to be standard Gaussian ($N(0,1)$), then Karhunen-Loeve expansion takes the following form,

$$\gamma(x):=\sum_{n=1}^{\infty}\sqrt{\lambda_n}\,\psi_n(x)Z_n. \tag{3.3.7}$$

KL expansion provides a way of modelling a random field of a single variable, which is considered to be the space variable, in terms of a set of orthonormal basis functions of a Hilbert space and a discrete set of standard Gaussian variables. We extend this development to model the velocity fluctuation of equation (3.2.6), $\xi(x,t)$, which is spatially and temporally correlated in such a way that $\xi(x,t)\in H^0=L_2(R)\times[0,T]$ where H^0 is a separable Hilbert space in which we assume $\xi(x,t)$ to be spatially correlated through a symmetric and positive definite covariance function $q(x_1,x_2)$, and δ-correlated in time (or white in time). As mentioned before this means that velocity changes in a porous medium are influenced by the porous matrix but behaves like white noise with respect to time, i.e., correlation in time is a Dirac delta function. Suppose that the mean velocity $\overline{V}(x,t)$ of a region is 1 m per day, then within a second a solute particle travels 0.01 mm on the average, and within 0.001 days it travels 1 mm, which increases the probability of solute particle changing its course. We can assume that in slow moving fluids, the velocity fluctuation at one small interval in time is independent of that of within another interval in time. By incorporating appropriate discretisation time and space intervals in the solution process, the white-in-time assumption leads to a simpler but physically plausible model of velocity fluctuation. Therefore, we can express $\xi(x,t)$ as a second-order random field with the moments as given in equation (3.2.9).

Based on stochastic calculus considerations (Unny, 1985), $\xi(x,t)\,dt$ can be considered as a Wiener process increment $d\beta(t)$ in Hilbert space H^0 for a given *x;* and to obtain strong solutions to the stochastic partial differential equation (3.2.14) numerically, this representation is particularly useful. The orthonormal functions, $\{\psi_i : i=1, 2, 3... \}$, provide a basis for H^0, and then we can use the standard Wiener increments ($db_i(t)$) to replace random variables in *KL* expansion (equation (3.3.7)) to construct the random field $d\beta(t)$:

$$d\beta(t) := \sum_{n=1}^{\infty} \sqrt{\lambda_n}\, \psi_n(x)\, db_n(t) = \xi(x,t)dt\,. \tag{3.3.8}$$

Intrinsic in this model is the fact that for any given element $e \in H^0$, the inner product $<\beta(t), e>$ is a real Wiener process having the correlation,

$$E[<\beta(t),e_1><\beta(t),e_2>] = \iint_{K\times K} q(x_1,x_2)e_1(x_2)e_2(x_1)dx_1\,dx_2\,. \tag{3.3.9}$$

An approximation for equation (3.3.8) can be constructed by considering the first *m* terms in the expansion which converges to a desired accuracy. As the increments in standard Wiener process have zero means and *dt* variances, care must be given to the choice of the time increments within the context of the problem. Smaller the time increments, higher the accuracy of KL expansion as in the case of solving stochastic differntial equations numerically (Kloeden and Platen, 1992).

Equation (3.3.8) gives a series expansion for the stochastic process $d\beta(t)$ but eigen functions and eigenvalues must be found for a given kernel. This task is not straight forward and often involves solving the Fredholm integral equations. Let us assume, based on previous discussion, an exponentially decaying kernel in the *x*-direction in this chapter,

$$q(x_1,x_2) = \sigma^2 e^{\frac{-|x_1-x_2|}{b}}\,. \tag{3.3.10}$$

where x_1 and x_2 are two neighbouring points on *x*. The correlation length *b* signifies the extent to which the correlation of the stochastic process is decayed along the *x*-axis. σ^2 is the variance which acts as an amplitude factor. To obtain the orthornormal functions for the kernel in equation (3.3.10), the following integral equation must be solved within the domain [0, *a*], where *a* is the length (scale) of the experiment,

$$\int_0^a q(x_1,x_2)\; f_i(x_2)\; dx_2 = \lambda_i f_i(x_1)\,. \tag{3.3.11}$$

Equation (3.3.11) can be written as,

$$f_i(x_1) = \frac{1}{\lambda_i}\int_0^a \sigma^2 e^{\frac{-|x_1-x_2|}{b}}\; f_i(x_2)\; dx_2\,. \tag{3.3.12}$$

As the upper limit of integration is a constant, equation (3.3.10) is a homogenous Fredholm integral equation of the second kind.

We now discuss the general solution of the integral equation generated by equation (3.3.10) considering the solutions of a general Fredholm integral equation of the form (Polyanin et al., 1998),

$$y(x) + A1 \int_a^b e^{\theta|x-t|} y(t)\, dt = f(x), \tag{3.3.13}$$

where $A1$ and θ are constants.

Then the function $y = y(x)$ obeys the following second order linear non-homogeneous differential equation with constant coefficients,

$$y''_{xx} + \theta(2A1 - \theta)y = f''_{xx}(x) - \theta^2 f(x). \tag{3.3.14}$$

The boundary conditions for this ordinary differential equation (ODE) have the form,

$$y'_x(a) + \theta y(a) = f'_x(a) + \theta f(a) \text{ ,and} \tag{3.3.15}$$

$$y'_x(b) - \theta y(b) = f'_x(b) - \theta f(b). \tag{3.3.16}$$

Polyanin et al. (1998) explain why the given ODE (equation (3.3.16)) under these boundary conditions determines the solutions of the original integral equation (3.3.12).

Case 1. For $\theta(2A1 - \theta) < 0$, the general solution of equation (3.3.13) is given by,

$$y(x) = C_1 Cosh(kx) + C_2 Sinh(kx) + f(x) - \frac{2A1\theta}{k} \int_0^x Sinh[k(x-t)] f(t) dt, \tag{3.3.17}$$

where $k = \sqrt{\theta(\theta - 2A1)}$, and C_1 and C_2 are arbitrary constants.

Case 2. For $\theta(2A1 - \theta) > 0$, the general solution of equation (3.3.13) is given by

$$y(x) = C_1 Cos(kx) + C_2 Sin(kx) + f(x) - \frac{2A1\theta}{k} \int_0^x Sin[k(x-t)] f(t) dt, \tag{3.3.18}$$

where $k = \sqrt{\theta(2A1 - \theta)}$.

Case 3. For $\theta = 2A1$, the general solution of equation (3.3.13) is given by,

$$y(x) = C_1 + C_2 x + f(x) - 4A1^2 \int_a^x (x-t) f(t) dt. \tag{3.3.19}$$

The constants C_1 and C_2 are determined by the boundary conditions.

These results (Cases 1, 2, and 3) can be applied to the integral equation (3.3.11) by changing notation, and observing that

$$(2A1 - \theta) = \left(\frac{1}{b}\right)\left(\frac{2\sigma^2}{\lambda} + \frac{1}{b}\right) > 0. \tag{3.3.20}$$

The eigenvalues of equation (3.3.13) for constant σ^2 over [0, *a*] are given by

$$\lambda_i = \frac{2\theta\sigma^2}{\omega_i^2 + \theta^2}, \qquad (3.3.21)$$

where $\theta = \frac{1}{b}$, and

ω_i s are the roots of the following equation,

$$Tan(\omega_i a) = \frac{2\omega_i\theta}{\omega_i^2 - \theta^2}. \qquad (3.3.22)$$

The orthonormal basis functions of the Hilbert space associated with the given exponential kernel (equation (3.3.10)) are the normalised eigenfunctions,

$$f_i(x) = \frac{1}{\sqrt{N}}\left(Sin(\omega_i x) + \frac{\omega_i}{\theta} Cos(\omega_i x) \right), \qquad (3.3.23)$$

where,

$$N = \frac{1}{2}a\left(1 + \frac{\omega_i^2}{\theta^2}\right) - \frac{1}{4\omega_i}\left(1 - \frac{\omega_i^2}{\theta^2}\right) Sin(2\omega_i a) - \frac{1}{2\theta}(Cos(2\omega_i a) + 1). \qquad (3.3.24)$$

As seen from equation (3.3.21), the eigenvalues are dependent on the correlation length *b* and the variance σ^2 directly and to the length of the experiment, *a*, indirectly through equation (3.3.22). Equation (3.3.22) is a transendental equation with roots ω_i. Firstly, equation (3.3.22) has to be solved numerically for a given *a* and *b*, then the eigenvalues λ_i s and finally the basis functions of H^0. Then the random field $d\beta(t)$ for a given number of terms, *m*, can be evaluated by using equation (3.3.8) in conjunction with the standard Wiener increments.

3.4 The Dispersion and Travel Length Fluctuations

In this section, we explore the dispersion term in the SSTM to understand its behaviour in simplified settings; as we have seen previously, $S(C(x,t)d\beta(t))$ can be expanded by using the spectral expansion,

$$S(C(x,t)d\beta(t)) = S(C(x,t)\sum_{j=1}^{m} f_j(x)\sqrt{\lambda_j}\, db_j(t)). \qquad (3.4.1)$$

Let us assume that we use the same realisation of the standard Wiener process across all *x* in evaluating this term, i.e., db_j is independent of x. Then we can express the dispersion term for this situation,

$$S(C(x,t)d\beta(t)) = \sum_{j=1}^{m} S(C(x,t)\, f_j\sqrt{\lambda_j})\, db_j(t). \qquad (3.4.2)$$

Now for the sake of argument, let us assume that all the Wiener increments are the same, a situation which is never encountered in computation. Then we can take db_j s out of the summation, and explore the behaviour of the term, $\sum_{j=1}^{m} S(C(x,t) f_j(x)\sqrt{\lambda_j})$.

By substituting for the differential operator S and for $f_j(x)$, after symbolic manipulations, we can express,

$$\sum_{j=1}^{m} S(C(x,t) f_j(x)\sqrt{\lambda_j}) = \left[\sum_{j=1}^{m} \Phi_j\right]\frac{\partial^2 C}{\partial x^2} + \left[\sum_{j=1}^{m} \Psi_j\right]\frac{\partial C}{\partial x} + \left[\sum_{j=1}^{m} \Gamma_j\right] C, \tag{3.4.3}$$

where,

$$\Phi_j = \frac{1}{2}\sqrt{\frac{\lambda_j}{N}}\left(-h_x\, Sin(\omega_j x) - \frac{h_x \omega_j}{\theta} Cos(\omega_j x)\right); \tag{3.4.3a}$$

$$\Psi_j = \sqrt{\frac{\lambda_j}{N}}\left(\left(\frac{\omega_j h_x}{\theta} - 1\right) Sin(\omega_j x) - \left(\omega_j h_x + \frac{\omega_j}{\theta}\right) Cos(\omega_j x)\right); \text{ and} \tag{3.4.3b}$$

$$\Gamma_j = \sqrt{\frac{\lambda_j}{N}}\left(\left(\frac{\omega_j^2 h_x}{2} + \frac{\omega_j^2}{\theta}\right) Sin(\omega_j x) - \left(\frac{\omega_j^3 h_x}{2\theta} + \omega_j\right) Cos(\omega_j x)\right). \tag{3.4.3c}$$

This exercise shows the complexity of the dispersion term and it is related to the local spatial gradient of the concentration, $\frac{\partial C}{\partial x}$, the second order spatial derivative $\frac{\partial^2 C}{\partial x^2}$, as well as $C(x,t)$. Φ_j, Ψ_j and Γ_j coefficients are also dependent on λ_i s, h_x, and ωi s, and they are analogous to Fourier series, i.e., the coefficients themselves have the form of spectral expansions. Recall that h_x is a scale length introduced to retain the second order derivative of fluxes in the SSTM. We can assume that $h_x \approx O(\Delta x)$, i.e., $\lim_{\Delta x \to 0}\left(\frac{h_x}{\Delta x}\right) \to 0$ where Δx is the discretization length in x direction. If we make h_x=0 then Φ_j =0, which eliminates the second order spatial derivative of the concentration in equation (3.4.3). Even in a simplified setting of having a common standard Wiener increment ($db_i(t)$) for all x, and assuming a differentiable function for $C(x,t)$, this analysis shows that the dispersion term depicts much more complicated behaviours that cannot be modelled by scale independent simplifying assumptions. Therefore, one should note that as time increases the effects of Wiener process increases, and it would be worthwhile to investigate the dependence of the random field $d\beta(t)$ for different scales of experiments. In other words, from equation (3.2.7), we see that,

$$dX(t) = \bar{V}(x,t)dt + \xi(x,t)dt, \tag{3.4.4}$$

where $X(t)$ is travel distance of a solute particle in x-direction.

As seen in equation (3.3.7), $d\beta(t) \approx \xi(x,t)dt$ is the fluctuating part of the travel length of a solute within the time dt at a given x. Assuming $\overline{V}(x,t)$ is a constant across the domain [0,*a*], by investigating the nature of the fluctuating component of the travel length as the scale of the experiments changes, we can understand the scale dependency of the dispersion term better.

$d\beta(t)$ is an irregular stochastic function of time with spatial component appearing in normalised eigen functions, $f_j(x)$ .A standard Wiener process increment (db_i) corresponding to a time increment, Δt_i , should be generated for each eigenfunction. $d\beta(t)$ can be approximated as a summation of M terms:

$$d\beta(t) \approx \sum_{i=1}^{M} \sqrt{\lambda_i}\, f_i(x) db_i(t) .$$

Let $\eta_i(x) = \sqrt{\lambda_i}\, f_i(x)$, then $d\beta \approx \sum_{i=1}^{M} \eta_i(x) db_i(t)$.

Recall $db_i(t)$ s are independent zero-mean Gaussian increments with Δt_i variance.

Therefore, $E[d\beta] = E\left[\sum \eta_i(x) db_i\right] = 0$, for a given x.

For a given x, $Var[d\beta] = \sum \eta_i^2(x)\ Var[db_i]$.

If we discretise the time axis equidistantly, $\Delta t = \Delta t_1 = \Delta t_2 = ... = \Delta t_i ...$, then,

$$Var[d\beta] = \left(\sum \eta_i^2(x)\right)\Delta t . \tag{3.4.5}$$

As seen from equation (3.4.5), $d\beta$ is a summation of independent Gaussian processes for a given x value making it a Gaussian process zero mean and variance proportional to Δt. We will make use of equation (3.4.5) in the approximate numerical solution of SSTM for large scale experiments in chapter 4.

3.5 Numerical Solutions of the 1-D SSTM and Their Behaviours

We solve equation (3.2.14) for strong solutions using a finite difference scheme which is based on Euler solution of Ito integral. One dimensional domain is discretised, and the basis of numerical solutions to SPDEs as given by Gaines and Lyons (1997) is adopted. A constant mean velocity is assumed in the scheme. The differential operator S in equation (3.2.11) was expressed as a differential operator using a backward difference scheme. One dimensional spatial length, a ($0 \le x \le a$) on x axis was divided into (k-1) equidistant intervals of small lengths of Δx . The total model time, T, was divided into (n-1) equidistant small intervals of Δt . The space-time grid for the explicit difference scheme that can be used to independently calculate the concentration value at time level t_{n+1} from the concentration values at time intervals t_n , thus preserving the non-antipating nature of Ito integral.

Figure 3.2 show the space-time grid for the explicit difference scheme that can be used to independently calculate the value at time t_{n+1} (denoted by •) from the values at time t_n (denoted by ○).

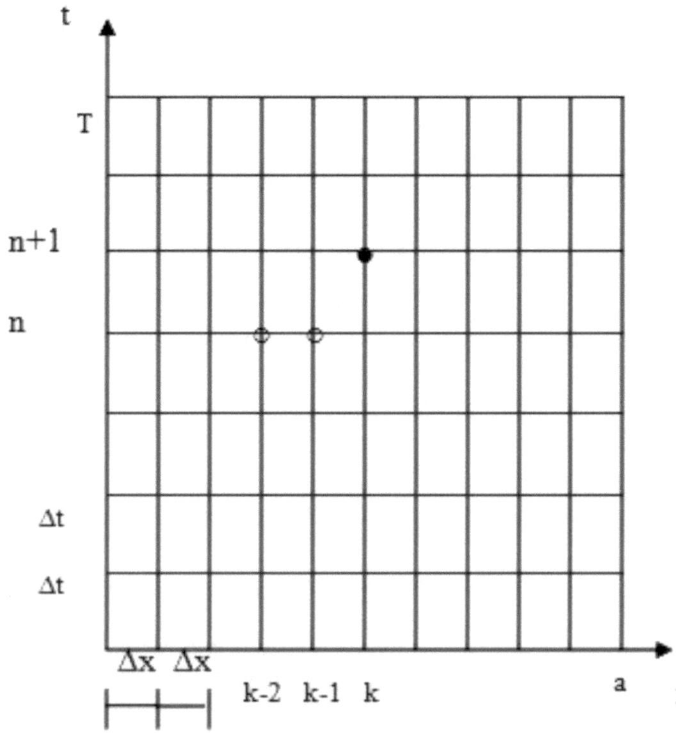

Figure 3.2. An explicit space-time scheme used for the computational solution.

The first derivative of a variable *U* can be described as (Morton and Mayers, 1994),

$$\left(\frac{\partial U}{\partial x}\right)_k^n = \frac{U_k^n - U_{k-1}^n}{\Delta x}, \tag{3.5.1}$$

where U_k^n = value of *U* at the grid point (*k*, *n*).

The second derivative can be given by,

$$\left(\frac{\partial^2 U}{\partial x^2}\right)_k^n = \frac{U_k^n - 2U_{k-1}^n + U_{k-2}^n}{\Delta x^2}. \tag{3.5.2}$$

The operator *S* can be written as,

$$SU = -\left(\frac{\partial U}{\partial x} + \frac{h_x}{2}\frac{\partial^2 U}{\partial x^2}\right),$$

Therefore, we can express the operator in the difference form

$$(SU)_k^n = -\left(\left(\frac{\partial U}{\partial x}\right)_k^n + \frac{h_x}{2}\left(\frac{\partial^2 U}{\partial x^2}\right)_k^n\right). \tag{3.5.3}$$

Substituting the backward difference schemes from (3.5.1) and (3.5.3) and taking $h_x = \Delta x$,

$$(SU)_k^n = -\left(\frac{1}{2\Delta x}\right)\left[3U_k^n - 4U_{k-1}^n + U_{k-2}^n\right]. \tag{3.5.4}$$

The first derivative of U with respect to time can be expressed using a forward difference scheme,

$$\frac{\partial U}{\partial t} = \frac{U_k^{n+1} - U_k^n}{\Delta t}. \tag{3.5.5}$$

Applying equation (3.5.1) and (3.5.3) to (3.5.5) and considering the mean velocity for the region as a constant, v, we can obtain the following scheme:

$$\begin{aligned} C_k^{n+1} &= C_k^n - \left(\frac{\Delta t.v}{2\Delta x}\right) * \left[3C_k^n - 4C_{k-1}^n + C_{k-2}^n\right] \\ &-\left(\frac{1}{2\Delta x}\right) * \left[3C_k^n d\beta(t)_k^n - 4C_{k-1}^n d\beta(t)_{k-1}^n + C_{k-2}^n d\beta(t)_{k-2}^n\right], \end{aligned} \tag{3.5.6}$$

where $d\beta(t)$ = Wiener process increments in Hilbert space for a given x.

The explicit difference model (3.5.6) gives the future values of a stochastic variable in terms of the past values preserving the properties of Ito definition of integration with respect to time. This scheme is stable and gives strong solutions to equation (3.2.14), as in many SPDEs, if $\Delta t \le 10^{-4}$. For example, if a=1000 meters, and if we simulate the solute transport for at least 1000 days, taking Δx =0.01 m and Δt =0.0001 days for stability reasons, we need a grid of $10^5 \, x \, 10^7$. In addition, the evaluation of $d\beta(t)$ for each x involves the summation of a large number of $\eta_i(x)\, db_i$ terms. Because of the computational time it requires to solve the SPDE, we use the scheme given in equation (3.5.6) when a< 10 m, and for larger a values we approximate $d\beta(t)$ term as described later.

We can now investigate the behaviour of the stochastic solute transport model (SSTM) in one-dimension. The main parameters of the SSTM are correlation length, b and variance, σ^2. As the statistical nature of the computational solution changes with different b and σ^2, we would like to understand the effect of these parameters on the solution of the model. Furthermore, we attempt to understand these parameters in relation to the hydrodynamic dispersion.

The finite difference numerical schemes are used in the investigation taking the numerical convergence and stability into account for the domain [0, 1]. First we solve equation (3.3.20) for the given values of b and σ^2. It is necessary to find and appropriate number of roots for equation (3.3.20) to produce the desired accuracy of the numerical solution. For the domain

[0, 1], the first 30 values of the roots (ω_i) are generally sufficient. We generate the standard Wiener process increments for 0.001 day time intervals for total of three days. Then the eigenvalues λ_n are computed for the given σ^2 using equation (3.3.21). With these roots, ω and λ_n, we calculate the basis functions using equation (3.3.23). These values are used to compute $d(t)$, the Hilbert space valued Wiener incremental processes, using the *KL* expansion (equation (3.3.7)). Then we calculate the concentration profile for the discretised values of spatial-temporal development for the mean velocity of 0.5 m/day. The numerical solution is implemented in a mathematical software package, Mathematica® (Wolfram Research, 1999).

We use a spatial grid length of 0.1 m for the numerical calculation. The initial concentration distribution profile of 1.0 unit at $x = 0$ is considered and it exponentially decreases through the rest of the domain according to the function, $e^{-5k\,\Delta x}$, where $k = 1, 2, \ldots, 10$ and Δx = grid size. We begin the numerical scheme with very small numerical concentration values, rather than zero concentrations, to reduce the numerical errors at the beginning of the scheme. The concentration of 1.0 unit is maintained at the boundary of $x = 0$ for the whole time period of the solution to mimic a continuous point source.

To investigate the general behaviour of the SSTM, we obtain the temporal development of the concentration profiles at the mid point of the domain, $x = 0.5$ m, for various parameter combinations of b and σ^2. The same realisation of the standard Wiener process increments and constant mean velocity of 0.5 m/day are used for all the experiments, so that we would not bias our comparisons.

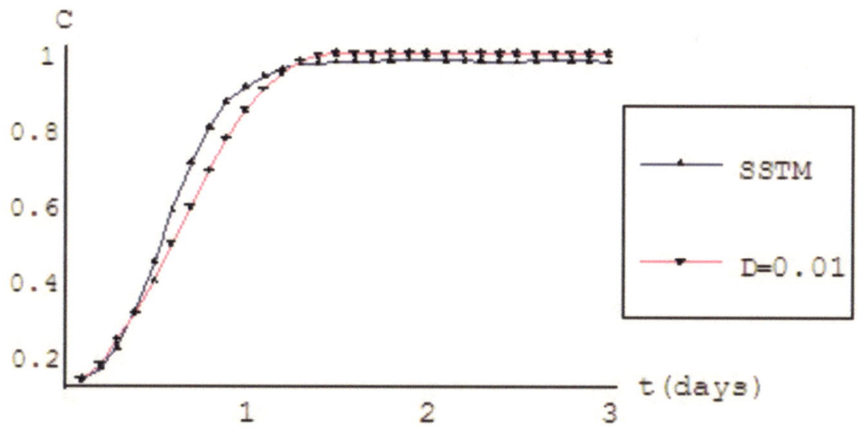

Figure 3.3. Comparison of deterministic advection-dispersion (D = 0.01) and stochastic (σ^2 = 0.001 and b = 0.0001) model concentration profiles. An explicit space-time scheme used for the computational solution.

Figure 3.3 shows that the stochastic model can mimic the solution of the advection-dispersion equation with reasonable accuracy. The concentration breakthrough curves (the time history of concentration at a fixed x) for the SSTM for $\sigma^2 = 0.001$ and $b = 0.0001$, and the deterministic curve for the advection-dispersion equation for dispersion coefficient (D)

of 0.01 m²/day are overlaid in Figure 3.3. We can always find a solution for the SSTM that reasonably represents the deterministic break through curve for any given dispersion coefficient using appropriate values for the parameters, σ^2 and b.

To study the influences of b and σ^2 on the solution of the problem, we keep one parameter constant and change the other within a reasonable range to examine the behavioural change of the concentration breakthrough curves. Figure 3.4 shows the concentration profile at x = 0.5 m for a small value of the variance, σ^2 = 0.0001, when the correlation length, b varies from 0.0001m to 0.25m. Although the range of b varies from 0.0001 to 0.25m (a change of 2500 times) the change of stochasticity (noise level) is negligible and the solutions of the SSTM are independent of b and behave like those of a deterministic model.

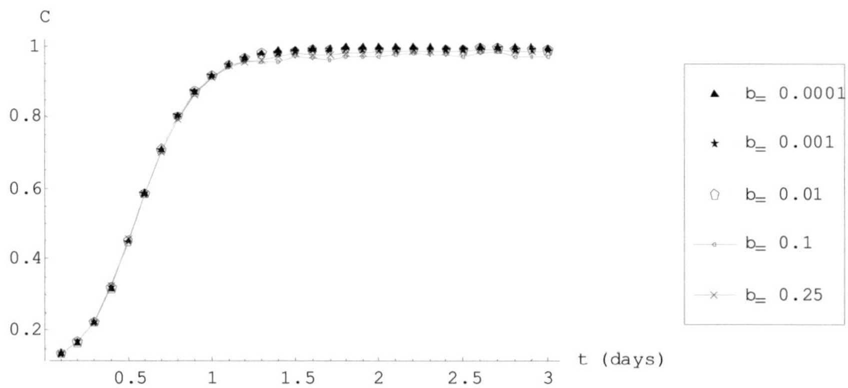

Figure 3.4. Concentration profiles at x = 0.5m for σ^2 = 0.0001.

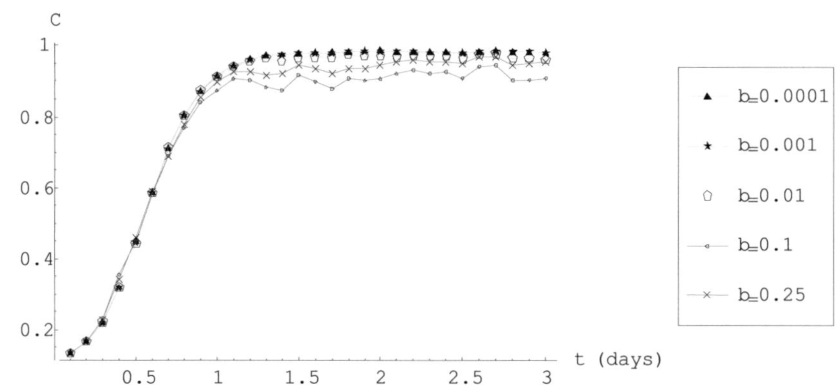

Figure 3.5. Concentration profiles at x = 0.5 m for σ^2 = 0.001.

We gradually increase σ^2 and obtain the concentration profiles for the same regime of b (0.0001 m to 0.25 m) to examine the effect of σ^2. With an increase in σ^2 by 10 times, Figure 3.5 shows that two types of changes have occurred in the concentration profiles;

individual concentration profiles have worse fluctuatiing stochasticity, and there are significant differences between concentration values for different b values at a given time. The high values of the variance not only directly increase the unpredictable nature of the flow but also influence the ways in which b affects the flow. We also observe that with high b values the asymptotic values (sills) of the concentration profiles are lower than the deterministic sill.

In the note that when b is very small, the concentration profile is smooth, but when b is 0.1 m it lowers the sill. By increasing σ^2 by 10 times, to 0.01, and by using the same standard Wiener process increments, we obtain the break through curves as shown in Figure 3.6. The flow tends to be significantly unsteady for larger correlation lengths and still shows smaller fluctuations smaller b values. Furthermore larger values of σ^2 intensities the fluctuation the effect of b significantly.

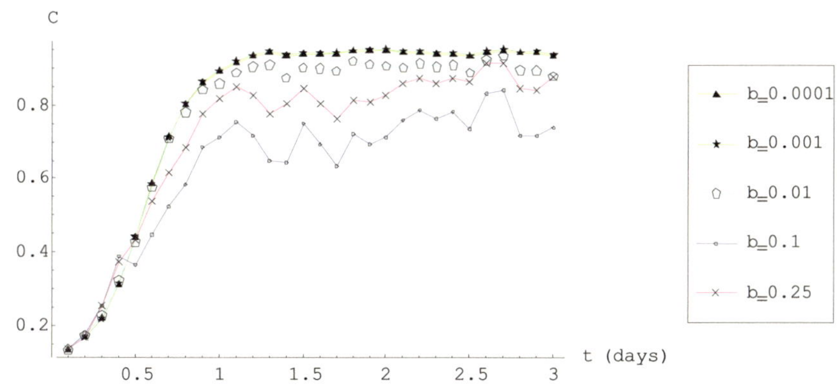

Figure 3.6. Concentration profiles at $x = 0.5$ m for $\sigma^2 = 0.01$.

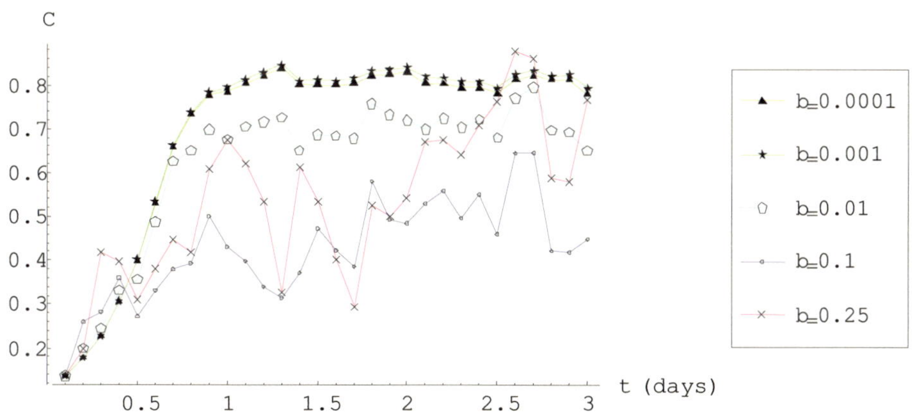

Figure 3.7. Concentration profiles at $x = 0.5$ m for $\sigma^2 = 0.1$.

The concentration profiles for higher b regimes for the increased value of σ^2 (=0.1) are highly random as shown in Figure 3.7. With higher values of b, the concentration profiles become highly irregular making the numerical scheme unstable. Therefore, limit our experiments to smaller b values, that are less than 0.01 m. Figure 4.8 shows that the fluctuation invariably increase with the high σ^2 values and the behaviour of the model continues with the same trend that we noticed earlier, but with enhanced effects.

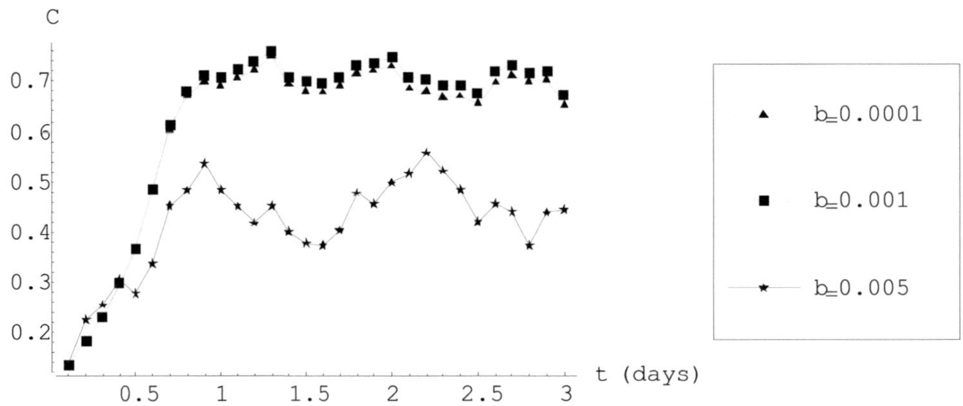

Figure 3.8. Concentration profiles at x = 0.5 m for σ^2 = 0.25.

Figure 3.9 shows the concentration profiles at b = 0.0001 for the range of σ^2 that varies from 0.0001 to 0.25. By comparing in Figure 3.4, when σ^2 was very small, the fluctuation are not distinguishable even for very high b values; however, in Figure 3.9, irrespective of smaller b, σ^2 influenced the behaviour of the flow. It is not possible to differentiate the concentration profiles for very small σ^2, such as 0.0001 and 0.001. With the increase of σ^2 stochasticity increases rapidly, and σ^2 influences the behaviour of the flow more than b does.

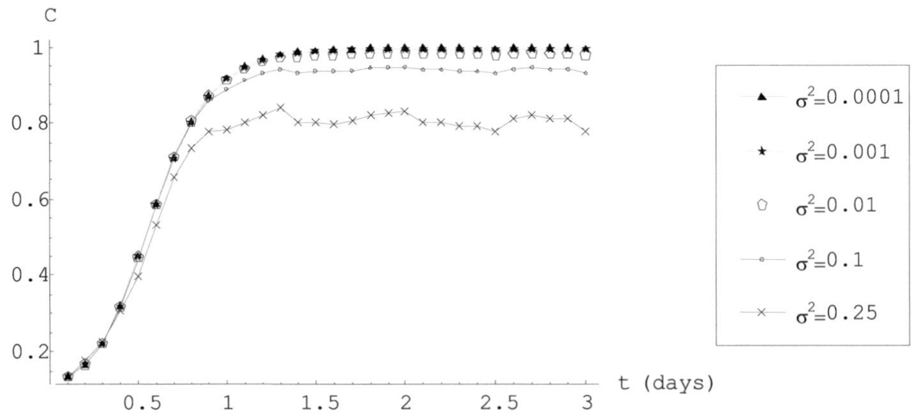

Figure 3.9. Concentration profiles at x = 0.5 m for b = 0.0001.

We increase b by 10 times to obtain Figure 3.10, which shows considerable changes in the breakthrough curves.

To understand the effects of different Wiener realizations on the concentration profiles by using 50 different Wiener realisations to calculate the 95% confidence intervals. They show that, for smaller values of parameters (for example, $\sigma^2 = 0.001$, $b= 0.01$), the variations in the concentration profile are negligible, but for larger values (for example, $\sigma^2 = 0.1$, $b= 0.1$) the fluctuation regimes increase but the solutions remain stable. Obviously, the confidence intervals widen with the larger values of the parameters.

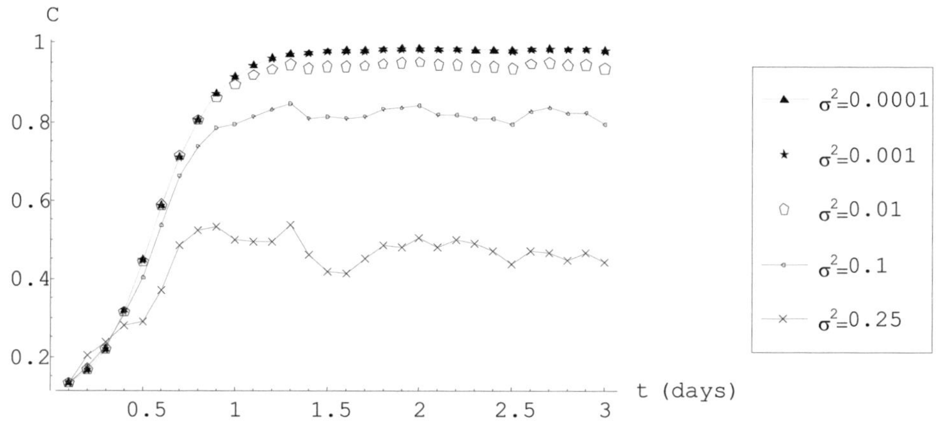

Figure 3.10. Concentration profiles at $x = 0.5$ m for $b = 0.001$.

We can now extend the investigation to a 10 m flow length. Similar to the 1 m investigation, a simple setting of the one-dimensional case is used to explore the behaviour of the model for different model parameters of the correlation length, b and the variance, σ^2. To obtain meaningful concentration profiles for the extended spatial domain, we also increase the time interval of the solution. The stochastic model is computationally solved for an average linear velocity of 0.5 m/day for 30 days, which allows sufficient time for the solute to travel the entire spatial domain. However, due to increases in the time length, a different realisation of the standard Wiener process increments was used for the 10 m length. This may raise the question of the validity in comparing of the model for two different spatial lengths. However, as we have shown earlier the model is reasonably stable for different Wiener process increments and therefore, it is reasonable to assume that the solutions of the model are not significantly affected by the different Wiener processes. A single realisation of the standard Wiener process is used throughout the investigation of the 10 m spatial domain.

Similar to 1 m case, the 10 m scale shows that a SSTM could mimic the solution of the advection - dispersion equation for the same distance (Figure 3.11)

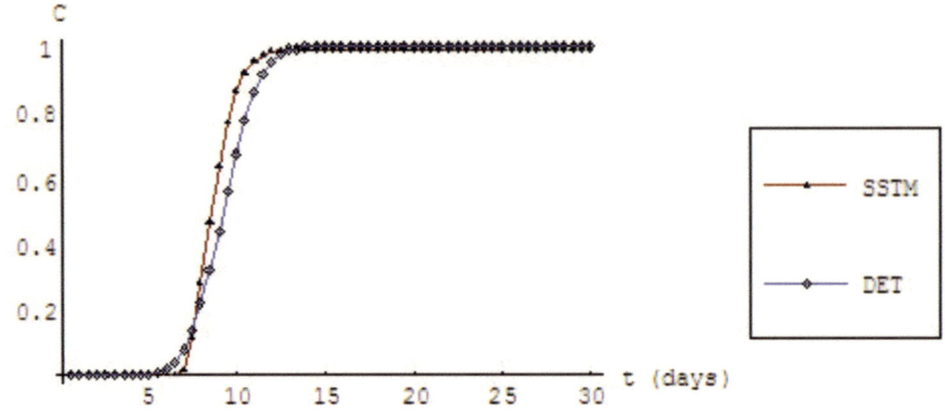

Figure 3.11. Comparison of deterministic advection-dispersion (D = 0.035 m2/day) and the SSTM (σ^2 = 0.001 and b = 0.0001) concentration profiles at x = 5m for 10 m domain.

The behaviours of the SSTM model for the 10-m flow length are quite similar to those for the 1-m flow length. The influence of the parameter b can be seen in Figure 3.12 for the fixed values of σ^2. High b values increase the propensity of the flow to be more stochastic and decrease the asymptotic values of the concentration. For a given b, the effects of increasing σ^2 are more profound in comparison to those associated with increasing b for a fixed σ^2.

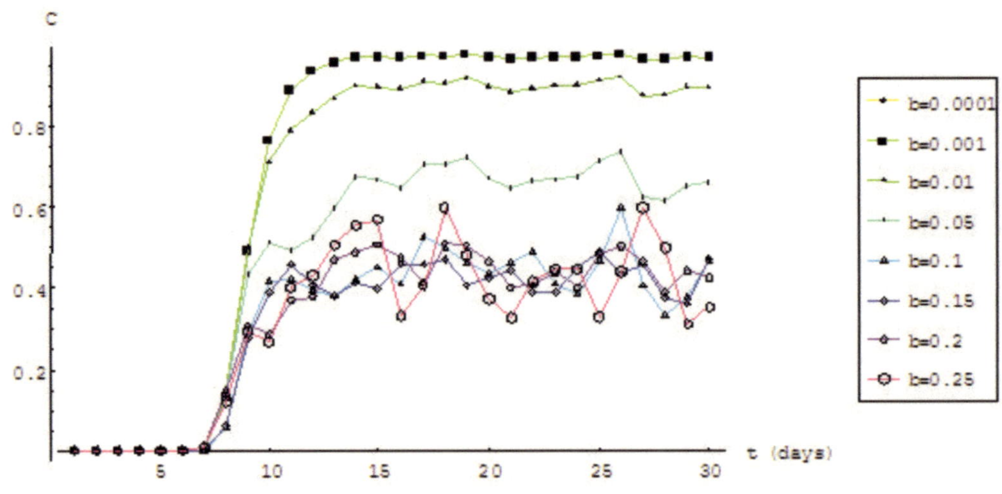

Figure 3.12. Comparison of deterministic advection-dispersion (D = 0.035 m2/day) and the SSTM (σ^2 = 0.001 and b = 0.0001) concentration profiles at x = 5m for 10 m domain.

How do we relate the parameter, σ^2 and b, to the physical porous structure? The relationship need to be understood through the influences on the concentration profiles. b is the correlation length of the velocity Kernel $q(x_1,x_2)$ (see equation 3.3.9), and higher the b slower the rate at which $q(x_1,x_2)$ decays. This means that pore structure contains larger pores; and b is indicative of the size of pores, and, may be, geometric shapes of pores. σ^2 affects the profiles more dramatically, especially depressing asymptotic of the profiles, indicating that solute mass is dissolved in a larger volume of water. This alludes again to pore geometry (shapes and interconnecting paths) and if pore structure is heterogeneous with high porosity, one could expect σ^2 as well as b to be high. σ^2 and b allow us more flexibility of defining the nature of solute dispersion, and the complex interaction between σ^2 and b would help us to characterise the pore structures for a given velocity kernel.

3.6 A Comparison of the SSTM with the Experiments Data

The Lincoln University aquifer is 9.49 m long, 4.66 m wide and 2.6 m deep. As shown in Figure 3.13, constant head tanks are the boundaries of the aquifer at its upstream and downstream ends. A porous wall provides the hydraulic connection between the aquifer and the head tanks. A weir controls the water surface elevation in each head tank, and each weir can be adjusted to provide different hydraulic gradients. However, a uniform hydraulic gradient of 0.0018 (head loss along the aquifer / flow length = 0.017 m / 9.49 m) is maintained during the entire experiment along the longitudinal direction of the tank.

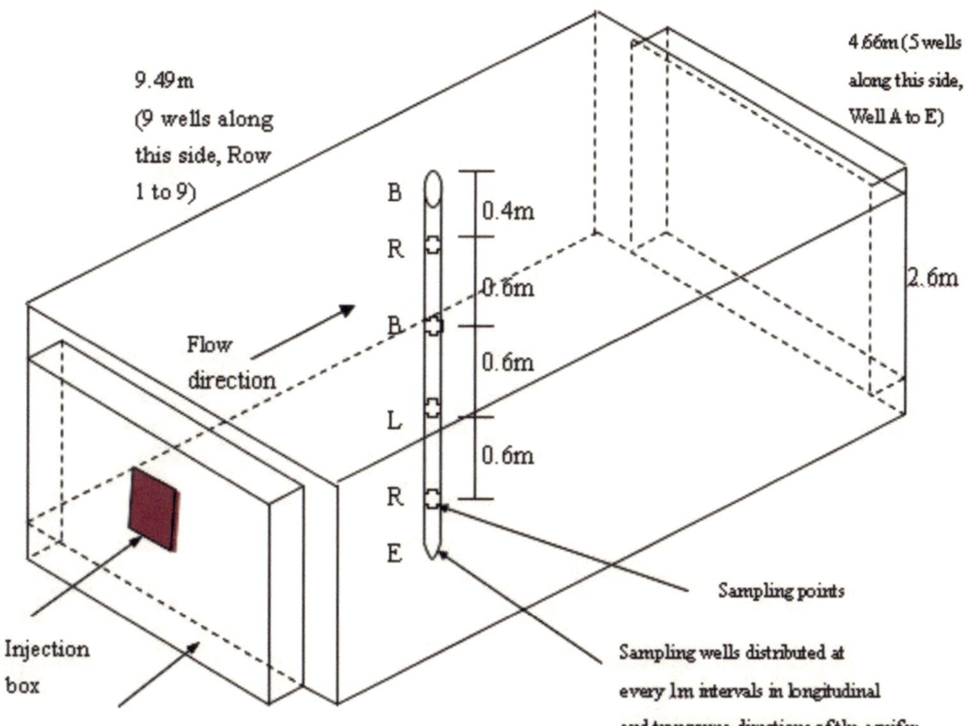

Figure 3.13. Schematic diagram of the artificial aquifer at Lincoln University, New Zealand (Courtesy of Dr.John Bright, Lincoln Ventures Ltd).

Multi-port monitoring wells are laid out on a 1m x 1m grid. The computer controlled peristaltic pumps enable fully automated, simultaneous solute water samples to be collected from sample points that are uniformly distributed throughout the aquifer (four sample points for each grid point at 0.4m, 1.0m, 1.6m and 2.2m depth from the top surface of the aquifer). The tracer used is Rhodamine WT (RWT) dye with an initial concentration of 200 parts per million and then allowed to decrease exponentially. Tracer is injected at the middle of the header tank using an injection box (dimensions of 50 cm length, 10 cm width and 20 cm depth). This tracer is rapidly mixed in the upstream header tank and, thus, infiltrates across the whole of the upstream face of the aquifer. This particular experiment described here lasted 432 hours, and two samples were taken at four-hour intervals from the wells.

Since, STTM described in this chapter is a one-dimensional model, we experiment in directly relating the one-dimension solute concentration profiles of the aquifer. However, as one can assume, the actual aquifer is subjected to transverse dispersion, and consideration of only a one-dimensional flow is not sufficiently accurate. Hence, we employ the following methodology to approximate the aquifer parameters.

Solute concentration values for the artificial aquifer are available for a large number of spatial points at different temporal intervals. The data are available mainly for header tank, row 1, row 3, row 5, row 7 and row 9 (see Figure 3.13) at all levels. Initially, we select a few spatial coordinates at row 5 of well A - level YE. We then develop a two-dimensional deterministic advection-dispersion transport model and obtain corresponding concentration values of the model that are similar to the selected spatial locations of the aquifer. As past studies show, we approximate that the transverse dispersion coefficient is 10% of the longitudinal dispersion (Fetter, 1999). The mean velocity is 0.5 m/day. The profiles of both the aquifer and the deterministic model are plotted in one axis system, to compare their similarities. This trial-and-error curve fitting technique is carried out to determine the most accurate dispersion coefficients of the deterministic model. In this procedure concentration values of the aquifer are normalised (i.e., the values vary from 0 to 1).

By trial and error, we find that the closest fit is given by the longitudinal dispersion coefficient of 0.15 m^2/day, i.e., transverse dispersion is 0.015 m^2/day, (Figure 3.14) for the aquifer.

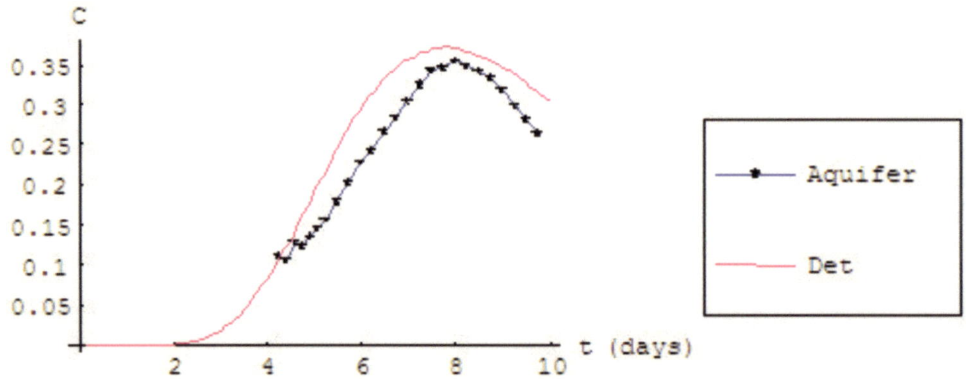

Figure 3.14. Concentration profile of trial and error curve fit for D = 0.15 m^2/day of the advection dispersion model with row 5 of the aquifer data.

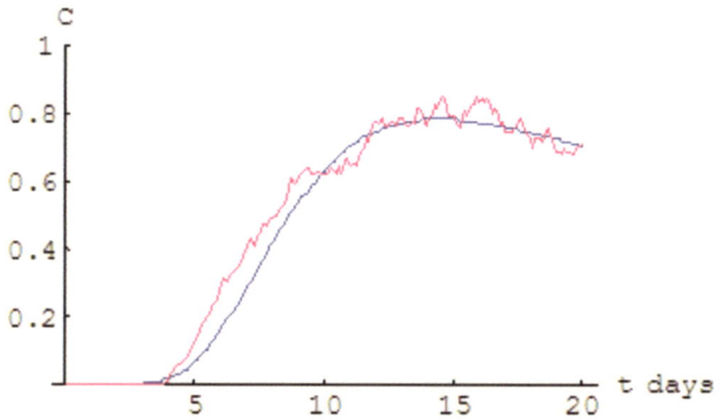

Figure 3.15. Concentration profiles of deterministic advection-dispersion model with D = 0.15 m²/day and SSTM with $\sigma^2 = 0.01$ and $b = 0.01$.

Subsequently, we develop a one-dimensional deterministic advection-dispersion model using the *D* obtained from a two-dimensional comparison. We then use a similar curve fitting technique with the 1-D deterministic model and 1-D stochastic model to find the most suitable σ^2 and *b* for the SSTM.

Figures 3.15 show the best fitting curves for both the SSTM and the 1-D advection-dispersion model. Having determined the appropriate parameters of the SSTM ($\sigma^2 = 0.01$ and $b = 0.01$) that simulate the Lincoln University aquifer at the spatial location under consideration (Row 5 - well A) we investigated the robustness of the model for different Wiener processes and found that the SSTM is reasonably stable for the seven different Wiener realisations tested.

Even though the results show, as mentioned above, that the parameter combination of $\sigma^2 = 0.01$ and $b = 0.01$ is a fairly accurate representation of the experimental aquifer for the given spatial point, we need to test these parameters other spatial locations. Figure 3.16 shows that the 2-D deterministic advection-dispersion model with the longitudinal dispersion coefficient of 0.15 m²/day fits the aquifer data reasonably well for the similar locations.

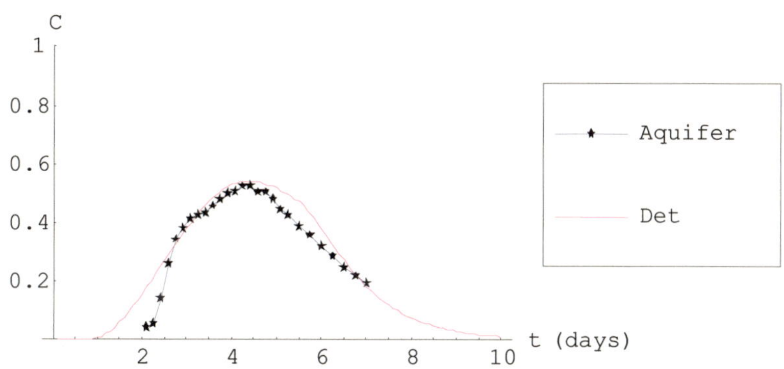

Figure 3.16. Concentration profiles of 2-D deterministic advection-dispersion model (D = 0.15 m²/day) and the experimental aquifer.

We compare the curves of the one-dimensional deterministic advection-dispersion model with D= 0.15 and of the SSTM with $\sigma^2 = 0.01$ and $b = 0.01$. Figure 3.17 illustrates that the curves for the deterministic model and the SSTM are in agreement.

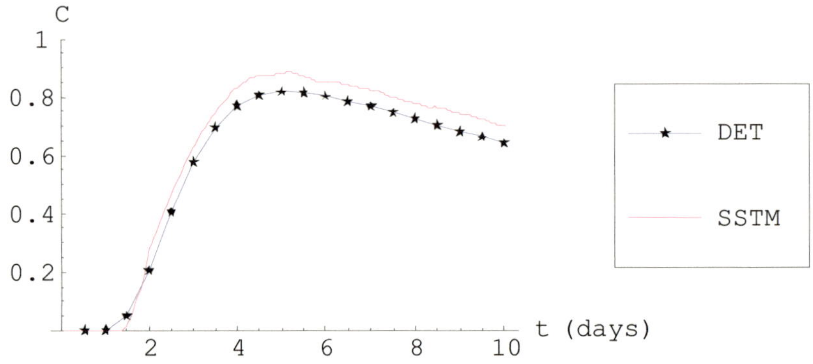

Figure 3.17. Concentration profiles of the deterministic advection-dispersion model (D = 0.15 m2/day) and SSTM with $\sigma^2 = 0.01$ and $b = 0.01$ for row 3 well A.

Figures 3.18 and 3.19 show that the same parameter combination is valid for the data from well A of row 7.

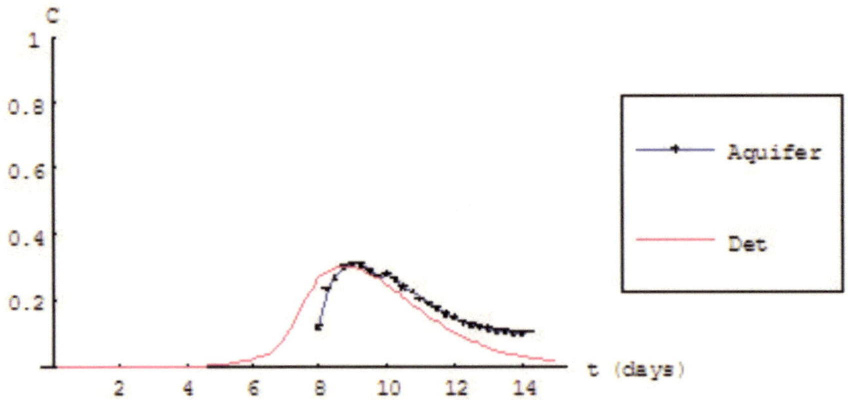

Figure 3.18. Concentration profiles of the 2-D deterministic advection-dispersion model (D = 0.15 m2/day) and the experimental aquifer at row 7.

The comparative study of the SSTM and the experimental data described here is to show that the SSTM would faithfully mimic the concentration breakthrough curves in a real experiment situation. However, we do not attempt to validate the SSTM using the trial-and-error curve fitting techniques for all the data sets as if is too labour intensive. As the experimental aquifer consists of sand of similar particle size, one would expect that one set of σ^2 and b values should be able to characterise the whole aquifer. It appears that σ^2 =0.01 and b=0.01 would be an acceptable set of parameters. However, we can not say much about the uniqueness of these set of parameters. A correlation length (b) of 0.01 m seems to be reasonable for a porous medium containing sand. But this has not been ascertained through the experiments in a laboratory. Therefore, one of the ways of determining the uniqueness of the parameters set is to develop the methodologies to estimate them using all the observations we have. We have used the maximum likelihood estimation (MLE) to determine the parameters of the deterministic advection and dispersion model for the aquifer data. However, MLE can not be used to estimate parameters of SSTM as the SSTM contains the stochastic integral for dispersion which can not be built into likelihood functions. Therefore, we make use of ANN to estimate the parameters of the SSTM for the experimental aquifer in section 3.6.

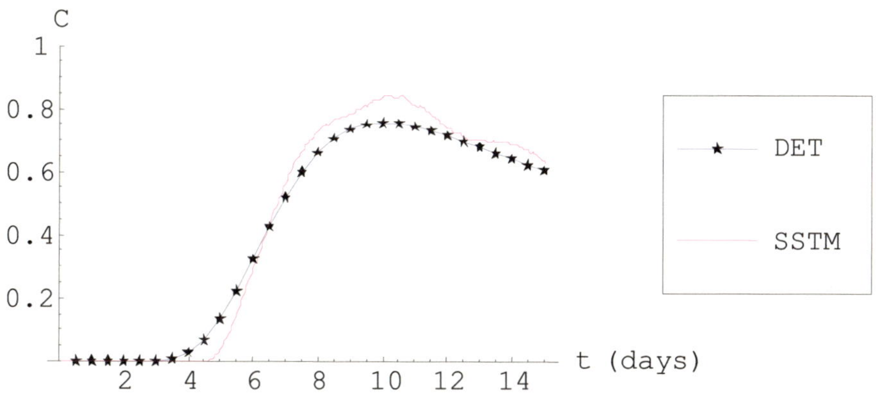

Figure 3.19. Concentration profiles of the deterministic advection-dispersion model (D = 0.15 m²/day) and SSTM with $\sigma^2 = 0.01$ and $b = 0.01$ for row 7 well A.

3.7 Parameter Estimation using Maximum Likelihood Method

In chapter 1, we discuss the parameter estimation of the partial differential equations when the additive noise terms are present. The development of the likelihood functions are based on the theory of parameter estimation for stochastic process (Kutoyants, 1984; Lipster and Shirayer, 1977; Basawa and Prakasa Rao, 1980) and we use this theory to estimate parameters.

Let us consider a one-dimensional stochastic advection-dispersion equation with additive fluctuations:

$$\frac{\partial C}{\partial t} = D_L\left(\frac{\partial^2 C}{\partial x^2}\right) - v_x\left(\frac{\partial C}{\partial x}\right) + \xi(x,t), \quad (3.7.1)$$

where D_L is the longitudinal hydrodynamic dispersion coefficient, in m²/day, and v_x is the velocity of water flow, in m/day.

The two parameters to be estimated are D_L and v_x, and we can express the right hand side of equation (3.7.1) as a linear function of the parameters (see section 1.4)

$$f(t,C,\theta) = a_0(C,\ t)+\theta_1 a_1(C,t)+\theta_2 a_2(C,\ t). \tag{3.7.2}$$

where

$$a_0(C_i,t)=0; \quad a_1(C_i,t) = \left(\frac{\partial^2 C}{\partial x^2}\right)_i; \quad a_2(C_i,t) = -\left(\frac{\partial C}{\partial x}\right)_i; \ \theta_1 = D_L; \quad \theta_2 = v_x .$$

Then the log-likelihood function can be written as,

$$\begin{aligned} l(\theta_1,\theta_2) &= \sum_{i=1}^{M}\int_0^T\{a_0(C_i,t)+\theta_1 a_1(C_i,t)+\theta_2 a_2(C_i,t)\}\,dC_i(t) \\ &\quad -\frac{1}{2}\sum_{i=1}^{M}\int_0^T\{a_0(C_i,t)+\theta_1 a_1(C_i,t)+\theta_2 a_2(C_i,t)\}^2\,dt \end{aligned} \tag{3.7.3}$$

Differentiating equation (3.7.3) with respect to θ_1 and θ_2, respectively, we obtain the following two simultaneous equations:

$$\sum_{i=1}^{M}\int_0^T\{a_1(C_i,t)\}\,dC_i(t) - \sum_{i=1}^{M}\int_0^T\{a_0(C_i,t)+\theta_1 a_1(C_i,t)+\theta_2 a_2(C_i,t)\}\{a_1(C_i,t)\}\,dt = 0 .$$

$$\sum_{i=1}^{M}\int_0^T\{a_2(C_i,t)\}dC_i(t) - \sum_{i=1}^{M}\int_0^T\{a_0(C_i,t)+\theta_1 a_1(C_i,t)+\theta_2 a_2(C_i,t)\}\ \{a_2(C_i,t)\}\,dt = 0 . \tag{3.7.4}$$

Suppose we have the observations of solute concentration, C_i at M independent space coordinates along the x-axis, where $1 \le i \le M$, at different time intervals, t (where $0 \le t \le T$, and T is an integer that represents the last reading taken at unit intervals on t-axis). In other words, we have M number of C_i observations for each time step. Hence, there are, altogether, $((T+1)M)$ C_i observations. We use these observations to estimate the parameter θ_1 and θ_2,

We substitute $a_0(C_i,t)$, $a_1(C_i,t)$, $a_2(C_i,t)$, θ_1 and θ_2 in equations (3.7.4) to obtain the following set of equations,

$$\sum_{i=1}^{M}\sum_{t=0}^{T}\left\{\frac{\partial^2 C_i}{\partial x^2}\right\}\Delta C_i - D_L\sum_{i=1}^{M}\sum_{t=0}^{T}\left\{\frac{\partial^2 C_i}{\partial x^2}\right\}^2\Delta t - v_x\sum_{i=1}^{M}\sum_{t=0}^{T}\left\{\frac{\partial C_i}{\partial x}\right\}\left\{\frac{\partial^2 C_i}{\partial x^2}\right\}\Delta t = 0$$

$$\sum_{i=1}^{M}\sum_{t=0}^{T}\left\{\frac{\partial C_i}{\partial x}\right\}\Delta C_i - D_L\sum_{i=1}^{M}\sum_{t=0}^{T}\left\{\frac{\partial C_i}{\partial x}\right\}\left\{\frac{\partial^2 C_i}{\partial x^2}\right\}\Delta t - v_x\sum_{i=1}^{M}\sum_{t=0}^{T}\left\{\frac{\partial C_i}{\partial x}\right\}^2\Delta t = 0. \tag{3.7.5}$$

Therefore, D_L and v_x values can be obtained by solving these two simultaneous equations.

Once v_x is known, the hydraulic conductivity (K) can be obtained from,

$$v_x = \frac{K}{n_e}\left(\frac{dh}{dl}\right) = \text{average linear velocity, m/day,} \tag{3.7.6}$$

C = solute concentration, mg/l,

K = hydraulic conductivity, m/day,

$\frac{dh}{dl}$ = hydraulic gradient, m/m, and

n_e = effective porosity.

We have used the experimental data from the artificial aquifer (Figure 3.13) to estimate D_L and v_x. Table 3.1 shows the estimated and experimental values for D_L and K (calculated from equation (3.7.6)) at different depths of the aquifer from the top surface.

Depth (m)	Hydraulic conductivity, K (m/day)		Longitudinal hydrodynamic dispersion, D_L (m²/day)	
	Estimated	Experimental	Estimated	Experimental
0.4	203.2	137	0.167	0.1596
1.0	210.6	137	0.143	0.1596
1.6	208.9	137	0.134	0.1596
2.2	262.3	137	0.242	0.1596

Table 3.1. Estimated and experimental parameters hydraulic conductivity, K (m/day) and longitudinal hydrodynamic dispersion, D_L (m²/day).

The results show the accuracy of D_L estimates is better than that of K. We estimate the v_x by using equation (3.7.6) for and for simplicity, we assume that the hydraulic gradient, $\frac{dh}{dl}$ and the effective porosity, n_e to be constants, or in other words, their spatial distributions are homogeneous. However, distribution of these values in the aquifer may be slightly heterogeneous. This assumption may have influenced the accuracy of less precise K estimates. However, the D_L values are estimated directly and not affected by such assumptions, and the maximum likelihood estimates are closer to the experimental.

Another possible phenomenon that can be present in solute transport is adsorption and the occurrence of short circuits which are, assumed to be included in the random component, $\xi(x,t)$, of the governing equation, equation (3.7.1). However, we assumed that in the experiments the tracer is mixed in the upstream header tank, hence, adsorption in the aquifer could be neglected.

As mentioned earlier, in the process of calibration to obtain parameters, it is assumed that the experimental aquifer is homogeneous. However, Figures 3.20, 3.21 and 3.22 show that the aquifer did not behave as expected (please refer to Figure 3.13 for notation). Figure 3.10 shows that the concentration values at a well which is closer to the middle of the artificial aquifer (Row 5 – Well B). This well is approximately 3 m away from the header tank as shown in Figure 3.13. Other Figures, 3.21 and 3.22, show that the concentration profiles of wells at Well B at Row 3 and Well A at Row 7, respectively. These figures demonstrate that the concentration values are not the same at all the depths and, hence, the behaviour of the aquifer is not similar throughout. The plots of other wells also exhibit heterogeneous behaviour. Therefore, we can state that the aquifer is not behaving homogeneously, meaning that the aquifer parameters, such as hydraulic gradient and effective porosity are not uniformly distributed throughout the system. The variables used to calibrate the aquifer parameters are subjected to randomness and the accuracy of the results could be affected, considerably.

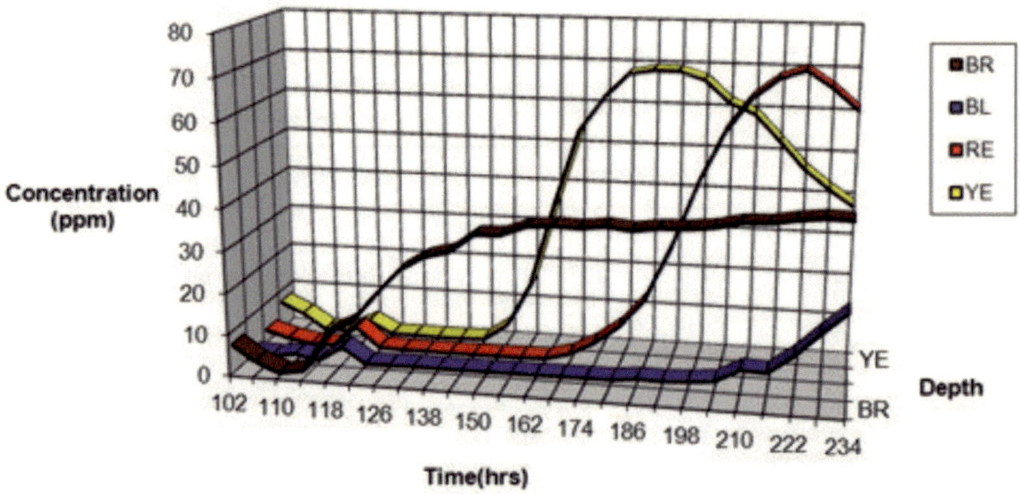

Figure 3.20. Concentration profiles at Row 5 - Well B.

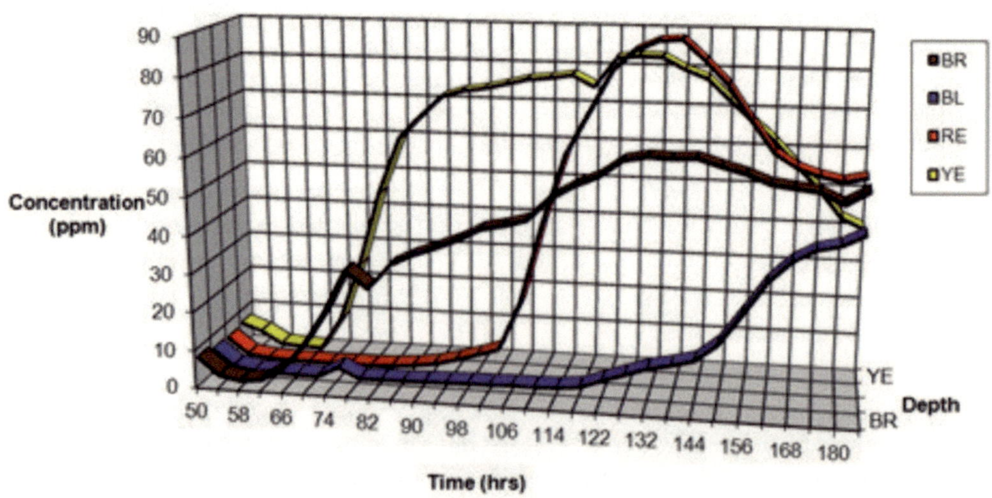

Figure 3.21. Concentrations profiles at Row 3 - Well B.

The reason that the artificial aquifer does not behave homogeneously may be due to the method of construction. The aquifer was constructed using sand blocks that were laid layer by layer. We assume that even though material used in the aquifer is uniform, joints in the blocks can create diverse flow patterns and different flow lengths. Besides, due to the high pressure on the bottom layers (from the top layers), they may be more compacted and, therefore, behave differently.

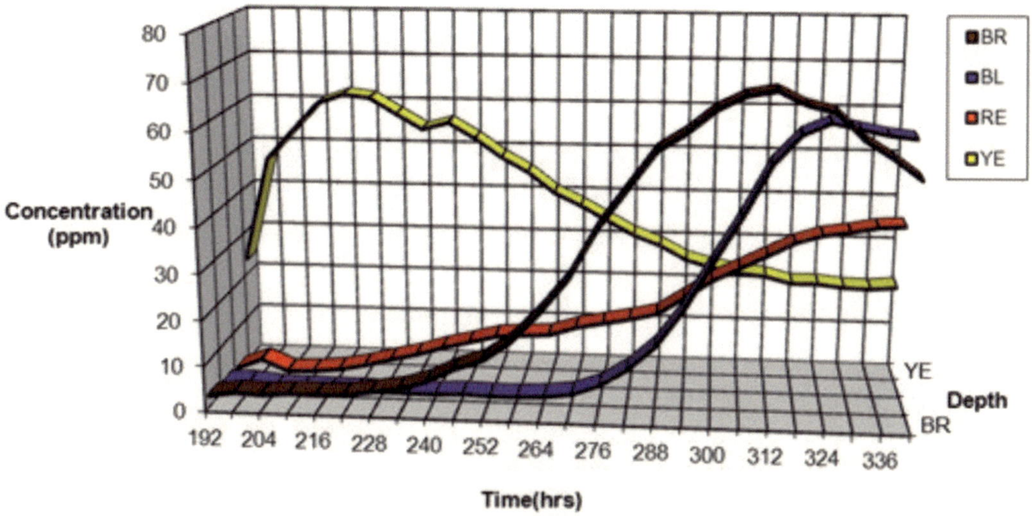

Figure 3.22. Concentrations profiles at Row 7 - Well A.

We can extend the parameter estimation procedure to determine parameters of a two-dimensional groundwater problem. In the two-dimensional case, an advancing solute front will also tend to spread in the directions normal to the direction of flow because at the pore scale the flow paths can diverge. This results in mixing in the directions normal to the flow path, which is called transverse dispersion. Considering the transverse dispersion, the two-dimensional advection-dispersion equation can be written as (Fetter, 1999),

$$\partial C = \left\{ D_L \left(\frac{\partial^2 C}{\partial x^2} \right) + D_T \left(\frac{\partial^2 C}{\partial y^2} \right) \right\} dt - v_x \left(\frac{\partial C}{\partial x} \right) dt \,, \tag{3.7.7}$$

where C = solute concentration (mg/l),

t = time (day),

D_L = hydrodynamic dispersion coefficient parallel to the principal direction of flow (longitudinal) (m^2/day),

D_T = hydrodynamic dispersion coefficient perpendicular to the principal direction of flow (transverse) (m^2/day), and

v_x = average linear velocity (m/day).

The randomness of heterogeneous groundwater systems can be accounted for by adding a noise component to equation (3.7.7), and it can be given by

$$\partial C = \left\{ D_L \left(\frac{\partial^2 C}{\partial x^2} \right) + D_T \left(\frac{\partial^2 C}{\partial y^2} \right) \right\} dt - v_x \left(\frac{\partial C}{\partial x} \right) dt + \xi(x,t)\, dt\,, \tag{3.7.8}$$

where $\xi(x,t)$ is assumed to be a zero-mean stochastic process.

We multiply equation (3.6.8) by dt throughout and replace $\xi(x,t)dt$ by $\sigma^2 dB(t)$ (Jazwinski, 1970), where σ^2 is the amplitude of the Wiener increments, $dB(t)$, to obtain equation (3.7.9). We can now obtain the stochastic partial differential equation as follows,

$$\partial C = \left\{ D_L \left(\frac{\partial^2 C}{\partial x^2} \right) + D_T \left(\frac{\partial^2 C}{\partial y^2} \right) \right\} dt - v_x \left(\frac{\partial C}{\partial x} \right) dt + \sigma^2 dB(t)\,. \tag{3.7.9}$$

As we described in equation (3.7.6) average linear velocity can be expressed by

$$v_x = \frac{K}{n_e} \left(\frac{dh}{dl} \right),$$

Hence, equation (3.7.9) becomes,

$$\partial C = \left\{ D_L \left(\frac{\partial^2 C}{\partial x^2} \right) + D_T \left(\frac{\partial^2 C}{\partial y^2} \right) \right\} dt - \frac{K}{n_e} \left(\frac{dh}{dl} \right) \left(\frac{\partial C}{\partial x} \right) dt + \sigma^2 dB(t)\,. \tag{3.7.10}$$

We assume that transverse dispersion (D_T) can be approximated to 10% of the longitudinal dispersion D_L , i.e., $D_T = 0.1\ D_L$ (Felter,1999).

Then equation (3.7.10) becomes,

$$\partial C = D_L \left\{ \left(\frac{\partial^2 C}{\partial x^2} \right) + 0.1 \left(\frac{\partial^2 C}{\partial y^2} \right) \right\} dt - \frac{K}{n_e} \left(\frac{dh}{dl} \right) \left(\frac{\partial C}{\partial x} \right) dt + \sigma^2 dB(t)\,. \tag{3.7.11}$$

Equation (3.7.11) can be written in the following form:

$$f(t,C,\theta) = a_0(C,t) + \theta_1 a_1(C,t) + \theta_2 a_2(C,t),$$

where,

$$a_0(C_i,\ t) = 0; \quad a_1(C,t) = \left\{ \frac{\partial^2 C}{\partial x^2} + 0.1 \left(\frac{\partial^2 C}{\partial y^2} \right) \right\}; \ a_2(C_i,t) = -\left(\frac{\partial C}{\partial x} \right)_i;$$

$$\theta_1 = D_L; \quad \theta_2 = v_x = \frac{K}{n_e} \left(\frac{dh}{dl} \right).$$

We use the observations for $C(x, y, t)$ at M discrete points in (x, y) coordinate space for a period of time t (where $0 \le t \le T$). Then we obtain the estimates for two unknown parameters as the solution to the following simultaneous equations:

We can simplify equation (3.7.11) to

$$\sum_{i=1}^{M}\int_{0}^{T}\left\{\frac{\partial^2 C}{\partial x^2}+0.1\left(\frac{\partial^2 C}{\partial y^2}\right)\right\}dC_i$$
$$-\sum_{i=1}^{M}\int_{0}^{T}\left\{D_L\left\{\frac{\partial^2 C}{\partial x^2}+0.1\left(\frac{\partial^2 C}{\partial y^2}\right)\right\}+\frac{K}{n_e}\left(\frac{dh}{dl}\right)\left(\frac{\partial C}{\partial x}\right)\right\}\left\{\frac{\partial^2 C}{\partial x^2}+0.1\left(\frac{\partial^2 C}{\partial y^2}\right)\right\}dt=0,$$

$$\sum_{i=1}^{M}\int_{0}^{T}\left\{\frac{\partial C}{\partial x}\right\}dC_i-\sum_{i=1}^{M}\int_{0}^{T}\left\{D_L\left\{\frac{\partial^2 C}{\partial x^2}+0.1\left(\frac{\partial^2 C}{\partial y^2}\right)\right\}+\frac{K}{n_e}\left(\frac{dh}{dl}\right)\left(\frac{\partial C}{\partial x}\right)\right\}\left\{\frac{\partial C}{\partial x}\right\}dt=0. \quad (3.7.12)$$

We can rewrite equations (3.7.12) as

$$D_L k_1+\frac{K}{n_e}\left(\frac{dh}{dl}\right)l_1+m_1=0,$$
$$D_L k_2+\frac{K}{n_e}\left(\frac{dh}{dl}\right)l_2+m_2=0, \quad (3.7.13)$$

where

$$k_1=-\sum_{i=1}^{M}\sum_{j=0}^{n-1}\left\{\frac{\partial^2 C_i^j}{\partial x^2}+0.1\,\frac{\partial^2 C_i^j}{\partial y^2}\right\}^2\left(t_{j+1}-t_j\right),$$

$$l_1=-\sum_{i=1}^{M}\sum_{j=0}^{n-1}\left\{\frac{\partial C_i^j}{\partial x}\right\}\left\{\frac{\partial^2 C_i^j}{\partial x^2}+0.1\,\frac{\partial^2 C_i^j}{\partial y^2}\right\}\left(t_{j+1}-t_j\right),$$

$$m_1=\sum_{i=1}^{M}\sum_{j=0}^{n-1}\left\{\frac{\partial^2 C_i^j}{\partial x^2}+0.1\,\frac{\partial^2 C_i^j}{\partial y^2}\right\}\left(C_i^{j+1}-C_i^j\right),$$

$$k_2=-\sum_{i=1}^{M}\sum_{j=0}^{n-1}\left\{\frac{\partial C_i^j}{\partial x}\right\}\left\{\frac{\partial^2 C_i^j}{\partial x^2}+\frac{\partial^2 C_i^j}{\partial y^2}\right\}\left(t_{j+1}-t_j\right),$$

$$l_2=-\sum_{i=1}^{M}\sum_{j=0}^{n-1}\left\{\frac{\partial C_i^j}{\partial x}\right\}^2\left(t_{j+1}-t_j\right), \text{ and}$$

$$m_2=\sum_{i=1}^{M}\sum_{j=0}^{n-1}\left\{\frac{\partial C_i^j}{\partial x}\right\}\left(C_i^{j+1}-C_i^j\right).$$

We can develop the finite difference approximations for $\frac{\partial C_i}{\partial x_i}$, $\frac{\partial^2 C_i}{\partial x_i^2}$ and $\frac{\partial^2 C_i}{\partial y_i^2}$, to obtain values of k_1, l_1, m_1, k_2, l_2, and m_2. Furthermore, by substituting average values for the hydraulic gradient, $\left(\frac{dh}{dl}\right)$, and the effective porosity, n_e, two simultaneous equations (3.7.13) can be solved to obtain D_L and K, for a two-dimensional groundwater system.

We estimate the parameters of the artificial aquifer at Lincoln University using the procedure developed. The observations of solute concentration are obtained at 1 m grid intervals at four different levels (0.4, 1.0, 1.6, and 2.2 m from the surface of the aquifer). Hence, we rearrange the dataset to be four two-dimensional datasets for each level.

Table 3.2 shows the estimated parameters for the two-dimensional aquifer and the estimates have come closer to the experimental values. However, as the experimental values may not represent the real values within the aquifer, further computational experiments by changing the lateral dispersion would not improve the estimates.

Depth (m)	Hydraulic conductivity, K (m/day)		Longitudinal hydrodynamic dispersion, D_L (m²/day)	
	Estimated	Experimental	Estimated	Experimental
0.4	198.2	137	0.165	0.1596
1.0	166.7	137	0.162	0.1596
1.6	171.5	137	0.143	0.1596
2.2	231.1	137	0.197	0.1596

Table 3.2. Estimated and experimental parameters, hydraulic conductivity, K (m/day), and longitudinal hydrodynamic dispersion, D_L (m^2/day), for the aquifer.

3.8 Parameter Estimation using ANN

In estimating parameters with ANN, first we employ a deterministic 2-D advection-dispersion transport numerical model to generate synthetic data. Afterwards, ANN are trained to learn the complex excitation and response relationship of the generated data. This is done by training the network sufficiently to minimise the error between the actual and network response while retaining the generalising capabilities of the network. We then estimate the associated parameters using noisy concentration data that represent real world aquifer systems. We also test the ability of the model to estimate hydraulic conductivity of an artificial experimental aquifer.

The two-dimensional deterministic advection–dispersion equation (Fetter, 1999), is used as the governing equation for this section. It is important to mention that other possible phenomenon that can be present in the solute transport, such as adsorption and the occurrence of short circuits, are neglected in the governing equation on the assumption that the introduction of noise into the solute concentration values used to estimate the parameters would compensate for them.

The deterministic solute concentration values are generated for a 10 m x 5 m 2-D aquifer using equation (3.6.7). Eight hundred data examples (patterns) are generated for different hydraulic conductivity, *K*, values that ranged from 40 to 240 m/day. It is assumed that all other parameters, control variables and subsidiary conditions are fixed. An initial concentration value of 100 ppm is considered as a point source at the middle of the header boundary of the aquifer and the same source is maintained at the boundary throughout the 10 day period considered. Exponentially distributed concentration values of the point source (at the middle of the header boundary) are considered along with the longitudinal and lateral directions as the initial conditions for the other spatial coordinates. We gather 50 input values for each example. These input values represent solute concentration values at 10 spatial locations (Figure 6.1) at five different time intervals; $t = 1$, $t = 3$, $t = 5$, $t = 7$, $t = 10$ day. We examine the possibility of amalgamating the time as an independent variable into the concentration input data. However, it is difficult to meaningfully integrate them into presently available ANN architectures and innovative model structures need to be developed.

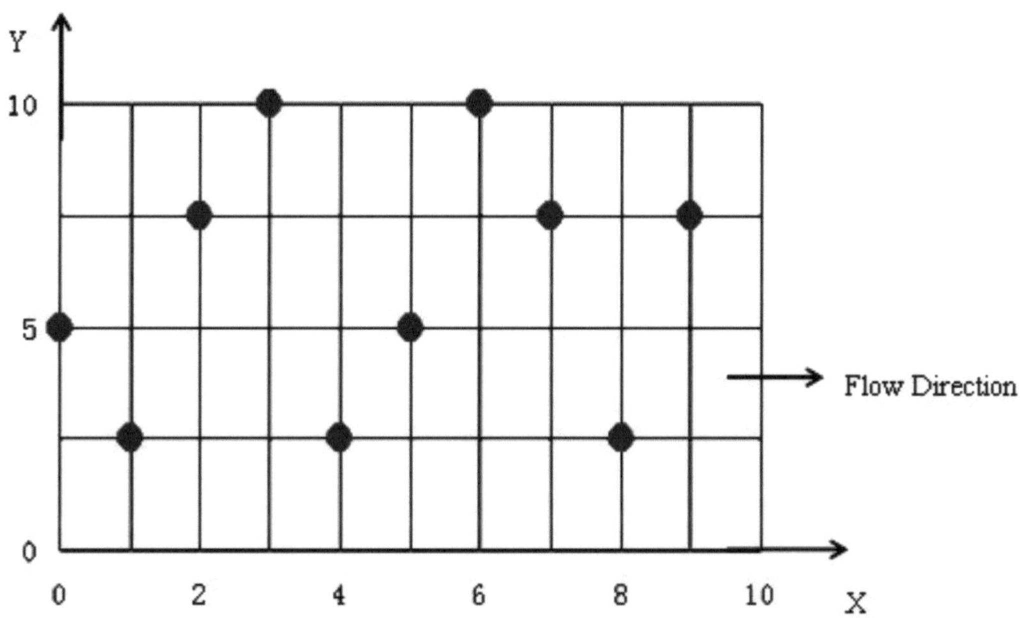

Figure 3.23. Spatial coordinates of concentration observations of the 2-D aquifer.

It is noted, in many studies, that determination of an appropriate network architecture is one of the most important but also one of the most difficult tasks in the model building process (Maier and Dandy, 2000). The network architecture determines the number of connection weights (free parameters) and the way information flows through the network. It is common practice to fix the number of hidden layers in the network and then to choose the number of nodes in each of these layers. Initially, it may be worthwhile to consider a network with simple properties. Such networks have higher processing speeds and can be implemented on hardware more economically (Towell et al., 1991; Bebis and Georgiopoulos,

1994; Castellano et al., 1997). Cybenko (1989) showed that only one hidden layer was required to approximate any continuous function, given that sufficient degrees of freedom (i.e. connection weights) are provided. However, in practice many functions are difficult to approximate with one hidden layer, requiring a prohibitive number of hidden layer nodes (Flood and Kartam, 1994). The use of more than one hidden layer provides greater flexibility and enables the approximation of complex functions with fewer connection weights in many situations (Sarle, 1994).

Despite numerous studies, no systematic approach has been developed for the selection of an optimal network architecture and its geometry. Hence, we employ a trial and error exercise to determine the network architecture (number of hidden layers and number of nodes for each layer). Initially, a simple three layer MLP network (only one hidden layer) is used to train the network to build the complex relationship of output, *K*, and the associated concentration values. Hecht-Nielsen (1987) suggested that an optimum number of hidden nodes for a single hidden layer network can be selected from following relationship, Number if hidden nodes = 2 (Number of input nodes) + 1.

This suggests we should have 101 hidden nodes for 50 inputs. Nevertheless, after a number of trial and error tests, it was found that the optimum results can be achieved by 20 hidden neurons. As reported elsewhere, Abrahart et al. (1999) presented a method based on genetic algorithms to identify the best number of suitable hidden nodes. Chakilam (1998) used principal component analysis to determine the optimal structure of the multi-layered feed forward neural network for a time series forecasting problems, thus reducing the generalisation error and overcoming the over fitting problems.

The dataset is divided into two categories with a random selection of 80% used for training and the rest for testing. The maximum and minimum values of the training network are set by selecting the values from both training (and testing) and estimating dataset, to prevent the ANN from extrapolating beyond its range. We apply scale functions of none, logistic and logistic for input, hidden and output layers, respectively. The default network parameters of NeuroShell2 (neural computing software package) are used; learning rate = 0.1, momentum = 0.1, initial weight = 0.3. The network reached the stopping criterion of average error on test set, fixed at 0.000002, in less than two minutes in a 1GHz personal computer with performance measurements of the coefficient of multiple determination, $R^2 = 0.9999$ and the square of the correlation coefficient, $r^2 = 0.9999$. The network that produces the best results on the test set is the one most capable of generalising, so this is saved as the best network.

Having completed the successful training, another dataset is employed to test the performance of the trained network. We make use of the same model to generate 800 new data values, however, the initial concentration is randomly changed by up to ±5%, and up to ±5% noise is arbitrarily added to all concentration input values. The reason for adding the noise is to simulate the real world problem of erratic behaviour of aquifers. The estimation error of each *K* value is given in Figure 3.4.4, which shows that the error increases with *K*.

Table 3.3 illustrates that the statistical measurements of error with mean square error (MSE) of 45.25, an average absolute percentage error (AAPE) of 5.63%, and a maximum error of 22.45 m/day. Such high error values may not be acceptable in the most practical cases. Since the objective range of parameters is fairly large (40 –240 m/day), the accuracy of the approximation tends to decrease (Figure 3.24). Therefore, we conduct the same estimation procedure with four smaller permissible parameter regimes of *K*; (i) 40-90, (ii) 90-140, (iii) 140-190, and (iv) 190-240 m/day. Table 3.3 shows that accuracy of the estimates has improved considerably.

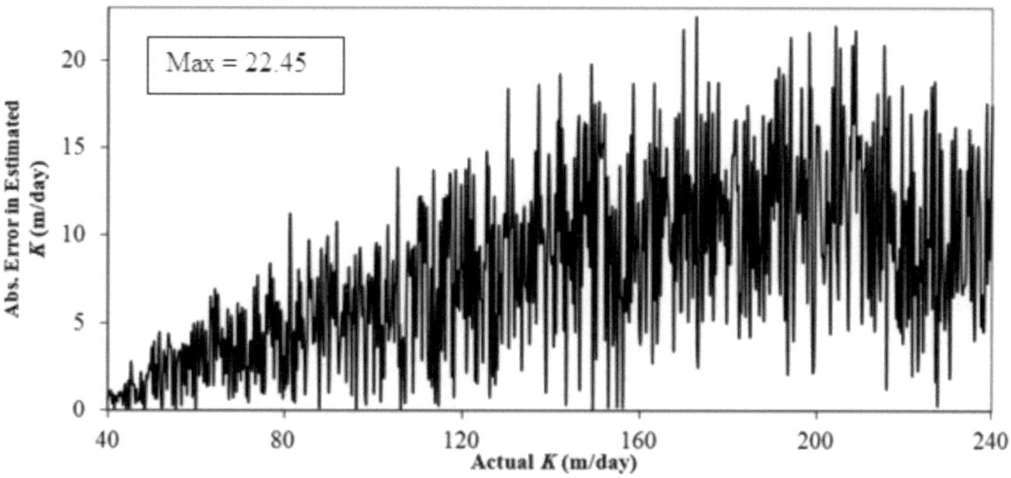

Figure 3.24. Absolute error of estimated parameter, *K*, when considering the whole range, 40–240 m/day.

The maximum error in the 190-240 range has been reduced by about 90% (Figure 3.25 and Table 3.3). Therefore, it is reasonable to assume that if we can gather prior information about the system under consideration, it is possible to obtain more accurate estimates. However, in the real world problems the prior knowledge of the system is limited. Later, we discuss a method to identify the range of parameters by using Self-Organising Maps (SOM). However, before using SOM, we explore the robustness of the ANN estimation models.

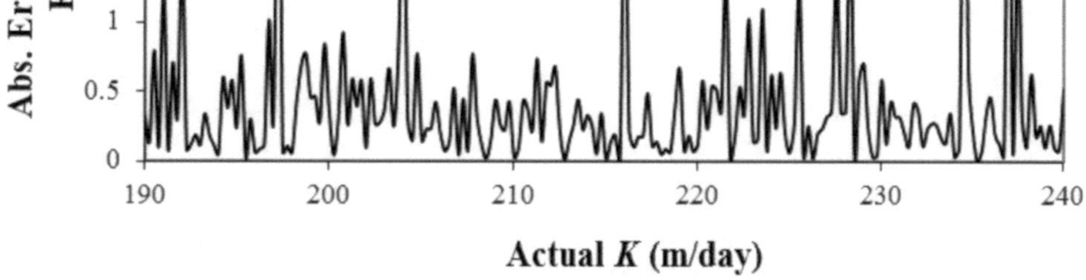

Figure 3.25. Absolute Error of estimated parameter *K*, only for the range 190 – 240 m/day.

Error	*K* Range (m/day)				
	40-240	40–90	90–140	140–190	190-240
Max	22.45	1.88	2.23	2.99	2.98
Mean	8.03	0.27	0.38	0.36	0.39
StDev	5.15	0.32	0.41	0.49	0.47
MSE	45.25	0.11	0.14	0.20	0.19
AAPE(%)	5.63	0.11	0.12	0.18	0.18

Table 3.3. Statistics of estimated error for different ranges of *K* with up to a ±5% difference in initial value and up to a ±5% noise in observations.

Initial condition		Error of *K* (m/day)				
Point C value	Noise	Maximum	Mean	Stdev	MSE	AAPE
50	-50%	9.72	3.48	1.68	12.66	0.95
60	-40%	7.55	2.06	1.57	3.36	0.94
70	-30%	6.18	2.01	1.42	3.01	0.92
80	-20%	4.36	1.59	0.97	2.58	0.77
90	-10%	2.84	0.97	0.72	1.46	0.43
Trained value (100)	0%	1.64	0.34	0.44	0.17	0.17
110	+10%	2.92	1.04	0.86	1.46	0.44
120	+20%	4.57	1.68	1.05	2.95	0.84
130	+30%	6.49	2.11	1.48	3.26	1.06
140	+40%	7.58	2.08	1.57	3.47	1.07
150	+50%	10.14	3.67	1.73	13.81	1.07

Table 3.4. Statistics of estimated error for different initial values with up to a ±5% error for the *K* range, 190-240.

As discussed in chapter 1, real world aquifer systems are subject to numerous random effects. One of them may be an initial value problem. First, we investigate in the range of *K* between 190 – 240 m/day for the stability of the model for different initial values. The point source value of the initial concentration are changed from –50% to 50%. Since, as explained above, an exponentially distributed pattern was used to determine the initial concentration values of other spatial points, change of initial value at the point source also resulted in changing the initial values of every spatial location. Furthermore, to illustrate the heterogeneity of the aquifers, up to ±5% extra noise is added to the generated concentration values of all time intervals. Table 3.4 shows the statistics of the estimates. The estimates exhibit a direct relationship to the noise; however, the most of the results are dependable even at higher noise levels.

Random boundary conditions and an irregular porous structure can result in an erratic distribution of flow paths. Therefore, solute concentration spreads could be highly stochastic. We address this issue by extending the investigation of the robustness by adding different level of randomness to the concentration values. First, the data is generated using the deterministic solutions of equation (3.6.7) for each case and then noise is added randomly to each deterministic concentration value to generate a noisy dataset. For example, to generate up to a ±10% noise component to a deterministic value, *d*, two random functions are used as follows,

random function 1 $\rightarrow$ generate a random number between 0-1 (say n)

random function 2 $\rightarrow$ generate either + or -.

Therefore, noisy data = $d\,(1 \pm 10\% * n)$.

Table 3.5 demonstrates the statistics of the estimates obtained for noisy concentration data. Estimates show that the ANN model is stable even for highly stochastic systems.

± %	Error of Estimate K (m/day)				
added noise	Max	Mean	StDev	MSE	AAPE
10	2.29	0.85	1.10	1.98	0.68
20	3.54	1.05	1.19	2.04	0.76
30	5.46	1.74	1.22	2.25	0.81
40	5.88	1.96	1.35	2.31	0.92
50	6.00	1.99	1.39	2.39	0.93

Table 3.5. Statistics of estimates for noisy data for the K range, 190-240 m/day.

The ANN model gives more accurate estimates when the target parameter range is small. However, in real world heterogeneous aquifers, it may not be a trivial task to identify the accurate parameter range without reliable prior information. Self Organising Maps (SOM) has the ability to sort items into categories of similar objects by nonlinearly projecting the data onto a lower dimensional display and by clustering the data (Kohonen, 1990). We use this power of SOM and develop a method to identify the parameter range for given solute concentration values. We employ SOM to cluster an 800 x 50 dimension noisy dataset used before with a parameter range of 40 –240 m/day into four different categories. The "Supervised Kohonen" network architecture of NeroShell2 successfully categorised four different groups with 201, 200, 197 and 202 data patterns in each cluster, respectively. The SOM put data into categories with a high accuracy, with few exceptions which can be expected with noisy data, at the boundaries of the parameter ranges. To test the accuracy of the prediction capability of the trained model, we then create and feed 12 different test datasets with the same number of input variables (50) into the trained SOM and it accurately identified the correct parameter range for all the datasets.

We extend the hybrid methodology to solve the groundwater inverse problem in the case of two unknown system parameters. We simulate the same aquifer as used above. The two parameters to be estimated are hydraulic conductivity, K (m/day) and longitudinal dispersion coefficient, D_L (m²/day). In line with earlier work, we fed 50 concentration values and two actual outputs (K and D_L) to train the network.

We use a simple three layer network and produce R^2 = 0.9999 and r^2 = 0.9999 for both outputs in 2 min and 50 sec. We then feed a different dataset, which has not been seen by the trained network before. The new dataset consisted of randomly varying (up to ±5%) initial conditions and added noise to replicate a natural system. We explore two different levels of noise; up to ±5% and ±50%. The parameter ranges are; K between 190 – 240 m/day, D_L between 0.03 – 0.08 m²/day. The ANN model produces reasonable estimates for both parameters and the summary of estimates is given in Table 3.6.

Parameter	Actual Range	± % noise	Error of Estimate			
			Max	Mean	MSE	AAPE
K	190-240	5	2.48	0.99	2.65	0.81
		50	6.78	2.35	3.18	1.12
D_L	0.03-0.08	5	0.00341	0.00092	0.0014	0.0005
		50	0.00875	0.00247	0.0029	0.0010

Table 3.6. Statistics of estimates for two parameter case

We apply the hybrid ANN inverse approach presented in the above sections to estimate parameters of the artificial aquifer at Lincoln University. Although, initial conditions, other parameters and the subsidiary conditions of the aquifer are somewhat known, we have to conduct a fairly tiresome, "trial and error" exercise to replicate the aquifer. Eight hundred data patterns are generated for the hydraulic conductivity range of 80 to 280 m/day. Each pattern consists of 100 concentration input variables for 10 distinct spatial locations for 10 different time intervals. We then use Kohonen's SOM (80% data for training and 20% for testing) to classify the input values into four clusters. Next we feed the actual aquifer data into the trained network and the selected subrange; it is established that the aquifer parameter should be within the second cluster (130 – 180 m/day). Based on this information, we generate a separate dataset for the specified range and train an MLP network with the associated K values.

The estimate of K given by the trained ANN is 152.86 m/day. The experimental value of hydraulic conductivity, K, is found to be 137 m/day, which is calculated by calibration tests conducted by aquifer testing staff. In these experiments they have assumed that the aquifer is homogeneous. The difference between two estimates is only 10.37 %. Considering the assumptions of homogeneity made by the aquifer researchers and other possible human errors, it is fair to state that the estimate obtained from the ANN model is reasonable and acceptable.

Our investigation emphasise that the importance of modelling a sufficiently true representation of the physical system and subsidiary conditions to obtain accurate parameter values. As Minns et al. (1996) pointed out, the ANN is susceptible to becoming "a prisoner of its training data". Therefore, prior information, such as type of contaminant source, boundary conditions and subsidiary conditions is crucial to modelling the system accurately. If we could gain such prior information and model the system with ANN, it would be capable of solving the inverse problem with greater accuracy, even with highly noisy data, as well as different system input values.

3.9 Parameter Estimation of SSTM

In this section, we apply the ANN hybrid approach presented in the previous section to estimate parameters of the Stochastic Solute Transport Model (SSTM) developed in this chapter. Since SSTM consists of two parameters ; variance (σ^2) and correlation length (b), we estimate both parameters simultaneously.

In section 3.8 we showed that the accuracy of the estimates was inversely proportional to the size of the objective range of the output (maximum error of the estimate of parameter K was reduced by about 90% for smaller output ranges). In addition, the accuracy of the estimates may reduce when two parameters are estimated simultaneously. To limit the diminution of accuracy of the results imposed by the above mentioned performance characteristics of the method and, as this research is conducted in a general personal computer, we select a smaller permissible output ranges. Additionally, it has shown that the higher parameter values of SSTM (especially σ^2 around 0.25) represent greater heterogeneous flow systems. Thus, we limit the parameter range for both parameters, σ^2 and b, to be between 0.0001 and 0.2.

The main objective of this section is to estimate parameters of SSTM using a hybrid ANN approach developed in the above section. We then extend the exercise using a case study to validate the method. As used in the previous section, the results from the artificial aquifer is used for the validation. However, we intend to achieve an auxiliary objective in the validation process by comparing the artificial aquifer parameters with the estimates obtained for the same aquifer using a curve fitting technique.

As the first step of the implementation process, we use SSTM to simulate a one-dimensional aquifer of 10 m in length. Eight hundred data patterns for different combinations of σ^2 and b are generated. Each parameter ranges from 0.0001 and 0.2. Every data pattern consists of 200 inputs for 10 various spatial locations of the aquifer for 20 distinct time intervals. The same standard Wiener process is used for generating all data sets. The initial condition of the concentration value of unit 1.0 at $x = 0.0$ and exponentially distributed values for other spatial locations are considered. Throughout the simulation the same concentration (unit 1.0) is maintained at the upper end boundary. It is assumed that the mean velocity of the solute is 0.5 m/day. As mentioned above, it is very important to limit the objective range of the parameters for smaller regimes to attain accurate approximations. Thus, Kohonen's Self Organising Map (SOM) is employed to cluster the data set into four categories.

Since the data set represents the stochastic behaviour of the flow, the time needed to classify the data into separate groups is much more than for the similar case, in the deterministic advection - dispersion data, in the previous section. Randomly selected 80% of data were used for training the network and the rest for the validation. Notwithstanding the random nature of the current dataset, the SOM has clustered the data to an adequate degree of accuracy that may be sufficient for the problem at hand.

To test the performance of the trained network model, we use eight different data patterns. Two datasets are generated for each group of clustered network. Moreover, each dataset is produced using different standard Wiener process. New data patterns are fed into the trained model and it accurately identified the parameter range it fitted into.

Having substantiated that the SOM could be successfully used to cluster large dataset that represent heterogeneous data, such as given by SSTM, we create four separate specialised network models for smaller parameter regimes of both parameters in the following ranges;

$$0.0001 - 0.05; 0.05 - 0.1; 0.1 - 0.15; \text{ and } 0.15 - 0.2.$$

Each dataset comprises 441 data patterns of different combinations of σ^2 and b at intervals of 0.0025. For instance, for the range of 0.05 - 0.1, there are 21 different values of each parameter; 0.05, 0.0525, 0.055, 0.0575, ... , 0.1 (21 x 21 = 441 data patterns). Same SSTM model used above for SOM cluster distribution is also used for data generation. Nevertheless, in this case each data pattern contains not only 200 inputs but also two corresponding output parameters. The number of training patterns has considerable influence on the performance of the ANN model (Flood and Kartam, 1994). Increasing the number of data patterns provides more information about the shape of the solution surface and, thus, improves the accuracy of the model prediction. However, in most real world applications, numerous logistical issues impose limitations on the amount of data available and, consequently, the size of the training set. Hence, in developing a method for practical applications, it is important to test the robustness of the method for such data limitations. For that reason, we limit the parameter range of each model to 21 values (between 0.0001 and 0.2 at intervals of 0.0025).

Maier and Dandy (2000) showed that it was important to select a suitable network architecture and model validation method in the development of ANN models to achieve optimum results. In addition, it may be necessary to select the most suitable model for handling highly random data such as SSTM data. Therefore, we conduct a few trial and error exercises to choose the appropriate model structure, and training and testing procedure. The following are the MLP ANN models that are considered for different combinations of hidden layers and various grouping of activation functions: three layer standard connections; four layer standard connections; five layer standard connections; one hidden layer with two parallel slabs with different activation functions; one hidden layer with three hidden slabs with different activation functions; one hidden layer of two parallel slabs, different activation functions and jump connection; three layer jump connections; four layer jump connections; and five layer jump connections.

After numerous attempts, it is found that the network model of five layer standard connections could produce the best trained model in the least time. In the selected model, each hidden layer consists of 30 neurons. Activation functions of linear <0, 1>, logistic, tanh,

Gaussian and logistic are used for layers of input, hidden (3 layers) and output, respectively. The default network parameters (NeuroShell2) are employed; learning rate = 0.1, momentum = 0.1, initial weight = 0.3. The stopping criterion is set to a minimum error of 0.000001. All four networks reach the stopping condition in about 30 minutes in a 1 GHz personal computer with the performance measurements shown in Table 3.7.

After the completion of successful training for each model, separate datasets are generated to test the prediction capability of each model. The same SSTM is employed to produce another dataset of 441 data patterns for each parameter range. However, different standard Wiener process increments are used. In addition, initial and boundary conditions are adjusted up to ±5% by adding random values. Input data values of each dataset are then fed into the corresponding trained network and processed to obtain model predictions.

Parameter range	Coefficient of multiple determination, R^2		Square of the correlation coefficient, r^2		Mean absolute error	
	σ^2	b	σ^2	b	σ^2	b
0.0001 - 0.05	0.9912	0.9876	0. 9911	0.9876	0.0	0.0
0.05 - 0.1	0.9911	0.9876	0. 9899	0.9876	0.0	0.0
0.1 - 0.15	0.9898	0.9870	0. 9872	0.9868	0.0	0.0
0.15 - 0.2	0.9728	0.9774	0. 9721	0.9661	0.0001	0.0001

Table 3.7. Performance measurements of trained ANN model for four different parameter ranges.

Figure 3.26 illustrates the absolute error of estimated parameter σ^2, for the range of 0.0001 - 0.05. It shows that the ANN model prediction is extremely satisfactory and that the average absolute error is approximately 0.04%. Figure 3.27 shows that prediction for the other parameter, *b* also met with similar accuracy for the same range.

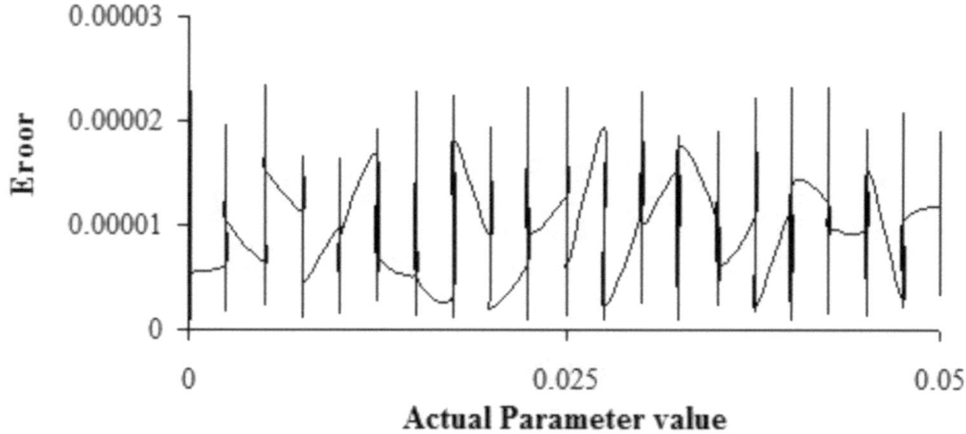

Figure 3.26. Absolute error of estimated parameter σ^2, for the range of 0.0001 - 0.05.

A similar approach is also applied to other parameter ranges. The precision of the estimates given by ANN models shrinks with highly heterogeneous data. As larger values of parameters indicate excessive stochastic flows, we can expect the accuracy of the prediction to diminish for highly stochastic flows. Nonetheless, the average absolute error for the estimates for a range of 0.15 to 0.2 is approximately 5.5% (for example, Figure 3.28 illustrates the error of estimated parameter σ^2 for parameter range of 0.15 to 0.2), which may be acceptable for the most of practical applications.

The above prediction accuracy analyses of the ANN models are based on similar ranges for both parameters. However, in real world applications we may have to deal with extremely different values for two parameters. Therefore, the robustness of the ANN method for different values of parameter regimes for two parameters need to be assessed.

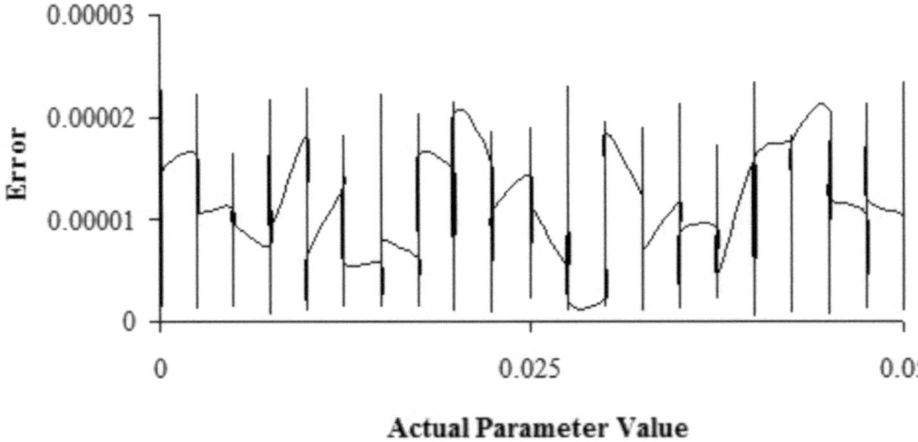

Figure 3.27. Absolute error of estimated parameter *b*, for the range of 0.0001 – 0.05.

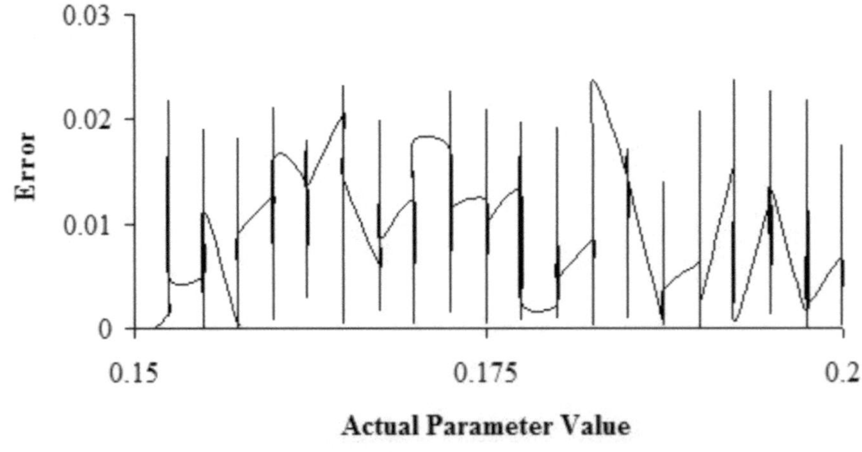

Figure 3.28. Absolute error of estimated parameter σ^2, for the range of 0.15– 0.2.

We generate two separate datasets for two extreme cases:

where σ^2 is smaller and *b* is higher - σ^2 ranges of 0.0001 – 0.05 and *b* ranges of 0.15 – 0.2; and where σ^2 is higher and *b* is smaller - σ^2 ranges of 0.15 – 0.2 and *b* ranges of 0.0001 – 0.05.

A similar method to that which was used for earlier investigations is employed to gauge the capability of the ANN model. Figures 3.29 and 3.30 reveal that the trained network has predicted the estimates with reasonable precision. In both cases the percentage average absolute error is approximately 4%.

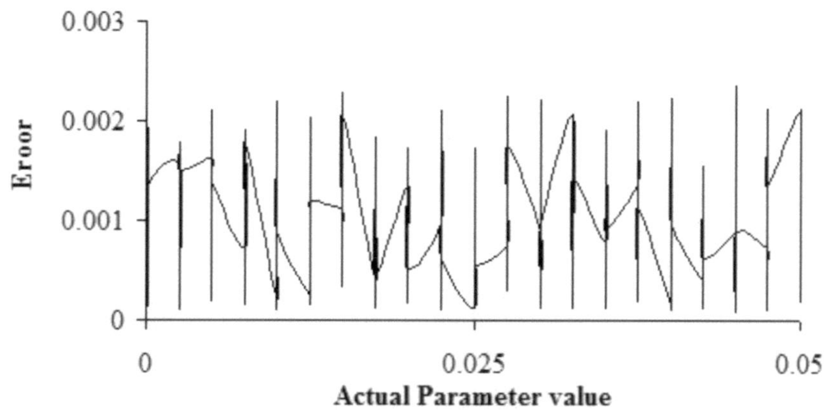

Figure 3.29. Absolute error of estimated parameter σ^2, for the σ^2 range of 0.0001 – 0.05 and *b* range of 0.15 – 0.2.

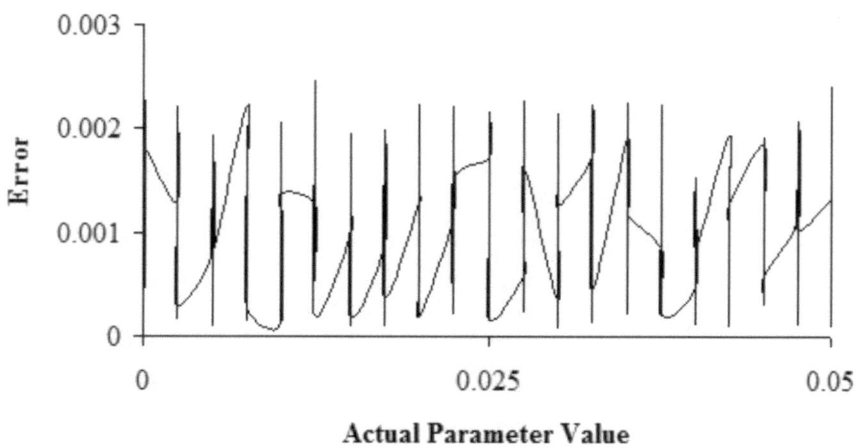

Figure 3.30. Absolute error of estimated parameter b, for the σ^2 range of 0.15 – 0.2 and *b* range of 0.0001 – 0.05.

We use the artificial aquifer data to validate the developed hybrid ANN method. We make use of the same aquifer dataset in this section to estimate the parameters of SSTM for the aquifer. Additionally, we use the same data to partially validate the stochastic model (SSTM) previously using a curve fitting technique to approximate the aquifer parameters. It was found that the approximate artificial aquifer parameters are variance, $\sigma^2 = 0.01$ and correlation length, $b = 0.01$.

In the present validation, first, we used the known conditions such as initial and boundary conditions, and hydraulic gradient to simulate the aquifer using the SSTM. The initial concentration at $x = 0$ is 1.0 unit and it is reduced exponentially with time. Initial values of other spatial points are considered as zero. 1681 data patterns are generated for different combinations of parameters, σ^2 and b. Single standard Wiener process increments are retained for every simulation run. Both parameters varied between 0.0001 and 0.2.

The 1681 generated data patterns are fed into Kohonen's self-organising map architecture to cluster them into four different groups. After classifying them with reasonable accuracy the aquifer dataset is fed into the SOM model to identify relevant groups that the data resemble the most. In this case, we make an assumption that the effect of the transverse dispersion of the flow is reflected in the stochastic flow described by SSTM. As shown in Figure 3.13, the data have been collected along five wells at four levels (A to E wells at levels BR, BL, RE and YE). We consider the data collected along each well at a certain level as a one-dimensional flow path. Hence, we reproduce 20 different one-dimensional datasets.

Concentration values of the aquifer are normalised to enable to weigh them against the normalised SSTM data.

Initially, a dataset closer to the middle of the aquifer, well C – level RE is chosen for the estimation of parameters. An aquifer dataset has to be interpolated to produce missing data and fabricate uniform spatial and temporal grids. Having constructed an exact number of data for similar spatial and time intervals as for the original ANN model, the aquifer dataset is fed into the trained model. The selected dataset is then separated from the larger set and trained for the smaller range selected. Based on the findings described previously, a five layer standard connections is used with the same activation functions, initial weights, momentum and learning rates.

After completing sufficient training, the artificial aquifer dataset is fed into the ANN model to estimate parameters. The estimates that are produced by the model are $\sigma^2 = 0.01364$ and $b = 0.01665$. The estimates produced by the ANN model show close resemblance to the values given by the curve fitting technique. Since we avoid considering lateral dispersions for estimation by ANN model, the results may be subject to slight errors.

We extend the estimation procedure to determine the parameters of the Lincoln University aquifer for other flow lines. Since the earlier dataset is closer to the middle of the aquifer, we choose the next dataset that is nearer to the boundary of the aquifer. Estimates obtained using well A – level YE are $\sigma^2 = 0.01483$ and $b = 0.00912$. These estimates are similar to earlier values.

3.10 Dispersivity Based on the SSTM

To estimate the parameter of the SSTM, we develop a procedure consisting of the following steps: (1) we generate a large number of realizations of concentration (usually 100) for a particular set of values of σ^2 and b using the SSTM; (2) estimate the diffusion coefficient

(*D*) using the maximum likelihood estimation procedure for the 1-D advection-dispersion equation for a given velocity using each of the realization; and (3) take the mean of the estimates of *D* as the dispersivity for the given set of parameters

We have demonstrated that the SSTM can be used to characterise an experimental homogeneous sand aquifer of 5 m width x 10 m length x 2.7 height using a single set of values of (σ^2 = 0.01 and b = 0.01) quite satisfactorily. It has also been shown that the numerical solutions of SSTM, in conjunction with the parameter estimation methods such as maximum likelihood method and artificial neural networks, can be used to estimate reliable effective dispersion coefficients, therefore, effective dispersivity, for different scale experiments up to 10 meters.

We use this procedure, which we call stochastic inversive method (SIM) to estimate *D* for other combinations of σ^2 and *b* for different flow lengths. Table 3.8 exhibits the estimated dispersion coefficients (*D*) for the range of scales; 1, 10, 20, 30, 50 and 100 m.

We need to remember that the SSTM is based on the velocity covariance kernel, $\sigma^2 e^{\frac{-|x_1 - x_2|}{b}}$, and a different kernel would give different D values. In addition, SIM is not accurate for very noisy realizations because the theory of estimation is strictly valid when noise is small and Gaussian (Kutoyants, 1984).

b	σ^2	Estimated *D*					
		1 m	10 m	20 m	30 m	50 m	100 m
0.0001	0.0001	0.01634	0.03502	0.05804	0.07328	0.09447	0.12493
0.0001	0.001	0.01942	0.03738	0.06126	0.07526	0.09930	0.13006
0.0001	0.01	0.03844	0.05287	0.08469	0.10502	0.13591	0.18294
0.0001	0.05	0.04758	0.07799	0.12986	0.16064	0.20645	0.27009
0.0001	0.1	0.06786	0.08690	0.14214	0.17914	0.23342	0.31205
0.0001	0.15	0.06968	0.09060	0.15044	0.18790	0.24022	0.31327
0.0001	0.2	0.07047	0.09259	0.15717	0.20209	0.25756	0.33937
0.0001	0.25	0.07188	0.09382	0.15905	0.19747	0.25542	0.33289
0.0001	0.3	0.07258	0.09466	0.16131	0.19895	0.26026	0.34742
0.001	0.0001	0.01917	0.03738	0.05519	0.07807	0.09628	0.12984
0.001	0.001	0.03749	0.05289	0.08020	0.11085	0.13335	0.18273
0.001	0.01	0.06739	0.08698	0.13530	0.18702	0.23005	0.31770
0.001	0.05	0.07424	0.09650	0.15306	0.21656	0.26236	0.36391
0.001	0.1	0.08492	0.09910	0.15522	0.21291	0.25431	0.35222

0.001	0.15	0.08671	0.10782	0.17443	0.24632	0.29578	0.40749
0.001	0.2	0.09482	0.11886	0.18858	0.26626	0.32559	0.44440
0.001	0.25	0.10701	0.12933	0.20057	0.28264	0.33817	0.46265
0.001	0.3	0.11008	0.13860	0.21898	0.30438	0.36830	0.50826
0.01	0.0001	0.02541	0.05302	0.08035	0.11327	0.14376	0.20657
0.01	0.001	0.05697	0.08773	0.13444	0.19613	0.24574	0.34753
0.01	0.01	0.07906	0.10003	0.15332	0.22578	0.28589	0.40472
0.01	0.05	0.09457	0.16952	0.26730	0.38284	0.48728	0.69328
0.01	0.1	0.11483	0.21334	0.33450	0.48658	0.61670	0.87920
0.01	0.15	0.13745	0.24065	0.37173	0.54195	0.67787	0.96664
0.01	0.2	0.15574	0.25994	0.40478	0.58780	0.73802	1.05102
0.01	0.25	0.18468	0.27120	0.41747	0.59966	0.75083	1.06491
0.01	0.3	0.18994	0.27751	0.43013	0.62369	0.78586	1.11591
0.05	0.0001	0.01874	0.07828	0.12467	0.17543	0.22998	0.34209
0.05	0.001	0.03559	0.10128	0.16245	0.22834	0.29946	0.44681
0.05	0.01	0.06957	0.15994	0.25211	0.34326	0.45352	0.68013
0.05	0.05	0.07651	0.26271	0.41319	0.56701	0.75557	1.13054
0.05	0.1	0.08450	0.29209	0.45872	0.63193	0.83988	1.26490
0.05	0.15	0.08725	0.29659	0.47462	0.66040	0.88362	1.33137
0.05	0.2	0.08987	0.29700	0.46840	0.64492	0.85205	1.27735
0.05	0.25	0.09219	0.29480	0.46693	0.65051	0.87047	1.30991
0.05	0.3	0.09294	0.29137	0.45748	0.63153	0.83935	1.26428
0.1	0.0001	0.01797	0.08546	0.14242	0.19805	0.26901	0.42102
0.1	0.001	0.02971	0.10536	0.16856	0.23555	0.31622	0.48560
0.1	0.01	0.05925	0.17795	0.29101	0.41507	0.56815	0.88488
0.1	0.05	0.06452	0.28179	0.45334	0.64813	0.87743	1.35846
0.1	0.1	0.07232	0.29698	0.48594	0.68641	0.93357	1.45105
0.1	0.15	0.07485	0.29776	0.47662	0.67992	0.91941	1.42114
0.1	0.2	0.07587	0.29876	0.48105	0.68887	0.93379	1.44814
0.1	0.25	0.07608	0.29928	0.48535	0.68808	0.93290	1.45029

0.1	0.3	0.07678	0.29791	0.48068	0.67575	0.91363	1.41871
0.15	0.0001	0.01731	0.08784	0.14149	0.20423	0.28678	0.45299
0.15	0.001	0.02570	0.10921	0.18047	0.25898	0.35905	0.56336
0.15	0.01	0.05454	0.16218	0.26117	0.37775	0.52802	0.82934
0.15	0.05	0.06574	0.24498	0.40463	0.57946	0.81625	1.27853
0.15	0.1	0.07627	0.24830	0.40532	0.58494	0.82098	1.28586
0.15	0.15	0.07722	0.24896	0.40327	0.58331	0.82088	1.29136
0.15	0.2	0.07785	0.25016	0.40435	0.58084	0.81027	1.27489
0.15	0.25	0.07807	0.25278	0.41587	0.59926	0.83683	1.32106
0.2	0.3	0.07527	0.27394	0.44577	0.65306	0.93236	1.47560
0.25	0.0001	0.01694	0.08642	0.14037	0.20553	0.29769	0.47547
0.25	0.001	0.02292	0.11779	0.19345	0.28363	0.41296	0.65983
0.25	0.01	0.04829	0.13433	0.22093	0.32259	0.46790	0.74928
0.25	0.05	0.06187	0.18828	0.30661	0.45919	0.67190	1.08123
0.25	0.1	0.07470	0.23226	0.37711	0.55761	0.81495	1.30630
0.25	0.15	0.07537	0.25020	0.41219	0.60827	0.88655	1.42797
025	0.2	0.07559	0.26583	0.42875	0.63902	0.92617	1.48670
0.25	0.25	0.07567	0.28102	0.46074	0.68281	0.99764	1.60438
0.25	0.3	0.07593	0.29162	0.46948	0.69110	1.00010	1.61016
0.3	0.0001	0.01785	0.08229	0.13906	0.21167	0.31537	0.51395
0.3	0.001	0.02169	0.11016	0.18535	0.28209	0.42416	0.69259
0.3	0.01	0.04787	0.14860	0.25288	0.38448	0.58112	0.95251
0.3	0.05	0.06316	0.22140	0.38149	0.57637	0.87271	1.42535
0.3	0.1	0.07527	0.25171	0.42778	0.64452	0.97782	1.58726
0.3	0.15	0.07728	0.27513	0.47773	0.73238	1.10681	1.80695
0.3	0.2	0.07799	0.28755	0.49003	0.73771	1.11325	1.81448
0.3	0.25	0.07824	0.29803	0.50666	0.77144	1.17052	1.91032
0.3	0.3	0.07911	0.30699	0.53747	0.80802	1.22297	1.98500

Table 3.8. Estimates of D obtained by using a stochastic inverse method for different combinations of parameters of SSTM for different flow lengths (velocity = 0.5 m/day).

We can summarise some of the estimates in the plots in Figures 3.31, 3.32 and 3.33 as functions of the scales of the experiments. What these plots show is that, for a given set of parameters, the SSTM would give the estimates of dispersivity increasing with the flow length.

As discussed in chapter 1, Pickens and Grisak (1981), and Lallemand-Barres and Peaudecerf (1978, cited in Fetter, 1999) showed that the scale dependency of α_L has a linear relationship of $\alpha_L = 0.1\ L$, where L is the mean travel distance. However, Pickens and Grisak (1981) recognised that the linear increase of dispersivity with the mean travel distance was unlikely for large travel distances. It was expected that tracer migration between aquifer layers could cause a reduction in the magnitude of the proportionality constants, since the transverse migration would tend to reduce the spreading effect caused by the stratification. Field measurements obtained by Gelhar (1986) illustrate that the scale dependence relationship between α_L and the flow length is non-linear (Figure 3.34).

To evaluate the comparative estimates of D obtained from the inverse method for the SSTM parameters and the field measurements observed by Gelhar (1986), we plot them on the same graph (Figure 3.35 – 3.37). Only reliable observations of Figure 3.34 (indicated by larger symbols) are considered. Since the parameter estimated from the inverse approach is D, α_L values of Figure 3.34 are converted to D ($D = \alpha_L v$). Furthermore, we plot the relationship of $\alpha_L = 0.1\ L$ in the same graph to assess our estimates. Three different ranges of b are chosen. Figure 3.35 shows the estimates for smaller b, 0.0001 m, for four values of σ^2 (0.0001, 0.05, 0.2 and 0.3). Figures 3.36 and 3.37 illustrate the similar σ^2 values for a mid range value b, 0.01 m, and larger b, 0.3, respectively.

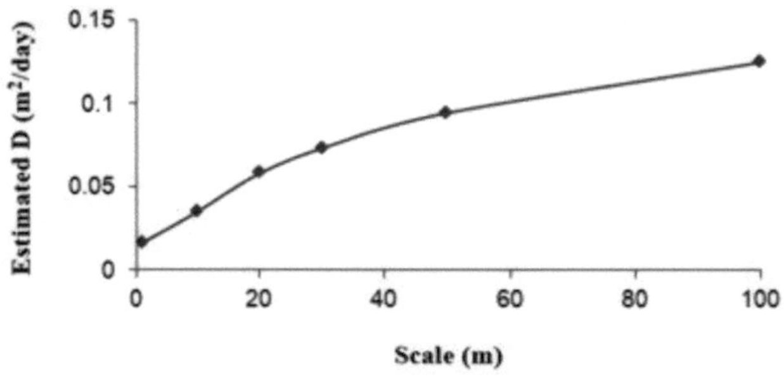

Figure 3.31. D for the parameter combination of $b = 0.0001$ and $\sigma^2 = 0.0001$.

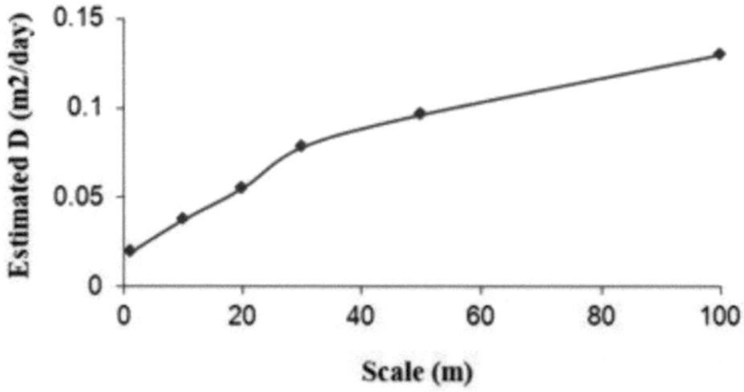

Figure 3.32 D for the parameter combination of $b = 0.001$ and $\sigma^2 = 0.0001$.

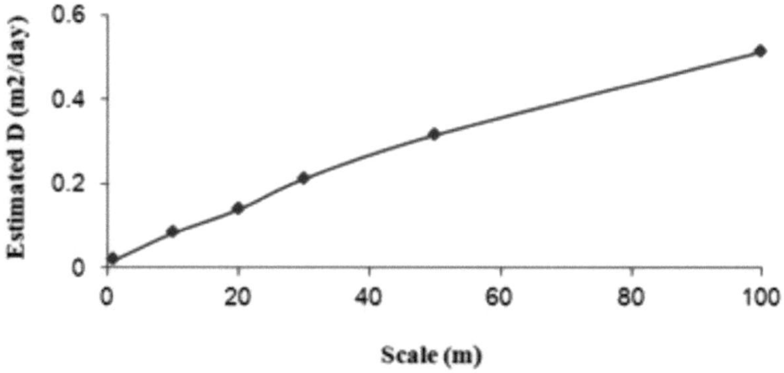

Figure 3.33. D for the combination of b = 0.3 and σ^2 = 0.0001.

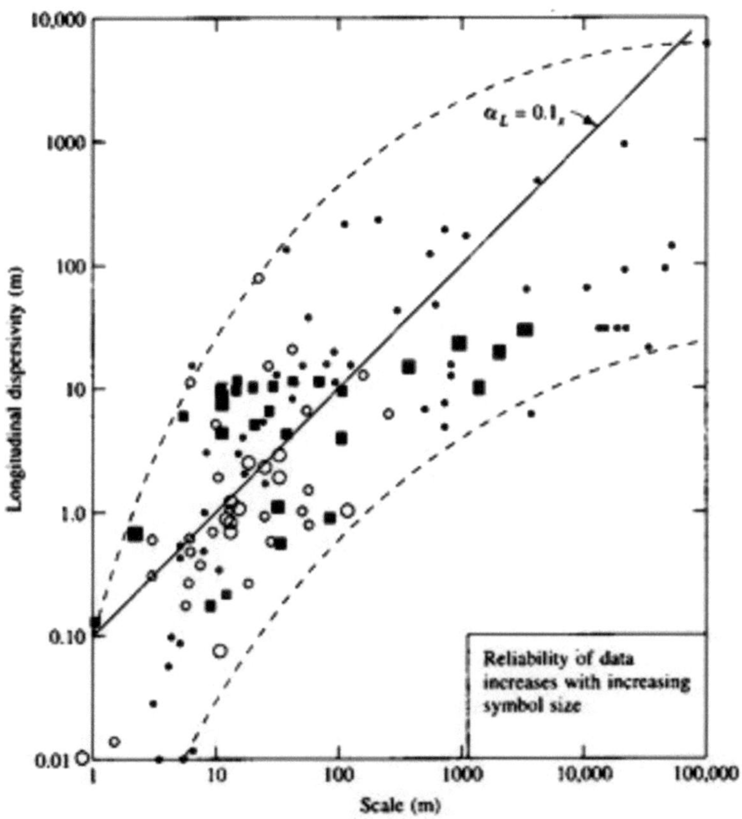

Figure 3.34. Field measured values of longitudinal dispersivity as a function of the scale of measurement. The largest circles represent the most reliable data. The estimated dispersivity from the SSTM are given by the squares. (Source: Gelhar (1986).)

Figures 3.35 – 3.37 demonstrate that corresponding D values obtained for SSTM parameters do not agree with the relationship of $\alpha_L = 0.1\ L$. However, for mid and larger ranges of b, estimated D s are in reasonable agreement with the most of the reliable field measurements

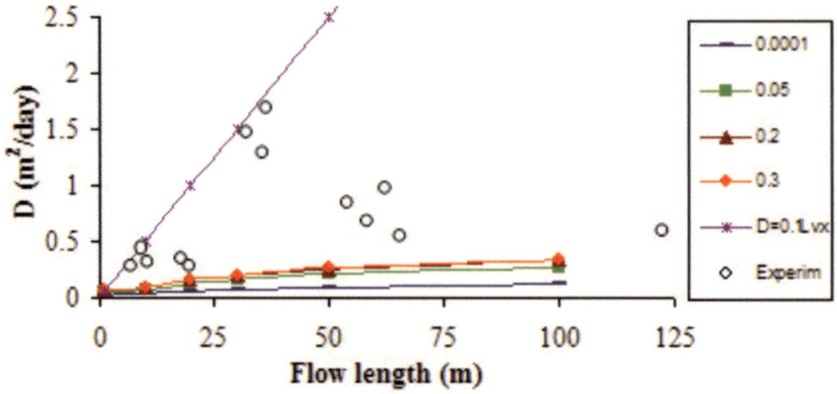

Figure 3.35. Estimated D values for b = 0.0001 m for range of σ^2 (0.0001 - 0.3), $D= 0.1\ L\ v$, and reliable field measurements observed by Gelhar (1986) for different flow lengths.

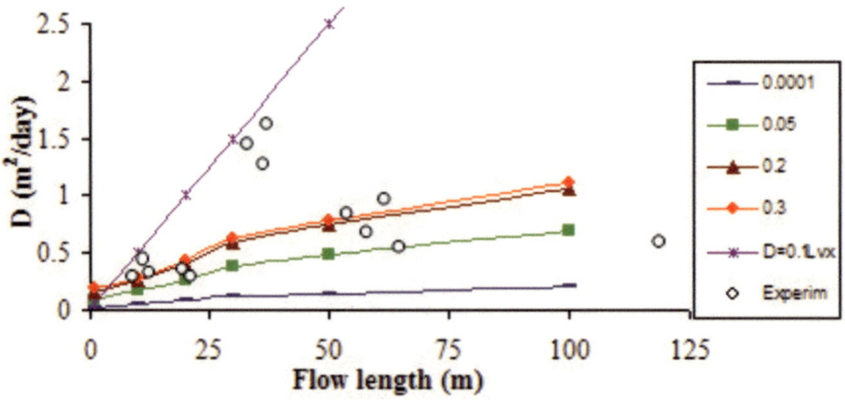

Figure 3.36. Estimated D values for b = 0.01 m for range of σ^2 (0.0001 - 0.3), $D= 0.1Lv$, and reliable field measurements observed by Gelhar (1986) for different flow lengths.

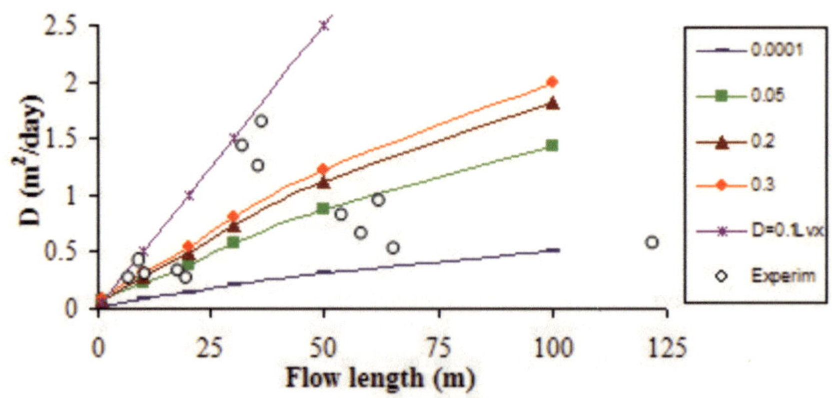

Figure 3.37 Estimated D values for b = 0.1 m for range of σ^2 (0.0001 - 0.3), $D= 0.1Lv$, and reliable field measurements observed by Gelhar (1986) for different flow lengths.

observed by Gelhar (1986). Data in Figure 3.35 represent a solute transport system with very low stochasticity, which may not be realistic in real world aquifers. Figures 3.38 and 3.39 may be a better representation of an actual aquifer. Note that the α_L values of Figure 3.36 were obtained from many sites around the world. The estimated data that agrees with field measurements may be obtained from a variety of soil and heterogeneity.

To simplify the computational burden, we make use of the fact that the expected value of mean $d\beta(t)$ is zero and the variance is given by equation (3.4.5). Instead of calculating $d\beta(t)$ for each *x* within *a*, we take the mean of $Var[d\beta]$ over the length *a*,

$$E[Var(d\beta(t))] = \frac{\int_0^a \left(\sum_{i=1}^{M} (\eta_i^2)\Delta t \right) dx}{a} = \left(\frac{\int_0^a \sum_{i=1}^{M} (\lambda_i f_i^2(x))dx}{a} \right) \Delta t \tag{3.10.1}$$

But by orthogonality, $\int_0^a f_i^2(x)dx = 1$, and, (3.10.2)

it can be shown that approximately, $\underset{M\to\infty}{Limit} \sum_{i=1}^{M} \lambda_i = \sigma^2 a$. (3.10.3)

Therefore, $E[Var(d\beta(t))] = \sigma^2 \Delta t$. (3.10.4)

To illustrate this approximation, the number of eigenvalues required for each *a* (*M*) is determined by calculating a number of roots that are sufficient for the *M*th eigenvalue to reach a value ε, where ε was set to be 5% of the value of the first eigenvalue. The relationship between *a* and the number of roots required is approximately 150 * *a*, for *a* = 1 to 10 000 metres. For example, when σ^2 =1.0 and b=0.01, *M* = {150,750,1500,7500,15000,75000,150000,300000,450000}, then for a = {1,5,10,50,100,500,1000,2000,3000}. $\sum_{i=1}^{M} \lambda_i$ = {0.8762, 4.2920, 8.5443, 42.5518, 85, 04312, 425.0663, 850.1131, 1710.6345, and 2684.8313}. This shows the extent of the computational problem without the approximation for $d\beta(t)$. We have computed ($E[Var(d\beta(t))] / \Delta t$) using equation (3.10.1) for different values of *a* with *b*=0.01, Δt =0.001, $\Delta x = 0.01$, σ^2 =1.0, and 150* *a* number of eigen values. For each *a* , the computation was done using a set of routines written in the Python™ language with the *Numeric* extension for fast array operations. Computing ($E[Var(d\beta(t))] / \Delta t$) for larger values of *a* is a computationally expensive operation with the computing times increasing exponentially with *a*. As an example, for *a* = 1000 meters, it takes approximately 200 minutes, with *a* = 2000 taking approximately 760 minutes on a 1.8 GHZ computer. For *a* ={1,5,10,50,100,500,1000,2000,3000}, the corresponding values for $E[Var(d\beta(t))] / \Delta t$ are {0.8653, 0.8647,0.8630,0.8615,0.8611,0.8610,0.8610,0.8655, 0.8983}, respectively, and we can expect that for an infinite number of eigen functions it will approach 1.0. Therefore, the spatially averaged $d\beta(t)$ is a Gaussian random variable with zero-mean and $\sigma^2 \Delta t$ - variance, which can be readily incorporated into the numerical solution scheme for SSTM.

Because of the high computational times involved, instead of using the SIM procedure, we estimate the dispersivity for a computational experiment by limiting ourselves to the SSTM parameters obtained for experimental sand aquifer (i.e., σ^2 =0.01; b=0.01 m) in the following way:

(a) Set the initial and boundary conditions as,

$$C(x,0)=0, \quad x \geq 0$$
$$C(0,t)=1.0, \; t \geq 0 \text{ and}$$
$$C(\infty,t)=0, \quad t \geq 0$$

(b) Solve equation (21) assuming mean velocity to be 1.0 m/day,

(c) Use a realization of $C(x,t)$ at x=a to estimate the dispersivity, α_L , using equation (3.10.5) (Fetter, 1999) given below using nonlinear regression: (Mathematica® was used for this purpose.)

$$C(x,t) = 0.5\left(erfc\left(\frac{a-t}{2\sqrt{\alpha_L t}}\right) + \exp\left(\frac{a}{\alpha_L}\right) erfc\left(\frac{a+t}{2\sqrt{\alpha_L t}}\right)\right). \quad (3.10.5)$$

Equation (3.10.5) is the analytical solution for the one-dimensional advection-dispersion equation for the initial and boundary conditions given in (a) above. To get a reliable estimate of α_L for given a, we need to have x-axis length of 1.5 a meters and should have $C(x,t)$ realization upto 2 a days. For example, to obtain an estimate of α_L for a = 3000 meters, we need to run the simulation of a domain of 4500 meters for 6000 days. However, to reduce the computational time, one can use higher Δx and Δt values than ideally suitable in solving SPDEs thereby sacrificing the reliability. (Δx =0.01 m and Δt =0.00001 days would give very good solutions to SSTM.) However, this approximate procedure is only valid for the velocity covariance kernel used in this chapter. This procedure is not as reliable as the SIM.

We overlay some representative values of dispersivities from the SSTM on a graph of the field measurements obtained by Gelhar (1986) from different experiments in Figure 3.34, which shows that SSTM could model the multi-scale dispersion with a single set of parameters, σ^2 =0.01; b=0.01 m, that would give rise to similar non-linear scale dependency of "deterministic" dispersivity evaluated using the realisations of SSTM.

In Figure 3.34, the larger (hollow) circles depict the most reliable experimental data whereas the smaller (filled) circles give the data with lesser experimental accuracy. The dotted lines show the bounded region of experimental data. The estimated dispersivity values (filled squares) from SSTM are within the bounded region and follow similar trends to the most reliable experimental data. We estimated the dispersivities from SSTM using only a limited number of computational experiments, and each computational experiment produces a random realisation. Therefore, the estimated dispersivities are stochastic quantities just like the experimental values, and it is reasonable to expect discrepancies within the bounded region.

4

A Generalized Mathematical Model in One-Dimension

4.1 Introduction

In the previous chapter we derived a stochastic solute transport model (equation (3.2.14)); we developed the methods to estimate its parameters, and investigated its behaviour numerically. We see some promise to characterise the solute dispersion at different flow lengths, and there are some indications that equation (3.2.14) produce the behaviours that would be interpreted as capturing the scale-dependency of dispersivity. However, there are weaknesses in the model as evident from Chapter 3. These weaknesses, which are discussed in the next section, are stemming from the very assumptions we made in the development of the model. One could argue that by relaxing the Fickian assumptions, we are actually complicating the problem quite unnecessarily. But as we see in Chapter 3 and in this chapter, we develop a new mathematical and computational machinery at a more fundamental level for the hydrodynamic dispersion in saturated porous media.

We see that equation (3.2.14) is based on assuming a covariance kernel for the velocity fluctuations, and the solution is dependent on solving an integral equation (see equation (3.3.11)). In Chapter 3, the integral equation is solved analytically for the covariance kernel given by equation (3.3.10) to obtain the eigen values and eigen functions, but analytical solutions of integral equations can not be easily derived for any arbitrary covariance kernel. This limits the flexibility of the SSTM in employing a suitable covariance kernel independent of the ability to solve relevant integral equations. Further, we need to solve the SSTM in a much more computationally efficient manner, and estimating dispersivity by always relating to the deterministic advection-dispersion equation is not quite satisfactory. Therefore, we seek to develop a more general form of equation (3.2.14) in this chapter.

4.2 The Development of the Generalized Model

We restate equation (3.2.14) in the differential form:

$$dC = S\left(\bar{V}(x,t)\,C(x,t)\right)dt + S\left(C(x,t)\,d\beta_m(t)\right), \tag{4.2.1}$$

$$\text{where}\quad d\beta_m(t) = \sigma\sum_{j=1}^{m}\sqrt{\lambda_j}\,f_j\,db_j(t). \tag{4.2.2}$$

We use the same notations and symbols as in Chapter 3. In equation (4.2.2), $d\beta_m(t)$ is calculated by summing m terms of ($\sqrt{\lambda_j}\,f_j\,db_j(t)$), and for each eigen function, f_j, there is an associated independent Wiener process increment ($db_j(t)$).

This Wiener process increment is δ-correlated in time only, and for a particular point in time, t_i, the Wiener process $B(\omega,f)$ generates the Wiener increments $db_j(t_i)$ for each of the eigen functions. At another time, t_k, $B(\omega,f)$ generates $db_j(t_k)$ for each of the eigen function. However, as the Wiener increments are Gaussian with Δt variance (see Chapter 2), i.e., $db_j(t_i)$ and $db_j(t_k)$ are essentially the same stochastic variable.

The number of terms that need to be summed up, m, has to be determined by considering the contribution each pair of eigen value λ_i and corresponding eigen function f_j make to approximate the covariance.

Instead of solving the integral equation to obtain eigen function, we assume the following function to be a generalized eigen function. (We will discuss the method to obtain this function for any given kernel in section 4.3.)

We define,

$$f_j(x) = g_{0j} + g_{1j}x + \sum_{k=2}^{p_j} g_{kj} e^{-r_{kj}(x-s_{kj})^2}, \tag{4.2.3}$$

where $f_j(x)$ is the jth eigen function of a given covariance kernel, g_{0j}, g_{1j} and g_{kj} are numerical coefficients, r_{jk} and s_{jk} are the coefficients in the exponent where k is an integer index ranging from 2 to p_j. p_j is determined by the computational method in section 4.3.

The differential operator is defined by,

$$S = -\left(\frac{h_x}{2} \frac{\partial^2}{\partial x^2} + \frac{\partial}{\partial x} \right),$$

and the second term on the right hand side of equation (4.2.1) can be written as,

$$S\left(C(x,t) \sum_{j=1}^{m} \sqrt{\lambda_j} f_j db_j(t) \right) = \sigma \sum_{j=1}^{m} \sqrt{\lambda_j} S\left(C(x,t) f_j \right) db_j(t), \tag{4.2.4}$$

after substituting equation (4.2.2) into the second terms of equation (4.2.1) and taking $\sqrt{\lambda_j}$ and $db_j(t)$ out of the operand. We can now expand the differential,

$$S\left(C(x,t) f_j \right) = S\left(C(x,t) \left(g_{0j} + g_{1j}x + \sum_{k=2}^{p_j} g_{kj} e^{-r_{kj}(x-s_{kj})^2} \right) \right). \tag{4.2.5}$$

Let us evaluate the derivatives separately;

$$\frac{\partial}{\partial x}\left(C(x,t)\left(g_{0j}+g_{1j}x+\sum_{k=2}^{p_j}g_{kj}e^{-r_{kj}\left(x-s_{kj}\right)^2}\right)\right)$$
$$=\frac{\partial}{\partial x}\left[g_{0j}C(x,t)+g_{1j}xC(x,t)+\sum_{k=2}^{p_j}g_{kj}C(x,t)e^{-r_{kj}\left(x-s_{kj}\right)^2}\right], \tag{4.2.6}$$
$$=g_{0j}\frac{\partial C(x,t)}{\partial x}+g_{1j}x\frac{\partial C(x,t)}{\partial x}+g_{1j}C(x,t)+\sum_{k=2}^{p_j}g_{kj}\frac{\partial}{\partial x}\left(C(x,t)e^{-r_{kj}\left(x-s_{kj}\right)^2}\right).$$

Now the derivative within the summation in equation (4.2.6) is evaluated.

$$\frac{\partial}{\partial x}\left(C(x,t)e^{-r_{kj}\left(x-s_{kj}\right)^2}\right)=C(x,t)\left(-2r_{kj}\left(x-s_{kj}\right)e^{-r_{kj}\left(x-s_{kj}\right)^2}\right)+e^{-r_{kj}\left(x-s_{kj}\right)^2}\frac{\partial C(x,t)}{\partial x}$$
$$=\left[-2r_{kj}C(x,t)\left(x-s_{kj}\right)+\frac{\partial C(x,t)}{\partial x}\right]e^{-r_{kj}\left(x-s_{kj}\right)^2}.$$

Substituting this derivation back to equation (4.2.6) and defining, $\psi_j(x,t)$ for eigen function j,

$$\psi_j(x,t)\equiv\frac{\partial}{\partial x}\left(C(x,t)\left(g_{0j}+g_{1j}x+\sum_{k=2}^{p_j}g_{kj}e^{-r_{kj}\left(x-s_{kj}\right)^2}\right)\right),$$
$$=g_{0j}\frac{\partial C(x,t)}{\partial x}+g_{1j}x\frac{\partial C(x,t)}{\partial x}+g_{ij}C(x,t)+\sum_{k=2}^{p_j}g_{kj}\left[\frac{\partial C(x,t)}{\partial x}-2r_{kj}\left(x-s_{kj}\right)C(x,t)\right]e^{-r_{kj}\left(x-s_{kj}\right)}, \tag{4.2.7}$$
$$=\left\{g_{1j}-2\sum_{k=2}^{p_j}g_{kj}\,r_{kj}\left(x-s_{kj}\right)e^{-r_{kj}\left(x-s_{kj}\right)^2}\right\}C(x,t)+\left\{g_{0j}+g_{1j}\,x+\sum_{k=2}^{p_j}g_{kj}e^{-r_{kj}\left(x-s_{kj}\right)^2}\right\}\frac{\partial C(x,t)}{\partial x}.$$

Then taking the derivative of $\psi_j(x,t)$ with respect to x,

$$\frac{\partial\psi(x,t)}{\partial x}=\left\{g_{1j}-2\sum_{k=2}^{p_j}g_{kj}r_{kj}\left(x-s_{kj}\right)e^{-r_{kj}\left(x-s_{kj}\right)^2}\right\}\frac{\partial C(x,t)}{\partial x}$$
$$+\left\{4\sum_{k=2}^{p_j}g_{kj}r_{kj}^2\left(x-s_{kj}\right)^2e^{-r_{kj}\left(x-s_{kj}\right)^2}-2\sum_{k=2}^{p_j}g_{kj}r_{kj}e^{-r_{kj}\left(x-s_{kj}\right)^2}\right\}C(x,t)$$
$$+\left\{g_{0j}+g_{1j}x+\sum_{k=2}^{p_j}g_{kj}e^{-r_{kj}\left(x-s_{kj}\right)^2}\right\}\frac{\partial^2C(x,t)}{\partial x^2}+\left\{g_{1j}-2\sum_{k=2}^{p_j}g_{kj}r_{kj}\left(x-s_{kj}\right)e^{-r_{kj}\left(x-s_{kj}\right)^2}\right\}\frac{\partial C(x,t)}{\partial x},$$

$$=2\left\{g_{1j}-2\sum_{k=2}^{p_j}g_{kj}r_{kj}\left(x-s_{kj}\right)e^{-r_{kj}\left(x-s_{kj}\right)^2}\right\}\frac{\partial C(x,t)}{\partial x}+\left\{g_{0j}+g_{1j}x+\sum_{k=2}^{p_j}g_{kj}e^{-r_{kj}\left(x-s_{kj}\right)^2}\right\}\frac{\partial^2 C(x,t)}{\partial x^2}$$
$$+\left\{4\sum_{k=2}^{p_j}g_{kj}r_{kj}^2\left(x-s_{kj}\right)^2e^{-r_{kj}\left(x-s_{kj}\right)^2}-2\sum_{k=2}^{p_j}g_{kj}r_{kj}e^{-r_{kj}\left(x-s_{kj}\right)^2}\right\}C(x,t) \qquad (4.2.8)$$

Therefore, equation (4.2.5) can be expressed as,

$$-S\left(C(x,t)f_j\right)=\frac{h_x}{2}\left[\frac{\partial^2\left(C(x,t)f_j\right)}{\partial x^2}\right]+\left[\frac{\partial\left(C(x,t)f_j\right)}{\partial x}\right],$$
$$=\psi_j(x,t)+\frac{h_x}{2}\frac{\partial\psi_j(x,t)}{\partial x}, \qquad (4.2.9)$$
$$=P_{0j}(x)C(x,t)+P_{1j}\frac{\partial C(x,t)}{\partial x}+P_{2j}\frac{\partial^2 C(x,t)}{\partial x^2},$$

Where

$$P_{0j}(x)=\left[g_{ij}-2\sum_{k=2}^{p_j}g_{kj}r_{kj}\left(x-s_{kj}\right)e^{-r_{kj}\left(x-s_{kj}\right)^2}\right]$$
$$+\left(\frac{h_x}{2}\right)\left[4\sum_{k=2}^{p_j}g_{kj}r_{kj}^2\left(x-s_{kj}\right)^2e^{-r_{kj}\left(x-s_{kj}\right)^2}-2\sum_{k=2}^{p_j}g_{kj}r_{kj}e^{-r_{kj}\left(x-s_{kj}\right)^2}\right], \qquad (4.2.10)$$

$$P_{1j}(x)=g_{0j}+g_{1j}x+\sum_{k=2}^{p_j}g_{kj}e^{-r_{kj}\left(x-s_{kj}\right)^2}+\left(\frac{h_x}{2}\right)\left[2\left(g_{ij}-2\sum_{k=2}^{p_j}g_{kj}r_{kj}\left(x-s_{kj}\right)e^{-r_{kj}\left(x-s_{kj}\right)^2}\right)\right], \qquad (4.2.11)$$

And

$$P_{2j}(x)=\left(\frac{h_x}{2}\right)\left[g_{0j}+g_{1j}x+\sum_{k=2}^{p_j}g_{kj}e^{-r_{kj}\left(x-s_{kj}\right)^2}\right]. \qquad (4.2.12)$$

We see that, in equation (4.2.9), the coefficients, $P_{ij}(x)\ (i=0,1,2)$ are functions of x only.

If we recall the premise on which stochastic calculus is discussed in Chapter 2, $C(x,t)$ is a continuous, non-differentiable function, and equation (4.2.1) should be interpreted as an Ito stochastic differential, which essentially mean equation (4.2.1) has to be understood only in the following form:

$$C(x,t)=\int A\left(C(x,t),t,x\right)dt+\sum_i\int B_i\left(C(x,t),t,x\right)dw_i, \qquad (4.2.13)$$

where $A\left(C(x,t),t,x\right)$ is the drift coefficient and $B_i\left(C(x,t),t,x\right)$ are diffusion coefficients of the Ito diffusion, equation (4.2.13); here $dw_i(t)$ are increments of the standard Wiener process. Ito diffusion are an interesting class of stochastic integrals and has many advantageous properties of practical importance (Klebaner, 1998).

The expression of stochastic partial differential equation (equation (4.2.1)) as an Ito diffusion in time would give us the mathematical justification in solving it using Ito calculus. In our development, the eigen functions, $f_j(x)$ are continuous, differentiable functions so are the coefficients, $P_{ij}(x)(i=0,1,2)$. Therefore, the Ito stochastic product rule is the same as the product rule in standard calculus (Klebaner, 1998), and we employ this fact in the previous derivations. Further, we assume that the mean velocity $\bar{V}(x,t)$ is a continuous, differentiable function which is a reasonable assumption given that the average velocity in aquifer situation is based on the hydraulic conductivity, porosity and the pressure gradient across a large enough domain within a much larger total flow length.

Therefore, we can write the drift term of equation (4.2.1) as follows:

$$\begin{aligned}
-S\left(\bar{V}(x,t)C(x,t)\right) &= \frac{\partial \bar{V}(x,t)}{\partial x}C(x,t) + \bar{V}(x,t)\frac{\partial C(x,t)}{\partial x} \\
&\quad + \frac{h_x}{2}\left(\frac{\partial^2 \bar{V}(x,t)}{\partial x^2}C(x,t) + 2\frac{\partial C(x,t)}{\partial x}\frac{\partial \bar{V}(x,t)}{\partial x} + \bar{V}\frac{\partial^2 C(x,t)}{\partial x^2}\right) \\
&= \left(\frac{\partial \bar{V}(x,t)}{\partial x} + \frac{h_x}{2}\frac{\partial^2 \bar{V}(x,t)}{\partial x^2}\right)C(x,t) + \left(\bar{V}(x,t) + \frac{h_x}{2}2\frac{\partial \bar{V}(x,t)}{\partial x}\right)\frac{\partial C(x,t)}{\partial x} \\
&\quad + \frac{h_x}{2}\bar{V}(x,t)\frac{\partial^2 C(x,t)}{\partial x^2}.
\end{aligned} \tag{4.2.14}$$

By substituting equations (4.2.14) and (4.2.9) into equation (4.2.1),

$$\begin{aligned}
dC(x,t) = -&\left\{\begin{aligned}&\left(\frac{\partial \bar{V}(x,t)}{\partial x} + \frac{h_x}{2}\frac{\partial^2 \bar{V}(x,t)}{\partial x^2}\right)C(x,t) + \left(\bar{V}(x,t) + \frac{h_x}{2}2\frac{\partial \bar{V}(x,t)}{\partial x}\right)\frac{\partial C(x,t)}{\partial x^2} \\ &+\left(\frac{h_x}{2}\bar{V}(x,t)\right)\frac{\partial^2 C(x,t)}{\partial x^2}\end{aligned}\right\} \\
&-\sigma\sum_{j=1}^{m}\sqrt{\lambda_j}\left(P_{0j}C(x,t) + P_{1j}\frac{\partial C(x,t)}{\partial x} + P_{2j}\frac{\partial^2 C(x,t)}{\partial x^2}\right)db_j(t),
\end{aligned}$$

and then,

$$dC(x,t) = -C(x,t)dI_0 - \frac{\partial C(x,t)}{\partial x}dI_1 - \frac{\partial^2 C(x,t)}{\partial x^2}dI_2, \tag{4.2.15}$$

where,

$$dI_0(x,t) = \left(\frac{\partial \bar{V}(x,t)}{\partial x} + \frac{h_x}{2}\frac{\partial^2 \bar{V}(x,t)}{\partial x^2}\right)dt + \sigma\sum_{j=1}^{m}\sqrt{\lambda_j}P_{0j}\,db_j(t), \tag{4.2.16}$$

$$dI_1(x,t) = \left(\bar{V}(x,t) + \frac{h_x}{2} \frac{2\partial \bar{V}(x,t)}{\partial x} \right) dt + \sigma \sum_{j=1}^{m} \sqrt{\lambda_j} P_{1j}\, db_j(t), \text{ and} \tag{4.2.17}$$

$$dI_2(x,t) = \left(\frac{h_x}{2} \bar{V}(x,t) \right) dt + \sigma \sum_{j=1}^{m} \sqrt{\lambda_j} P_{2j}\, db_j(t). \tag{4.2.18}$$

In equation (4.2.15), dI_0, dI_1 and dI_2 are Ito stochastic differentials with respect to t as well, and we can rewrite a generalized SSTM given by equation (4.2.1) in terms of another set of stochastic differentials,

$$C(x,t) = -\int_t C(x,t)\, dI_0 - \int_t \frac{\partial C(x,t)}{\partial x} dI_1 - \int_t \frac{\partial^2 C(x,t)}{\partial x^2} dI_2 + C(x,\phi). \tag{4.2.19}$$

We note that dI_0, dI_1 and dI_2 are only functions of the mean velocity, $\bar{V}(x,t)$, and $P_{ij}(x)(i=0,1,2)$; and $C(x,t)$ is separated out in equation (4.2.19), which can be interpreted as $C(x,t)$ and its spatial derivatives are modulating $dI_i(i=0,1,2)$s. I_i are Ito stochastic integrals of the form given by equation (4.2.13), and can be expressed as,

$$I_i(x,t) = \int F_i(x,t)\, dt + \sigma \sum_{j=1}^{m} \int G_{ij}(x,t)\, db_j(t), \quad (i,0,1,2) \text{ and } (j,1,m), \tag{4.2.20}$$

where,

$$F_0(x,t) = \left(\frac{\partial \bar{V}(x,t)}{\partial x} + \frac{h_x}{2} \frac{\partial^2 \bar{V}(x,t)}{\partial x^2} \right), \tag{4.2.21}$$

$$F_1(x,t) = \left(\bar{V}(x,t) + \frac{h_x}{2} 2 \frac{\partial \bar{V}(x,t)}{\partial x} \right), \tag{4.2.22}$$

$$F_2(x,t) = \left(\frac{h_x}{2} \bar{V}(x,t) \right), \tag{4.2.23}$$

$$G_{0j} = \sqrt{\lambda_j} P_{0j}(x), \tag{4.2.24}$$

$$G_{1j} = \sqrt{\lambda_j} P_{1j}(x), \tag{4.2.25}$$

$$\text{and } G_{2j} = \sqrt{\lambda_j} P_{2j}(x). \tag{4.2.26}$$

As the stochastic integrals, $I_i(x,t)$ are dependent only on the behaviours of $\bar{V}(x,t)$, the eigen values of the velocity covariance kernel and $P_{ij}(x)$ functions, i.e., $I_i(x,t)$s are only dependent on the velocity fields within the porous media. A corollary to that is if we know the velocity fields and characterize them as stochastic differentials, we can then develop an empirical SSTM based on equation (4.2.19). We explore the behaviours of $I_i(x,t)$ in section 4.5. Next we discuss the derivation of the generalized eigen function, the form of which is given by equation (4.2.3).

4.3 A Computational Approach for Eigen Functions

We discuss the approach in this section to obtain the eigen functions for any given kernel in the form given by equation (4.2.3). We calculate the covariance kernel matrix (COV) for any given kernel function and COV can be decomposed in to eigen values and the corresponding eigen vectors using singular value decomposition method or principle component analysis. This can easily be done using mathematical software. Then we use the eigen vectors to develop eigen functions using neural networks.

Suppose that we already have an exponential covariance kernel as given by,

$$q(x_1,x_2)=\sigma^2\ e^{-\frac{y}{b}}\ , \tag{4.3.1}$$

where $y=|x_1-x_2|$,

b is the correlation length , and

σ^2 is the variance when $x_1=x_2$.

In terms of x_1 and x_2, both of them have the domain of [0,L]; we equally divide this range into (n) equidistant intervals of Δx for both variables. Thus, the particular position for x_1 and x_2 can be displayed as:

$$x_{1k}=k\,\Delta x\ ,\quad \text{for } k=0,1,2,\cdots,\ n\ \text{, and} \tag{4.3.2}$$

$$x_{2j}=j\,\Delta x\ ,\quad \text{for } j=0,1,2,\cdots,\ n\ . \tag{4.3.3}$$

By substituting equations (4.3.2) and (4.3.3) into equation (4.3.1), we can obtain,

$$COV(k,j)=\sigma^2\ e^{-\frac{|(k-j)\,\Delta x|}{b}}\quad \text{for } k,j\in[\ 1,\ n-1\ ]. \tag{4.3.4}$$

In equation (4.3.4), COV is the covariance matrix which contains all the variances and covariances, and it is a symmetric matrix with size $n\times n$ where n is the number of intervals. The diagonals of COV represent variances where x_1 is equal to x_2 and off-diagonals represent covariances between any two different discrete x_1 and x_2.

After the covariance matrix is defined, we can transform the COV matrix into a new matrix with new scaled variables according to Karhunen-Loève (KL) theorem. In this new matrix, all the variables are independent of each other having their own variances. i.e, the covariance between any two new variables is zero. The new matrix can be represented by using the Karhunen-Loève theorem as,

$$COV1=\sum_{j=1}^{n}\lambda_j\,\phi_j(x)\,\overline{\phi_j(x)}\,, \tag{4.3.5}$$

where n is the total number of variables in the new matrix; λ_j represents the variance of the jth rescaled variable and λ_j is also the jth eigen values of the $COV1$ matrix; and $\phi_j(x)$ is the eigen vectors of the $COV1$ matrix. The number of eigen vectors depends on the number of discrete intervals. This decomposition of the $COV1$ matrix which is called the singular value decomposition method can easily be done by using mathematical or statistical software.

Once we have the eigen vectors, the next step is to develop suitable neural networks to represent or mimic these eigen vectors. In fact, it is not necessary to simulate all the eigen vectors. The number of neural networks is decided by the number of eigen values which are significant in the KL representation. In some situations, for example, we may have 100 eigen values in the KL representation but only 4 significant eigen values. Then, we just create four networks to simulate these four eigenvectors which correspond to the most significant eigen values. The way we decide on the number of significant eigen values is based on the following equation:

$$R[i] = \frac{\lambda_i}{\sum_{j=1}^{n} \lambda_j} \quad \text{for} \quad i \in [1, n], \tag{4.3.6}$$

$$Th = \sum_{i}^{k} R[i], \tag{4.3.7}$$

where $R[i]$ represents the contribution of the ith eigen value in capturing the total original variance, k represents the number of the significant eigen values, and Th is the contribution of all significant eigen values in capturing the total original variance. In this chapter, Th is chosen to vary between 0.95 and 1. This means that if the total number of eigen values is 100 from the KL expansion and the contribution of the first 4 eigen values takes up more than 95% of the original variance, there are only four individual neural networks that need to be developed.

The main factors that need to be decided in the development of neural networks are the number of neurons needed, the structure of neural networks and the learning algorithm. The number of neurons in neural networks is case-dependent. It is difficult to define the number of neurons before the learning stage. In general, the number of neurons is adjusted during training until the network output converges on the actual output based on least square error minimization. A neural network with an optimum number of neurons will reach the desired minimum error level more quickly than other networks with more complex structures. The proposed neural network is a Radial Basis Function (RBF) Network. The approximation function is the Gaussian Function given below:

$$G(s, r) = e^{-r\ (x-s)^2}, \tag{4.3.8}$$

where r and s are constants. In this symmetric function, s defines the centre of symmetry and r defines the sharpness of Gaussian function.

Based on numerical values of the significant eigen vectors, several RBF networks with one input (x) and one output (eigen vector) are developed to approximate each significant eigenvector. Now let us have the following function the form of which is previously given in equation (4.2.3) to define the RBF network,

$$\phi(x) = g_0 + g_1\, x + \sum_{k=2}^{p+1} g_k\, e^{-r_k\,(x-s_k)2} = g_0 + g_1\, x + \sum_{k=2}^{p+1} g_k\, G(s_k, r_k) \qquad (4.3.9)$$

where g_0 is the bias weight of the network, g_1 and g_k is the 1st and k^{th} weight of the network, and p is the total number of neurons in this RBF network (the reason for using p+1 for the summation is that k starts at 2). Figure 4.1 displays the architecture of a neural network for the case of one-dimensional input and $\varphi(x)$ is used to represent the output of the neural network given by equation (4.3.9).

After we decide the input-output mapping and architecture of deterministic neural networks, the next step is to choose the learning algorithm, i.e., the method used to update weights and other parameters of networks. The backpropagation algorithm is used as the learning algorithm in this work. The backpropagation algorithm is used to minimize the network's global error between the actual network outputs and their corresponding desired outputs. The backpropagation leaning method is based on gradient descent that updates weights and other parameters through partial derivatives of the network's global error with respect to the weights and parameters. A stable approach is to change the weights and parameters in the network after the whole sample has been presented and to repeat this process iteratively until the desired minimum error level is reached. This is called batch (or epoch based) learning.

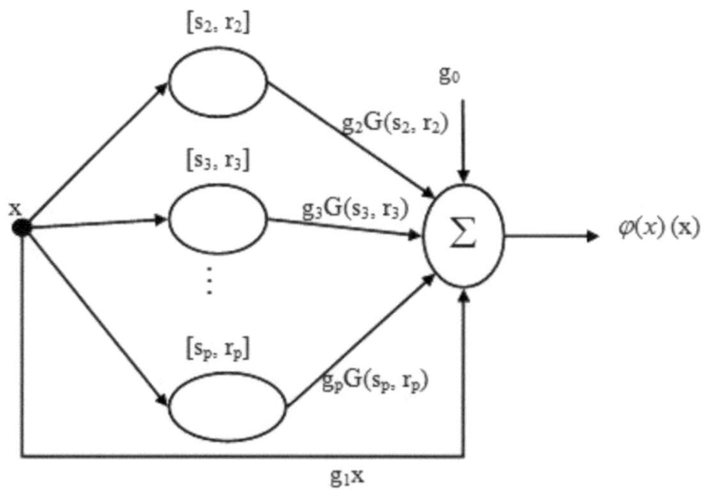

Figure 4.1. Architecture of the one-dimensional RBF network given by equation (4.3.9).

Their values are based on the summation over all training examples of the partial derivative of the network's global error with respect to the weights and parameters in the whole sample.

Now let us assume that the actual network output is $T(\varphi(x))$, the desired network output is $Z(\varphi(x))$. The network's global error between the network output and actual output is

$$E = \frac{1}{2N}\sum_{i}^{N}(T_i - Z_i)^2, \tag{4.3.10}$$

where T_i and Z_i are the actual output and the network output for the ith training pattern, and N is the total number of training patterns. The multiplication by $1/2$ is a mathematical convenience (Samarasinghe, 2006).

The method of modifying a weight or a parameter is the same for all weights and parameters so we show the change to an arbitrary weight as an example. The change to a single weight of a connection between neuron j and neuron i in the RBF network based on batch learning can be defined as,

$$\Delta g_{ji} = \eta \sum_{p=1}^{k}\left(\frac{dE}{dg_{ji}}\right)_p, \tag{4.3.11}$$

where η is called the learning rate with a constant value between 0 and 1. It controls the step size and the speed of weight adjustments. k is the total number of input vectors. The process that propagates the error information backwards into the network and updates weights and the parameters of network is repeated until the network minimizes the global error between the actual network outputs and their corresponding desired outputs. In the learning process, the weights and the parameters of the network converge on the optimal values.

To illustrate the computational approach, we give some examples here. The first covariance kernel is chosen to be

$$g(x_1, x_2) = \sigma^2 e^{-\frac{y}{b}}, \tag{4.3.12}$$

where $y = |x_1 - x_2|^2$,

b is constant, and

σ^2 is variance when $x_1 = x_2$.

This covariance kernel needs a relatively lower number of significant eigen values to capture 95% or more of the total variance; therefore we choose to work with this kernel and later we use two other forms of kernels: one discussed previously in Chapter 3 and other one is empirically based.

Figure 4.2 displays the covariance matrix based on the covariance kernel (equation (4.3.12)) when $\sigma^2 = 1$ and $b = 0.1$.

Table 4.1 reports all eigen values in the KL representation of the covariance matrix. The most of the eigen values is equal to zero and these eigen values can not affect the covariance matrix and just a few are significant and capture the total variance in the original data.

Therefore, we need to focus on the significant eigen values as well as their corresponding eigen functions. There are 6 significant eigen values whose contribution takes up 99.9035% of the original variance and table 4.1 shows the value of each significant eigen value and the proportion of variance captured by the corresponding eigen value.

Thus, the six eigenvectors corresponding to the significant eigenvalues are simulated by the individual RBF network. Although we use a different RBF network to approximate each of these six eigenvectors, the structure of RBF network is the same but the weights and parameters inside the individual RBF network are different.

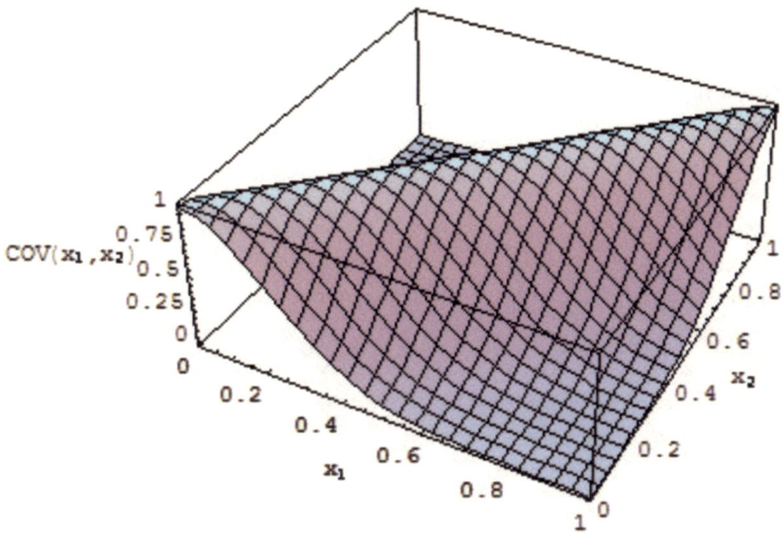

Figure 4.2. The covariance matrix calculated by the given covariance kernel (equation 4.3.12) when $\sigma^2 = 1$ and $b = 0.1$.

The number of eigen values	Values	Contribution as a propotion
λ_1	48.128	0.477
λ_2	30.636	0.303
λ_3	14.692	0.145
λ_4	5.446	0.054
λ_5	1.61	0.016
λ_6	0.392	0.004

Table 4.1. Significant eigen values obtained from the KL expansion of the covariance kernel given by equation (4.3.12) (six significant eigen values take up 99.9035% of total variance)

Then each individual RBF network was trained to learn their related eigen vector, while the weights and all the parameters of Gaussian functions were updated until each network reaches global minimum error given by

$$E = \frac{1}{N-1}\sum_{n=1}^{N}\left[\varphi_n^i(x) - S_n^i(x)\right]^2. \tag{4.3.13}$$

where $S_n^i(x)$ is an approximation to $\varphi_n^i(x)$, i th eigen function; and N is the total number of eigen values.

Figure 4.3 displays all the six eigen functions and Table 4.2 gives their functional forms. Figure 4.3 shows the eigen functions given by the KL theory (dots), obtained by solving the corresponding integral equation, overlaid with the outputs from the neural networks (lines), and the approximation functions are the same as the theoretically derived functions.

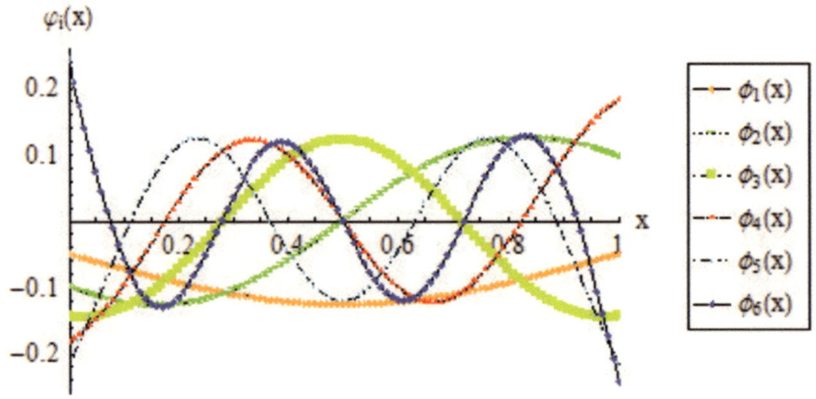

Figure 4.3. The approximated six eigen functions from BRF networks for equation (4.3.12) when $\sigma^2 = 1$ and b=0.1.

For the second example, we use the same covariance kernel with $b = 0.2$ and $\sigma^2 = 1$, and decomposed the matrix for the domain [0, 1]. Figure 4.4 shows the covariance matrix calculated by the given covariance kernel. Based on the standard of choosing the number of significant eigen values, it can be seen that five significant eigen values together capture 99.9582% of the original variance. Thus, there are five RBF networks to be developed for the corresponding eigenvectors. Table 4.3 gives the value of each significant eigen value and the proportion of variance captured by the corresponding eigen value; Table 4.4 provides the eigen functions obtained from the neural networks; the graphical forms of the eigen functions are given by Figure 4.5. As before, the analytically derived eigen function as an very well approximated by the approximations from the neural networks. (The theoretical eigen functions are not displayed in Figure 4.5).

Eigen values	Values	The analytical forms of eigen functions $(\phi_i(x))$ for $x \in [0,1]$
λ_1	48.128	$0.0456723 - 1.61025 \times 10^{-12}\, x - 0.170974\, e^{-2.34049\,(x-0.5)^2}$
λ_2	30.636	$0.689211 - 0.560102\, x - 0.360116\, e^{-5.37562\,(x-0.290915)^2}$ $-0.745057\, e^{-2.56631\,(x+0.335246)^2}$
λ_3	14.692	$-0.00132933 + 0.0185462\, x - 3.7566\, e^{-6.62157\,(x-0.703168)^2}$ $+3.7712\, e^{-6.6592\,(x-0.683601)^2} - 0.183884\, e^{-9.56556\,(x-0.0999343)^2}$
λ_4	5.446	$10.4236 - 5.90955\, x - 0.3771\, e^{-13.4883\,(x-0.68965)^2}$ $+0.282871\, e^{-14.6016\,(x-0.306358)^2} - 12.8992\, e^{-0.385895\,(x+0.699959)^2}$
λ_5	1.61	$0.0403405 - 3.13566 \times 10^{-14}\, x + 9.47326\, e^{-8.95446\,(x-0.727565)^2}$ $+19.0735\, e^{-8.41938\,(x-0.5)^2} - 31.1501\, e^{-5.67596\,(x-0.5)^2}$ $+9.47326\, e^{-8.95446\,(x-0.272435)^2}$
λ_6	0.392	$-0.318516 + 0.548883\, x + 127.699\, e^{-7.08944\,(x-0.658744)^2}$ $-429.099\, e^{-5.57986\,(x-0.511944)^2} + 237.989\, e^{-5.3708\,(x-0.46363)^2}$ $+88.8399\, e^{-8.18627\,(x-0.433595)^2}$

Table 4.2. The final formula from the developed RBF networks to approximate each significant eigen vector and their corresponding eigen values.

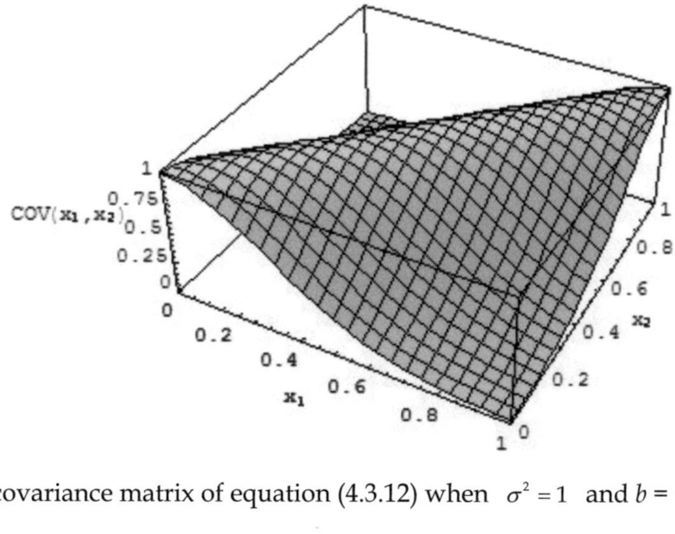

Figure 4.4. The covariance matrix of equation (4.3.12) when $\sigma^2 = 1$ and $b = 0.2$.

Eigen values	Values	Contribution as a proportion
λ_1	61.242	0.606
λ_2	28.820	0.285
λ_3	8.747	0.087
λ_4	1.853	0.018
λ_5	0.29597	0.00293

Table 4.3. Relative amounts of variance in the data captured by each significant eigenvalue obtained from the KL expansion of equation (4.3.12) when $\sigma^2 = 1$ and b=0.2.

Eigen values	Values	The analytical forms of eigen functions $(\phi_i(x))$ for $x \in [0,1]$
λ_1	61.242	$0.0179462 - 7.11262 \times 10^{-17} x - 0.137587 e^{-2.18805 (x-0.5)^2}$
λ_2	28.820	$0.000620869 - 0.00124174 x - 0.147148 e^{-4.39837 (x-0.820696)^2}$ $-0.147148 e^{-4.39837 (x-0.179304)^2}$
λ_3	8.747	$-0.201764 - 3.67217 \times 10^{-8} x + 0.197208 e^{-13.4824 (x-0.625896)^2}$ $+0.197207 e^{-13.4824 (x-0.374103)^2}$
λ_4	1.853	$0.0357425 - 0.0604364 x - 176.588 e^{-3.81696 (x--0.559606)^2}$ $+231.215 e^{-3.70961 (x-0.536422)^2} - 56.2021 e^{-3.5887 (x-0.459753)^2}$
λ_5	0.29597	$-0.195412 - 0.641926 x + 0.834518 e^{-11.2297 (x-0.826432)^2}$ $+0.479846 e^{-14.0892 (x-0.212252)^2} - 0.649793 e^{-14.9973 (x+0.226353)^2}$

Table 4.4. The eigen functions from the developed RBF networks to approximate each significant eigen vector for the kernel given by equation (4.3.12) when $\sigma^2 = 1$ and b=0.2.

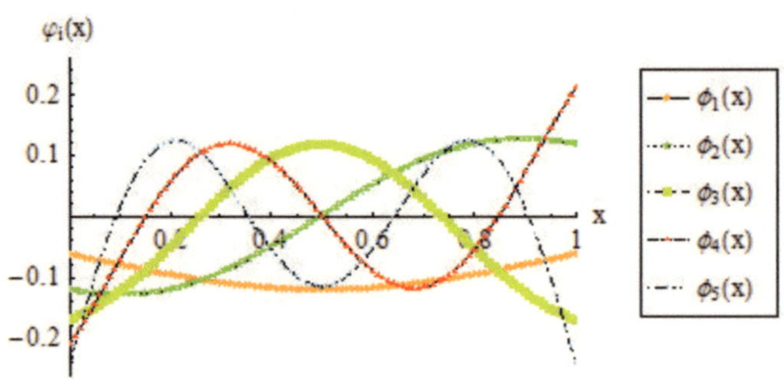

Figure 4.5. The approximated six eigen functions from BRF networks for equation (4.3.12) when $\sigma^2 = 1$ and $b = 0.2$.

From the previous two examples, we have seen that the covariance kernel given by equation (4.3.12) provides a relative small number of eigen functions and therefore one may say that the kernel given by equation (4.3.12) has fast convergence. This is quite a desirable property to have, especially in terms of computational efficiency of the algorithms. In the next example, we find the eigen values and the eigen functions of the covariance kernel we use in the development of the SSTM in Chapter 3. In Chapter 3 the covariance kernel given by equation (4.3.14) - we reproduce the equation here- constitutes an integral equation which we solve analytically to obtain eigen values and eigen functions:

$$g(x_1, x_2) = \sigma^2 e^{-\frac{-|x_1 - x_2|}{b}}, \qquad (4.3.14)$$

when σ^2 and b have the same meanings as before.

This covariance kernel is depicted graphically in Figure 4.6.

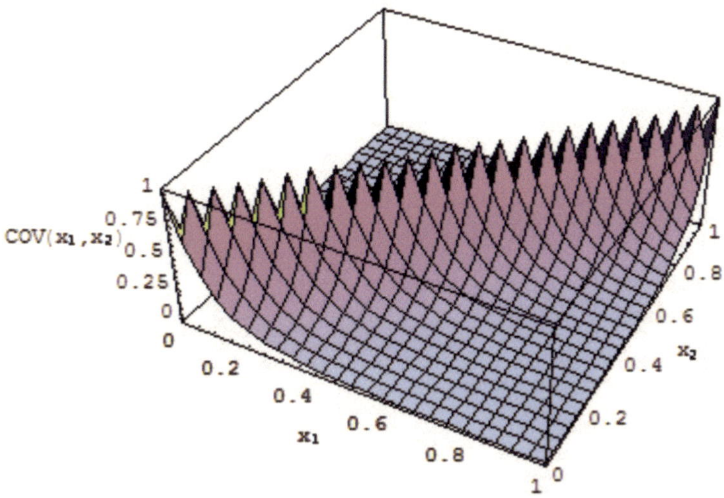

Figure 4.6. The covariance matrix calculated by the given equation (4.3.14) under the condition $\sigma^2 = 1$.

Eigen values	Values	Contribution as a proportion
λ_1	18.745	0.186
λ_2	15.681	0.155
λ_3	12.218	0.121
λ_4	9.241	0.091
λ_5	6.976	0.069
λ_6	5.332	0.053
λ_7	4.149	0.041
λ_8	3.293	0.033

λ_9	2.661	0.026
λ_{10}	2.188	0.022
λ_{11}	1.826	0.018
λ_{12}	1.545	0.015
λ_{13}	1.323	0.013
λ_{14}	1.145	0.011
λ_{15}	0.9999	0.0099
λ_{16}	0.881	0.0087
λ_{17}	0.782	0.0077
λ_{18}	0.699	0.0069
λ_{19}	0.628	0.0062
λ_{20}	0.568	0.0056
λ_{21}	0.516	0.0051
λ_{22}	0.471	0.0047
λ_{23}	0.432	0.0043
λ_{24}	0.398	0.0039
λ_{25}	0.367	0.0036
λ_{26}	0.341	0.0034
λ_{27}	0.317	0.0031
λ_{28}	0.295	0.0029
λ_{29}	0.276	0.0027
λ_{30}	0.259	0.0026
λ_{31}	0.244	0.0024
λ_{32}	0.229	0.0023

Table 4.5. The eigen values for the kernel given by equation (4.3.14) (32 significant eigen values which take up 94.29% of original variance)

In Table 4.5, we give the 32 eigen values which capture up to 94% of the only original variance; Table 4.6 gives only the first six eigen functions obtained from the networks for brevity. Figure 4.7 shows the first eight eigen functions.

Eigen values	Values	The analytical forms of eigen functions $(\phi_i(x))$ for $x \in [0,1]$
λ_1	18.745	$0.238941 + 7.92548 \times 10^{-16}\, x - 0.368191\, e^{-1.19444\,(x-0.5)^2}$
λ_2	15.681	$0.128953 - 0.257905\, x + 0.23274\, e^{-5.79605\,(x-0.830952)^2}$ $-0.23274\, e^{-5.79605\,(x-0.169048)^2}$
λ_3	12.218	$0.297969 + 0.071349\, x - 1.99033\, e^{-5.41338\,(x-0.640904)^2}$ $+1.74606\, e^{-7.13097\,(x-0.592419)^2} - 0.339719\, e^{-10.6256\,(x-0.0883508)^2}$
λ_4	9.241	$-0.520716 + 0.848337\, x - 182.653\, e^{-5.89655\,(x-0.636135)^2}$ $+214.465\, e^{-5.66061\,(x-0.603547)^2} - 38.6999\, e^{-6.81302\,(x-0.448057)^2}$
λ_5	6.976	$-1.10289 + 1.12328 \times 10^{10}\, x - 55.2051\, e^{-9.19718\,(x-0.611767)^2}$ $+99.6664\, e^{-7.12542\,(x-0.5)^2} - 55.2051\, e^{-9.19718\,(x-0.388233)^2}$
λ_6	5.332	$822.58 - 496.01\, x - 6.74448\, e^{-17.354\,(x-0.590219)^2}$ $-190.785\, e^{-4.883\,(x-0.215442)^2} + 2539.25\, e^{-1.85592\,(x-0.0783536)^2}$ $-3181.28\, e^{-1.30206\,(x+0.0105042)^2}$
λ_7	4.149	$-2.16846 + 0.148883\, x + 1451.69\, e^{-14.2086\,(x-0.592557)^2}$ $-2198.81\, e^{-13.3089\,(x-0.577832)^2} + 1013.85\, e^{-10.1574\,(x-0.488994)^2}$ $-358.254\, e^{-13.1355\,(x-0.350845)^2}$
λ_8	3.293	$-31.8294 - 108.195\, x + 6255.59\, e^{-9.37148\,(x-0.813402)^2}$ $-7941.31\, e^{-8.63616\,(x-0.807765)^2} + 1838.53\, e^{-5.03775\,(x-0.766933)^2}$ $-282.847\, e^{-13.5694\,(x-0.3499)^2} + 52.6999\, e^{-22.3578\,(x-0.307475)^2}$

Table 4.6. The final formula from the developed RBF networks to approximate the first 8 significant eigen vectors and their corresponding eigen values.

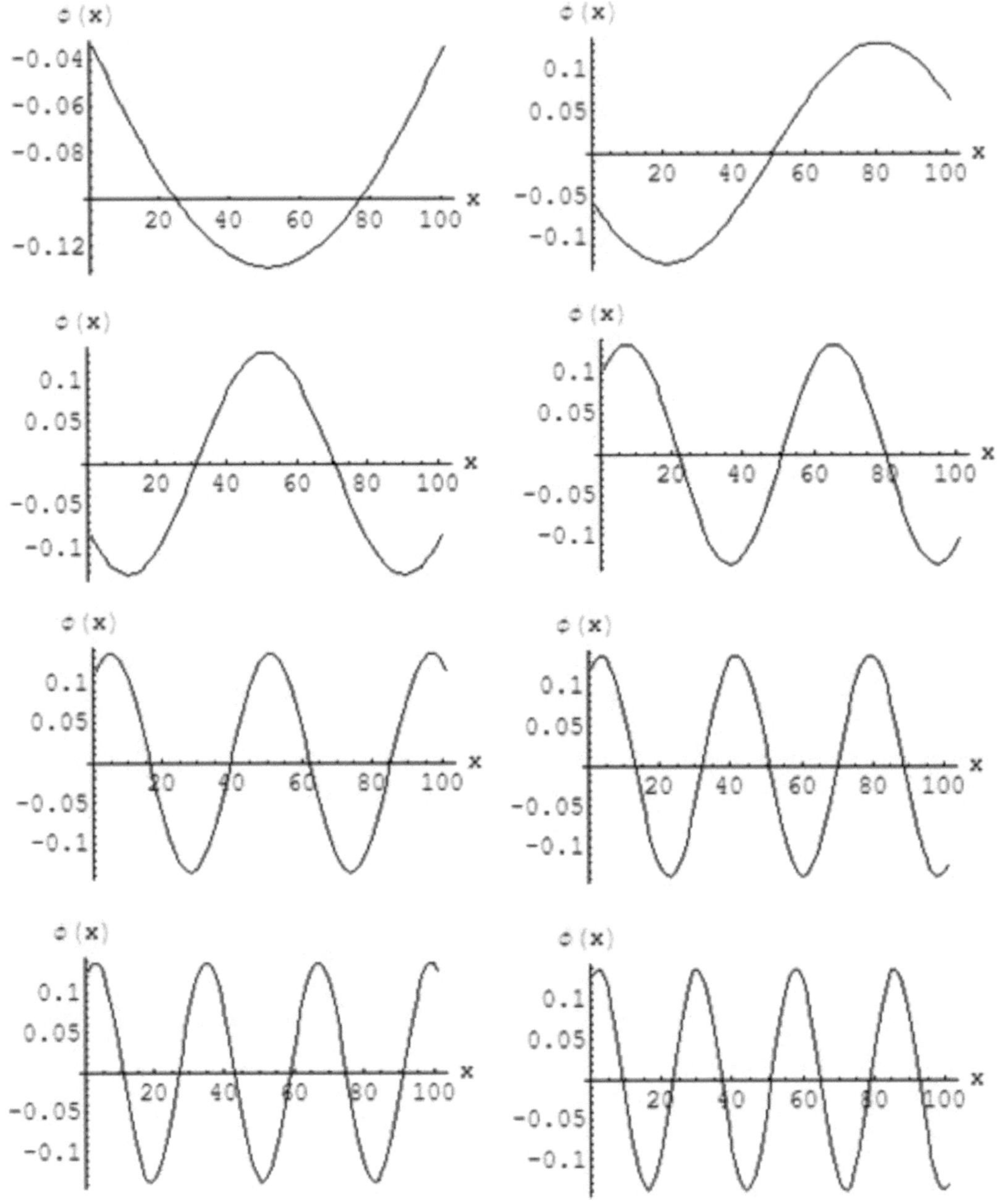

Figure 4.7. The approximated first eight eigen functions from RBF network for the equation (4.3.14) when $\sigma^2 = 1$ and $b = 0.1$.

We can also use an empirically derived covariance kernel. As an example, let us consider equation (4.3.15).

$$Cov(x_1,x_2)=\begin{cases} -|x_1-x_2|+1 & for \quad 0\le|x_1-x_2|\le 0.5 \\ -\frac{5}{3}(|x_1-x_2|-0.8) & for \quad 0.5<|x_1-x_2|\le 0.8\,, \\ 0 & for \quad 0.8<|x_1-x_2|\le 1 \end{cases} \tag{4.3.15}$$

Equation (4.3.15) is depicted in Figure 4.8, and Figure 4.9 shows the corresponding covariance matrix.

Table 4.7 gives the most significant eigen values (the first nine values); Table 4.8 shows the functional forms of eigen functions and Figure 4.10 shows the graphical forms of eigen functions.

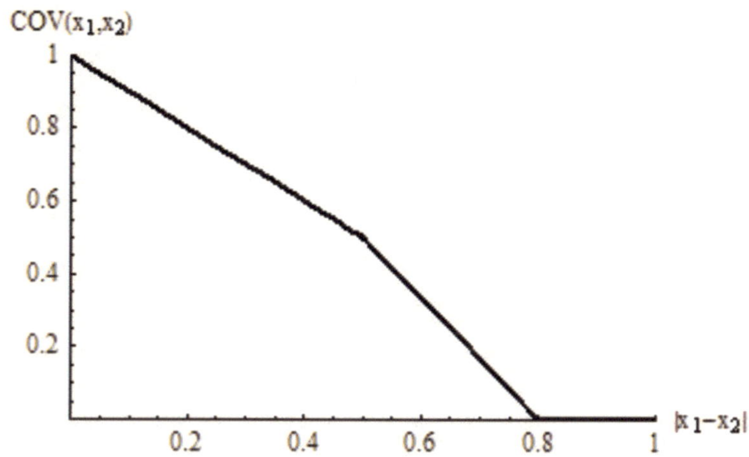

Figure 4.8. An empirical distribution.

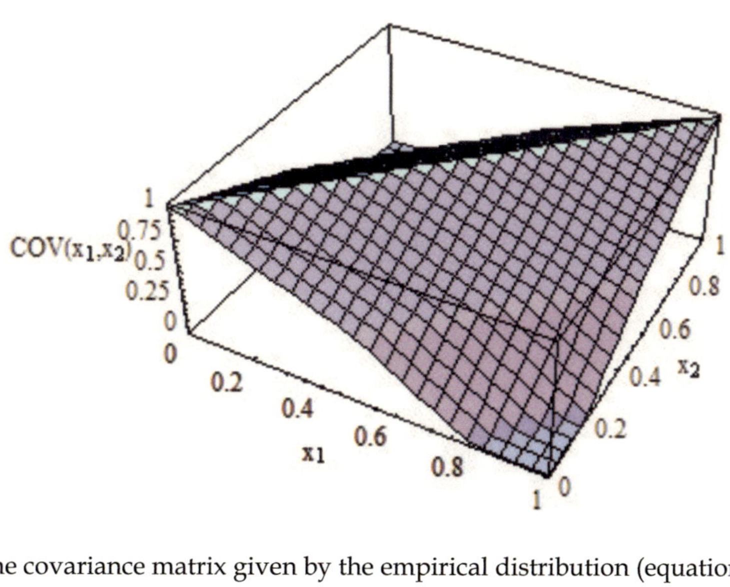

Figure 4.9. The covariance matrix given by the empirical distribution (equation (4.3.15)).

Eigen values	Values	Contribution as a proportion
λ_1	66.022	0.6537
λ_2	24.216	0.2398
λ_3	3.163	0.0313
λ_4	1.989	0.0197
λ_5	0.447	0.0189
λ_6	0.445	0.00443
λ_7	0.395	0.0044
λ_8	0.390	0.00391
λ_9	0.201	0.00386

Table 4.7. Relative amount of variance in the data captured by each significant eigen value for the kernel in equation (4.3.15). (9 significant eigen values capture 98% of original variance)

Eigen values	Values	The analytical forms of eigen functions $(\phi_i(x))$ for $x \in [0,1]$
λ_1	66.022	$0.0495323 + 3.28499 \times 10^{-16}\, x - 0.165441\, e^{-1.38223\,(x-0.5)^2}$
λ_2	24.216	$-0.0156028 + 0.0312062\, x + 0.127272\, e^{-8.33766\,(x-0.951692)^2}$ $-0.127273\, e^{-8.33761\,(x-0.0483079)^2}$
λ_3	3.163	$-672.733 + 332.866\, x + 1.19376 \times 10^{7}\, e^{-0.810094\,(x+0.374112)^2}$ $-1.60589 \times 10^{7} e^{-0.807196\,(x+0.375468)^2}$ $+4.12218 \times 10^{6}\, e^{-0.798664\,(x+0.379503)^2}$
λ_4	1.989	$93.5157 - 68.0722\, x - 813.179\, e^{-3.71071\,(x-0.0967842)^2}$ $+1577.84\, e^{-3.15124\,(x-0.0721231)^2} - 860.897\, e^{-2.33563\,(x-0.0182454)^2}$
λ_5	0.447	$4.82583 - 4.6287\, x - 1.32608\, e^{-14.504\,(x--0.624954)^2}$ $-4.73704\, e^{-4.31785\,(x+0.0230752)^2} - 0.196755\, e^{-174.457\,(x+0.074625)^2}$
λ_6	0.445	$-9.87408 \times 10^{7} + 3.76629 \times 10^{6}\, x$ $+1.39729 \times 10^{6}\, e^{-2.78874\,(x-1.40277)^2}$ $+4.53545 \times 10^{7}\, e^{-1.17605\,(x-0.688669)^2}$ $-3.41918 \times 10^{8}\, e^{-0.360088\,(x--0.448068)^2}$ $+3.84429 \times 10^{8} e^{-0.206739\,(x-0.405528)^2}$ $+1.13264 \times 10^{7}\, e^{-2.08493\,(x-0.139661)^2}$ $+1.06435 \times 10^{7} e^{-2.10254\,(x+0.336545)^2}$

λ_7	0.395	$-2.02737 - 7.9356\,x - 5263.75\,e^{-27.8868\,(x-0.860872)^2}$ $+1.03168 \times 10^7\,e^{-25.9199\,(x-0.765634)^2}$ $-7.83776 \times 10^7\,e^{-26.0007\,(x-0.764335)^2}$ $+6.80653 \times 10^7\,e^{-26.0126\,(x-0.764145)^2}$ $+4.26386\,e^{-4.50902\,(x-0.43218)^2} + 0.388207\,e^{-183.561\,(x-0.100811)^2}$
λ_8	0.390	$-386986 + 334630\,x + 1.13814 \times 10^8\,e^{-4.2926\,(x-0.649682)^2}$ $-1.52714 \times 10^8\,e^{-3.99793\,(x-0.630907)^2}$ $+8.57437 \times 10^7\,e^{-2.777\,(x-0.591124)^2} + 702189\,e^{-7.32322\,(x-0.57722)^2}$ $-5.31436 \times 10^7\,e^{-2.43237\,(x-0.572872)^2}$ $+6.4929 \times 10^6\,e^{-5.69446\,(x-0.396187)^2}$ $+1.62219 \times 10^6\,e^{-1.15913\,(x-0.0920272)^2}$
λ_9	0.201	$6589.2 + 102.051\,x - 277640\,e^{-8.1404\,(x-0.811728)^2}$ $-151130\,e^{-3.04348\,(x-0.528018)^2} + 1.6007 \times 10^7\,e^{-5.70678\,(x-0.480254)^2}$ $-1.67931 \times 10^7\,e^{-5.91597\,(x-0.47122)^2}$ $+2.8962 \times 10^6\,e^{-8.42978\,(x-0.395813)^2}$ $-1.79879 \times 10^6\,e^{-8.86148\,(x-0.388545)^2}$ $-25798.1\,e^{-3.56779\,(x-0.288557)^2}$

Table 4.8. The final formulas from the developed RBF networks to approximate each significant eigenvector and their corresponding eigen values.

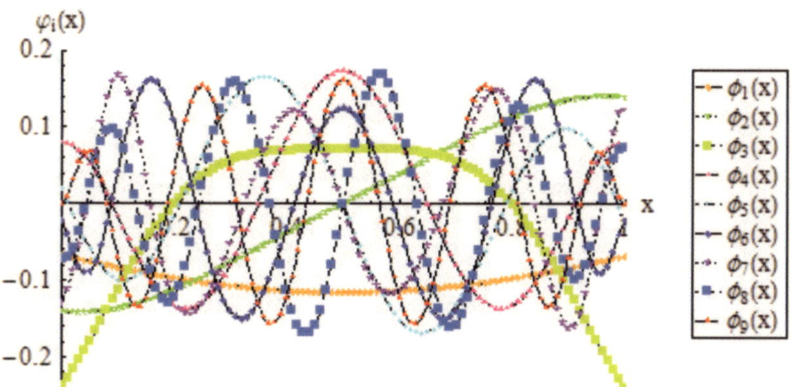

Figure 4.10. The approximated nine eigenfunctions from the BRF networks for the kernel given in equation (4.3.15).

We have seen that some covariance kernels provide relatively small number of significant eigen values for the given domain [0,1] and whereas for others, obtaining the significant eigen functions could be tedious. The main point in this exercise is to show that any given covariance kernel can be used to obtain the eigen functions of the form given by equation (4.2.3). A corollary to this statement is that if we express the eigen functions in the form given by equation (4.2.3), then we can assume that these is an underlying covariance kernel responsible for these eigen functions. In deriving the SSTM in the form of equation (4.2.15), we assume that the form of equation (4.2.3) is given. But we see now that any covariance-kernel driven SSTM can be represented by equation (4.2.15).

4.4 Effects of Different Kernels and h_x

We have seen in sections 4.2 and 4.3 that the SSTM developed in Chapter 2 and 3 can be recasted so that we could employ any given velocity kernel. In fact, we can even use an empirical set of data for the velocity covariance. We can anticipate that the generalized SSTM would behave quite similar to the one developed in Chapter 2 given that same covariance kernel is used. We compute the 95% confidence intervals for the concentration breakthrough curves (concentration realizations) at $x = 0.5$ m when the flow length is 1 m to compare the differences that occur in using different kernels in the generalized SSTM. The mean velocity is kept constant at 0.5 m/day, and the covariance kernel given by equation (4.3.14) is used to obtain Figure 4.11, and Figure 4.12 is obtained by employing the kernel, $\sigma^2 e^{-\frac{-(x_1-x_2)^2}{b}}$. First, the confidence intervals shown in Figure 4.11 are very similar to those ones could obtain by using the SSTM developed in Chapter 2. Comparing the effects of the kernels on the behaviours of the generalized SSTM, we see that the confidence interval bandwidth in Figure 4.12 is almost non-existent. The reason is that the kernel used has a faster convergence when decomposed in the eigen vector space. For smaller values of σ, the randomness in the concentration realization are minimal but as σ^2 is increased, we see increased randomness in the realizations. This also allows us to use the kernel used in Figure 4.12 for larger scale computations. We conclude that the choice of the velocity covariance kernel has a significant effect on the behaviour of the generalized SSTM increasing the flexibility of the SSTM.

		The Kernel 1		The Kernel 2	
σ^2	b	$Cov(x_1,x_2)=\sigma^2 e^{-\frac{\lvert x_1-x_2\rvert}{b}}$		$Cov(x_1,x_2)=\sigma^2 e^{-\frac{(x_1-x_2)^2}{b}}$	
		D_L	α	D_L	α
0.0001	0.1	0.02305	0.04611	0.02460	0.04921
0.001	0.1	0.02699	0.05199	0.02513	0.05025
0.01	0.1	0.03059	0.06117	0.02782	0.05361
0.1	0.1	0.06852	0.13705	0.06407	0.12815

Table 4.9. Comparison of the dispersivity values for the two kernels.

We investigate the effects of the kernels on the dispersivity values; we compute them using the stochastic inverse method (SIM) discussed in Chapter 3. Table 4.9 shows the results. For all practical purposes they are essentially the same. The mechanic of dispersion is more influenced by σ^2 for a given b or if both σ^2 and b are allowed to vary, on both σ^2 and b. The mechanics of dispersion in general can also be assumed to be influenced by the mathematical form of the kernel. The both of these kernels are exponential decaying functions. Because of the case of computations, we continue to use kernel 2 in Table 4.9 in the most of the work discussed in this book.

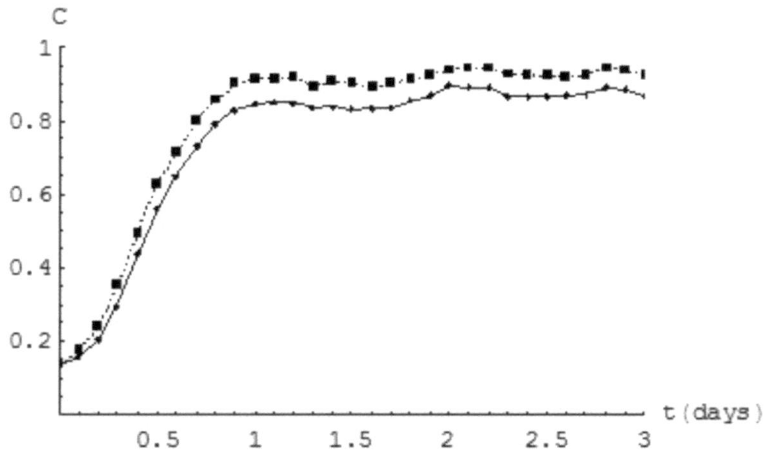

Figure 4.11. The generalized SSTM 95% confidence intervals for the concentration realization for the kernel, $\sigma^2 e^{-\frac{-|x_1 - x_2|}{b}}$ when $\sigma^2 = 0.1$ and $b = 0.1$.

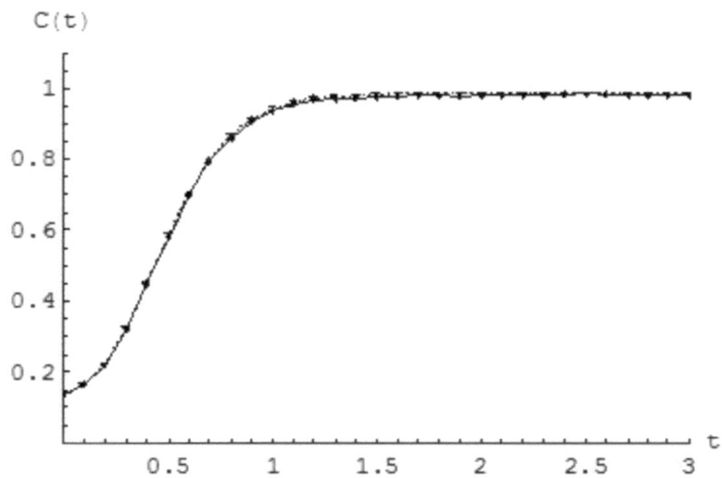

Figure 4.12. The generalized SSTM 95% confidence intervals for the concentration realization for the kernel, $\sigma^2 e^{-\frac{-(x_1 - x_2)^2}{b}}$ when $\sigma^2 = 0.1$ and $b = 0.1$.

4.5 Analysis of Ito Diffusions $I_i(x,t)$

We have developed the Ito diffusions $I_i(x,t)$ in section 4.2 (see equation (4.2.20)), and we rewrite the diffusions in the differential form:

$$dI_i(x,t) = F_i(x,t)dt + \sigma \sum_{j=1}^{m} G_{ij}(x,t)db_j(t), \text{ for } (i=0,1,2) \text{ and } (j=1,\ldots,m). \quad (4.5.1)$$

In equation (4.5.1), $F_i(x,t)$ are given by equations (4.2.21), (4.2.22) and (4.2.23), which can be considered as regular continuous and differentiable functions of x and t because we assumed the mean velocity $(\bar{V}(x,t))$ to be a continuous, differentiable function with finite variation in the development of the SSTM.

For many situations, we can assume $(\bar{V}(x,t))$ to be a function of x alone, and some regions of x it can be considered as a constant. G_{ij}'s are continuous differentiable functions of x only, with finite variation with respect to x (see equations (4.2.24) to (4.2.26)). Therefore, for a fixed value of x, we can write equation (4.5.1) as,

$$dI_{x,i}(t) = F_{x,i}(t)dt + \sigma \sum_{j=1}^{m} G_{x,ij}db_j(t), \quad (i=0,1,2) \text{ and } (j=1,\ldots,m). \quad (4.5.2)$$

From the derivation of equation (4.2.19), we see that the $db_j(t)s$ are the same standard Wiener process increments for each $I_{x,i}$ and each $db_j(t)$: equation (4.5.2) is a diffusion in m dimensions, and we can write $\underline{I}_x(t)$ as a multidimensional stochastic differential equation (SDE) (Klebaner, 1998).

In coordinate form we can write,

$$dI_{x,i}(t) = F_{x,i}(t)dt + \sigma \begin{bmatrix} G_{x,i1} & G_{x,i2} & \ldots & G_{x,im} \end{bmatrix} \begin{bmatrix} db_1(t) \\ db_2(t) \\ \cdot \\ \cdot \\ db_m(t) \end{bmatrix}. \quad (4.5.3)$$

In matrix form, we can write,

$$d\underline{I}_x(t) = \underline{F}_x dt + \sigma \underline{G}_x dB(t) \quad (4.5.4)$$

when, $\underline{G}_x = \begin{bmatrix} G_{x,01} & G_{x,02} & \ldots & G_{x,0m} \\ G_{x,11} & G_{x,12} & \ldots & G_{x,1m} \\ G_{x,21} & G_{x,22} & \ldots & G_{x,2m} \end{bmatrix}_{3\times m}$,

$$d\underline{B} = \begin{bmatrix} db_1(t) \\ db_2(t) \\ . \\ . \\ db_m(t) \end{bmatrix}_{m\times 1},$$

$$\underline{F}_x = \begin{bmatrix} F_{x,0} \\ F_{x,1} \\ F_{x,2} \end{bmatrix}.$$

The drift and diffusion coefficients of the multi-dimensional SDEs are vector $\underline{F}_x$ and the matrix $\sigma\underline{G}_x$ is independent of t, and the drift coefficient $\underline{F}_x$ can also be assumed to be independent of t in many cases. Therefore, equation (4.2.4) is a linear multi-dimensional SDE. The associated with this SDE, the matrix $\underline{a}$ called the diffusion matrix can be defined,

$$\underline{a} = (\sigma\underline{G}_x)(\sigma\underline{G}_x)^T \tag{4.5.5}$$

when superscript T indicates the transposed matrix. Under the conditions such as the coefficients use locally Lipschitz, equation (4.5.4) has strong solutions (see Theorem 6.22 in Klebaner (1998)).

The diffusion matrix, $\underline{a}$, is important to obtain the covariation of $\underline{I}_x$:

$$d[I_i, I_j](t) = dI_i(t)dI_j(t) = a_{ij}dt, \tag{4.5.6}$$

when, $a_{ij} = \begin{cases} \sigma^2 \sum_{K=1}^{m} G_{x,ik}^2 & \text{if } i = j \\ \sigma^2 \sum_{K=1}^{m} G_{x,ik} G_{x,jk} & \text{if } i \neq j \end{cases}, \quad i = 0,1,2, \text{ and } j = 0,1,2.$

$\underline{a}$ is a symmetric matrix.

In obtaining equation (4.2.6), we employ the fact that independent Brownian motions have quadratic covariation. The most important use of quadratic covariation is that we can determine the movement of $\underline{I}_x(t)$ with respect to time using the following well known results for Ito diffusions, which are also continuous Markov processes. It can be shown that, for an infinitesimal time increment,

$$E(I_{x,i}(t+\Delta) - I_{x,i}(t)) = F_{x,i}\Delta + O(\Delta), \tag{4.5.7}$$

$$E\{(I_{x,i}(t+\Delta) - I_{x,i}(t))(I_{x,j}(t+\Delta) - I_{x,j}(t)) | I_{x,i}(t)\} = a_{ij}\Delta + O(\Delta), \tag{4.5.8}$$

and when $i = j$, equation (4.6.8) becomes,

$$E\left\{\left(I_{x,i}(t+\Delta)-I_{x,i}(t)\right)^2 \middle| I_{x,i}(t)\right\} = a_{ii}\Delta + O(\Delta), \tag{4.5.9}$$

As the solution to the SDE equation (4.5.4) exists, from equation (4.5.8) it is seen that $\underline{F}_x$ is the form of $\underline{I}_x$ at time t, and $\underline{a}$ is the coefficients in the covariance of the infinitesimal displacement from $\underline{I}_x$. Using those results we can construct the realizations of $\underline{I}_x(t)$ by using the fact that $\underline{I}_x(t)$ are Gaussian processes. By dividing a given time interval into equidistant infinitesimal time interval, Δ, we can generate normally distributed $d\underline{I}_x$ increments for a given x, using the mean and variance obtained by equations (4.5.7) and (4.5.9). It should be noted that in generating the standard Wiener process increments, we use the zero-mean and Δ-variance Gaussian increments.

We take $\underline{I}_x(t)=\underline{0}$ when $t=0$ because

$$\underline{I}_x(t) = \int_0^t \underline{F}_x(t)dt + \sigma\int_0^t \underline{G}_x(t)d\underline{B}(t). \tag{4.5.10}$$

Figure 4.13 shows some realizations of $\underline{I}_x(t)$ when $x = 0.5$.

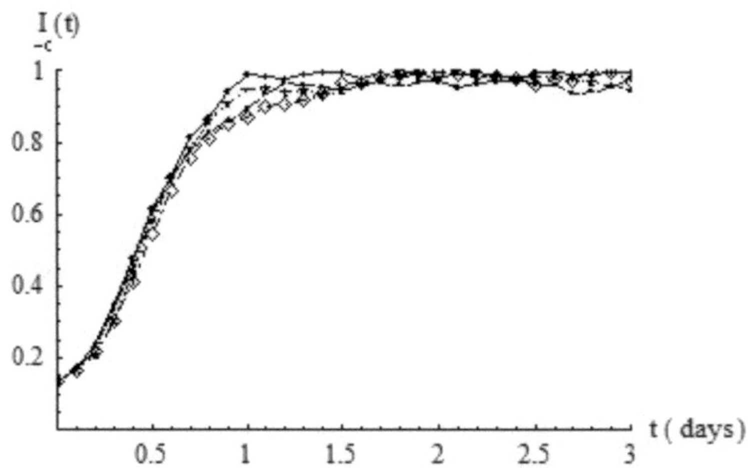

Figure 4.13. Some realizations of $\underline{I}_x(t)$ when $x = 0.5$.

The increments of $\underline{I}_x(t)$ are Gaussian random variables having the mean and variance given by equations (4.5.7) and (4.5.8).

The SDE given in equation (4.5.4) is linear and strong solutions do exist. When $F_{x,i}$ are not functions of t, then the solution of equation (4.5.4) is given by

$$\underline{I}_x(t) = \underline{F}_x t + \sigma \underline{G}_x \underline{B}(t). \tag{4.5.11}$$

Equation (4.5.11) provides realizations which have the statistical properties of the realizations depicted in Figure 4.13. The vector $\underline{B}(t)$ consists of independent Wiener processes; Figure 4.14 shows some realizations based on equation (4.5.11).

The statistical properties of these realizations are essentially the same to those of the realizations given in Figure 4.13.

As we have mentioned earlier, $\underline{I}_x(t)$ are only dependent on the velocity patterns in the medium, and it is important ask the question how the correlation length, b, affects the realization of $\underline{I}_x(t)$. (In this discussion we focus on the kernel $\sigma^2 e^{\frac{-|x_1-x_2|^2}{b}}$ only). It is seen that σ (the square root of the variance of the kernel) acts as the multiplication factor to the diffusion form of the SDE given in equation (4.5.11). However, the correlation length b influence $\underline{I}_x(t)$ nonlinearly through $\underline{G}_x$, but this influence can always be captured by suitable changes in σ . Therefore, we can keep b at a constant value that is appropriate for the porous medium under study. We found that b =0.1 is suitable for our computational experiments in this chapter as well as in chapters 6, 7 and 8.

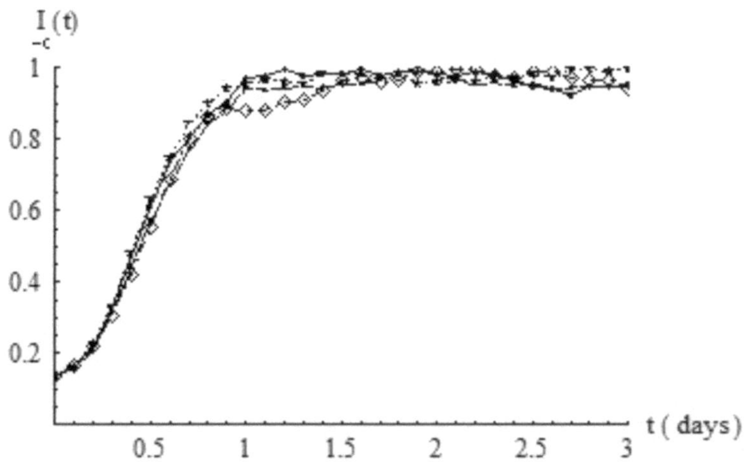

Figure 4.14. Some realization of $\underline{I}_x(t)$ for fixed $F_{x,i}s$ when $x=0.5$ based on equation (4.5.11).

Equation (4.5.11) can be written in component forms,

$$I_{x,0}(t)=F_{x,0}(t)+\sigma\sum_{j=1}^{m}G_{x,0j}B_j(t), \tag{4.5.12a}$$

$$I_{x,1}(t)=F_{x,1}(t)+\sigma\sum_{j=1}^{m}G_{x,1j}B_j(t), \tag{4.5.12b}$$

$$\text{and } I_{x,2}(t) = F_{x,2}(t) + \sigma \sum_{j=1}^{m} G_{x,2j} B_j(t). \tag{4.5.12c}$$

In the above equations, m is the number of significant eigen functions and is dependent on b. From equation (4.2.24), (4.2.25) and (4.2.26), we see that G_{ij} are related to $P_{ij}(x)$ which are given by equations (4.2.10), (4.2.11) and (4.2.12). For $b = 0.05$, $m = 8$, Figure 4.15 give $P_{ij}(x)s$ when $0.0 \le x \le 1.0$. The following observations can be noted from Figure 4.15: (a) $P_{ij}s$, therefore $G_{ij}s$ are sinesodial in nature; (b) amplitutes of $P_{ij}s$ increase with m (eigen function number) but as eigen values decrease with m, $G_{ij}s$ diminish with m (not shown); (c) $P_{2j}s$ are insignificant in comparision to $P_{0j}s$ and $P_{1j}s$ and therefore could be ignored; and (d) frequency of P_{ij} functions increases as m increase.

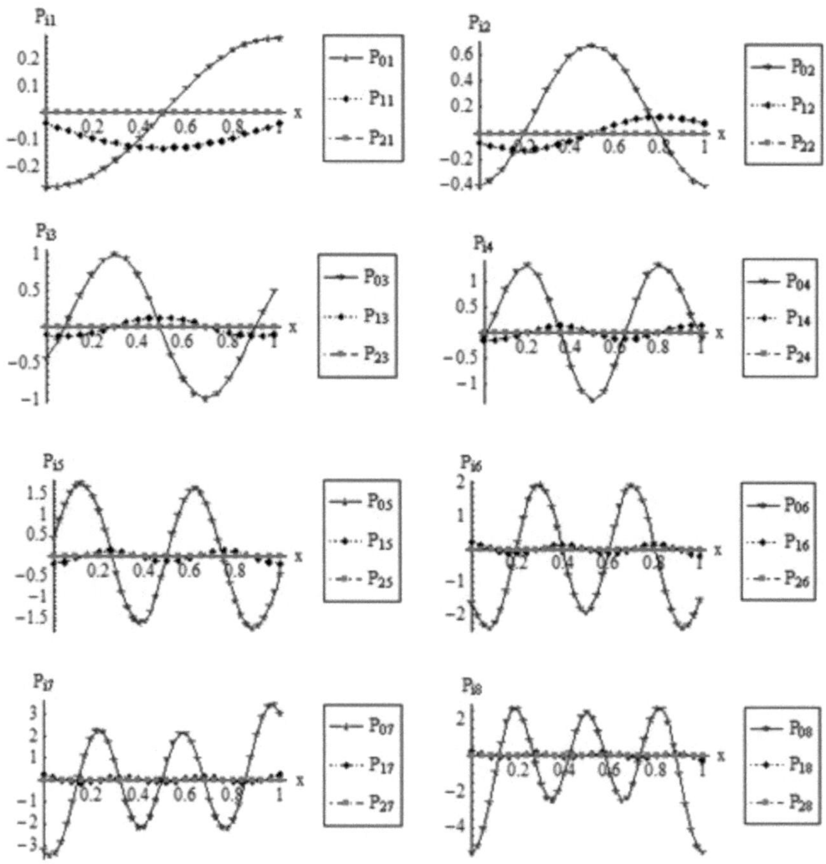

Figure 4.15. The approximated $P_{ij}(x)s$ given by equations (4.2.10), (4.2.11) and (4.2.12) when $0.0 \le x \le 1.0$ for $b = 0.05$.

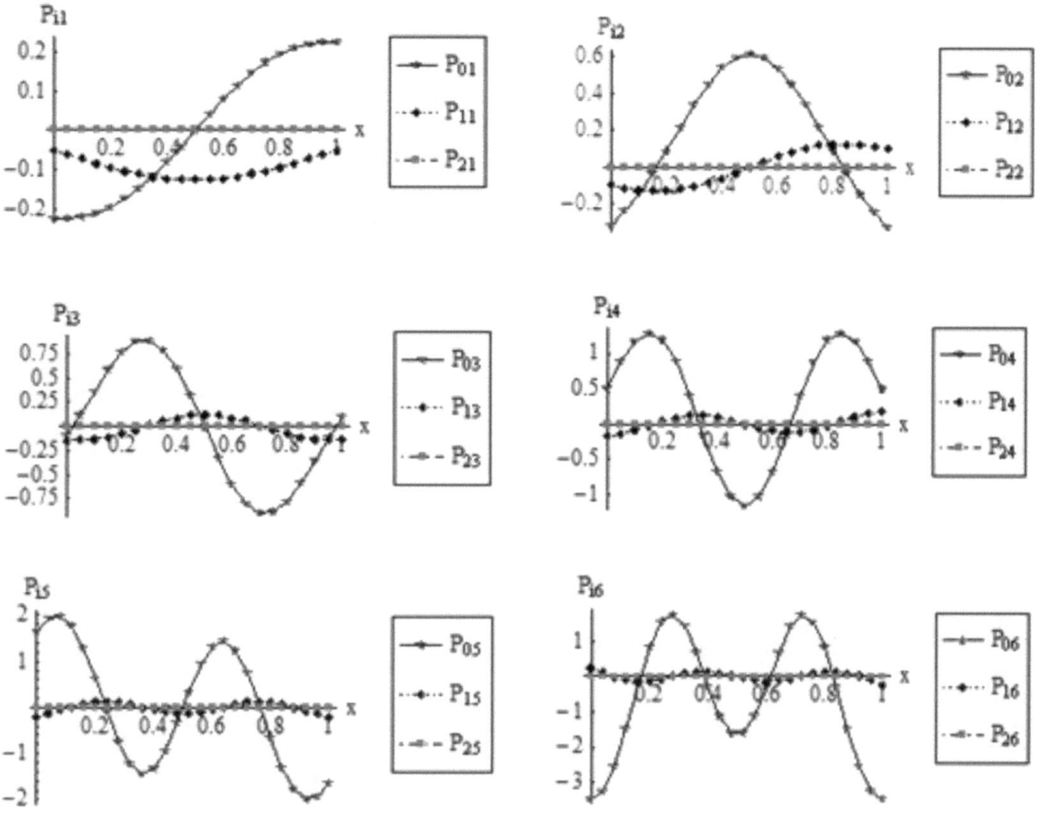

Figure 4.16. The approximated $P_{ij}(x)s$ given by equations (4.2.10), (4.2.11) and (4.2.12) when $0.0 \le x \le 1.0$ for $b = 0.1$.

When $b = 0.1$, the required number of significant eigen values is reduced to 6 and P_{ij} functions are depicted in Figure 4.16. Similar observation as before, when $b = 0.05$, can be made. Figure 4.17 shows P_{ij} functions when $b = 0.2$, and now the number of significant eigen values is 5 (i.e, $m = 5$). The same observations can be made for P_{ij} s when $b = 0.2$.

We produce the 3-dimensional graphs of P_{ij} when $i = 0,1$ and $j = 1,2,3,4,5$ in Figure 4.18 and Figure 4.19; b is plotted as the y-axis. As one could expect, it is reasonable to assume that function surface of P_{ij} is a smooth, continuous function of b. We can define continuous functions of x and b to define $P_{2j}s$.

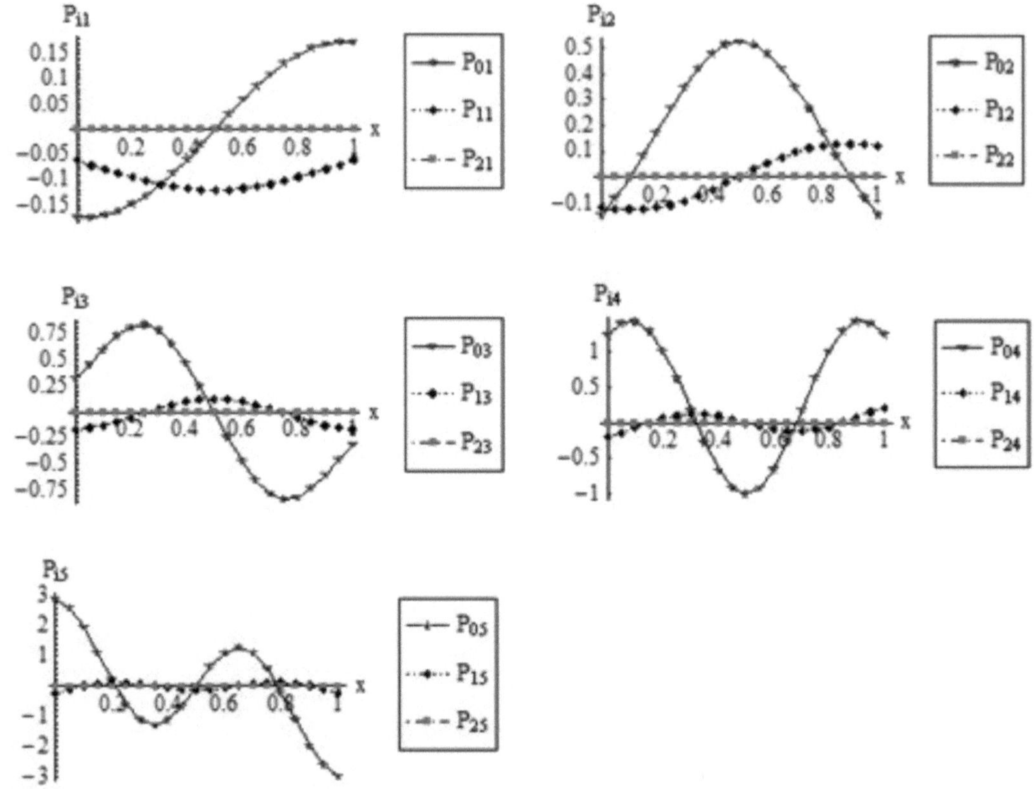

Figure 4.17. The approximated $P_{ij}(x)s$ given by equations (4.2.10), (4.2.11) and (4.2.12) when $0.0 \le x \le 1.0$ for $b = 0.2$.

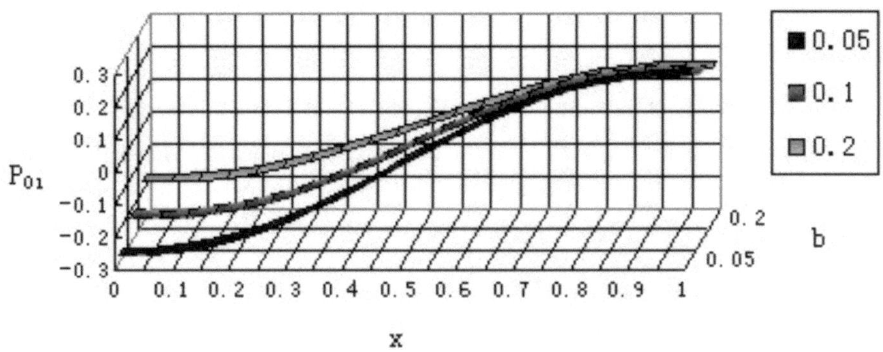

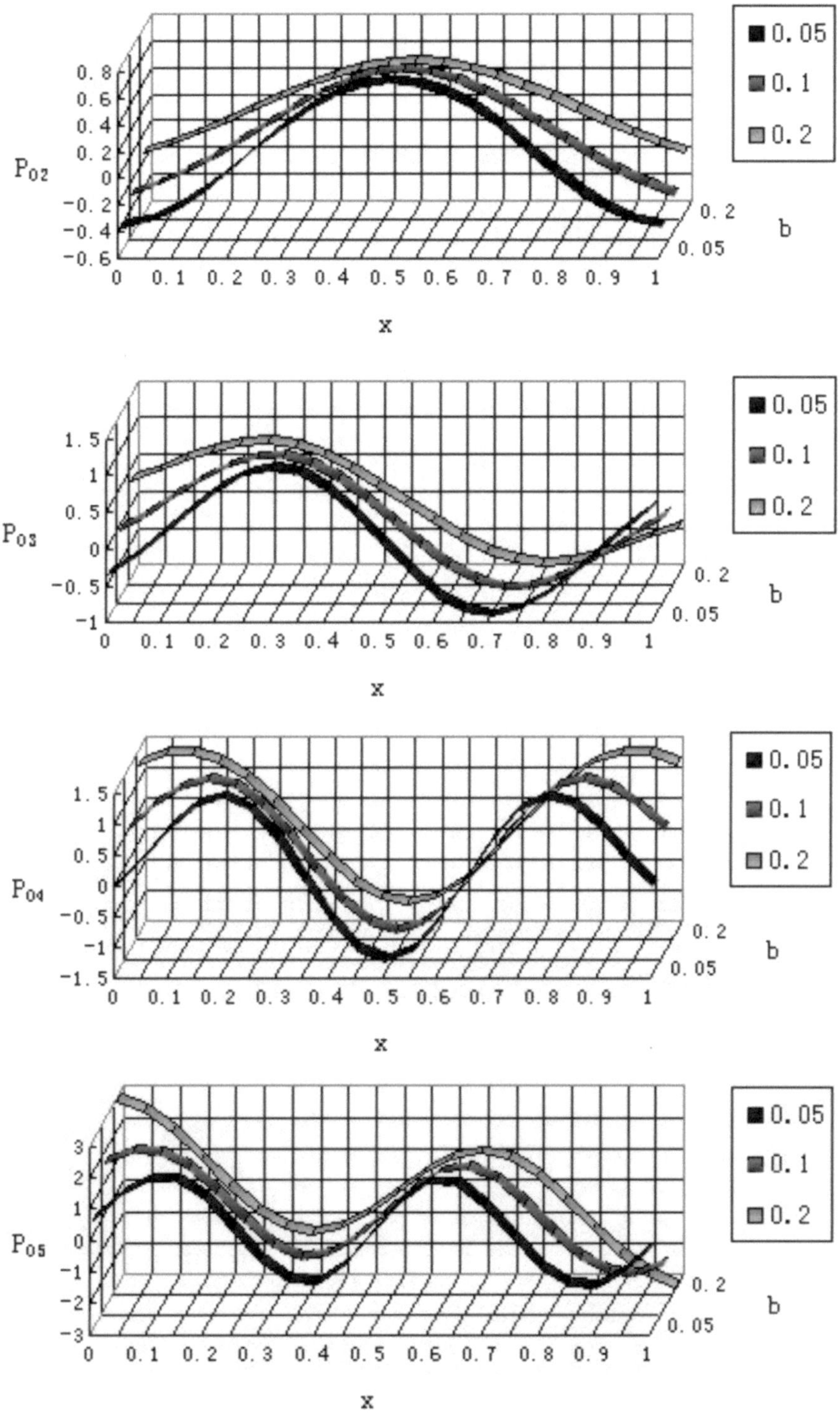

Figure 4.18. The 3-dimensional graphs of P_{ij} when $i=0$ and $j=1,2,3,4,5$

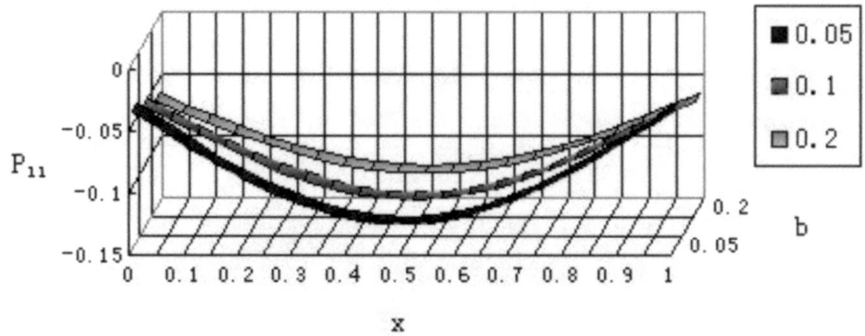
0.05
0.1
0.2
0
-0.05
-0.1
-0.15
P_{11}
0 0.1 0.2 0.3 0.4 0.5 0.6 0.7 0.8 0.9 1
x
0.2
0.05
b

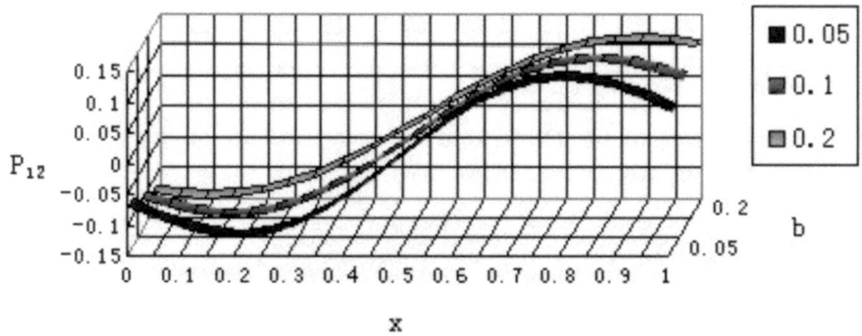
0.05
0.1
0.2
0.15
0.1
0.05
0
-0.05
-0.1
-0.15
P_{12}
0 0.1 0.2 0.3 0.4 0.5 0.6 0.7 0.8 0.9 1
x
0.2
0.05
b

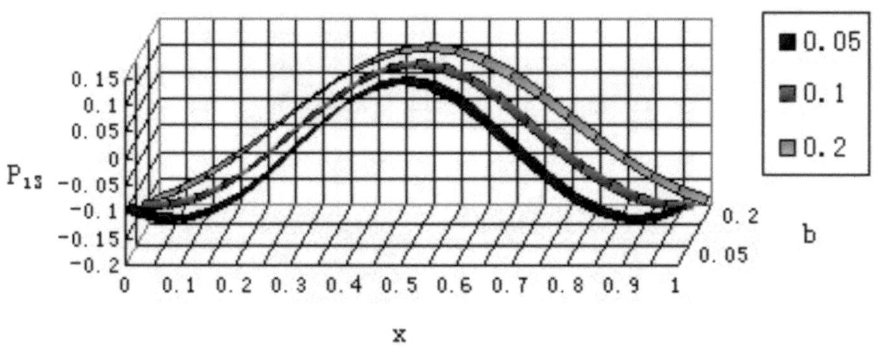
0.05
0.1
0.2
0.15
0.1
0.05
0
-0.05
-0.1
-0.15
-0.2
P_{13}
0 0.1 0.2 0.3 0.4 0.5 0.6 0.7 0.8 0.9 1
x
0.2
0.05
b

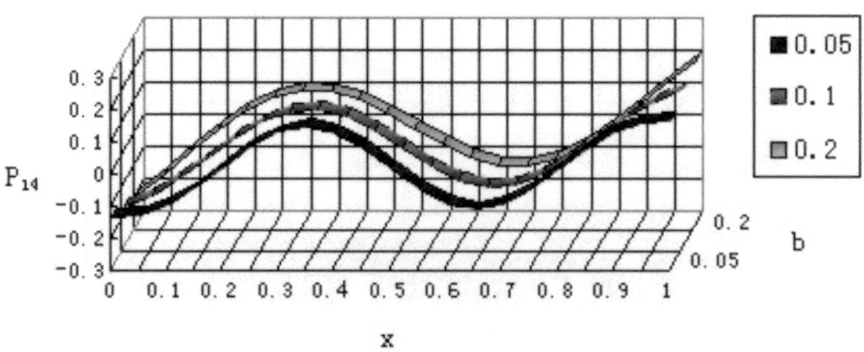
0.05
0.1
0.2
0.3
0.2
0.1
0
-0.1
-0.2
-0.3
P_{14}
0 0.1 0.2 0.3 0.4 0.5 0.6 0.7 0.8 0.9 1
x
0.2
0.05
b

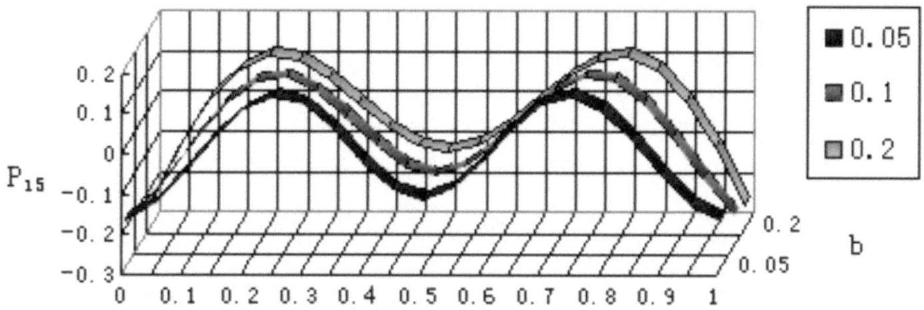

Figure 4.19. The 3-dimensional graphs of P_{ij} when $i=1$ and $j=1,2,3,4,5$

As we recall that the SSTM can be expressed as a diffusion process with martingale properties in time dimensions when another set of diffusion processes, $\underline{I}_x(t)$ are used:

$$dC_x(t) = -C_x(t)dI_{x,0} - \left(\frac{\partial C_x}{\partial x}\right)_x dI_{x,1} - \left(\frac{\partial^2 C_x}{\partial x^2}\right)_x dI_{x,2}. \tag{4.5.13}$$

We need to interpret this equation as follows: the solute concentration at a given point x consists of a combination of three diffusion processes which are solely based on velocity.

The spatial influence on the concentration is mediated through the prevailing concentration, and its spatial gradients. In keeping with the Ito definition of stochastic integration (Klebaner, 1998) we must use the concentration and its spatial gradients at a previous time. As a difference equation, we can write equation (4.5.13) as,

$$C_x(t+1) - C_x(t_n) = -C_x(t_n)dI_{x,0}(t_n) - \left(\frac{\partial C}{\partial x}\right)_{x,t_n} dI_{x,1}(t_n) - \left(\frac{\partial^2 C}{\partial x^2}\right)_{x,t_n} dI_{x,2}(t_n), \tag{4.5.14}$$

where t_n denotes the discretized time and the spatial gradients act as the coefficients of $d\underline{I}_x(t)$, and therefore can be written as,

$$dC_x(t) = \begin{bmatrix} -C_x & -\frac{\partial C_x}{\partial x} & -\frac{\partial^2 C_x}{\partial x^2} \end{bmatrix} \begin{bmatrix} dI_{x,0} \\ dI_{x,1} \\ dI_{x,2} \end{bmatrix} = \underline{F} d\underline{I}_x, \tag{4.5.15}$$

when, $\underline{F} = \begin{bmatrix} -C_x & -\frac{\partial C_x}{\partial x} & -\frac{\partial^2 C_x}{\partial x^2} \end{bmatrix}$.

Therefore, we can write,

$$C_x(t) = \int_0^t \underline{F} dI_x(t).$$

As P_{2j} functions are insignificant compared to the other two functions, we can approximate equation (4.5.15) as

$$dC_x(t) = \begin{bmatrix} -C_x & -\dfrac{\partial C_x}{\partial x} \end{bmatrix} \begin{bmatrix} dI_{x,0} \\ dI_{x,1} \end{bmatrix}. \tag{4.5.16}$$

This approximation enables us to reduce the computational time further in obtaining solutions.

Equation (4.2.3) gives the general form of eigen functions, $f_j(x)$ s. By inspecting equation (4.2.10), (4.2.11) and (4.2.12), we can deduce the following relationships between P_{ij} s and f_j s:

$$P_{0j}(x) = \frac{df_j(x)}{dx} + h_x \frac{d^2 f_j(x)}{dx^2}, \tag{4.5.17}$$

$$P_{1j}(x) = f_i(x) + h_x \frac{df_j(x)}{dx}, \tag{4.5.18}$$

$$\text{and } P_{2j}(x) = \frac{h_x}{2} f_j(x). \tag{4.5.19}$$

Therefore G_{ij} are given by,

$$G_{0j} = \sqrt{\lambda_j}\frac{df_j}{dx} + h_x\sqrt{\lambda_j}\frac{d^2 f_j}{dx^2}, \tag{4.5.20}$$

$$G_{1j} = \sqrt{\lambda_j} f_j + h_x \sqrt{\lambda_j}\frac{df_j}{dx}, \tag{4.5.21}$$

$$\text{and } G_{2j} = \frac{h_x}{2}\sqrt{\lambda_j} f_j. \tag{4.5.22}$$

The components of diffusion matrix $\underline{a}$ (see equation (4.5.5)) can be written as,

$$a_{ii} = \sigma^2 \sum_{k=1}^{m} G_{(i-1)k}^2, \qquad (i,1,2,3), \tag{4.5.23}$$

$$\text{and } a_{ij} = \sigma^2 \sum_{k=1}^{m} G_{i-1k} G_{j-1k}, \qquad (j,1,2,3) \;. \tag{4.5.24}$$

For example,

$$\begin{aligned} a_{11} &= \sigma^2 \sum_{k=1}^{m} G_{0k}^2 \\ &= \sigma^2 \sum_{k=1}^{m} \left(\sqrt{\lambda_k}\frac{df_k}{dx} + h_x \sqrt{\lambda_k}\frac{d^2 f_k}{dx^2} \right)^2, \end{aligned}$$

$$a_{11} = \sigma^2 \sum_{k=1}^{m} \left(\lambda_k \left(\frac{\partial f_k}{\partial x} \right)^2 + 2h_x \lambda_k \left(\frac{df_k}{dx} \right) \frac{d^2 f_k}{dx^2} + h_x^2 \lambda_k \left(\frac{\partial^2 f_k}{\partial x^2} \right)^2 \right). \tag{4.5.25}$$

Similarly,

$$a_{22} = \sigma^2 \sum_{k=1}^{m} G_{1k}^2 = \sigma^2 \sum_{k=1}^{m} \left(\lambda_k f_k^2 + 2h_x \lambda_k f_k \frac{df_k}{dx} + h_x^2 \lambda_k \left(\frac{df_k}{dx} \right)^2 \right). \tag{4.5.26}$$

$$a_{33} = \sigma^2 \sum_{k=1}^{m} \frac{h_x}{4} \lambda_j f_j^2. \tag{4.5.27}$$

$a_{ij}s$ can also be evaluated using equation (4.5.24).

This menas that once we have eigen functions in the form given by equation (4.2.3), the diffusion matrix $\underline{a}$ can be evaluated and equation (4.5.7) and (4.5.9) can be used to calculate the strong solutions for $\underline{I}_x(t)$.

4.6 Propagator of $\underline{I}_x(t)$

The propagator of $\underline{I}_x(t)$ can be defined as

$$\varepsilon_i\left(\Delta t; I_{x,i}(t), t\right) \equiv \left(I_{x,i}(t+\Delta t) - I_{x,i}\right) \big| I_{x,i}(t). \tag{4.6.1}$$

ε_i denotes the displacement of $I_{x,i}(t)$ during the infinitesimally small time interval Δt given the position (value) of $I_{x,i}(t)$ at time t. As $I_{x,i}(t)$ is an Ito diffusion, it is also a Markov process; the propagator $\varepsilon_i\left(\Delta t; I_{x,i}(t), t\right)$ is also a Markov process having a Gaussian probability density function, which completely specifics the propagator variable. To abbreviate the notation, we denote the propagator as $\varepsilon_i(\Delta t)$. It can be shown that the moments of $\varepsilon_i(\Delta t)$ has the analytical structure (Gillespie,1992),

$$E\left(\varepsilon_i^n(\Delta t)\right) \equiv \int_{-\infty}^{\infty} d\varepsilon \varepsilon^n P(\varepsilon|\Delta t) = B_u(t)\Delta t + O(\Delta t), \tag{4.6.2}$$

when B_n s are well behaved functions of t for a given $I_{x,i}(t)$ ($B_n(t)$ are also called the n th propagator moment function.) ; and $P(\varepsilon|\Delta t)$ is the probability density function of $\varepsilon_i(\Delta t)$.

It can be shown that, for a given value of $I_{x,i}(t)$ at time t, the mean and variance of the propagator function can be expressed as follows (Gillespie, 1992):

$$E\left(\varepsilon_i(\Delta t)\right) = A_i(t)\Delta t + O(\Delta t), \text{and} \tag{4.6.3}$$

$$Var\left(\varepsilon_i(\Delta t)\right) = D_i(t)\Delta t + O(\Delta t), \tag{4.6.4}$$

when $A_i(t)$ and $D_i(t)$ are independent of Δt. As the variance can not be negative, $D_i(t)$ should be a non-negative function. As mentioned before, $\varepsilon_i(\Delta t)$ is a Gaussian variable, i.e., it is normally distributed; therefore, we can write,

$$\varepsilon_i(\Delta t) \simeq N(A_i(t)\Delta t, D_i(t)\Delta t), \tag{4.6.5}$$

where "$\simeq$" indicates the random variable is generated from the normal density function having the mean, $A_i(t)\Delta t$ and the variance $D_i(t)\Delta t$.

If we recall, equation (4.5.9) gives,

$$E\left\{\left(I_{x,i}(t+\Delta) - I_{x,i}(t)\right)^2 \middle| I_{x,i}(t)\right\} = a_{ii}\Delta t + O(\Delta). \tag{4.6.6}$$

This can be written as,

$$E\left\{\varepsilon_i^2(\Delta t) \middle| I_{x,i}(t)\right\} = a_{ii}\Delta t. \tag{4.6.7}$$

when $t = t,$ i.e., $\Delta t = 0,$ therefore $\varepsilon_i(\Delta t) = 0$.

$E(\varepsilon_i / \Delta t) = 0$ at $t = t,$.

This leads to

$$Var(\varepsilon_i(\Delta t)) = a_{ii}\Delta + O(\Delta). \tag{4.6.8}$$

By comparing equation (4.5.7) with equation (4.6.3), and equation (4.6.4) with equation (4.6.8), we deduce that,

$$A_i(t) = F_{x,i}, \text{ and} \tag{4.6.9}$$

$$D_i(t) = a_{ii}. \tag{4.6.10}$$

We can now write the Langevin equation for the Ito diffusion, $I_{x,i}(t)$.

4.7 Langevin Equation for $I_{x,i}(t)$

From equation (4.6.1), the propagator can be written as,

$$dI_{x,i}(\Delta t) \equiv I_{x,i}(t+\Delta t) - I_{x,i}(t), \text{ for a given } I_{x,i}(t). \tag{4.7.1}$$

At the same time, we can write equation (4.6.5) as,

$$dI_{x,i}(t) = N\left[a_{ii}(t)\Delta t\right]^{1/2} + F_{x,i}\Delta t, \tag{4.7.2}$$

where N is a unit normal random variable generated from $N(0,1)$ density function. In the limit, $\Delta t \to 0,$

$$dI_{x,i}(t) = F_{x,i}dt + \left[a_{ii}(t)dt\right]^{1/2} N. \tag{4.7.3}$$

This is the first form of the Langevin equation for $I_{x,i}(t)$.

It can be shown that, if $N \simeq Normal(0,1)$,

$$\beta N + \lambda = Normal(\lambda, \beta^2), \tag{4.7.4}$$

Therefore, $\sqrt{dt}N$ is a normally distributed random variable having the density function $Normal(0, dt)$. This is the density function of the standard Wiener process increments, $dw(t)$. Therefore, we can rewrite equation (4.7.3) as,

$$dI_{x,i}(t) = F_{x,i}dt + \sqrt{a_{ii}}\,dw_i(t). \tag{4.7.5}$$

Equation (4.7.5) is the second form of the Langevin equation.

The advantage of this Langevin approximation for $I_{x,i}(t)$ over equation (4.5.2) is that it is not a multidimensional SDE but a one-dimensional one. This would allow us to compute $I_{x,i}(t)$ s more efficiently.

The moment evolution equations for $I_{x,i}(t)$ can be given as follows: (See Gillespie (1992) for derivations.)

$$\frac{d\left[E(I_{x,i}(t))\right]}{dt} = E\left[F_{x,i}\right], \tag{4.7.6}$$

$$\frac{d\left[Var(I_{x,i}(t))\right]}{dt} = 2\left(E\left[I_{x,i}(t)F_{x,i}\right] - E\left[I_{x,i}(t)\right]E\left[F_{x,i}\right]\right) + E\left[a_{ii}\right], \tag{4.7.7}$$

with initial conditions,

$$E\left[I_{x,i}(0)\right] = 0, \text{ and} \tag{4.7.8}$$

$$Var\left[I_{x,i}(0)\right] = 0. \tag{4.7.9}$$

If $F_{x,i}$ and a_{ii} are deterministic functions of x then the moment evolution equations can be simplified to equations (4.5.7) and (4.5.8).

4.8 The Evaluation of $C_x(t)$ Diffusions

The SSTM can be written as, for given x, (see equation (4.5.13)),

$$dC_x(t) = -C_x(t)dI_{x,0} - \left(\frac{\partial C_x}{\partial x}\right)_x dI_{x,1} - \left(\frac{\partial^2 C_x}{\partial x^2}\right)_x dI_{x,2} \quad , \tag{4.8.1}$$

where subscript x refers to the first and second derivatives with respect to x. Note that the coefficients are functions of t for given x, and $I_{x,i}$ s are Ito diffusions based on the velocity structure. Equation (4.8.1) is a stochastic diffusion and a SDE which displays the interplay between the concentration profile and velocity structures in the medium. By substituting the equations of the form of equation (4.7.5) for $dI_{x,i}$ s we obtain,

$$\begin{aligned} dC_x(t) = & -C_x(t)\left(F_{x,0}dt + \sqrt{a_{00}}dw_0(t)\right) \\ & -\left(\frac{\partial C}{\partial x}\right)_x \left(F_{x,1}dt + \sqrt{a_{11}}dw_1(t)\right) \\ & -\left(\frac{\partial^2 C}{\partial x^2}\right)_x \left(F_{x,2}dt + \sqrt{a_{22}}dw_2(t)\right). \end{aligned} \quad (4.8.2)$$

In equation (4.8.2), dw_0, dw_1 and dw_2 are independent standard Wiener increments.

Equation (4.8.2) can be written as,

$$dC_x(t) = -\alpha\left(C_x(t),t\right)dt - \sum_{k=0}^{2}\beta_k\left(C_x(t),t\right)dw_k, \quad (4.8.3)$$

where,

$$\alpha\left(C_x(t),t\right) = \alpha = \left(C_x(t)F_{x,0} + \left(\frac{\partial C}{\partial x}\right)F_{x,1} + \left(\frac{\partial^2 C}{\partial x^2}\right)F_{x,2}\right), \quad (4.8.4)$$

$$\beta_0 = C_x(t)\sqrt{a_{00}}, \quad (4.8.5a)$$

$$\beta_1 = \left(\frac{\partial C}{\partial x}\right)_x \sqrt{a_{11}}, \text{ and} \quad (4.8.5b)$$

$$\beta_2 = \left(\frac{\partial^2 C}{\partial x^2}\right)_x \sqrt{a_{22}}. \quad (4.8.5c)$$

Now the equation (4.8.3) can be written as

$$\begin{aligned} dC_x(t) &= -\alpha dt - \sum_{k=0}^{2}\beta_k dw_k, \\ &= -\alpha dt + \left[-\beta_0 \quad -\beta_1 \quad -\beta_2\right]\begin{bmatrix} dw_0 \\ dw_1 \\ dw_2 \end{bmatrix}. \end{aligned} \quad (4.8.6)$$

Equation (4.8.6) gives a diffusion matrix,

$$\begin{aligned} f &= \left[-\beta_0 \quad -\beta_1 \quad -\beta_2\right]\left[-\beta_0 \quad -\beta_1 \quad -\beta_2\right]^T, \\ &= \beta_0^2 + \beta_1^2 + \beta_2^2 \end{aligned} \quad (4.8.7)$$

Following Klebaner (1998), the expectations of infinitesimal differences of $C_x(t)$ can be written as (see also equation (4.5.7) and (4.5.9)),

$$E\left(C_x(t+\Delta)-C_x(t)\middle|C_x(t)\right)=-\alpha\Delta+O(\Delta) \quad , \tag{4.8.8}$$

and

$$E\left(\left(C_x(t+\Delta)-C_x(t)\right)^2\middle|C_x(t)\right)=\left(\beta_0^2+\beta_1^2+\beta_2^2\right)\Delta+O(\Delta). \tag{4.8.9}$$

Following the same arguments as in the case of deriving the Langevin equation for $I_{x,i}(t)$, we can obtain the Langevin equation for $C_x(t)$:

$$dC_x(t)=-\alpha dt+\sqrt{\beta_0^2+\beta_1^2+\beta_2^2}\,dw(t), \tag{4.8.10}$$

where $dw(t)$ is independent increments of the standard Wiener process, and if

$$\beta_x \equiv \sqrt{\beta_0^2+\beta_1^2+\beta_2^2}, \text{ then}$$

$$dC_x(t)=-\alpha dt+\beta_x dw(t). \tag{4.8.11}$$

This shows that the concentration at given x can be characterised by a Langevin type stochastic differential equation. This equation can be used to develop numerical solutions of the concentration profiles.

The time evolution of the probability density function of $C_x(t)$, $P_x\left(C_x,t|C_x(t),t_0\right)$, is described by Fokker-Plank equation (Klebaner, 1998; Gillespie, 1992). The Fokker-Plank equation for $P_x\left(y,t|y_0,t_0\right)$ is,

$$\frac{\partial P_x\left(y,t|y_0,t_0\right)}{\partial t}=\frac{\partial\left(\alpha P_x\right)}{\partial y}+\frac{1}{2}\frac{\partial^2\left(\beta_x^2 P_x\right)}{\partial y^2}, \tag{4.8.12}$$

where y denotes $C_x(t)$ and P_x stands for $P_x\left(y,t|y_0,t_0\right)$.

Equation (4.8.12) has the initial condition,

$$P\left(y,t=t_0|y_0,t_0\right)=\delta\left(y-y_0\right), \tag{4.8.13}$$

where δ is the Dirac-delta function.

Once we solve the Fokker-Plank equation (4.8.12) along with its initial condition, the time evolution of probability density function can be found. This is also a weak solution to equation (4.8.10). Equation (4.8.10) also has strong solutions which can be obtained by integrating the SDE (4.8.11) using Ito integration. The drift coefficient $(-\alpha)$ in equation (4.8.11) is a stochastic variable in x and t.

Similar to equations (4.7.6) and (4.7.7), we can write time evolution of the moments $C_x(t)$. The derivation of these equations are very similar to those given by Gillespie (1992).

The time evolution of the mean of $C_x(t)$ is given by,

$$\frac{d\left(E\left(C_x(t)\right)\right)}{dt}=E[-\alpha], \tag{4.8.14}$$

therefore,

$$E\left(C_x(t)\right)=\int_0^t E[-\alpha]dt. \tag{4.8.15}$$

The mean of $C_x(t)$ at a given x is expressed as an integral of the expectation of $(-\alpha)$. As can be seen from equation (4.8.4), α is not only dependent on $C_x(t)$ and its first and second derivatives with respect to x, but also dependent on the mean velocity and its first and second derivatives with respect to x, according to equations (4.2.20), (4.2.21) and (4.2.22). The initial condition for equation (4.8.15) is $C_x(0)$, the value of the concentration at time is zero for a given x.

The evolution of the variance of $C_x(t),\left(Var\left(C_x(t)\right)\right)$ is given by,

$$\frac{d\left[Var\left(C_x(t)\right)\right]}{dt}=2\left(E\left(-\alpha C_x(t)\right)+E\left(C_x(t)\right)E(\alpha)\right)+E\left[\beta_x^2\right], \tag{4.8.16}$$

and the variance of $C_x(t)$ can be obtained by integrating equation (4.8.16) with respect to t,

$$Var\left(C_x(t)\right)=2\int_0^t E\left(-\alpha C_x(t)\right)dt+2\int_0^t E\left(C_x(t)\right)E(\alpha)dt+\int_0^t E\left[\beta_x^2\right]dt. \tag{4.8.17}$$

By Fubini's theorem (Klebaner,1998), for continuous stochastic variable such as α, $C_x(t)$ and β_x, we can rewrite equation (4.8.17) as,

$$Var\left(C_x(t)\right)=-2E\left[\int_0^t \alpha C_x(t)dt\right]+2\int_0^t E\left(C_x(t)\right)E(\alpha)dt+E\left[\int_0^t \beta_x^2\right]dt. \tag{4.8.18}$$

In equation (4.8.18), Fubini's theorem is only applied to the first and third term of equation (4.8.17).

Once we evaluate the mean and variance of $C_x(t)$, we can obtain the probability density function, $P_x\left(y,t|y_0,t_0\right)$ of $C_x(t)$ (y represents the value of $C_x(t)$). As Ito diffusions are Martingales with Markovian properties (Klebaner, 1998), and $C_x(t)$ is Gaussian,

$$P_x\left(y,t|y_0,0\right) \equiv P_x\left(y,t\right) = \frac{1}{\left[2Var(y)\right]^{1/2}} \exp\left(\frac{-\left(y-E(y)\right)^2}{2Var(y)}\right). \quad (4.8.19)$$

when $E(y)$ and $Var(y)$ are given by equations (4.8.15) and (4.8.18). When time is zero, $P_x\left(C_x(0)\right) = 1.0$.

Equation (4.8.19) should also be the solution to the Fokker-Plank equation (4.8.12). The Fokker-Plank equation (4.8.12) is a stochastic partial differential equation for which analytical equations can not easily be obtained. Therefore, we can make use of this fact to verify the numerical solutions for the Fokker-Planck equation.

4.9 Numerical Solutions

We have seen in the previous section 4.8, the following SDE gives the time course of concertration $C_x(t)$ for a given x in the vicinity of x:

$$dC_x(t) = -\alpha dt + \beta_x dw(t), \quad (4.9.1)$$

where $dw(t)$ is the standard Wiener increments with a zero mean and dt variance, if dt is sufficiently small; the drift coefficient α is given by (see equation (4.8.4)),

$$\alpha = C_x(t)F_{x,0} + \left(\frac{\partial C}{\partial x}\right)_x F_{x,1} + \left(\frac{\partial^2 C}{\partial x^2}\right)_x F_{x,2}. \quad (4.9.2)$$

In equation (4.9.2),

$$F_{x,0} = \frac{\partial \bar{V}(x,t)}{\partial x} + \frac{h_x}{2}\frac{\partial^2 \bar{V}(x,t)}{\partial x^2}, \quad (4.9.3)$$

$$F_{x,1} = \bar{V}(x,t) + h_x \frac{\partial \bar{V}(x,t)}{\partial x}, \quad (4.9.4)$$

and,

$$F_{x,3} = \frac{h_x}{2}\bar{V}(x,t); \quad (4.9.5)$$

where $\bar{V}(x,t)$ in the mean velocity which is assumed to be regular differentiable continuous function.

β_x in equation (4.9.1) is given by,

$$\beta_x = \left(\beta_0^2 + \beta_1^2 + \beta_2^2\right)^{1/2}, \quad (4.9.6)$$

where,

$$\beta_0 = C_x(t)\sqrt{a_{00}}, \quad (4.9.7)$$

$$\beta_1 = \left(\frac{\partial C}{\partial x}\right)_x \sqrt{a_{11}}, \text{ and}$$

$$\beta_2 = \left(\frac{\partial^2 C}{\partial x^2}\right)_x \sqrt{a_{22}}, \tag{4.9.8}$$

The following equation gives the expressions of a_{00}, a_{11}, and a_{22},

$$a_{ii} = \sigma^2 \sum_{j=1}^{m} G_{ij}^2, \qquad (i,0,1,2), \tag{4.9.9}$$

where m is the number of effective eigen functions, and

$$G_{ij} = \sqrt{\lambda_j} P_{ij}, \quad (i,0,1,2). \tag{4.9.10}$$

In the numerical solutions, we make use of the finite differences, for a given dependent variable, say U, based on the grid given in Figure 4.20

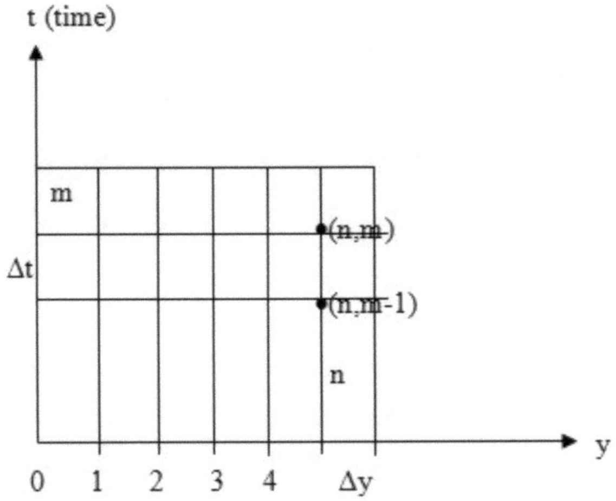

Figure 4.20. Space-time grid used in the numerical solutions with respect to y

$$\left(\frac{\partial U}{\partial y}\right)_n^m = \frac{\left(U_n^m - U_{n-1}^m\right)}{\Delta y}, \tag{4.9.11}$$

$$\left(\frac{\partial^2 U}{\partial y^2}\right)_n^m = \frac{\left(U_n^m - 2U_{n-1}^m + U_{n-2}^m\right)}{\Delta y^2}, \tag{4.9.12}$$

and

$$\left(\frac{\partial U}{\partial t}\right)_n^m = \frac{\left(U_n^{m+1} - U_n^m\right)}{\Delta t}. \tag{4.9.13}$$

By using a numerical scheme developed, we obtain realizations of $C_x(t)$ as strong solutions to equation (4.9.1). We can also obtain solutions to the Fokker-Plank equation (4.8.12) using the same finite differences.

4.10 Remarks for the Chapter

In this Chapter, we develop a generalized form of SSTM that can include any arbitrary velocity covariance kernel in principle. We have demonstrates that for a given kernel, a generalized analytical forms for eigen functions can be obtained by using the computational methods developed. We have also developed a Langevin form of the SSTM for a given x, and the time evolution of concentration, $C_x(t)$, follows a stochastic differential equation having the coefficients α and β_x which are again functions of $C_x(t)$ and eigen functions. In other words, if one monitors the concentration $C_x(t)$ at a given point in space, the data collected along with time would constitute a realization of the strong solution of the SDE. The solution is a function of the covariance kernel, i.e. a function of σ^2 and b for an exponentially decaying kernel, and also a function of $C_x(t)$ itself and its first- and second derivatives with respect to x. This focus of SDE provides a very convenient and computationally efficient way to solve the stochastic partial differential equation associated with the SSTM.

By deriving a Langevin form of the SSTM, we essentially prove that any time course of the concentration at a given point behaves according to the underlying SDE, which would characterize the nature of local porous medium and is a statement of mass concentration of the solute.

5

Theories of Fluctuations and Dissipation

5.1 Introduction

In the previous chapters, we see that the hydrodynamic dispersion is in fact a result of solute particles moving along a decreasing pressure gradient and encountering the solid surfaces of a porous medium. The pressure gradient provides the driving force which translates into kinetic energy, and the porous medium acts as the dissipater of the kinetic energy; any such energy dissipation associated with small molecules generates fluctuations among molecules. Looking at a molecular-level picture, the dissolved solute particles in water travelling through the porous medium slow down nearing a surface and then increase in velocity once the molecules get scattered after the impact with solid surface. Refining this picture a bit more, we see that the velocity boundary layers along the solid surfaces are helping this process. Not all the molecules hit solid surfaces either; some of these would be subjected to micro-level local pressure gradients and move away from the surfaces. A physical ensemble of these solute molecules would depict behaviours that are measurable using appropriate extensive variables. (Extensive variables depend on the extent of the system of molecules. i.e., the number of molecules, concentrations, kinetic energy etc., where as intensive variables do not change with size of the system, i.e., pressure, temperature, entropy etc.) These measurable quantities at macroscopic level have origins in microscopic level. Therefore, we can anticipate that molecular level description would justify the operational models that we develop at an ensemble level. Naturally one could expect that the statistical moments of the variables of an ensemble would lead to meaningful models of the process we would like to observe.

In the development of the SSTM, we express the velocity of solute as the sum of the mean velocity and a fluctuating component around the mean. The mean velocity may then be evaluated by using the Darcy's law. We then express the fluctuating component in terms of the spectral expansion dependent on a covariance kernel. However, we need to understand that this type of picture in a more fundamental way should be based on the established theories. Towards that end, in this chapter, we review some of the fundamental theoretical frameworks associated with molecular fluctuation. We show the connectivity of thermodynamical, molecular and stochastic description of fluctuations and dissipations, and then we make use of Ito diffusions to obtain the models of statistical moments of relevant variables. While we do not cite the reference within this chapter -- as the works we refer to are well accepted knowledge in the disciplines such as thermodynamics, statistical mechanics and stochastic processes-- all the relevant works are given in the references list at the end of the book. However, we refer to Keizer's work (1987) primarily in this chapter.

Any description of a process once expressed in mathematical abstraction, becomes a "contracted" description or a contracted model. What is important to understand is that different levels of contracted descriptions could be useful for different purposes, and at the same time, the insights gained from one level of description should be obtained by another level of description and vice versa. However, this is a very difficult task in many of the molecular level processes. One of the main reasons for this difficulty is that the most of the molecular processes are thermodynamically irreversible. In addition, physics of the processes at different levels of descriptions are based on different conceptual frameworks, albeit being very meaningful at a given level. In our discussion here, we consider the thermodynamic level of description, the Boltzmann level of description, and physical ensemble description which is inherently stochastic, hence described in stochastic processes.

5.2 Thermodynamic Description

To facilitate the discussion here, we make use of the Brownian motion as an example with the aim of developing a general framework for discussion. The total differential of entropy of an idealized system of the Brownian particles can be written as,

$$dS = \frac{dU}{T} + \left(\frac{P}{T}\right)dV - \left(\frac{\mu}{T}\right)dN, \tag{5.2.1}$$

where U is the internal energy; V is the volume of the system; N is the number of particles (molecules); P is the pressure; μ is the chemical potential; and, T is the absolute temperature. Equation (5.2.1) is a statement for a system of molecules and the system has the well-defined physical boundaries through which mass and heat transfer could occur. The momentum of the particles is included in the internal energy term, and by including the momentum (M), the total energy is $E = U + \frac{M^2}{2m}$, where m is the mass of a particle. We can write equation (5.2.1) in the following form after including the momentum as a thermodynamic variable:

$$dS = \frac{dE}{T} - \left(\frac{\underline{v}}{T}\right)d\underline{M} + \left(\frac{P}{T}\right)dV - \left(\frac{\mu}{T}\right)dN. \tag{5.2.2}$$

In equation (5.2.2), $\underline{v}$ is the row vector of particle velocities and $\underline{M}$ is the column vector of particle moments. The total differential of entropy (dS) can be expressed in terms of partial derivatives:

$$dS = \left(\frac{\partial S}{\partial E}\right)dE + \left(\frac{\partial S}{\partial \underline{M}}\right)d\underline{M} + \frac{\partial S}{\partial V}dV + \frac{\partial S}{\partial N}dN, \tag{5.2.3}$$

where $\frac{\partial S}{\partial \underline{M}}$ indicates the row vector of $\frac{\partial S}{\partial M_i}$; $\frac{\partial S}{\partial E}$, $\frac{\partial S}{\partial \underline{M}}, \frac{\partial S}{\partial V}$ and $\frac{\partial S}{\partial N}$ are thermodynamically conjugate to the respective variables in equation (5.2.3), namely E, $\underline{M}, V$ and N.

The Onsager principle for the linear laws for irreversible processes states that the rate of change of an extensive variable is linearly related to the difference of the corresponding thermodynamically conjugate variable from its value at the thermodynamic equilibrium. According to this Onsager linear law we can express the expected value of the momentum conditional on the initial value in component form as follows:

$$\frac{dE}{dt}\left[M_i(t)\middle|M_i(0)\right]=\sum_j L_{ij}\left[E\left[\frac{\partial S}{\partial M_i}(t)\middle|\frac{\partial S}{\partial M_i}(0)\right]\right]-E\left[\frac{\partial S}{\partial M_i}(t_e)\middle|\frac{\partial S}{\partial M_i}(0)\right], \tag{5.2.4}$$

with $E[\ ]$ denoting the expectation operator; $L[\ ]$ denoting the coupling matrix, which is symmetric and non-negative definite; and subscript "e" refers to the values at the thermodynamic equilibrium. To simplify the notation, we denote conditional expectation as $E[\ ]^0$ when the variable within square brackets is conditional upon a well defined value at $t=0$. Using this notation, equation (5.2.4) can be written as,

$$\frac{dE}{dt}\left[M_i(t)\right]^0=\sum_j L_{ij}\left[E\left[\frac{\partial S}{\partial M_i}(t)\right]^0-E\left[\frac{\partial S}{\partial M_i}(t_e)\right]^0\right]. \tag{5.2.5}$$

According to equation (5.2.5), the rate of change of the conditional average of the momentum of the particle is linearly related to the deviation of conditional average of the thermodynamic conjugate of the momentum from its value at the equilibrium. The conjugate variables are intensive variables and the conjugate for the momentum is $\frac{-v_i}{T}$ according to equation (5.2.2); i.e.,

$$\frac{\partial S}{\partial M_i}=-\frac{v_i}{T} \tag{5.2.6}$$

The coefficient matrix L needs to be found to complete the linear law. In this case, we can make use of the Langevin description of the Brownian motion. (See section 5.3 for a discussion of the Langevin equation.) By disregarding the random force term, the expected value of the particle momentum can be expressed as,

$$\frac{dE}{dt}\left[\underline{M}(t)\right]^0=-\left(\frac{\nu}{m}\right)E\left[\underline{M}(t)\right]^0, \tag{5.2.7}$$

with ν as the fiction constant m is the mass of the particle, according to the Newton law of motion.

Because $\underline{M}(t)=m\underline{v}(t)$, we can rewrite equation (5.2.7) as,

$$\frac{dE}{dt}\left[\underline{M}(t)\right]^0=-\nu E\left[\underline{v}(t)\right]^0. \tag{5.2.8}$$

Combining with equation (5.2.6), equation (5.2.8) becomes,

$$\frac{dE}{dt}\left[\underline{M}(t)\right]^{0} = -\nu TE\left[\frac{\partial S}{\partial \underline{M}}(t)\right]^{0}. \tag{5.2.9}$$

As the equilibrium value of $\underline{v}(t_e)$ is 0, we could express equation (5.2.9) in form of the Onsager linear law,

$$\frac{dE}{dt}\left[M_i(t)\right]^{0} = \sum_j L_{ij}\left[E\left[\frac{\partial S}{\partial M_j}(t)\right]^{0} - E\left[\frac{\partial S}{\partial M_j}(t_e)\right]^{e}\right]. \tag{5.2.9a}$$

with $L_{ij} = T\nu\delta_{ij}$ when δ_{ij} is the Kronecker delta.

Another example of linear law is the Newton's law of cooling. Consider the heat transfer between two solids, one at temperature T_1 and the other at T_2, and the equilibrium temperature the two solids reach is T_e. The thermodynamic conjugates of the internal energies, U_1 and U_2, are $\frac{1}{T_1}$ and $\frac{1}{T_2}$ (equation (5.2.1)). The Onsager principle states that,

$$\frac{dE\left[U_1(t)\right]^{0}}{dt} = -\frac{dE\left[U_2(t)\right]^{0}}{dt} = \frac{L}{T_e^2}E\left[T_2(t)\right]^{0} - E\left[T_1(t)\right]^{0}. \tag{5.2.10}$$

Equation (5.2.10) can be derived from applying the Onsager principle for the two solids separately and taking into the account of the fact that the energy loss of one solid is the energy gained of the other solid. L in equation (5.2.10) is non-negative and needs to be determined experimentally. Further, equation (5.2.10) is only valid in the vicinity of the equilibrium.

The extensive variables, the momentum and the internal energy, are expressed as thermodynamic rule laws in equation (5.2.9) and (5.2.10); however, the momentum and the internal energy have quite distinct forms of functional characteristics. For example, if we reverse the velocities of the molecules, the magnetic field and the time associated with a physical ensemble, the momentum changes the direction but the internal energy remains the same. As the time progresses in the reverse direction, the ensemble will move along the past trajectory. When an extensive variable changes its sign under the reversal of the time or the magnetic field or velocities, we call that variable an odd variable; the variables that are invariant under the reversal are call even variables. In the Brownian molecule and the heat transfer examples discussed previously, the internal energy and the momentum are decoupled, i.e. the coupling effects are ignored. The coupling are only among the variables having the same symmetry under time reversal. Onsager principle can be extended to the situation where the coupling between the variables with different time reversal symmetry exists. The matrix L_{ij} in the linear laws now change to

$$L_{ij}\left(\underline{B}\right) = \varepsilon_i\varepsilon_j L_{ij}\left(-\underline{B}\right) \tag{5.2.11}$$

when L is dependent on the external magnetic filed, $\underline{B}$, when either the effects of the external magnetic field are ignored or the magnetic field is absent, the even or odd variables are coupled by a symmetric matrix where as the odd and even variables are coupled by a antisymmetric matrix. Equation (5.2.11) are called the Onsager-Casimir reciprocal relations.

To simplify the notation in the linear laws such as equation (5.2.5), we introduce the following variables:

1. $Y_j = E\left[\frac{\partial S}{\partial x_j}(t)\right]^0 - E\left[\frac{\partial S}{\partial x_j}(t_e)\right]^0$ to denote the conditional average difference of the thermodynamic conjugate of the extensive variable x_j from the corresponding equilibrium value; and

2. $a_i(t) = E[x_i(t)]^0 - E[x_i(t_e)]^0$ to denote the conditional average of the difference between an extensive variable of our choice and its value at the thermodynamic equilibrium. Then the Onsager linear laws can be written as,

$$\frac{da_i}{dt} = \sum L_{ij} Y_j \tag{5.2.12}$$

and equation (5.2.12) can be interpreted in terms of fluxes and thermodynamic forces: Y_j is the "thermodynamic force" which drives a_i towards zero, i.e., x_i approaches its equilibrium value on the average. The rate of change of a_i can be considered as the average thermodynamic flux, J_i, giving,

$$\frac{da_i}{dt} = J_i = \sum_i L_{ij} Y_j \tag{5.2.13}$$

In the linear laws, the thermodynamic forces are descriptions of the entropy of the system. At thermodynamic equilibrium, the entropy of a given system is maximum as the Second Law of thermodynamics says that entropy increases on the average of any spontaneous process. Let us consider the entropy of an isolated system in the vicinity of its thermodynamic equilibrium. The extensive variable $\underline{a}$ as defined before has finite values, and the entropy associated with the system, $S(\underline{a})$, can be expressed in terms of Taylor series:

$$S(\underline{a}) = S(0) + \sum_j \left(\frac{\partial S}{\partial x_j}\right)^e a_j + \frac{S}{2}\sum_i \sum_j \left(\frac{\partial^2 S}{\partial x_i \partial x_j}\right)^e a_i a_j . \tag{5.2.14}$$

at the maximum of $S(\underline{a})$,

$$\left(\frac{\partial S}{\partial x_j}\right)^e = 0 ,$$

And

$$S_{ij} = \left(\frac{\partial^2 S}{\partial x_i \partial x_j} \right)^e < 0;$$

as these conditions are true for any $\underline{a}$, the matrix S_{ij} must be negative semi-definite. By incorporating equation (5.2.12) in equation (5.2.14), and using the conditions for the thermodynamic equilibrium stated previously, we obtain,

$$S(\underline{a}) = S(0) + \frac{1}{2} \sum_i \sum_j S_{ij} a_i a_j . \quad (5.2.15)$$

But as an approximation, we can write,

$$Y_i = \sum_j S_{ij} a_j , \quad (5.2.16)$$

Because our definition of Y_i is the first derivative of S with respect to x_i on the average. Therefore, we can write equation (5.2.15),

$$S(\underline{a}) = S(0) = \frac{1}{2} \sum_i Y_i a_i . .$$

This can be expressed on the average

$$\frac{dS(\underline{a})}{dt} = \frac{1}{2} \sum_i Y_i \frac{da_i}{dt} \quad (5.2.17)$$

Using equation (5.2.12),

$$\frac{dS(\underline{a})}{dt} = \sum_i \sum_j L_{ij} Y_i Y_j , \quad (5.2.18)$$

As the derivative of the entropy with respect to time is positive, L is a positive semi-definite matrix. What equation (5.2.17) and (5.2.18) convey is that the mean fluctuations of an extensive variable give rise to increase in the entropy, and therefore $\frac{dS(\underline{a})}{dt}$ alludes to dissipation of energy due to the fluctuations of an extensive variable. We define the Rayleigh-Onsager dissipation function as

$$\Phi(\underline{a}) = \frac{dS(\underline{a})}{dt} = \sum_i \sum_j L_{ij} Y_i Y_j \geq 0. \quad (5.2.19)$$

The dissipation function Φ is also called the entropy production and is dependent on our choice of the system.

Using equation (5.2.16) and (5.2.12), one can write,

$$\frac{da_i}{dt} = \sum_j L_{ij} \sum_j S_{ij} a_j = \sum_j H_{ij} a_j , \quad (5.2.20)$$

where $H_{ij} = \sum_k L_{ik} S_{kj}$, which is the relaxation matrix H governing the return of mean values of the extensive variables to equilibrium; equation (5.2.20) can be written in the matrix form,

$$\frac{d\underline{a}}{dt} = \underline{H}\underline{a}, \tag{5.2.21}$$

which has the solution,

$$\underline{a}(t) = \exp(\underline{H}t)a^0 \tag{5.2.22}$$

where $\underline{a}^0$ is the initial value of the selected process. The matrix H must be negative semi-definite as the entropy increases on the average during the relaxation process.

Using equation (5.2.22), we can deduce the covariance function, $\underline{C}(t_1,t_2)$,

$$\underline{C}(t_1,t_2) = E[\underline{a}(t_1)\underline{a}^T(t_2)] = E[(\exp(\underline{H}t_1)\underline{a}^0)(\exp(\underline{H}t_2)\underline{a}^0)^T] = E[\underline{a}^0\underline{a}^{0T}]\exp(\underline{H}t_1 + \underline{H}^T t_2). \tag{5.2.23}$$

If $t_2 = t_1 + \tau$, and closer to the equilibrium the process is stationary,

$$\underline{C}(\tau) = E[\underline{a}^0\underline{a}^T(\tau)] = E[\underline{a}^0\underline{a}^{0T}]\exp(\underline{H}^T\tau). \tag{5.2.24}$$

As we can see, from a thermodynamic point of view, equation (5.2.23) and (5.2.24) state that the covariances have an exponential character to them, and they are decaying functions with respective to time.

Equation (5.2.21) shows the behaviour of the conditional average value of $a_i(t) = E[x_i(t)]^0 - E[x_i(t_e)]^0$. in relation to matrix H_{ij}. By substituting for $\underline{a}$ the component form of equation (5.2.21) can be written as,

$$\frac{d}{dt}\left\{E[x_i(t)]^0 - E[x_i(t_e)]^0\right\} = H_{ij}E[x_i(t)]^0 - H_{ij}E[x_i(t_e)]^0.$$

At equilibrium, $E[x_i(t_e)]^0$ remains unchanged; therefore,

$$\frac{d}{dt}\left\{E[x_i(t)]^0\right\} = H_{ij}E[x_i(t)]^0 - H_{ij}E[x_i(t_e)]^0.$$

As discussed before any dissipative system would have fluctuations in extensive variables. Let us define the fluctuations with reference to the expected value conditioned upon the initial value as,

$$\delta x_i(t) = x_i(t) - E[x_i(t)]^0. \tag{5.2.25}$$

Then,

$$\frac{d}{dt}\{x_i(t) - \delta x_i(t)\} = H_{ij}\left(x_i(t) - \delta x_i(t)\right) - H_{ij}\left(x_i(t_e) - \delta x_i(t_e)\right);$$

$$\frac{dx_i(t)}{dt} - \frac{d\delta x_i(t)}{dt} = H_{ij}x_i(t) - H_{ij}\delta x_i(t) - H_{ij}x_i(t_e) + H_{ij}\delta x_i(t_e).$$

Rearranging,

$$\frac{d\delta x_i(t)}{dt} = H_{ij}\delta x_i(t) + \frac{dx_i(t)}{dt} H_{ij}x_i(t_e) + H_{ij}x_i(t) - H_{ij}\delta x_i(t_e).$$

Near equilibrium,

$\delta x_i(t_e) \approx 0$; and $\left\{\frac{dx_i(t)}{dt} - H_{ij}(x_i(t_e) - x_i(t_e))\right\}$ is small compared to $\frac{d}{dt}[\delta x_i(t)]$ following equation (5.2.21), we can simplify the above equation to

$$\frac{d\delta x_i(t)}{dt} = H_{ij}\delta x_i(t) + f_i.$$

where f_i is a random term. Expressing this in matrix form,

$$\frac{d\delta \underline{X}}{dt} = \underline{H}\delta\underline{X} + \underline{f}. \tag{5.2.26}$$

This equation is the Onsager's regression hypothesis for fluctuations. This hypothesis is based on the thermodynamic arguments not on the particles behaviour in a physical ensemble. However, as we will see in the next sections, equation (5.2.26) has a similar character to those derived from the particle dynamics.

To complete the Onsager picture of random fluctuations in equation (5.2.26), we need to consider equation (5.2.26) as linear stochastic differential equation. Then $\underline{f}$ term can be defined in terms of the Wiener process and $\underline{H}$ as a function of $\delta\underline{X}$ to develop the simplest form of a stochastic differential equation. We will address this in section 5.4.

5.3 The Boltzmann Picture

As mentioned in the previous section, the Onsager regression hypothesis is based on the entropy and the coefficients which form the coupling matrix, L. The Boltzmann equation is on the other hand dependent entirely on the molecular dynamics of collisions and the resulting fluctuations. We do not intent to derive the Boltzmann equation here; instead, we describe the equation and the variables here. For the technical details of the derivation, there are many excellent texts on statistical mechanics and some of the original works are given in the references.

Boltzmann's work was on the dynamics of dilute gases and the average behaviour of gas molecules was the main focus on his work. The Boltzmann's equation describes the nonlinear dynamics of the molecular collisions, while Onsager theory is on linear dynamics without fluctuations. It can be shown that the linearized Boltzmann equation is a special case of Onsager theory.

In the derivation of the Boltzmann equation, we have a six-dimensional space in which the position of, $\underline{r}$, and the velocity, $\underline{v}$, of the centre of mass of a single molecule are defined.

We call this six-dimensional space the μ-space or molecule phase space. We can divide the six-dimensional space into small cellular volumes and each volume elements is assigned an index $i = 1,2,3,...$ as a unique number for identification purposes. The number of molecules, $N_i(t)$ would be the macroscopic Boltzmann variable associated in the volume element i, and we choose the volume element i to be sufficiently large that $N_i(t)$ is a large number.

It is assumed that binary collisions between the molecules of only two volume elements located at $\underline{r},\underline{v}$ and $\underline{r},\underline{v}_1$ occur in the μ-space. Each of these volumes lose one molecule each and volume elements located at $\underline{r},\underline{v}'$ and $\underline{r},\underline{v}_1'$ gain one molecule each at the end of each collisions. (The primes denote the velocities at the centre of mass velocities after the collisions.) We can define the extensive property of the number density is μ-space, $\rho(\underline{r},\underline{v},t)$, so that $\rho(\underline{r},\underline{v},dt)d\underline{r}d\underline{v}$ is the number of molecules with centre of mass position and velocity in the ranges $[\underline{r},\underline{r}+d\underline{r}]$ and $[\underline{v},\underline{v}+d\underline{v}]$.

Then the Boltzmann equation gives,

$$\frac{\partial \rho}{\partial t} = -\underline{v} \bullet \nabla_r \rho - \underline{F} \bullet \nabla_v \rho + \int \hat{\sigma}_T g \left[\rho' \rho_1' - \rho \rho_1 \right] d\underline{v}_1, \tag{5.3.1}$$

where $\rho(\underline{r},\underline{v}',t) = \rho', \rho(\underline{r},\underline{v}'_{-1},t) = \rho_1'$, $\underline{F}$ is an external force field acting in the μ-space, and ∇_r and ∇_v are the derivatives with respective to $\underline{r}$ and $\underline{v}$, respectively. The third term on the right hand side of equation (5.3.1) is the dissipative effect of collisions; $\hat{\sigma}_T$ is a linear operator and g is the constant relative velocity magnitude. In the absence of an external force equation (5.3.1) can be written as,

$$\frac{\partial \rho}{\partial t} = -\underline{v} \bullet \nabla_r \rho + d_e, \tag{5.3.2}$$

with d_e lumping the dissipation due to collisions.

Unlike the Onsager's linear laws, which are true only near the thermodynamic equilibrium, the Boltzmann equation is true not only in the vicinity of the equilibrium but also away from the equilibrium. However, near the equilibrium these two pictures are similar and while the Boltzmann equation is valid strictly speaking only for diluted gases, the Onsager linear laws are valid for any ensemble.

Boltzmann's theory includes a function called the H-function which behaves in an entropy-like manner; for a closed system *H*-function is a non-increasing function, i.e., $\frac{dH}{dt} \leq 0$. H function is defined as

$$H = \int\int \rho \ln \rho d\underline{r}d\underline{v}. \tag{5.3.3}$$

This attribute of *H* function is *H*-theorem, and *H* function has similar character to the Gibb's free energy in thermodynamics.

It can be shown that when $\frac{dH}{dt} = 0$, if $\rho = \rho^e$ then

$$\rho^e \rho_1^e = \rho^{e'} \rho_1^{e'} \tag{5.3.4}$$

where 'e' indicates the equilibrium state.

In the vicinity of equilibrium, we can write,

$$\rho(\underline{r},\underline{v},t) = \rho^e(\underline{v}) + \Delta\rho(\underline{r},\underline{v},t) \tag{5.3.5}$$

where $\Delta\rho(\underline{r},\underline{v},t)$ is a small change in the μ-space density. By substituting equation (5.3.5) in the Boltzmann equation and ignoring the higher order terms of $\Delta\rho$, we obtain,

$$\frac{\partial \rho}{\partial t} = -\underline{v} \bullet \nabla_r \rho + C[\Delta\rho], \tag{5.3.6}$$

with $C[\Delta\rho]$ replacing the dissipation integral as a linear functional.

It can be shown that (Fox and Uhlenbeck, 1970 a and b) by adopting the Onsager hypothesis,

$$\frac{\partial \Delta\rho}{\partial t} = L[X] + \tilde{f}(\underline{r},\underline{v},t), \tag{5.3.7}$$

where, $X = -k_B \ln\left(\frac{\rho}{\rho_e}\right)$ the local thermodynamic force in μ-space;

$$L[X] \equiv \left(\frac{\underline{v}\rho^e}{k_B}\right) \bullet \nabla_r X + \int L^S(\underline{v},\underline{v}_1) X_1 d\underline{v}_1,$$

with L^S is a linear operator (see Fox and Uhlenbeck, 1970 a and b); and $\tilde{f}$ is a random term which needs to be characterised.

The random term now can be defined by,

$$E\left[\tilde{f}(\underline{r},\underline{v},t)\right] = 0 \text{ and}$$

$$E\left[\tilde{f}(\underline{r},\underline{v},t)\tilde{f}(\underline{r}',\underline{v}',t')\right] = 2k_B L^S(\underline{v},\underline{v}_1)\delta(\underline{r}-\underline{r}')\delta(t-t'). \tag{5.3.8}$$

In equation (5.3.7), the rate of change of the μ-space density increments are expressed in terms of thermodynamic forces (X).

By deriving the random term $\tilde{f}$ as in (5.3.8), we see that the random term is a zero-mean stochastic process in the μ-space, δ-correlated in $\underline{r}$ and t but influenced by the velocity of the centre of mass through a linear operator derived from the dissipation term, d_S, in the Boltzmann equation. Equation (5.3.7) and (5.3.8) show that the Boltzmann and Onsager pictures are united near equilibrium. Equally importantly, equation (5.3.8) justifies the δ-

correlated stochastic processes to model the fluctuations. Moving away from the μ-space, we describe the fluctuations and dissipation using the theory of stochastic processes in an effort to develop operational models of molecular fluctuations.

5.4 Onsager Regression Hypothesis, Langevin Equation and Itō processes

The Onsager regression hypothesis, equation (5.2.26), states that the fluctuations of extensive variables around their expected values conditional on the initial values can be expressed in terms of a system of differential equations through a relaxation matrix which is defined in equation (5.2.20). Equation (5.2.26) is similar in form to equations (5.3.6) and (5.3.7) which are derived from Boltzmann's equation (5.3.1). Both of these theories support the hypothesis that the time derivatives of fluctuations on the average follow differential equations with additive random terms. The average fluctuations are driven by thermodynamically coupled driving forces because of energy dissipation according to Boltzmann. We have seen in the previous section that both of these descriptions are phenomenologically equivalent. However, none of those descriptions are amenable for operational models of fluctuation and dissipation.

Starting point of the development of such models is the Langevin equation which describes the motion of Brownian particles. Even though Langevin used the Newtonian laws to describe the particle motion, he developed a differential equation with an addictive random term, which is quite similar to the Onsager regression hypothesis. Langevin started by considering a particle of mass m at a distance $\underline{r}$ from an initial point, if $\bar{p}$ is the momentum vector of the particle and $\underline{V}$ is the velocity, we can write from the Newton laws,

$$\frac{dr}{dt} = \frac{\bar{p}}{m}, \tag{5.4.1}$$

$$\underline{F} = \frac{d\bar{p}}{dt}, \tag{5.4.2}$$

$$\text{and } \bar{p} = m\underline{V}. \tag{5.4.3}$$

We have slightly changed the notation to indicate that the variables are associated with a particle rather than with an ensemble.

In equation (5.4.2), $\underline{F}$ is the force vector on the particle (the particle is bombarded by the surrounding water molecules). We can express the $\underline{F}$ as $(\underline{F}_d + \underline{F}_e)$ where $\underline{F}_d$ is the drag component due to friction and $\underline{F}_e$ is the external force; the force due to molecular collisions on the particle is assumed to be random. $\underline{F}_d$ can be expressed through the friction constant η,

$$\underline{F}_d = -\eta\underline{V}. \tag{5.4.4}$$

Now we can write, $\frac{d\underline{r}}{dt} = \frac{\bar{p}}{m}$ as in equation (5.4.1),

$$\text{and } \frac{d\bar{p}}{dt} = -\eta\left(\frac{\bar{p}}{m}\right) + \underline{F}_e + \underline{f}. \tag{5.4.5}$$

In equations (5.4.5) and (5.4.1), the position of the particle, $\underline{r}$ and the momentum, $\vec{p}$ are coupled, and $\underline{f}$ is a random additive noise. In a dissipative system, the random forcing term $\underline{f}$ can be assumed to have an expected value of zero:

$$E\left[\underline{f}\right]=\underline{0}. \tag{5.4.6}$$

At the given time, the random force term, $\underline{f}$ at time t_1 is uncorrelated to that of t_2, and it is a result if molecular impacts on the particle. Therefore, we can assume that $\underline{f}$ to be a δ-correlated function:

$$Cov\left(\underline{f}(t_1)\right)\underline{f}(t_2)=\sigma^2\delta(t_1-t_2), \tag{5.4.7}$$

where σ^2 is the variance.

It is now clear that the Wiener process described in Chapter 2 is a good model for $\underline{f}$, and therefore we can write equation (5.4.5) as,

$$d\vec{p}=-\left(\frac{\eta}{m}\right)\vec{p}dt+F_e dt+\sigma d\underline{w}(t), \tag{5.4.6}$$

where, $\underline{w}(t)$ is the standard Wiener process.

In the absence of an external force,

$$d\vec{p}=-\left(\frac{\eta}{m}\right)\vec{p}dt+\sigma d\underline{w}(t). \tag{5.4.7}$$

Therefore, the solution of the stochastic differential equation (5.4.7), can be written as,

$$\vec{p}(t)=\vec{p}(0)-\int\left(\frac{\eta}{m}\right)\vec{p}dt+\int\sigma d\underline{w}(t), \tag{5.4.8}$$

and equation (5.4.8) in an stochastic integral. The last integration can be interpreted in two ways: as an Itō integral or as a Stratonovich integral. Because of the martingale of property of Itō integrals, we choose to interpret the second integral on the right hand side of equation (5.4.8) as an Itō integral. The implications of this choice is important to understand: it makes stochastic processes such as equation (5.4.8) Markov processes with the transitional conditional probabilities obeying Fokker-Planck type equations. The stochastic differential equations of the type given by equation (5.4.7) describe the time evolution of stochastic variables. We generalize the stochastic differential of a vector valued stochastic process by,

$$d\underline{n}=\underline{h}(\underline{n},t)dt+\underline{\sigma}\underline{g}(\underline{n},t)d\underline{w}, \tag{5.4.9}$$

where $\underline{n}$ is an extensive variable, $\underline{h}$ is a vector function of $\underline{n}$ and t, $\underline{\sigma}$ is a diagonal matrix with σ_{ii} as the diagonal element, $\underline{g}(\underline{n},t)$ is a matrix function of $\underline{n}$ and t and $\underline{w}$ is the standard Wiener process vector. By taking $\underline{\sigma}$ to be diagonal matrix, we assume that covariance $\left(\sigma_{ij}\right)^2$ is not cross correlated, i.e., where $i=j$, $\sigma_{ij}=\sigma_{ii}$ and when $i \neq j$, $\sigma_{ij}=0$. Then by defining,

$$\underline{G}(n,t)=\underline{\sigma}\underline{g}(\underline{n},t),$$

We can write a general Ito integral,

$$\int d\underline{n} = \int \underline{h}(\underline{n},t)dt + \int \underline{G}(n,t)d\underline{w}, \text{ and}$$

$$\underline{n}(t)=\underline{n}(t_0)+\int_{t_0}^{t}\underline{h}(\underline{n},t)dt+\int_{t_0}^{t}\underline{G}(n,t)d\underline{w}. \tag{5.4.10}$$

Equation (5.4.10) depicts a Markov process and is a martingale.

The probability density or the transitional probability function of $\underline{n}(t)$, $p(\underline{n},\underline{t}\,|\,n_1,t_1)$ obeys the Fokker-Planck equation (given in the repeated summation indices):

$$\frac{\partial p(\underline{n},t\,|\,\underline{n}_1,t_1)}{\partial t}=\frac{\partial h_i}{\partial n_j}(\underline{n},t)\bar{p}(\underline{n},t\,|\,\underline{n}_1,t_1)+\frac{1}{2}\frac{\partial^2 g_{ik}}{\partial n_i \partial n_j}(\underline{n},t)g_{ik}(\underline{n},t)p(\underline{n},t\,|\,\underline{n}_1,t_1), \tag{5.4.11}$$

and $\bar{p}(n,0\,|\,\underline{n}_1,0)=\delta(\underline{n}-\underline{n}_1)$.

Once the Fokker-Plank equation is solved for the conditional density, the Markov process $\underline{n}(t)$ can be described completely. For the most of the Markov process of practical interest $\underline{h}(\underline{n},t)$ is linear in $\underline{n}$ and $\underline{G}(\underline{n},t)$ is independent of $\underline{n}$, and therefore the Fokker-Plank equation (5.4.10) can also be solved using integration by parts without resorting to Ito calculus. However, in general stochastic integrals are solved using Ito definition.

5.5 Velocity as a Stochastic Variable

Equation (5.4.6) expresses the dynamics of a single Brownian particle based on the first principles. We can write the infinitesimal change in momentum in a slightly modified form:

$$d\bar{p}=-\left[\left(\frac{\eta}{m}\right)\bar{p}+F_e\right]dt+\sigma_p dw_p, \tag{5.5.1}$$

where the subscript " p " indicates that they are associated with particle momentum. F_e denotes the external force acting on the particle. If the particle is in a porous media saturated with water, the porous matrix exerts a force opposite to the direction of flow, whereas the pressure gradient acting in the flow direction would be largely responsible for $\bar{p}$. The first term on the right hand side of equation (5.5.1) can be thought of as the change of momentum on the average if we lump the fluctuating component of F_e in to $\sigma_p dw_p$.

Therefore, we can write equation (5.5.1) as,

$$d\bar{p} = -\left[\left(\frac{\eta}{m}\right)\bar{p} + F_e\right]dt + \sigma_p' dw_p', \tag{5.5.2}$$

where $\sigma_p' dw_p'$ now contains the fluctuating component of the momentum change due to the porous media. F_e is in the mean force acting on the particle, and in the saturated medium, it may be dominating the first term of the right hand side of equation (5.5.2). Therefore, we could approximate equation (5.5.2) for an i th particle in an ensemble particles with,

$$dp_i = F_i dt + \sigma_{p,i} dw_{p,i}, \tag{5.5.3}$$

where F_i now depicts the mean force acting on a particle i, and all the variables are vectors and $\sigma_{p,i}$ is a matrix. Now we can write,

$$p_i = m_i v_i,$$

where m_i is the mass of a particle i and v_i is the particle velocity, which is a random variable. We can express equation (5.5.3) as,

$$d(m_i v_i) = m_i \frac{dv_i}{dt} dt + \sigma_{p,i} dw_{p,i}, \text{ and}$$

the instantaneous change in the velocity, dv_i, can be approximated by $v_i dt$ where $\bar{v}_i$ is the mean velocity of the i th particle at the locality of the particle at time, t. Now we can write

$$dv_i = \bar{v}_i dt + \sigma_{v,i} dw_{v,i}, \tag{5.5.4}$$

where $w_{v,i}$ is the standard Wiener process related to velocity fluctuations and $\sigma_{v,i} = \sigma_{v,i}/m_i$ is the associated amplitude. As discussed in Chapter 2, we can express the fluctuating component as,

$$\sigma_{v,i} dw_{v,i} = \xi_i dt \tag{5.5.5}$$

where ξ_i is the noise associated with velocity. We can rewrite equation (5.5.4) as,

$$dv_i = \bar{v}_i dt + \xi_i dt = (\bar{v}_i + \xi_i)dt = d(\bar{v}_i + \xi_i), \tag{5.5.6}$$

for very small increments of dt.

Therefore, we can write,

$$v_i = \bar{v}_i + \xi_i, \tag{5.5.7}$$

where particle velocity is decomposed into the mean velocity and a fluctuating component. For an ensemble of n particles,

$\sum v_i = \sum \overline{v}_i + \sum \xi_i$, and diving this equation by n,

$$V = \overline{V} + \xi ,$$

where V is the Gausssian velocity of the ensemble, $\overline{V}$ is the mean velocity and ξ is the "average" noise representing the fluctuations.

We have shown that the velocity can be expressed as consisting of a mean component and an additive fluctuating component, based on the Langevin description of Brownian particles. From an application point of view, the additive form of the velocity can be used to explain the local heterogeneity of the porous medium, i.e., we can always calculate the average velocity in a region and then the changes in the porous structure may be assumed to cause the fluctuations around the mean. This is the working assumption on which the stochastic solute transport model (SSTM) in Chapter 3 is based.

5.5.1 Thermodynamic Character of SSTM

As we have seen in section 5.3, equation (5.3.7) unites the Onsager and Boltzmann pictures close to equilibrium (Keizer, 1987). The SSTM given by equation (4.2.1) has a similar form to that of equation (5.3.7) and equation (5.3.2) where the fluctuating component is separated out as an additive component but the fluctuating part is now more complicated reflecting the influence of the porous media. According to equation (5.3.8), the "noisy" random functions have zero means and the two-time covariances are δ-correlated in time and space; and these Dirac's delta functions are related through a linear operator. In the development of SSTM, we assume only the δ-correlation in time because the spatial aspect is separated into a continuous function of space. This assumption can be justified as the porous medium influencing the fluctuations can be considered as a continuum.

6

Multiscale, Generalised Stochastic Solute Transport Model in One Dimension

6.1 Introduction

In Chapter 3 and 4, we have developed a stochastic solute transport model in 1-D without rosorting to simplifying Fickian assumptions, but by using the idea that the fluctuations in velocity are influenced by the nature of porous medium. We model these fluctuations through the velocity covariance kernel. We have also estimated the dispersivity by taking the realisations of the solution of the SSTM and using them as the observations in the stochastic inverse method (SIM) based on the maximum likelihood estimation procedure for the stochastic partial differential equation obtained by adding a noise term to the advection-dispersion equation. We have confined the estimation of dispersivities to a flow length of 1 m (i.e, $x \in [0,1]$) except in Chapter 3, section 3.10, where we have estimated the dispersivities up to 10 km using the SIM by simplifying the SSTM. This approach was proven to be computationally expensive and the approximation of the SSTM we have developed was based on the spatial average of the variance of the fluctuation term over the flow length. Further, the solution is based on a specific kernel. This development in Chapter 3 is inadequate to examine the scale dependence of the dispersivity. Therefore, we set out to develop a dimensionless model for any given arbitrary flow length, L, in this Chapter for any given velocity kernel provided that we have the eigen functions in the form given by equation (4.2.3). Then we examine the dispersivities in relation to the flow lengths to understand the multi-scale behaviour of the SSTM.

The starting point of the development of the multi-scale SSTM is the Langevin equation for the SSTM, which is interpreted locally. From equation (4.9.1), the Langevin equation can be written as,

$$dC_x(t) = -\alpha_x(C_x(t), \bar{V}(x,t), x)dt + \beta_x(C_x(t), \frac{\partial C_x}{\partial x}, \frac{\partial^2 C_x}{\partial x^2}, x)dw(t) \qquad (6.1.1)$$

where the coefficients α_x and β_x are dependent on $x, C_x(t)$ and $\bar{V}(x,t)$; and $C_x(t), \frac{\partial C_x}{\partial x}, \frac{\partial^2 C_x}{\partial x^2}$ and x, respectively. $dw(t)$ are the standard Wiener increments with zero-mean and dt variance. As discussed in Chapter 4, equation (6.1.1) has to be interpreted carefully to understand it better. Equation (6.1.1) is a SDE and also an Ito diffusion with the coefficients depending on the functions of space variables. It gives us the time evolution of the concentration of solute at a given point x which is denoted by subscript x . Obviously, the computation of C_x also depends on how the spatial derivatives of C_x are calculated. In that sense, equation (6.1.1) is a stochastic partial differential equation as the coefficients are functions of random quantities. But we avoid solving a SPDE by treating equation (6.1.1) as a SDE and interpreting it as an Ito integral which makes us to evaluate coefficients at the previous time point with respect to the current point of evaluation.

For simplicity, we will denote the coefficients as α_x and β_x. In Chapter 4, we have derived explicit function for α_x and β_x:

$$\alpha = C_x(t)F_{x,0} + \left(\frac{\partial C}{\partial x}\right)_x F_{x,1} + \left(\frac{\partial^2 C}{\partial x^2}\right)_x F_{x,2}. \tag{6.1.2}$$

Where

$$F_{x,0} = \frac{\partial \bar{V}(x,t)}{\partial x} + \frac{h_x}{2}\frac{\partial^2 \bar{V}(x,t)}{\partial x^2}, \tag{6.1.3}$$

$$F_{x,1} = \bar{V}(x,t) + h_x \frac{\partial \bar{V}(x,t)}{\partial x}, \tag{6.1.4}$$

and,

$$F_{x,3} = \frac{h_x}{2}\bar{V}(x,t); \tag{6.1.5}$$

$$\beta_x = \left(\beta_0^2 + \beta_1^2 + \beta_2^2\right)^{1/2}, \tag{6.1.6}$$

where,

$$\beta_0 = C_x(t)\sqrt{a_{00}}, \tag{6.1.7}$$

$$\beta_1 = \left(\frac{\partial C}{\partial x}\right)_x \sqrt{a_{11}}, \tag{6.1.8}$$

$$\beta_2 = \left(\frac{\partial^2 C}{\partial x^2}\right)_x \sqrt{a_{22}}, \tag{6.1.9}$$

and

$$a_{ii} = \sigma^2 \sum_{j=1}^{m} \lambda_j P_{ij}^2, \qquad (i,0,1,2), \tag{6.1.10}$$

In equation (6.1.10), σ^2 is the variance of the covariance kernel, λ_j are eigen functions, and for the domain of $x \in [0,1]$,

$$P_{0j}(x)=\left[g_{ij}-2\sum_{k=2}^{p_j}g_{kj}r_{kj}\left(x-s_{kj}\right)e^{-r_{kj}\left(x-s_{kj}\right)^2}\right]$$
$$+\left(\frac{h_x}{2}\right)\left[4\sum_{k=2}^{p_j}g_{kj}r_{kj}^2\left(x-s_{kj}\right)^2e^{-r_{kj}\left(x-s_{kj}\right)^2}-2\sum_{k=2}^{p_j}g_{kj}r_{kj}e^{-r_{kj}\left(x-s_{kj}\right)^2}\right], \quad (6.1.11)$$

$$P_{1j}(x)=g_{0j}+g_{1j}x+\sum_{k=2}^{p_j}g_{kj}e^{-r_{kj}\left(x-s_{kj}\right)^2}$$
$$+\left(\frac{h_x}{2}\right)\left[2\left(g_{ij}-2\sum_{k=2}^{p_j}g_{kj}r_{kj}\left(x-s_{kj}\right)e^{-r_{kj}\left(x-s_{kj}\right)^2}\right)\right], \quad (6.1.12)$$

and

$$P_{2j}(x)=\left(\frac{h_x}{2}\right)\left[g_{0j}+g_{1j}x+\sum_{k=2}^{p_j}g_{kj}e^{-r_{kj}\left(x-s_{kj}\right)^2}\right]. \quad (6.1.13)$$

Equation (6.1.1) to (6.1.13) constitute the Langevin form of the SSTM. It should be noted that the functions P_{ij} are only valid for $x\in[0,1]$. If we normalize the spatial variable x to remain with in $[0,1]$, then we can use the results in Chapter 4 to obtain P_{ij}. We develop the dimensionless Langevin form of the SSTM in section 6.2.

One should note that the Langevin equation for any system reflect the role of external noise to the system under consideration (van Kampen, 1992). Even though we have derived equation (6.1.1) starting from the mass conservation of solute particles, the fluctuations associate with hydrodynamics dispersion are a result of dissipation of energy of particles due to momentum changes associated near to the surfaces of porous medium. For α physical ensemble of solute particles, porous medium through which it flows act as an external source of noise. From this point of review, the Langevin type equation for solute concentration is justified. As a SDE, equation (6.1.1) is a Wiener process with stochastic, at best nonlinear, time-dependent coefficients, and it is also an Ito diffusion which should be interpreted locally, i.e., for a given x and t, equation (6.1.1) is valid only for short time intervals beyond t. This naturally leads us to evaluate the associated spatial derivatives at the previous time, which is valid according to Ito's interpretation of stochastic integral. In terms of discretized times, $t_0,t_1,...,t_i,t_{i+1},...,$ equation (6.1.1) can be written as,

$$dC_x(t)=C_x(t+1)-C_x(t)=\alpha_x\left(C_x(t_i),\bar{V}(x,t_i),\left(\frac{\partial\bar{V}}{\partial x}\right)_{t_i},\left(\frac{\partial^2\bar{V}}{\partial x^2}\right)_{t_i}\right)(t_{i+1}-t_i)$$
$$+(\beta_x)\left(C_x(t_i),\bar{V}(x,t_i),\left(\frac{\partial\bar{V}}{\partial x}\right)_{t_i},\left(\frac{\partial^2\bar{V}}{\partial x^2}\right)_{t_i}\right)d\omega(t_i) \quad (6.1.14)$$

where the drift coefficient, α_x, and the diffusion coefficient, β_x, are evaluated at time $=t_i$. This restrictive nature of equation (6.1.14) in evaluating the coefficient has to be taken in to account in developing numerical algorithms to solve it.

6.2 Partially Dimensionless SSTM with Flow Length L

We start the derivation of partially dimensionless SSTM by defining the dimensionless distance, Z, as:

$$Z = x/L \tag{6.2.1}$$

where L is the total flow length.

When $x \in [0,L]$, $Z \in [0,1]$.

If C_0 is a constant concentration defined such a way that $C_0 =$ maximum of $C_x(t)$ for all x and t, then $C_0 \geq C_x(t)$ for any t and x. We can define dimensional concentration $\Gamma(t)$ as,

$$\Gamma(t) = \frac{C_x}{C_0} \quad . \tag{6.2.2}$$

From equation (6.2.1),

$$\frac{\partial Z}{\partial x} = \frac{1}{L}, \tag{6.2.3a}$$

$$\frac{\partial C_x}{\partial x} = \frac{\partial(C_0\Gamma)}{\partial Z} \cdot \frac{\partial Z}{\partial x} = \frac{C_0}{L}\frac{\partial \Gamma}{\partial Z}, \tag{6.2.3b}$$

$$\frac{\partial^2 C_x}{\partial x^2} = \frac{\partial}{\partial x}\left(\frac{\partial C_x}{\partial x}\right) = \frac{\partial}{\partial x}\left(\frac{C_0}{L}\frac{\partial \Gamma}{\partial Z}\right) = \frac{\partial}{\partial Z}\left(\frac{C_0}{L}\frac{\partial \Gamma}{\partial Z}\right) \cdot \frac{\partial Z}{\partial x} = \frac{C_0}{L^2}\frac{\partial^2 \Gamma}{\partial Z^2}. \tag{6.2.3c}$$

As the domain of x is the generalized SSTM is from 0 to 1, we can replace x with Z in the dimensionless generalized SSTM. For example, $F_{x,0}$ becomes $F_{Z,0}$.

$$\begin{aligned} F_{Z,0} &= \frac{\partial \bar{V}(Z,t)}{\partial x} + \frac{h_Z}{2}\frac{\partial^2 \bar{V}(Z,t)}{\partial x^2} = \frac{\partial \bar{V}(Z,t)}{\partial Z} \cdot \frac{\partial Z}{\partial x} + \frac{h_Z}{2}\frac{\partial}{\partial x}\left(\frac{\partial \bar{V}}{\partial Z} \cdot \frac{\partial Z}{\partial x}\right) \\ &= \frac{1}{L}\frac{\partial \bar{V}}{\partial Z} + \frac{h_Z}{2L}\frac{\partial}{\partial Z}\left(\frac{\partial \bar{V}}{\partial Z}\right)\left(\frac{\partial Z}{\partial x}\right) = \frac{1}{L}\frac{\partial \bar{V}}{\partial Z} + \frac{h_Z}{2L^2}\frac{\partial^2 \bar{V}}{\partial Z^2}. \end{aligned} \tag{6.2.4}$$

Similarly,

$$F_{Z,1} = \bar{V}(Z,t) + \frac{h_Z}{L}\frac{\partial \bar{V}}{\partial Z}; \text{ and} \tag{6.2.5}$$

$$F_{Z,2} = \frac{h_Z}{2}\bar{V}(Z,t). \tag{6.2.6}$$

$P_{0j}(Z), P_{1j}(Z)$ and $P_{2j}(Z)$ are obtained by simply replacing x in $P_{0j}(x), P_{1j}(x)$ and $P_{2j}(x)$ expressions by Z, because these expressions are derived for $[0,1]$ domain.

Similarly,

$$\beta_0(Z) = C_0\Gamma(t)\sqrt{a_{00}(Z)} \tag{6.2.7}$$

$$\beta_1(Z) = \frac{C_0}{L}\frac{\partial\Gamma}{\partial Z}\sqrt{a_{11}(Z)}, \text{ and} \tag{6.2.8}$$

$$\beta_2(Z) = \frac{C_0}{L^2}\frac{\partial^2\Gamma}{\partial Z^2}\sqrt{a_{22}(Z)} \tag{6.2.9}$$

Now we can write equation (6.1.1) in the following manner:

$$d(C_0\Gamma) = -\alpha_Z(Z)dt + \beta_Z(Z)d\omega(t), \tag{6.2.10}$$

$$d\Gamma = \frac{-\alpha Z(Z)}{C_0}dt + \frac{\beta_Z(Z)}{C_0}d\omega(t). \tag{6.2.11}$$

where

$$\frac{\alpha_Z(Z)}{C_0} = \Gamma F_{Z,0} + \frac{1}{L}\frac{\partial\Gamma}{\partial Z}F_{Z,1} + \frac{1}{L^2}\frac{\partial^2\Gamma}{\partial Z^2}F_{Z,2}, \tag{6.2.12}$$

$$\frac{\beta_Z(Z)}{C_0} = \left\{\left(\Gamma^2 a_{00}(Z)\right) + \frac{1}{L^2}\left(\frac{\partial\Gamma}{\partial Z}\right)^2 a_{11}(Z) + \frac{1}{L^4}\left(\frac{\partial^2\Gamma}{\partial Z^2}\right)^2 a_{22}(Z)\right\}^{1/2} \tag{6.2.13}$$

Therefore, the Langevin form of the generalized SSTM is given by

$$d\Gamma = -\alpha_Z dt + \beta_Z d\omega(t), 0 \le Z \le 1. \tag{6.2.14}$$

where $\bar{\alpha}_Z = \frac{\alpha_Z(Z)}{C_0}$ and $\bar{\beta}_Z = \frac{\beta_Z(Z)}{C_0}$.

Using equation (6.2.14) we can compute the time course of the dimensionless concentration for any given L.

The dimensionless/concentration, Γ, varies from 0 to 1. $C_Z(t)$ is proportioned to the number of solute moles within a unit volume of porous/water matrix, and C_0 is proportional to the maximum possible number of solute moles within the same matrix. Therefore, $\Gamma = C_Z(t)/C_0$ can be interpreted as the likelihood (probability) of finding solute moles within the matrix.

It should be noted that time, t, is not a dimensionless quantity and therefore, equation (6.2.14) is partially dimensionless equation. We will explore the dispersivity using equation (6.2.14) first before discussing a completely dimensionless equation.

6.3 Computational Exploration of the Langevin form of SSTM

Equation (6.2.14) is not only an expression of how the solute disperses within a porous media but also an expression of nature of dispersion. Being a SDE, the drift coefficient $(\bar{\alpha}_Z)$ portrays the dispersion due to the convective forces and the diffusive coefficient $(\bar{\beta}_Z)$ shows the dynamical behaviour of hydrodynamic dispersion. As Z has the range from 0 to 1 in equation (6.2.14), we can compute α_Z and β_Z values for a specific Z value and examine how they change over time. (We use $C_0 = 1.0$ for computations, and therefore, $\bar{\alpha}_Z = \alpha_Z$ and $\bar{\beta}_Z = \beta_Z$.) We have developed a finite difference algorithm to compute α_Z and β_Z adhering to the Ito integration as we have done before. Figure 6.1a and 6.1b show the time courses of $-\alpha_Z$ and β_Z at $Z = 0.5$, respectively, for different σ^2 values when $L = 1m$ (All times are given in days and $b = 0.1$. At low σ^2 values, $-\alpha_Z$ behaves almost as a smooth deterministic function but at high σ^2 values it shows irregular behaviours. In these calculations, we have kept the mean velocity $\bar{V}$ at a constant value (0.5), therefore only fluctuating component affecting α_Z function is the solute concentration and its spatial derivatives. Further, Figure 6.1a and 6.1b only show a single realization for each σ^2 values. When we explore multiple realizations (not shown here), we see that randomness of α_Z and β_Z increases with higher σ^2. One distinct feature of Figure 6.1b for β_Z is that β_Z is almost negligible for very small values of σ^2 but increases quite sharply for higher σ^2 values. α_Z does not behave in this manner. However, we can not ignore the effect of σ^2 at low values in computing $\Gamma(Z)$, which has a follow-on affect on subsequent calculation. In other words, the affects of porous media, which σ^2 and the covariance kernel signify, can not be ignored as they affect the flow velocities significantly in making them stochastic. Figure 6.2a and 6.2b show $-\alpha_Z$ and β_Z realization at $Z = 0.5$ when $L = 5m$. The behaviours of $-\alpha_Z$ and β_Z realizations are similar to those shown in Figures 6.1a and 6.1b. Figure 6.3a and Figure 6.3b show the similar trends for $L = 10m$. It should be noted that as L is increased, the time duration for the numerical solution of equation (6.2.14) should be increased. For example, when $L = 10m$, the model was run for 25 days to obtain Figures 6.3a and 6.3b. However, the order of magnitude for α_Z and β_Z has not changed as we change L in an order of magnitude.

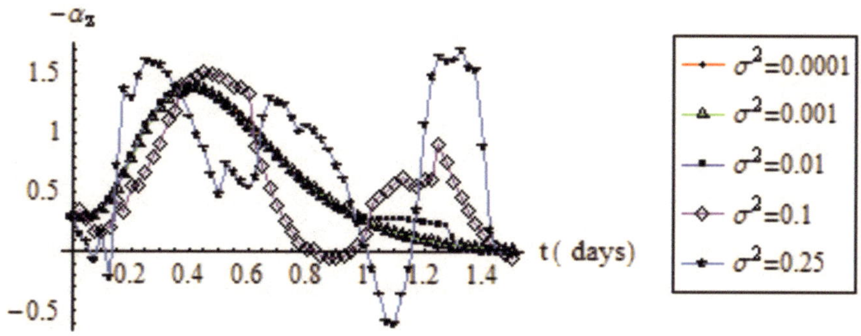

(a)

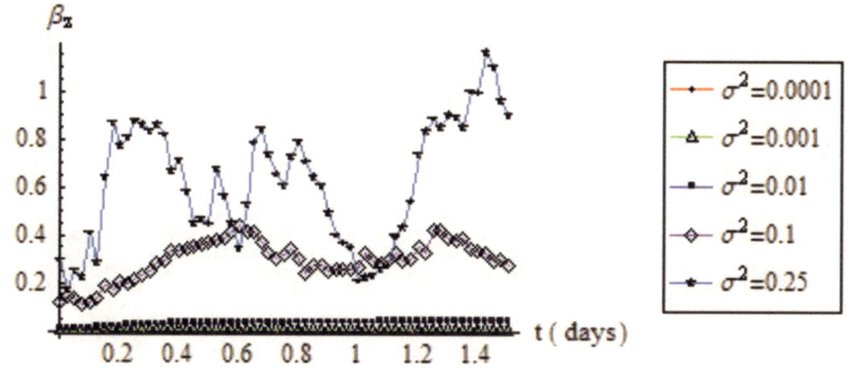

(b)

Figure 6.1. (a) Realizations of $-\alpha_Z$ at $Z=0.5$ when $L=1m$, $b=0.1$ and $\bar{V}=0.5m/day$ for different σ^2 values; (b) Realizations of β_Z at $Z=0.5$ when $L=1m$, $b=0.1$ and $\bar{V}=0.5m/day$ for different σ^2 values.

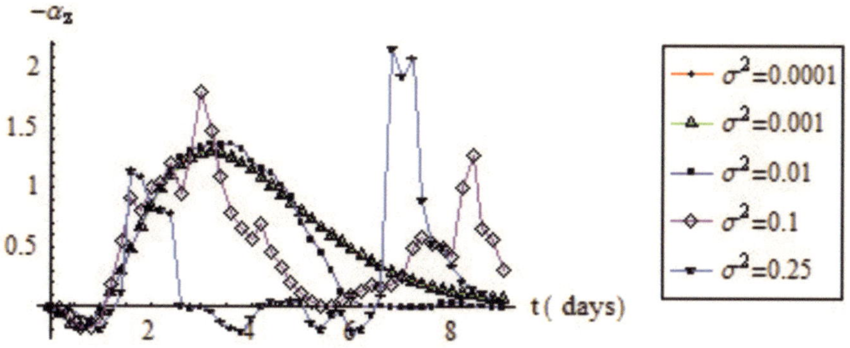

(a)

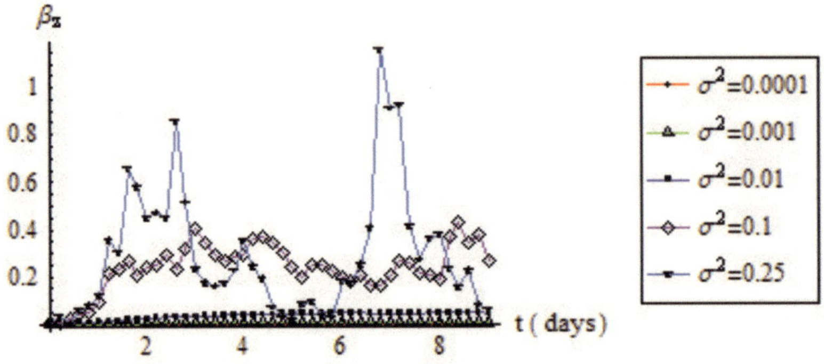

(b)

Figure 6.2. (a) Realizations of $-\alpha_Z$ at $Z = 0.5$ when $L = 5m$, $b = 0.1$ and $\bar{V} = 0.5\,m\,/\,day$ for different σ^2 values; (b) Realizations of β_Z at $Z = 0.5$ when $L = 5m$, $b = 0.1$ and $\bar{V} = 0.5\,m\,/\,day$ for different σ^2 values.

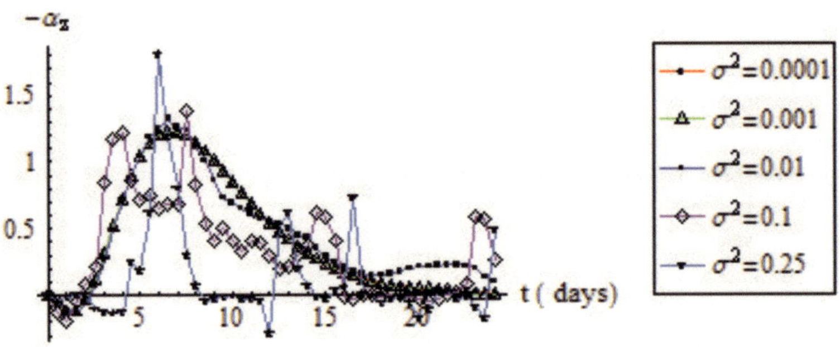

(a)

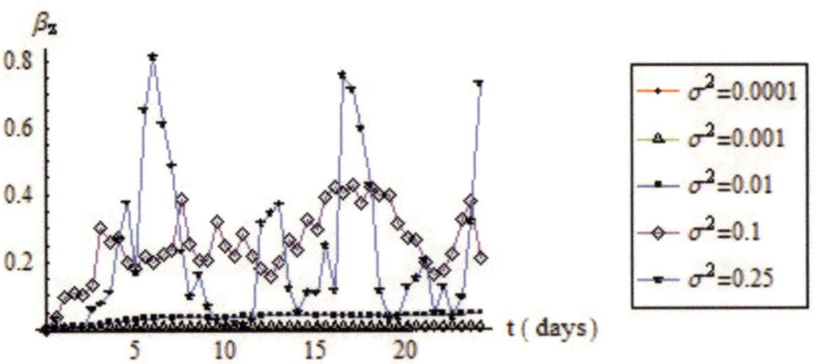

(b)

Figure 6.3. (a) Realizations of $-\alpha_Z$ at $Z = 0.5$ when $L = 10$ m, b = 0.1 and $\bar{V}$ =0.5 m/day for different σ^2 values; (b) Realizations of β_Z at $Z = 0.5$ when $L = 10$ m, b = 0.1 and $\bar{V}$ =0.5 m/day for different σ^2 values.

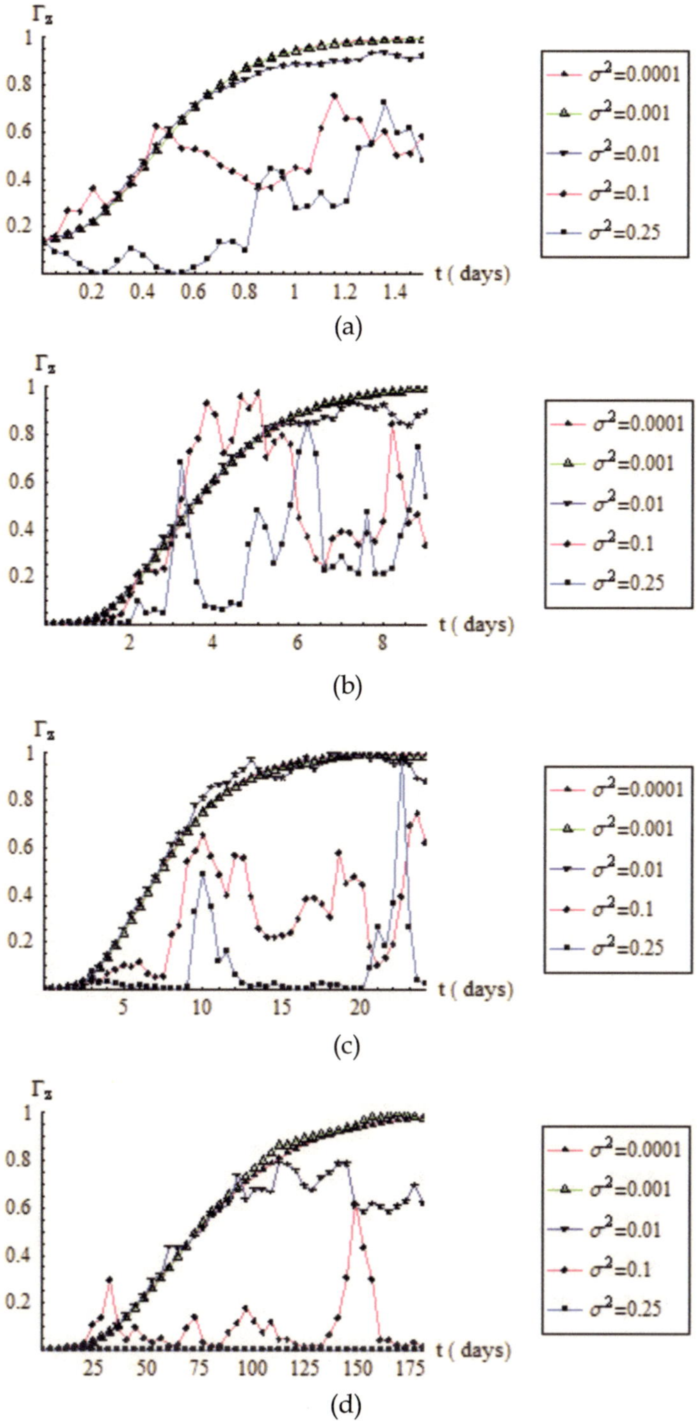

Figure 6.4. Realizations of Γ_Z at $Z = 0.5$ when b = 0.1, $\bar{V}$ =0.5 for (a) $L = 1$, (b) $L = 5$, (c) $L = 10$ and (d) $L = 100$

Figure 6.4a, 6.4b, 6.4c, and 6.4d show the realization of $\Gamma(Z)$ at $Z=0.5$ when $L=1,5,10,$ and 100, respectively, for different values of σ^2. (For all the calculations, we have used b = 0.1). When $L=100$ m, we computed $\Gamma(Z)$ values for 175 days and the affects of σ^2 on $\Gamma(Z)$ is quite dramatic, and this shows that equation (6.2.14) can display very complex behaviour patterns albeit its simplicity. It should be noted however that σ^2 plays major role in delimiting the nature of realizations; σ^2 values high than 0.25 in these situations produces highly irregular concentration realizations which could occur in highly heterogeneous porous formations such as fractured formations.

6.4 Dispersivities Based on the Langevin Form of SSTM for $L \le 10$ m

One of the advantages of the partially dimensionless Langevin equation for the SSTM (equation 6.2.14) is that we can use it to compute the solute concentration profiles when the travel length (L) is large. Equation (6.2.14) allows us to compute the dispersitivities using the stochastic inverse method (SIM) by estimating dispersivity for each realization of $\Gamma(Z)$. For the SIM, we need to modify the deterministic-advection and dispersion equation into a partially dimensionless one. We start with the deterministic advection-dispersion equation with additive Gaussian noise,

$$\frac{\partial C}{\partial t} = D_L \frac{\partial^2 C}{\partial x^2} - V_x \frac{\partial C}{\partial x} + \xi(x,t), \tag{6.4.1}$$

where D_L is the dispersion coefficient (dispersivity $\times V_x$).

The partially dimensionless form of equation (6.4.1) is,

$$\frac{\partial \Gamma}{\partial t} = \frac{D_L}{L^2}\frac{\partial^2 \Gamma}{\partial Z^2} - \frac{V_x}{L}\frac{\partial \Gamma}{\partial Z} + \xi(Z,t), \tag{6.4.2}$$

where $\frac{D_L}{L^2}$ is now estimated using SIM when V_x is known. Then the dispersivity value is (estimated $\frac{D_L}{L^2}$) $\times L^2 / V_x$.

Figure 6.5 show the scatter plots of dispersivity values estimated using the SIM for $L=1,5,$ and 10 m. Each plot in Figure 6.5 gives 30 estimates of the dispersivity for a given value σ^2. $\Gamma(Z)$ realizations were computed at $Z=0.5$ and $b=0.1$ for all plots. Table 6.1 summarizes the results giving the mean of each plot. We will compare these results with available data for dispersivities later in this chapter.

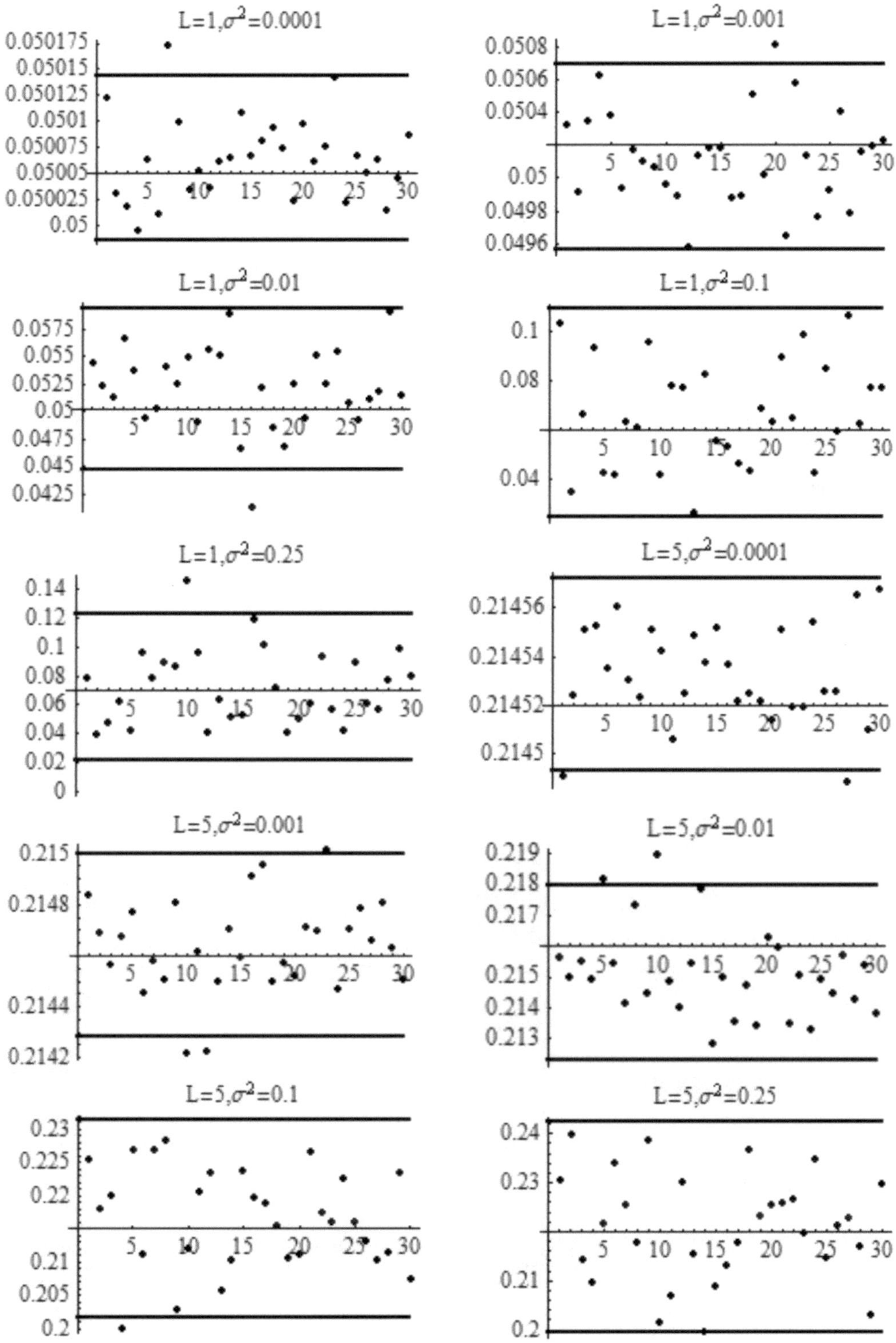
L=1,σ²=0.0001
0.050175
0.05015
0.050125
0.0501
0.050075
0.05005
0.050025
0.05
5 10 15 20 25 30
L=1,σ²=0.001
0.0508
0.0506
0.0504
0.05
0.0498
0.0496
5 10 15 20 25 30
L=1,σ²=0.01
0.0575
0.055
0.0525
0.05
0.0475
0.045
0.0425
5 10 15 20 25 30
L=1,σ²=0.1
0.1
0.08
0.04
5 10 15 20 25 30
L=1,σ²=0.25
0.14
0.12
0.1
0.08
0.06
0.04
0.02
0
5 10 15 20 25 30
L=5,σ²=0.0001
0.21456
0.21454
0.21452
0.2145
5 10 15 20 25 30
L=5,σ²=0.001
0.215
0.2148
0.2144
0.2142
5 10 15 20 25 30
L=5,σ²=0.01
0.219
0.218
0.217
0.215
0.214
0.213
5 10 15 20 25 30
L=5,σ²=0.1
0.23
0.225
0.22
0.21
0.205
0.2
5 10 15 20 25 30
L=5,σ²=0.25
0.24
0.23
0.21
0.2
5 10 15 20 25 30

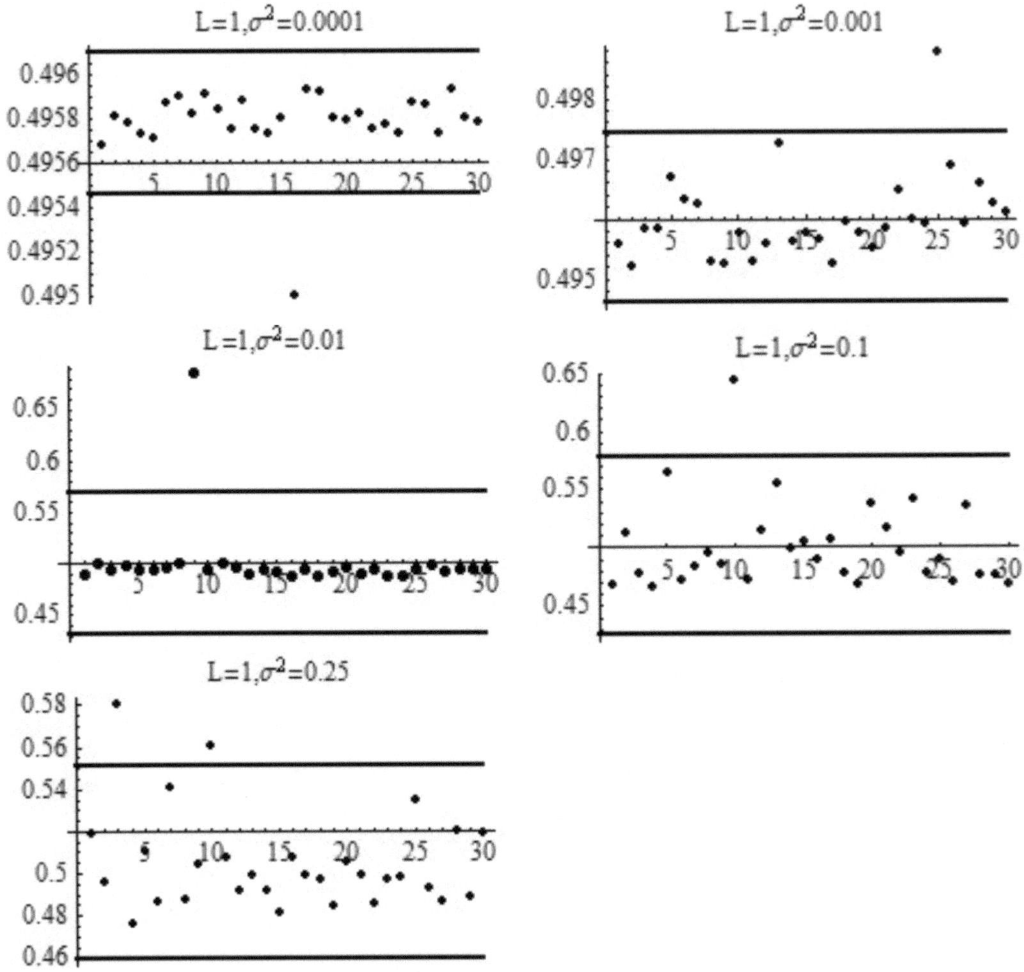

Figure 6.5. Dispersivities estimated from SSTM for $L = 1, 5$, and 10.

σ^2	Dispersivity		
	L=1	L=5	L=10
0.0001	0.050064	0.050112	0.0495545
0.001	0.0501232	0.05082	0.0511587
0.01	0.0520638	0.0604215	0.0778382
0.1	0.0669766	0.0832735	0.11899
0.25	0.0723413	0.111142	0.253195
0.4	0.0783754	0.142422	0.354335
0.6	0.0843219	0.170975	0.427603
0.8	0.0962623	0.225344	0.549473
1	0.110849	0.256348	0.609508

Table 6.1. Mean dispersivities for the data in Figure 6.5.

As mentioned previously, the partially dimensionless equation (6.2.14) still requires us to compute for a large number of days when L is large. While the computational times are still manageable, we would like to develop a completely dimensionless Langevin equation for the SSTM. This could be especially useful and insightful when the mean velocity $\bar{V}$ could be considered as a constant.

6.5 Dimensionless Time

We introduce dimensionless time, θ, as,

$$\theta = \bar{V}(Z,t).\frac{t}{L}, \tag{6.5.1}$$

where, $\bar{V}(Z,t)$ is mean velocity when $0 \le Z \le 1$, (m/day); L is travel length, m; and t is time in days.

Therefore, if $\bar{V} = 0.5$, $L = 100$ and $0 \le t \le 200$, then, $0 \le \theta \le 1.0$. This allows us to compute $\Gamma(Z)$ realization for larger times.

Equation (6.2.14) can be written as,

$$\Gamma(Z) = -\alpha_Z dt + \beta_z d\omega(t).$$

We can now change $dt = \frac{L}{\bar{V}} d\theta$, and the variance of $d\omega(t) = \Delta t = \frac{L}{\bar{V}} \Delta\theta$.

Therefore,

$$\Gamma(Z) = \frac{-\alpha_Z L}{\bar{V}} d\theta + \beta_z d\omega(t), \tag{6.5.2}$$

where $dw(\theta) \sim \mathrm{N}\left(0, \frac{L}{\bar{V}} d\theta\right)$.

The completely dimentionless Langevin form of the SSTM is therefore,

$$\Gamma(Z) = \alpha_{Z,\theta} d\theta + \beta_z d\omega(\theta), \tag{6.5.3}$$

where $d\omega(\theta)$ are the Wiener increment with zero-mean and $\frac{L}{\bar{V}} d\theta$ variance, and

$$\alpha_{Z,\theta} = \frac{-\alpha_Z L}{\bar{V}}. \tag{6.5.4}$$

To use equation (6.5.3), we need to choose $\Delta\theta$ and the range of θ appropriately. Ideally $\frac{L}{\bar{V}} d\theta < 0.0001$ for the Ito integration to be accurate; therefore, we should have for maximum $\Delta\theta$ as $\frac{0.0001\bar{V}}{L}$. Suppose $\bar{V} = 0.5, L = 1000$, then $\Delta\theta < \frac{10^{-4} \times 0.5}{1000}$, i.e, $\Delta\theta < 5 \times 10^{-8}$.

As we can see we may not gain much computational advantage with a completely dimensionless Langevin form of the SSTM.

6.6 Estimation of Field Scale Dispersivities

We have estimated the longitudinal dispersivities using SSTM for two different boundary conditions:

(A) $\Gamma_Z = 1$ at $Z = 0$ and for $t \geq 0$; and

(B) $\Gamma_Z = 1$ at $Z = 0$ and for $0 \leq t \leq t_R$, ; and $\Gamma_Z = 0$ at Z=0 for $t > t_R$.

t_R is taken to be 1/3 of the total time (*T*) of the computational experiment. Table 6.1 and 6.2 show the dispersivity values for the boundary conditions A and B, respectively, when $L \leq 10$ m based on 100 realisations for each of the boundary condition.

σ^2	Dispersivity		
	L=1	L=5	L=10
0.0001	0.050013	0.050013	0.049828
0.001	0.050035	0.050223	0.050226
0.01	0.050646	0.055152	0.06112
0.1	0.055176	0.079403	0.136904
0.25	0.068846	0.108899	0.257902
0.4	0.083342	0.16346	0.333472
0.6	0.093185	0.191919	0.334818
0.8	0.109335	0.251033	0.54346
1	0.129395	0.331389	0.613823

Table 6.2. Longitudinal dispersivities (mean) for the boundary condition A.

The values in Table 6.1 and 6.2 are similar for the similar values of σ^2 and L showing that (1) the SSTM procedure is robust in evaluating the dispersivities, and (2) the computed mean dispersivities do not depend on the boundary conditions, A and B. In these calculations, we have $\bar{V}_Z = 0.5$ m/day.

We have also computed the dispersivities for larger scales up to 10,000 m, and Table 6.3 gives the mean values for the range of L from 1 m to 10^4 m under the boundary condition A, and Table 6.4 gives the mean values for the range of *L* from 1 m to 10^8 m for the boundary condition B. All mean values are calculated based on different sets of 100 realisations for each boundary condition. Except for the smallest σ^2 values (0.0001 and 0.001), the dispersivities have similar mean values for both boundary conditions, A and B. Therefore, it is quite reasonable to compute the dispersivities only for the boundary condition A for larger values of *L*. We can also hypothesise that the dispersivities are independent of the boundary conditions used to solve the SSTM. We have tested the SSTM for different values of t_R > (1/3) *T* when *L*>10 m. Figure 6.6 depicts the dispersivity plotted against σ^2 and *L* in Log10 scale, and Log10 (Dispersivity) is a linear function of Log10(*L*) and Log10(σ^2) for the most parts of the Log10 (Dispersivity) surface. Figure 6.7 shows the linear relationship of Log10 (Dispersivity) vs Log10 (L) for different values of σ^2, and Figure 6.8 shows the same for Log10 (Dispersivity) vs Log10(σ^2) for different values of L. The gradient of the graphs are the same except for lower values of σ^2 (0.0001) and lower values of L (1 and 5). Therefore, we develop the following statistical nonlinear regression models for these significant relationships:

$$D_s = C_1\left(\sigma^2\right)^{m1}, \text{ and} \tag{6.6.1}$$

$$D_s = C_2\left(L\right)^{m2}, \tag{6.6.2}$$

where D_s is the dispersivity, and C_1 and C_2 are given in Tables 6.5 and 6.6 , respectively, along with $m1$ and $m2$ values. R-square values for equations (6.6.1) and (6.6.2) are 0.96 and 0.94, respectively.

σ^2	Dispersivity					
	L=1	L=5	L=10	L=50	L=100	L=500
0.0001	0.0498	0.0500	0.0497	0.0498	0.0507	0.0686
0.001	0.0498	0.0499	0.0495	0.0477	0.0639	0.4982
0.01	0.0492	0.0510	0.0511	0.1642	0.5073	4.0672
0.1	0.0449	0.0592	0.1372	0.9309	2.9601	28.6151
0.25	0.0451	0.1123	0.2391	2.5441	6.1225	40.5301
0.4	0.0573	0.1340	0.3413	3.4365	8.1834	48.7567
0.6	0.0784	0.1824	0.4619	4.9440	10.9837	64.7589
0.8	0.0958	0.1987	0.7057	6.6800	14.9122	82.4423
1	0.1247	0.2159	0.8102	8.9878	19.9003	112.5246
	L=1000	L=2000	L=4000	L=6000	L=8000	L=10000
0.0001	0.2697	0.7964	2.0630	4.1138	5.9939	8.1065
0.001	2.5154	7.2616	20.5460	32.6517	45.9978	69.0446
0.01	12.6500	30.0361	81.0270	155.2103	231.3154	324.3036
0.1	70.0564	156.8923	333.6665	523.4295	708.0212	903.6889
0.25	87.8303	185.7131	381.1019	569.9892	766.8287	978.5914
0.4	101.1441	203.0552	425.5467	625.6709	866.0189	1061.9651
0.6	131.0882	259.4990	528.0956	828.7496	1079.0040	1355.8468
0.8	173.1833	344.9935	691.7747	1070.9582	1399.5126	1771.3449
1	227.3204	453.3977	925.0844	1396.8663	1864.1378	2337.5588

Table 6.3. Longitudinal dispersivities (mean) for the range of L from 1 m to 10^4 m under the boundary condition A

σ^2	Dispersivity						
	L=1	L=5	L=10	L=50	L=100	L=500	L=1000
0.0001	0.0498	0.0500	0.0497	0.0498	0.0507	0.0686	0.1426
0.001	0.0498	0.0499	0.0495	0.0477	0.0639	0.4982	1.4690
0.01	0.0492	0.0510	0.0511	0.1642	0.5073	4.0672	12.0999
0.1	0.0449	0.0592	0.1372	0.9309	2.9601	28.6151	69.2489
0.25	0.0451	0.1123	0.2391	2.5441	6.1225	40.5301	87.0760
0.4	0.0573	0.1340	0.3413	3.4365	8.1834	48.7567	100.6075
0.6	0.0784	0.1824	0.4619	4.9440	10.9837	64.7589	132.1320
0.8	0.0958	0.1987	0.7057	6.6800	14.9122	82.4423	173.1823
1	0.1247	0.2159	0.8102	8.9878	19.9003	112.5246	221.6737

Table 6.4. Longitudinal dispersivities (mean) for the range of L from 1 m to 10^8 m under the boundary condition B

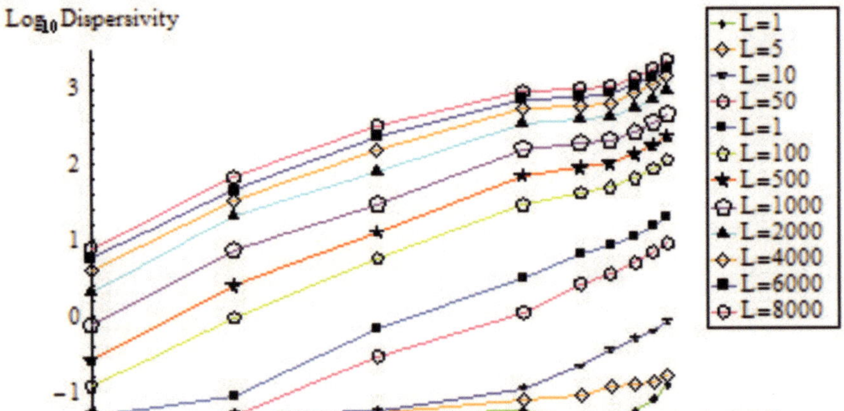

Figure 6.6. The linear relationship of Log10 (Dispersivity) vs Log10 (σ^2) for different values of L.

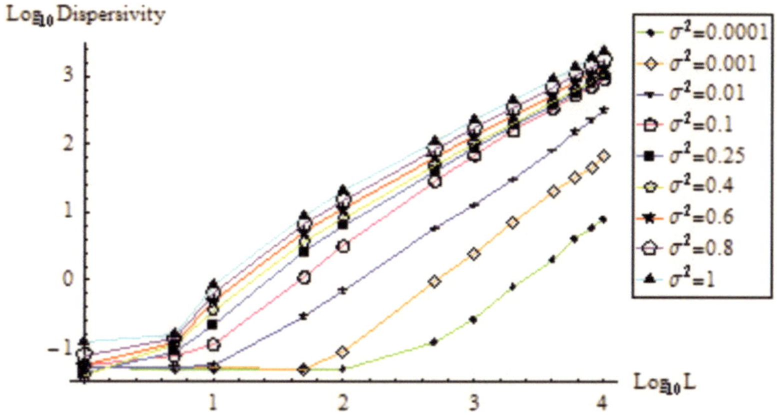

Figure 6.7. The linear relationship of Log10 (Dispersivity) vs Log10 (L) for different values of σ^2.

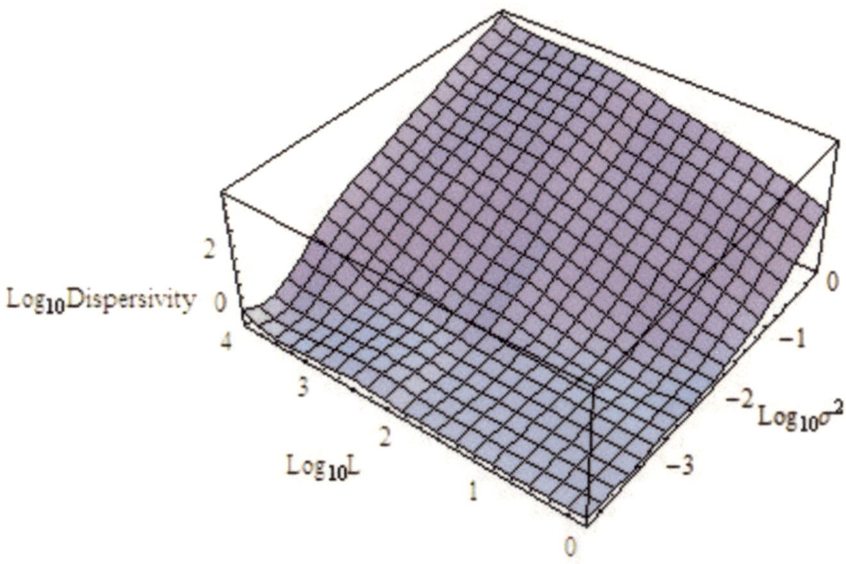

Figure 6.8. The plot of Log10 (Dispersivity) vs Log10 (σ^2) and Log10 (L)

L (m)	**1**	**5**	**10**	**50**	**100**	**500**
m1	0.039	0.125	0.311	0.605	0.677	0.704
C_1	0.063	0.124	0.468	6.275	16.23	109.6
L (m)	**1000**	**2000**	**4000**	**6000**	**8000**	**10000**
m1	0.690	0.642	0.605	0.578	0.567	0.552
C_1	229.5	451.3	912.4	1368.7	1823.1	2281.4

Table 6.5. $m1$ and C_1 values for different L for equation (6.6.1).

σ^2	**0.0001**	**0.001**	**0.01**	**0.1**	**0.25**	**0.4**	**0.6**	**0.8**	**1.0**
m2	0.589	0.897	1.067	1.150	1.148	1.148	1.148	1.148	1.144
C_2	0.0122	0.0078	0.0103	0.0168	0.0242	0.0311	0.0409	0.0535	0.0725

Table 6.6. *m2* and C_2 values for different σ^2 for equation (6.6.2).

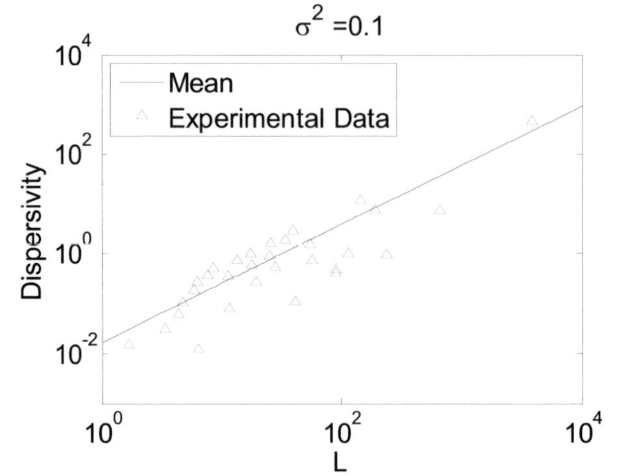

Figure 6.9. Mean dispersivity from the SSTM and experimental dispersivity vs flow length (log10 scale).

We can estimate the approximate dispersivity values either from Figures 6.7 and 6.8, or from equations (6.6.1) and (6.6.2). It is quite logical to ask the question whether we can characterise the large scale aquifer dispersivities using a single value of σ^2? To answer this question, we resort to the published dispersivity values for aquifers. We use the dispersivity data first published by Gelhar et al. (1992) and reported to Batu (2006). We extracted the tracer tests data related to porous aquifers in 59 different locations characterised by different geologic materials. The longest flow length was less than 10000 m. We then plotted the experimental data and overlaid the plot with the dispersivity vs *L* curves from the SSTM for each σ^2 value. Figure 6.9 shows the plots, and σ^2 =0.1 best fit to the experimental data. In other words, by using one value of σ^2, we can obtain the dispersivity for any length of the flow by using the SSTM. We can also assume that each experimental data point represents the mean dispersivity for any length of the flow by using the SSTM. We can also assume that each experimental data point represents the mean dispersivity at a particular flow length. If that is the case, Figure 6.9 can be interpreted as follows: by using the SSTM, we can obtain sufficiently large number of realisations for particular values of σ^2 and the mean flow velocity, and the mean values of the dispersivities estimated for those concentration realisations do represent the experimental dispersivities. σ^2 can be hypothesised to indicate the type of media (e.g. fractured, porous etc.). These findings support the hypothesis that the dimensionless SSTM is scale-independent, i.e., one value of σ^2 would be sufficient to characterise the dispersivity at different flow lengths. It is important to note that the role of the mean velocity in these calculations. We used 0.5 m/day to represent an indicative value in real aquifers, but the character of solutions do not change, if we assume a different value; only the specific values of σ^2 would be changed to represent a given flow situation.

7

The Stochastic Solute Transport Model in 2-Dimensions

7.1 Introduction

In Chapter 6, we developed the generalised Stochastic Solute Transport Model (SSTM) in 1-dimension and showed that it can model the hydrodynamic dispersion in porous media for the flow lengths ranging from 1 to 10000 m. For computational efficiency, we have employed one of the fastest converging kernels tested in Chapter 6 for illustrative purposes, but, in principle, the SSTM should provide scale independent behaviour for any other velocity covariance kernel. If the kernel is developed based on the field data, then the SSTM based on that particular kernel should give realistic outputs from the model for that particular porous medium. In the development of the SSTM, we assumed that the hydrodynamic dispersion is one dimensional but by its very nature, the dispersion lateral to the flow direction occurs. We intend to explore this aspect in this chapter.

First, we solve the integral equation with the covariance kernel in two dimensions, and use the eigen values and functions thus obtained in developing the two dimensional stochastic solute transport model (SSTM2d). Then we solve the SSTM2d numerically using a finite difference scheme. In the last section of the chapter, we illustrate the behaviours of the SSTM2d graphically to show the robustness of the solution.

7.2 Solving the Integral Equation

We consider the flow direction to be x and the coordinate perpendicular to x to be y in the 2 dimensional flow with in the porous matrix saturated with water. Then the distance between the points (x_1,y_1) and (x_2,y_2), r, is given by $\left[(x_1-x_2)^2+(y_1-y_2)^2\right]^{1/2}$. We can then define a velocity covariance kernel as follows:

$$q(x_1,y_1,x_2,y_2)=\sigma^2 \exp\left[-\frac{r^2}{b}\right], \tag{7.2.1}$$

where σ^2 is a constant. σ^2 is the variance at a given point, i.e., when $x_1=x_2$ and $y_1=y_2$. The covariance can be written as,

$$\begin{aligned} q(x_1,y_1,x_2,y_2)&=\sigma^2 \exp\left[-\frac{\left[(x_1-x_2)^2+(y_1-y_2)^2\right]}{b}\right], \\ &=\sigma^2 \exp\left[-\frac{(x_1-x_2)^2}{b}\right]\exp\left[-\frac{(y_1-y_2)^2}{b}\right]. \end{aligned} \tag{7.2.2}$$

Then the integral equation can be written for 2 dimensions,

$$\sigma^2 \int_0^1\int_0^1 \exp\left[-\frac{(x_1-x_2)^2}{b}\right]\exp\left[-\frac{(y_1-y_2)^2}{b}\right] f(x_2,y_2)dx_2dy_2 = \lambda f(x_1,y_1), \quad (7.2.3)$$

where $f(x,y)$ and λ are eigen functions and corresponding eigen values, respectively.

The covariance kernel is the multiplication of a function of x and a function of y, and from the symmetry of equation (7.2.3), we can assume that the eigen function is the multiplication of a function of x and a function of y:

$$f(x,y) = f_x(x) f_y(y). \quad (7.2.4)$$

Then the integral equation can be written as,

$$\sigma^2 \int_0^1\int_0^1 \left(f_x e^{-\frac{(x_1-x_2)^2}{b}} dx_2 \right)\left(f_y e^{-\frac{(y_1-y_2)^2}{b}} dy_2 \right) = \lambda f_x f_y$$

, and

$$\left\{\int_0^1 \left(f_x e^{-\frac{(x_1-x_2)^2}{b}} dx_2 \right)\right\}\left\{\int_0^1 \left(f_y e^{-\frac{(y_1-y_2)^2}{b}} dy_2 \right)\right\} = \frac{\lambda}{\sigma^2} f_x f_y \quad . \quad (7.2.5)$$

Therefore, if

$$\int_0^1 f_x e^{-\frac{(x_1-x_2)^2}{b}} dx_2 = \lambda_x f_x(x_1), \text{ and}$$

$$\int_0^1 f_y e^{-\frac{(y_1-y_2)^2}{b}} dy_2 = \lambda_y f_y(y_1)$$

Then we can see, $f(x,y) = f_x f_y$, and $\lambda = \sigma^2 \lambda_x \lambda_y$.

This shows that we can use the eigen functions and eigen values obtained for 1-dimensional covariance kernels in Chapter 4 can be used in constructing the eigen functions and eigen values for two dimensional covariance kernel given in equation (7.2.2). Once we have obtained eigen functions and eigen values as solutions of the integral equation, we can derive the two dimensional mass conservation equation for solutes.

7.3 Derivation of Mass Conservation Equation

Consider the two dimensional infinitesimal volume element depicted in Figure 7.1. We can write the mass balance for solutes with in the element as,

$$\Delta C(x,y,t) n_e l\,\Delta x\,\Delta y = \left\{J_x(x,y,t) - J_x(x+\Delta x,y,t)\right\} l\,\Delta y\, n_e \Delta t + \left\{J_y(x,y,t) - J_y(x,,y+\Delta y,t)\right\} l\,\Delta x\, n_e \Delta t$$

$$\text{and} \quad \frac{\Delta C(x,y,t)}{\Delta t} = \frac{(J_x - J_{x+\Delta x})}{\Delta x} + \frac{(J_y - J_{y+\Delta y})}{\Delta y}, \tag{7.3.1}$$

where $C(x,y,t)$ is the solute concentration and J represents the solute flux at the location indicated by a subscript. We can expand J using Taylor expansions as follows:

$$J_{x+\Delta x} - J_x = \frac{1}{1!}\frac{\partial J_x}{\partial x}\Delta x + \frac{1}{2!}\frac{\partial^2 J_x}{\partial x^2}(\Delta x)^2 + \frac{1}{3!}\frac{\partial^3 J_x}{\partial x^3}(\Delta x)^3 + \text{ higher order terms, and}$$

$$J_{y+\Delta y} - J_y = \frac{1}{1!}\frac{\partial J_y}{\partial y}\Delta y + \frac{1}{2!}\frac{\partial^2 J_y}{\partial y^2}(\Delta y)^2 + \frac{1}{3!}\frac{\partial^3 J_y}{\partial y^3}(\Delta y)^3 + \text{ higher order terms.}$$

Lumping the higher order terms greater than 2, and denoting R_x and R_y as the remainders of the series,

$$J_{x+\Delta x} - J_x = \frac{\partial J_x}{\partial x}\Delta x + \frac{1}{2!}\frac{\partial^2 J_x}{\partial x^2}(\Delta x)^2 + R_x(\varepsilon), \text{ and} \tag{7.3.2a}$$

$$J_{y+\Delta y} - J_y = \frac{\partial J_y}{\partial y}\Delta y + \frac{1}{2!}\frac{\partial^2 J_y}{\partial y^2}(\Delta y)^2 + R_y(\varepsilon). \tag{7.3.2b}$$

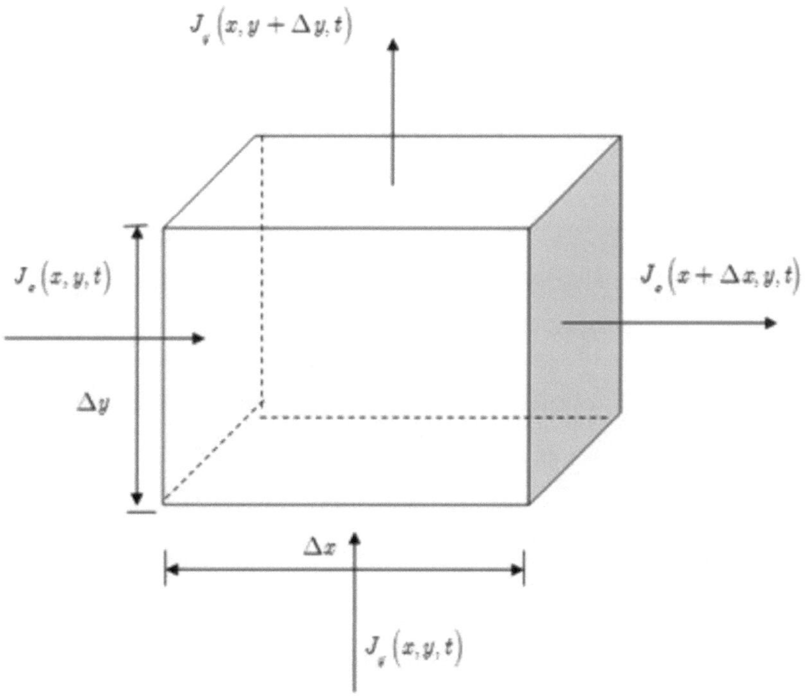

Figure 7.1. Two dimensional infinitesimal volume element with a depth l and porosity n_e. Δx and Δy are side lengths in x and y directions, respectively.

Substituting equations (7.3.2a) and (7.3.2b) back to equation (7.3.1) and taking the limit $\Delta t \to 0$,

$$\begin{aligned}\frac{\partial C(x,y,t)}{\partial t} &= -\frac{\partial J_x}{\partial x} - \frac{1}{2}\frac{\partial^2 J_x}{\partial x^2}\Delta x - \frac{\partial J_y}{\partial y} - \frac{1}{2}\frac{\partial^2 J_y}{\partial y^2}\Delta y + R_x^{'}(\varepsilon) \\ &= -\left(\frac{\partial J_x}{\partial x} + \frac{\partial J_y}{\partial y}\right) - \frac{h_x}{2}\left(\frac{\partial^2 J_x}{\partial x^2}\right) - \frac{h_y}{2}\left(\frac{\partial^2 J_y}{\partial y^2}\right) + R_x^{'}(\varepsilon) + R_y^{'}(\varepsilon)\end{aligned}, \tag{7.3.3}$$

where $h_x = \Delta x$ and $h_y = \Delta y$.

$$dC = -\left[\frac{\partial J_x}{\partial x} + \frac{h_x}{2}\frac{\partial^2 J_x}{\partial x^2}\right]dt - \left[\frac{\partial J_y}{\partial y} + \frac{h_y}{2}\frac{\partial^2 J_y}{\partial y^2}\right]dt + \left(R_x^{'}(\varepsilon) + R_y^{'}(\varepsilon)\right)dt.$$

Assuming $\left(R_x^{'}(\varepsilon) + R_y^{'}(\varepsilon)\right)dt \approx 0$,

$$dC(x,y,t) = -\left[\frac{\partial J_x}{\partial x} + \frac{h_x}{2}\frac{\partial^2 J_x}{\partial x^2}\right]dt - \left[\frac{\partial J_y}{\partial y} + \frac{h_y}{2}\frac{\partial^2 J_y}{\partial y^2}\right]dt . \tag{7.3.4}$$

Now we can express the solute flux in terms of solute concentration and velocity,

$$J_x(x,y,t) = V_x(x,y,t)C(x,y,t), \text{ and} \tag{7.3.5a}$$

$$J_y(x,y,t) = V_y(x,y,t)C(x,y,t). \tag{7.3.5b}$$

We can express the velocity in terms of the mean velocity vector and a noise vector,

$$\underline{V}(x,y,t) = \overline{\underline{V}}(x,y,t) + \underline{\xi}(x,y,t), \tag{7.3.6}$$

where $\underline{V}(x,y,t)$, $\overline{\underline{V}}(x,y,t)$ and $\underline{\xi}(x,y,t)$ are velocity, mean velocity and noise vectors respectively. Instantaneous velocity vector can now be expressed as,

$$\underline{V}(x,y,t) = V_x(x,y,t)\underline{i} + V_y(x,y,t)\underline{j}, \tag{7.3.7}$$

where $\underline{i}$ and $\underline{j}$ are unit vectors in x and y directions, respectively; and, $V_x(x,y,t)$ and $V_y(x,y,t)$ are the magnitudes of the velocities in x and y directions. By substituting the vector components in equation (7.3.6) in to equation (7.3.7), we obtain,

$$\begin{aligned}\underline{V}(x,y,t) &= \left(\overline{V}_x(x,y,t) + \xi_x(x,y,t)\right)\underline{i} + \left(\overline{V}_y(x,y,t) + \xi_y(x,y,t)\right)\underline{j} \\ &= \left(\overline{V}_x\underline{i} + \overline{V}_y\underline{j}\right) + \left(\xi_x(x,y,t)\underline{i} + \xi_y(x,y,t)\underline{j}\right)\end{aligned}, \tag{7.3.8}$$

where ξ_x and ξ_y are the noise components in x and y directions. We can see the noise term appearing as, $\left(\xi_x(x,y,t)\underline{i} + \xi_y(x,y,t)\underline{j}\right) = \underline{\xi}(x,y,t)$.

To simplify the notation,

$$V_x = \bar{V}_x + \xi_x \text{, and} \tag{7.3.9}$$

$$V_y = \bar{V}_y + \xi_y . \tag{7.3.10}$$

By substituting these equations in to equations (7.3.5a) and (7.3.5b), and then substituting the resulting equations in to equation (7.3.4), we obtain,

$$dC = S_x\left(\bar{V}_x C\right)dt + S_y\left(\bar{V}_y C\right)dt + S_x\left(C_x\xi_x\right)dt + S_y\left(C_y\xi_y\right)dt, \tag{7.3.11}$$

where $S_x = -\left(\frac{\partial}{\partial x} + \frac{h_x}{2}\frac{\partial^2}{\partial x^2}\right)$, and

$S_y = -\left(\frac{\partial}{\partial y} + \frac{h_y}{2}\frac{\partial^2}{\partial y^2}\right)$.

We can now write,

$dC = \left(S_x\left(\bar{V}_x C\right) + S_y\left(\bar{V}_y C\right)\right)dt + S_x\left(C_x\xi_x\right)dt + S_y\left(C_y\xi_y\right)dt$, and bringing dt in to the parenthesis in the third and fourth terms of the right hand side,

$$dC = \left(S_x\left(\bar{V}_x C\right) + S_y\left(\bar{V}_y C\right)\right)dt + S_x\left(C\xi_x dt\right) + S_y\left(C\xi_y dt\right). \tag{7.3.12}$$

As in the one dimensional case, we can define,

$\beta_x = \xi_x dt$ and $\beta_y = \xi_y dt$, and these are the components of a noise vector, β, which operates in a Hilbert space having eigen functions as co-ordinates. Equation (7.3.12) can now be expressed as,

$$dC = \left(S_x\left(\bar{V}_x C\right) + S_y\left(\bar{V}_y C\right)\right)dt + S_x\left(Cd\beta_x\right) + S_y\left(Cd\beta_y\right). \tag{7.3.13}$$

The resultant noise term is given by,

$$d\beta = \sigma\sum_{j=1}^{m}\sqrt{\lambda_{x,j}\lambda_{y,j}}\, f_{x,j} f_{y,j} db_j(t), \tag{7.3.14}$$

where $f_{x,j} =$ eigen functions in x direction, and

$f_{y,j} =$ eigen functions in y direction.

Now we can express the components in x and y directions,

$$d\beta_x = d\beta\cos\theta \text{, and} \tag{7.3.15}$$

$$d\beta_y = d\beta\sin\theta . \tag{7.3.16}$$

We make an assumption that θ is defined by

$\cos\theta = \frac{x}{\sqrt{|x|^2+|y|^2}}$; $\sin\theta = \frac{y}{\sqrt{|x|^2+|y|^2}}$. This is a simplifying approximation which makes the modelling more tractable; as the noise term is quite random, this approximation does not make significant difference to final results.

Then

$$dC = \left(S_x\left(\bar{V}_x C\right) + S_y\left(\bar{V}_y C\right)\right)dt + S_x\left(C(x,y,t)\,d\beta\cos\theta\right) + S_y\left(C(x,y,t)\,d\beta\sin\theta\right). \quad (7.3.17)$$

Analogous to equation (4.2.4),

$$S_x\left(C(x,y,t)\,d\beta\cos\theta\right) = S_x\left(C(x,y,t)\left\{\sigma\sum_{j=1}^{m}\sqrt{\lambda_{x,j}\lambda_{y,j}}\,f_{x,j}f_{y,j}\,db_j(t)\right\}\cos\theta\right).$$

$$\begin{aligned} -S_x\left(Cd\beta\cos\theta\right) &= -\sigma\sum_{j=1}^{m}\sqrt{\lambda_{x,j}\lambda_{y,j}}\,f_{y,j}S_x\left(Cf_{x,j}\cos\theta\right)db_j(t) \\ &= \sigma\sum_{j=1}^{m}\sqrt{\lambda_{x,j}\lambda_{y,j}}\,f_{y,j}\left\{-S_x\left(Cf_{x,j}\cos\theta\right)\right\}db_j(t) \end{aligned}. \quad (7.3.18)$$

Now we can expand the terms in the brackets in equation (7.3.18),

$$-S_x\left(Cf_{x,j}\cos\theta\right) = \left(\frac{\partial}{\partial x} + \frac{h_x}{2}\frac{\partial^2}{\partial x^2}\right)\left(Cf_{x,j}\cos\theta\right).$$

We see that,

$$\frac{\partial}{\partial x}\left(Cf_{x,j}\cos\theta\right) = Cf_{x,j}\frac{\partial\cos\theta}{\partial x} + C\cos\theta\frac{\partial f_{x,j}}{\partial x} + f_{x,j}\cos\theta\frac{\partial C}{\partial x}, \text{ and}$$

$$\begin{aligned} \frac{\partial^2}{\partial x^2}\left(Cf_{x,j}\cos\theta\right) = &\left(Cf_{x,j}\frac{\partial^2\cos\theta}{\partial x^2} + C\frac{\partial\cos\theta}{\partial x}\frac{\partial f_{x,j}}{\partial x} + f_{x,j}\frac{\partial\cos\theta}{\partial x}\frac{\partial C}{\partial x}\right) \\ &+\left(C\cos\theta\frac{\partial^2 f_{x,j}}{\partial x^2} + C\frac{\partial\cos\theta}{\partial x}\frac{\partial f_{x,j}}{\partial x} + \frac{\partial f_{x,j}}{\partial x}\cos\theta\frac{\partial C}{\partial x}\right) \\ &+\left(f_{x,j}\cos\theta\frac{\partial^2 C}{\partial x^2} + f_{x,j}\frac{\partial\cos\theta}{\partial x}\frac{\partial C}{\partial x} + \cos\theta\frac{\partial f_{x,j}}{\partial x}\frac{\partial C}{\partial x}\right) \end{aligned}$$

Now,

$$
\begin{aligned}
&-S_x\left(Cf_{x,j}\cos\theta\right)\\
&=C(x,y,t)\left[f_{x,j}\frac{\partial\cos\theta}{\partial x}+\cos\theta\frac{\partial f_{x,j}}{\partial x}+\frac{h_x}{2}\left(f_{x,j}\frac{\partial^2\cos\theta}{\partial x^2}+\frac{\partial\cos\theta}{\partial x}\frac{\partial f_{x,j}}{\partial x}+\cos\theta\frac{\partial^2 f_{x,j}}{\partial x^2}+\frac{\partial\cos\theta}{\partial x}\frac{\partial f_{x,j}}{\partial x}\right)\right]\\
&+\frac{\partial C(x,y,t)}{\partial x}\left[f_{x,j}\cos\theta\frac{\partial f_{x,j}}{\partial x}+\frac{h_x}{2}\left(f_{x,j}\frac{\partial\cos\theta}{\partial x}+\frac{\partial f_{x,j}}{\partial x}\cos\theta+f_{x,j}\frac{\partial\cos\theta}{\partial x}+\cos\theta\frac{\partial f_{x,j}}{\partial x}\right)\right]\\
&+\frac{\partial^2C(x,y,t)}{\partial x^2}\left[\frac{h_x}{2}\left(f_{x,j}\cos\theta\right)\right]
\end{aligned}
$$

Then,

$$
\begin{aligned}
&-S_x\left(Cf_{x,j}\cos\theta\right)\\
&=C(x,y,t)\left\{\left(f_{x,j}\frac{\partial\cos\theta}{\partial x}+\cos\theta\frac{\partial f_{x,j}}{\partial x}\right)+\frac{h_x}{2}\left(f_{x,j}\frac{\partial^2\cos\theta}{\partial x^2}+2\frac{\partial\cos\theta}{\partial x}\frac{\partial f_{x,j}}{\partial x}+\cos\theta\frac{\partial^2 f_{x,j}}{\partial x^2}\right)\right\}\\
&+\frac{\partial C(x,y,t)}{\partial x}\left\{f_{x,j}\cos\theta+\frac{h_x}{2}\left(2f_{x,j}\frac{\partial\cos\theta}{\partial x}+2\cos\theta\frac{\partial f_{x,j}}{\partial x}\right)\right\}\\
&+\frac{\partial^2C(x,y,t)}{\partial x^2}\left\{\frac{h_x}{2}f_{x,j}\cos\theta\right\}.
\end{aligned}
$$

Simplifying, we obtain,

$$
\begin{aligned}
-S_x\left(Cf_{x,j}\cos\theta\right)=C(x,y,t)&\left\{\frac{\partial\left(f_{x,j}\cos\theta\right)}{\partial x}+\frac{h_x}{2}\frac{\partial^2\left(f_{x,j}\cos\theta\right)}{\partial x^2}\right\}\\
&+\frac{\partial C(x,y,t)}{\partial x}\left\{f_{x,j}\cos\theta+h_x\frac{\partial\left(f_{x,j}\cos\theta\right)}{\partial x}\right\}\\
&+\frac{\partial^2C(x,y,t)}{\partial x^2}\left\{\frac{h_x}{2}\left(f_{x,j}\cos\theta\right)\right\}.
\end{aligned}
$$

Similarly,

$$
\begin{aligned}
&S_y\left(Cf_{y,j}\cos\theta\right)\\
&=C(x,y,t)\left\{\frac{\partial\left(f_{y,j}\sin\theta\right)}{\partial y}+\frac{h_x}{2}\frac{\partial^2\left(f_{y,j}\sin\theta\right)}{\partial y^2}\right\}+\frac{\partial C(x,y,t)}{\partial y}\left\{f_{y,j}\sin\theta+h_y\frac{\partial\left(f_{y,j}\sin\theta\right)}{\partial y}\right\}\\
&+\frac{\partial^2C(x,y,t)}{\partial y^2}\left\{\frac{h_y}{2}\left(f_{y,j}\sin\theta\right)\right\}.
\end{aligned}
$$

$$\therefore S_x\left(Cd\beta\cos\theta\right)$$
$$= -\sigma\sum_{j=1}^{m}\sqrt{\lambda_{x,j}\lambda_{y,j}}\left\{\left(P_{0\ x,y,j}C(x,y,t)+P_{1\ x,y,j}\frac{\partial C(x,y,t)}{\partial x}+P_{2\ x,y,j}\frac{\partial^2 C(x,y,t)}{\partial x^2}\right)\right\},$$

Where

$$P_{0,j}=P_{0,x,y,j}=f_{y,j}\left(\frac{\partial\left(f_{x,j}\cos\theta\right)}{\partial x}+\frac{h_x}{2}\frac{\partial^2\left(f_{x,j}\cos\theta\right)}{\partial x^2}\right); \tag{7.3.19}$$

$$P_{1,j}=P_{1,x,y,j}=f_{y,j}\left(f_{x,j}\cos\theta+h_x\frac{\partial\left(f_{x,j}\cos\theta\right)}{\partial x}\right);\ \text{and} \tag{7.3.20}$$

$$P_{2,j}=P_{2,x,y,j}=f_{y,j}\left(\frac{h_x}{2}\left(f_{x,j}\cos\theta\right)\right). \tag{7.3.21}$$

Similarly,

$$S_y\left(Cd\beta\sin\theta\right)=-\sigma\sum_{j=1}^{m}\sqrt{\lambda_{x,j}\lambda_{y,j}}\left\{Q_{0,j}C(x,y,t)+Q_{1,j}\frac{\partial C(x,y,t)}{\partial y}+Q_{2,j}\frac{\partial^2 C(x,y,t)}{\partial y^2}\right\},$$

$$Q_{0,j}=f_{x,j}\left(\frac{\partial\left(f_{y,j}\sin\theta\right)}{\partial y}+\frac{h_y}{2}\frac{\partial^2\left(f_{y,j}\sin\theta\right)}{\partial y^2}\right); \tag{7.3.22}$$

$$Q_{1,j}=f_{x,j}\left(f_{y,j}\sin\theta+h_y\frac{\partial\left(f_{y,j}\sin\theta\right)}{\partial y}\right);\ \text{and} \tag{7.3.23}$$

$$Q_{2,j}=f_{x,j}\left(\frac{h_y}{2}\left(f_{y,j}\sin\theta\right)\right). \tag{7.3.24}$$

$$\therefore S_x\left(Cd\beta_x\right)+S_y\left(Cd\beta_y\right)$$
$$=-\sigma\sum_{j=1}^{m}\sqrt{\lambda_{x,j}\lambda_{y,j}}\left\{\left(P_{0j}+Q_{0,j}\right)C(x,t)+\left(P_{1,j}\frac{\partial C}{\partial x}+Q_{1,j}\frac{\partial C}{\partial y}\right)+\left(P_{2,j}\frac{\partial^2 C}{\partial x^2}+Q_{2,j}\frac{\partial^2 C}{\partial y^2}\right)\right\}db_j(t)$$

Therefore,

$$\begin{aligned} dC = &-C(x,y,t)\,dI_{0x}-\frac{\partial C}{\partial x}dI_{1x}-\frac{\partial^2 C}{\partial x^2}dI_{2x}\\ &-C(x,y,t)\,dI_{0y}-\frac{\partial C}{\partial y}dI_{1y}-\frac{\partial^2 C}{\partial y^2}dI_{2y} \end{aligned}, \tag{7.3.25}$$

$$\text{where}\quad dI_{0x}=\left(\frac{\partial\bar{V}_x}{\partial x}+\frac{h_x}{2}\frac{\partial^2\bar{V}_x}{\partial x^2}\right)dt+\sigma\sum_{j=1}^{m}\sqrt{\lambda_{x,j}\lambda_{y,j}}P_{0j}db_j(t), \tag{7.3.26}$$

$$dI_{1x} = \left(\bar{V}_x + h_x \frac{\partial \bar{V}_x}{\partial x} \right) dt + \sigma \sum_{j=1}^{m} \sqrt{\lambda_{x,j} \lambda_{y,j}} P_{1j} db_j(t), \tag{7.3.27}$$

$$dI_{2x} = \left(\frac{h_x}{2} \bar{V}_x \right) dt + \sigma \sum_{j=1}^{m} \sqrt{\lambda_{x,j} \lambda_{y,j}} P_{2j} db_j(t), \tag{7.3.28}$$

$$dI_{0y} = \left(\frac{\partial \bar{V}_y}{\partial y} + \frac{h_y}{2} \frac{\partial^2 \bar{V}_y}{\partial y^2} \right) dt + \sigma \sum_{j=1}^{m} \sqrt{\lambda_{x,j} \lambda_{y,j}} Q_{0j} db_j(t), \tag{7.3.29}$$

$$dI_{1y} = \left(\bar{V}_y + h_y \frac{\partial \bar{V}_y}{\partial y} \right) dt + \sigma \sum_{j=1}^{m} \sqrt{\lambda_{x,j} \lambda_{y,j}} Q_{1j} db_j(t), \tag{7.3.30}$$

and

$$dI_{2y} = \left(\frac{h_y}{2} \bar{V}_y \right) dt + \sigma \sum_{j=1}^{m} \sqrt{\lambda_{x,j} \lambda_{y,j}} Q_{2j} db_j(t). \tag{7.3.31}$$

Equations (7.3.25) - (7.3.31) constitute the SSTM2d with the definitions for P s and Q s given by equations (7.3.19) to (7.3.24). The SSTM2d has similar Ito diffusions for velocities as in the one dimensional case. Equation (7.3.19) shows an elegant extension of SSTM into 2-dimensions. It should be noted that the eigen values for both directions are the same for the [0,1] domain, further simplifying the equations.

The development of the SSTM2d is based on the fact that any kernel can be expressed as a multiplication of two kernels, for example, as in equation (7.2.2); and we know the methodology of obtaining the eigen values and eigen functions for any kernel. Therefore, we can solve the SSTM2d for any kernel. However, for the illustrative purposes, we only focus on the kernel given in equation (7.2.2) in this chapter.

7.3.1 A Summary of the Finite Difference Scheme

To understand the behaviour of the SSTM2d, we need to solve the equations numerically by using a finite difference scheme developed for the purpose. We only highlight the pertinent equations in the algorithm.

Now let $x_i = i\Delta x$, $y_j = j\Delta y$, $t_n = n\Delta t$, and $C^n_{[i,j]} = C^{t_n}_{[x_i, y_j]}$, Equation (7.3.25) can be redisplayed as,

$$dc^{t_n}_{[x_i,y_j]} = dc^n_{[i,j]} = -c^n_{[i,j]} dI_{0,x_i} - \frac{dc^n_{[i,j]}}{dx_i} dI_{1,x_i} - \frac{d^2 c^n_{[i,j]}}{dx_i^2} dI_{2,x_i} - c^n_{[i,j]} dI_{0,y_j} - \frac{dc^n_{[i,j]}}{dy_j} dI_{1,y_j} - \frac{d^2 c^n_{[i,j]}}{dy_j^2} dI_{2,y_j}.$$

We use the forward difference to calculate the first first-order derivatives with respect to time (t), the backward difference to calculate the first-order derivative in x and y directions and the central difference to calculate the second-order derivatives, i.e.,

$$\frac{dc^n_{[i,j]}}{dt}=\frac{c^{n+1}_{[i,j]}-c^n_{[i,j]}}{\Delta t},\quad \frac{dc^n_{[i,j]}}{dx}=\frac{c^n_{[i,j]}-c^n_{[i-1,j]}}{\Delta x},\quad \frac{dc^n_{[i,j]}}{dy}=\frac{c^n_{[i,j]}-c^n_{[i,j-1]}}{\Delta y},$$
$$\frac{d^2c^n_{[i,j]}}{dx^2}=\frac{c^n_{[i+1,j]}-2c^n_{[i,j]}+c^n_{[i-1,j]}}{\Delta x^2},\quad \frac{d^2c^n_{[i,j]}}{dx^2}=\frac{c^n_{[i,j+1]}-2c^n_{[i,j]}+c^n_{[i,j-1]}}{\Delta y^2}. \tag{7.3.32}$$

We can develop the finite difference scheme to solve the SSTM2d based on the following equation:

$$\begin{aligned} c^{n+1}_{[i,j]}-c^n_{[i,j]} &= -c^n_{[i,j]}dI_{0,x_i}-\left(\frac{c^n_{[i,j]}-c^n_{[i-1,j]}}{\Delta x}\right)dI_{1,x_i}-\left(\frac{c^n_{[i+1,j]}-2c^n_{[i,j]}+c^n_{[i-1,j]}}{\Delta x^2}\right)dI_{2,x_i} \\ &\quad -c^n_{[i,j]}dI_{0,y_j}-\left(\frac{c^n_{[i,j]}-c^n_{[i,j-1]}}{\Delta y}\right)dI_{1,y_j}-\left(\frac{c^n_{[i,j+1]}-2c^n_{[i,j]}+c^n_{[i,j-1]}}{\Delta y^2}\right)dI_{2,y_j} \end{aligned}. \tag{7.3.33}$$

We illustrate some realisations of the solutions graphically in the next section.

7.3.2 Graphical Depictions of Realisations

In the following figures, we present a sample of solution realisations of the SSTM2d to illustrate the behaviours of the model under different parameter values for the boundary condition: $C(t, x, y)$=1.0 at (x=0.0 and y=0.0) for any given t. The value of b is kept at 0.1for all computations.

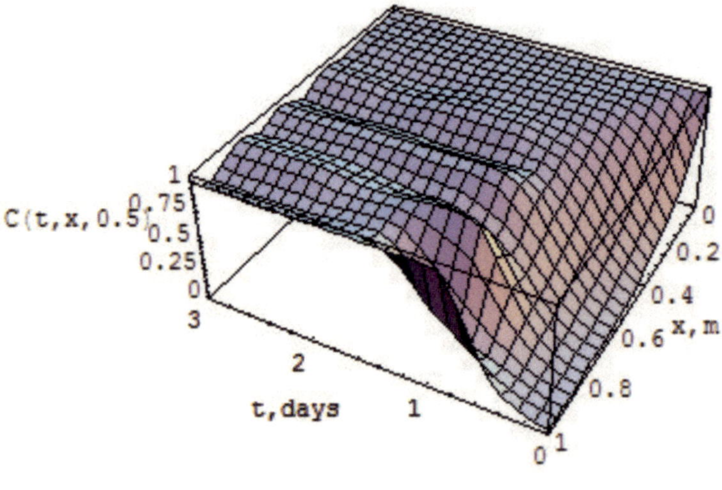

Figure 7.2. A realisation of concentration at y=0.5 m when σ^2 =0.0001.

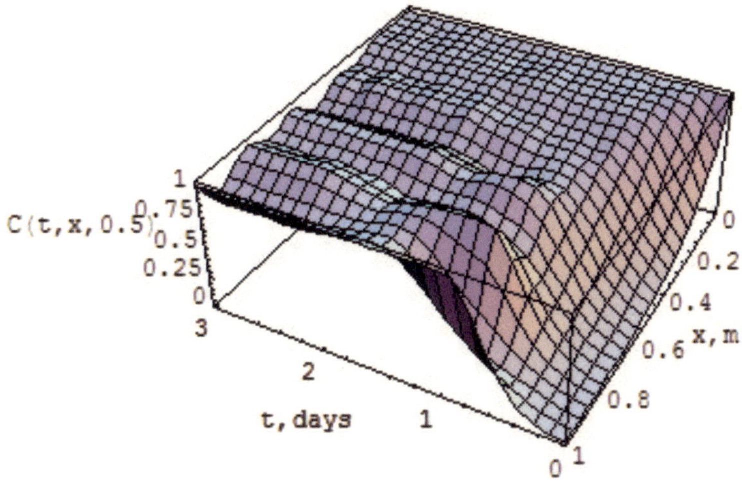

Figure 7.3. A realisation of concentration at y=0.5 m when σ^2 =0.001.

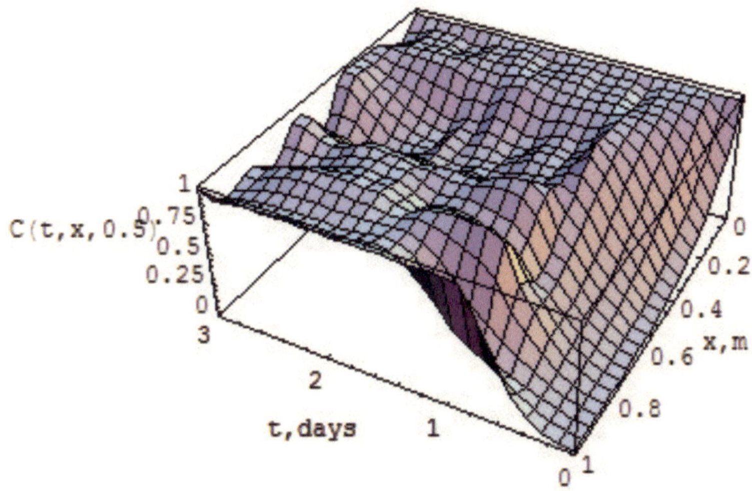

Figure 7.4. A realisation of concentration at y=0.5 m when σ^2 =0.01.

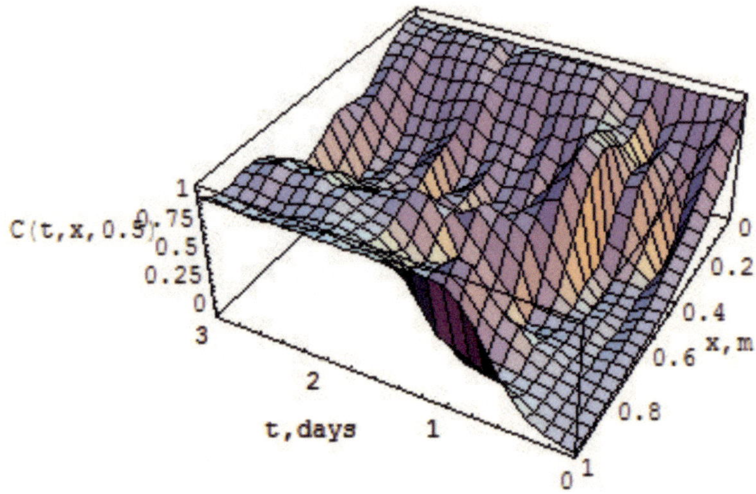

Figure 7.5. A realisation of concentration at y=0.5 m when σ^2 =0.1

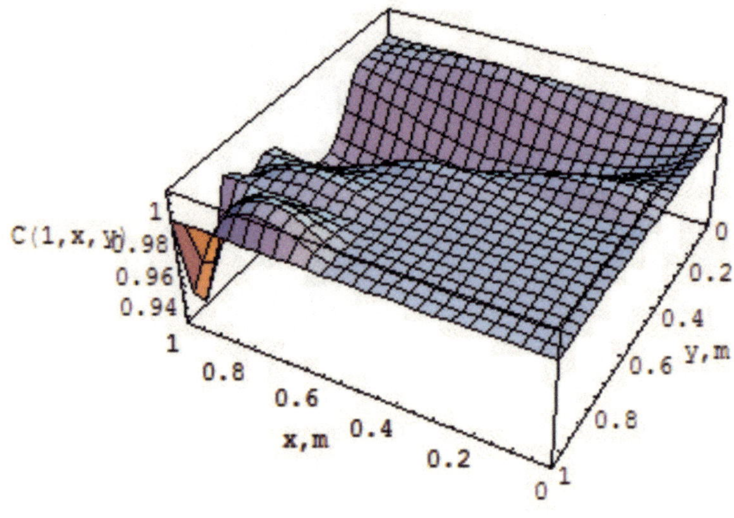

Figure 7.6. A realisation of concentration at t=1 day when σ^2 =0.0001.

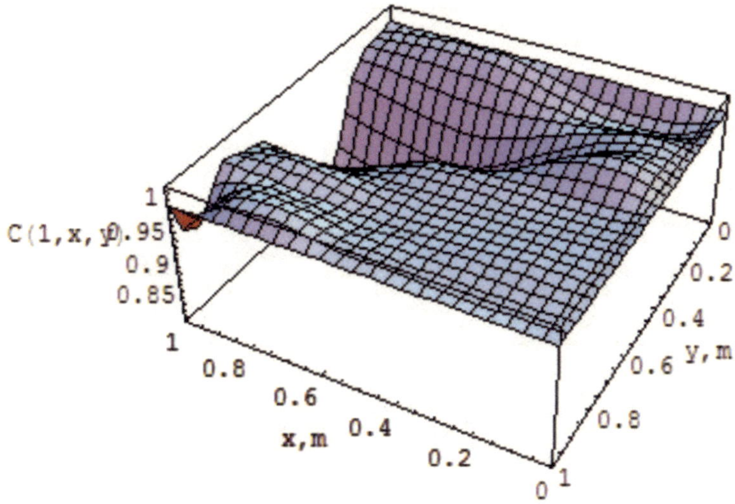

Figure 7.7. A realisation of concentration at t=1 day when σ^2 =0.001.

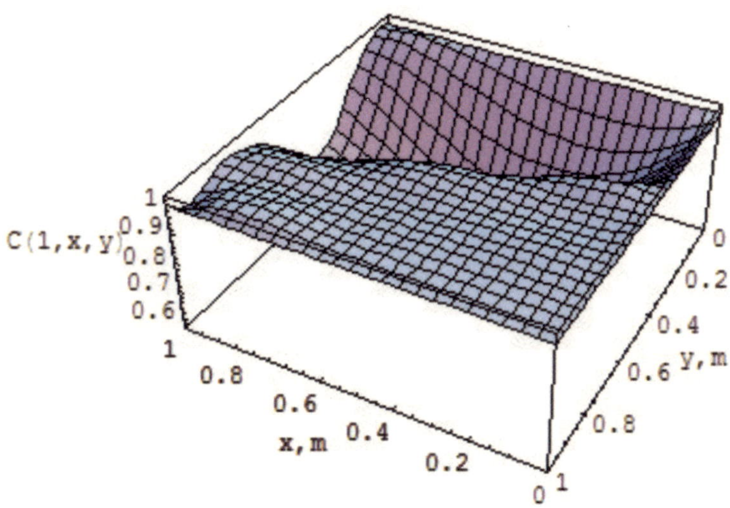

Figure 7.8. A realisation of concentration at t=1 day when σ^2 =0.01.

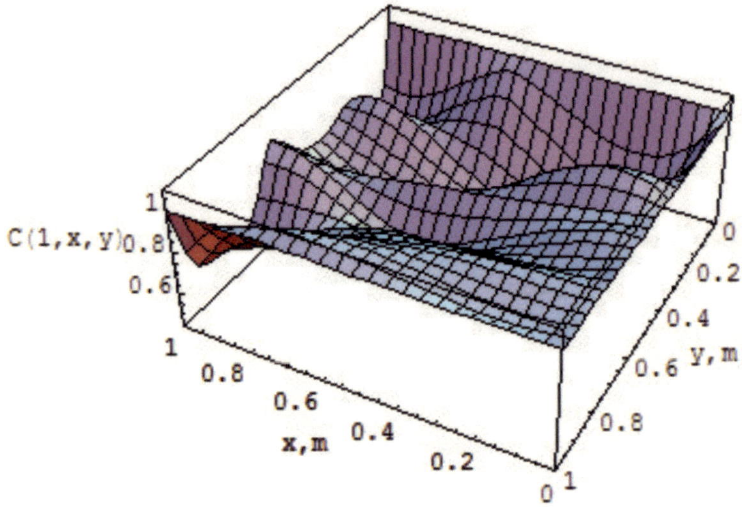

Figure 7.9. A realisation of concentration at t=1 day when σ^2=0.1.

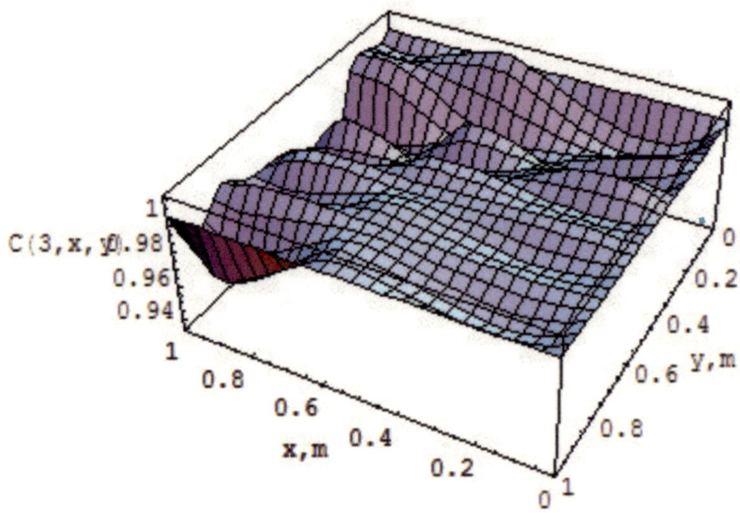

Figure 7.10. A realisation of concentration at t=3 days when σ^2=0.0001.

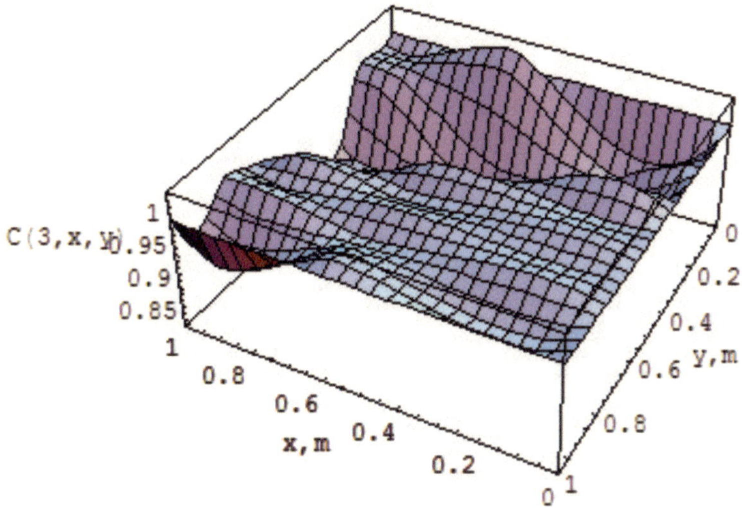

Figure 7.11. A realisation of concentration at t=3 days when σ^2=0.001.

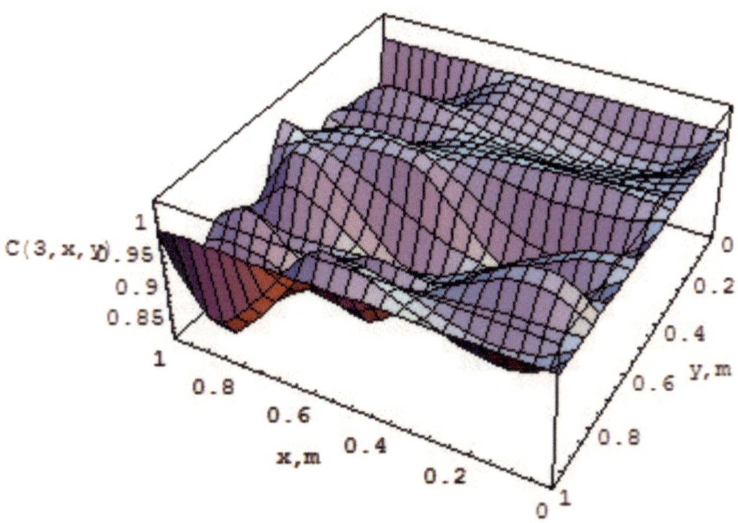

Figure 7.12. A realisation of concentration at t=3 days when σ^2=0.01.

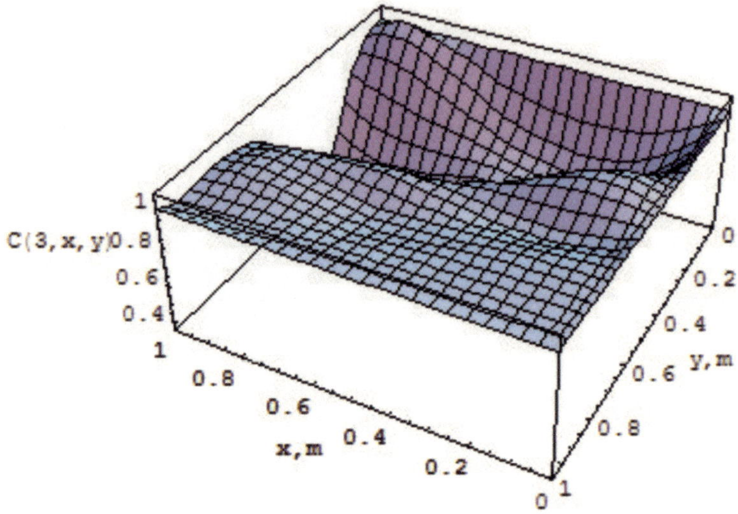

Figure 7.13. A realisation of concentration at t=3 days under σ^2=0.1.

The figures above shows that the numerical scheme is robust to obtain the concentration realisations for a range of values of σ^2. As σ^2 increases the stochasticity of the realisations increases.

7.4 Longitudinal and Transverse Dispersivity according to SSTM2D

To estimate the longitudinal and transverse dispersivities, we start with the partial differential equation for advection and dispersion, taking x axis to be the direction of the flow.

The two-dimensional advection-dispersion equation can be written as,

$$\frac{\partial C}{\partial t} = \left\{ D_L \left(\frac{\partial^2 C}{\partial x^2} \right) + D_T \left(\frac{\partial^2 C}{\partial y^2} \right) \right\} - v_x \left(\frac{\partial C}{\partial x} \right) \tag{7.4.1}$$

where C = solution concentration (mg/l),

t = time (day),

D_L = hydrodynamic dispersion coefficient parallel to the principal direction of flow (longitudinal) (m^2/day),

D_T = hydrodynamic dispersion coefficient perpendicular to the principal direction of flow (transverse) (m^2/day), and

v_x = average linear velocity (m/day).

The randomness of heterogeneous groundwater systems can be accounted for by adding a stochastic component to equation (7.4.1), and it can be given by

$$\frac{\partial C}{\partial t} = \left\{ D_L \left(\frac{\partial^2 C}{\partial x^2} \right) + D_T \left(\frac{\partial^2 C}{\partial y^2} \right) \right\} - v_x \left(\frac{\partial C}{\partial x} \right) + \xi(x,t) \quad , \tag{7.4.2}$$

where $\xi(x,t)$ is described by a zero-mean stochastic process.

We multiple equation (7.4.2) by dt throughout and, formally replace $\xi(x,t)dt$ by ζ(t). We can now obtain the stochastic partial differential equation as follows,

$$dC = \left\{ D_L \left(\frac{\partial^2 C}{\partial x^2} \right) + D_T \left(\frac{\partial^2 C}{\partial y^2} \right) \right\} dt - v_x \left(\frac{\partial C}{\partial x} \right) dt + \varsigma(t) \, . \tag{7.4.3}$$

The two parameters to be estimated are D_L and D_T (while $v_x = 0.5$ in this case). For the two parameter case, we can write the right hand side of equation (7.4.3) as follows:

$$f(t,C,\theta_1,\theta_2) = a_0(C,t) + \theta_1 a_1(C,t) + \theta_2 a_2(C,t) \, , \tag{7.4.4}$$

where,

$$a_0(C,t) = -v_x \left(\frac{\partial C}{\partial x} \right) = -0.5 \left(\frac{\partial C}{\partial x} \right) \; ; \qquad a_1(C,t) = \frac{\partial^2 C}{\partial x^2} \; ; \qquad a_2(C,t) = \frac{\partial^2 C}{\partial y^2} \; ;$$

$$\theta_1 = D_L \; ; \qquad \text{and} \qquad \theta_2 = D_T \, .$$

The log-likelihood function can be written as (see Chapter 1),

$$\begin{aligned} l(\theta_1,\theta_2) = & \sum_{i=1}^{M} \int_0^T \{a_0(C_i,t) + \theta_1 a_1(C_i,t) + \theta_2 a_2(C_i,t)\} dC_i(t) \\ & - \frac{1}{2} \sum_{i=1}^{M} \int_0^T \{a_0(C_i,t) + \theta_1 a_1(C_i,t) + \theta_2 a_2(C_i,t)\}^2 dt \end{aligned} \quad . \tag{7.4.5}$$

If we have values for $C(x,y,t)$ at M discrete points in (x, y) coordinate space for a period of time t (where $0 \le t \le T$), then differentiating equation (7.4.5) with respect to θ_1 and θ_2, respectively, we get the following two simultaneous equations:

$$\begin{aligned} & \sum_{i=1}^{M} \int_0^T a_1(C_i,t) dC_i(t) - \sum_{i=1}^{M} \int_0^T \{a_0(C_i,t) + \theta_1 a_1(C_i,t) + \theta_2 a_2(C_i,t)\} \{a_1(C_i,t)\} dt = 0 \\ & \sum_{i=1}^{M} \int_0^T a_2(C_i,t) dC_i(t) - \sum_{i=1}^{M} \int_0^T \{a_0(C_i,t) + \theta_1 a_1(C_i,t) + \theta_2 a_2(C_i,t)\} \{a_2(C_i,t)\} dt = 0 \end{aligned} \quad . \tag{7.4.6}$$

We simplify equation (7.4.6) to

$$\begin{gathered}\left\{\sum_{i=1}^{M}\int_{0}^{T}a_1(C_i,t)dC_i(t)-\sum_{i=1}^{M}\int_{0}^{T}a_0(C_i,t)a_1(C_i,t)dt\right\}\\ -\theta_1\sum_{i=1}^{M}\int_{0}^{T}\{a_1(C_i,t)\}^2dt-\theta_2\sum_{i=1}^{M}\int_{0}^{T}\{a_1(C_i,t)\}\{a_2(C_i,t)\}dt=0\\ \left\{\sum_{i=1}^{M}\int_{0}^{T}a_2(C_i,t)dC_i(t)-\sum_{i=1}^{M}\int_{0}^{T}a_0(C_i,t)a_2(C_i,t)dt\right\}\\ -\theta_1\sum_{i=1}^{M}\int_{0}^{T}\{a_1(C_i,t)\}\{a_2(C_i,t)\}dt-\theta_2\sum_{i=1}^{M}\int_{0}^{T}\{a_2(C_i,t)\}^2dt=0\end{gathered}. \tag{7.4.7}$$

Now we substitute $a_0(C_i,t)$, $a_1(C,t)$, $a_2(C,t)$, θ_1 and θ_2 in equations (7.4.7) to obtain the following set of equations:

$$\begin{gathered}\left\{\sum_{i=1}^{M}\sum_{t=0}^{T}\left\{\frac{d^2C_i}{dx^2}\right\}dC_i(t)+0.5\sum_{i=1}^{M}\sum_{t=0}^{T}\left\{\frac{dC_i}{dx}\right\}\left\{\frac{d^2C_i}{dx^2}\right\}dt\right\}\\ -\theta_1\sum_{i=1}^{M}\sum_{t=0}^{T}\left\{\frac{d^2C_i}{dx^2}\right\}^2dt-\theta_2\sum_{i=1}^{M}\sum_{t=0}^{T}\left\{\frac{d^2C_i}{dx^2}\right\}\left\{\frac{d^2C_i}{dy^2}\right\}dt=0\\ \left\{\sum_{i=1}^{M}\sum_{t=0}^{T}\left\{\frac{d^2C_i}{dy^2}\right\}dC_i(t)+0.5\sum_{i=1}^{M}\sum_{t=0}^{T}\left\{\frac{dC_i}{dx}\right\}\left\{\frac{d^2C_i}{dy^2}\right\}dt\right\}\\ -\theta_1\sum_{i=1}^{M}\sum_{t=0}^{T}\left\{\frac{d^2C_i}{dx^2}\right\}\left\{\frac{d^2C_i}{dy^2}\right\}dt-\theta_2\sum_{i=1}^{M}\sum_{t=0}^{T}\left\{\frac{d^2C_i}{dy^2}\right\}^2dt=0\end{gathered}. \tag{7.4.8}$$

We can rewrite equations (7.4.8) as,

$$\begin{gathered}m_1-D_Lk_1-D_Tl_1=0\\ m_2-D_Lk_2-D_Tl_2=0\end{gathered}. \tag{7.4.9}$$

Where $m_1=\sum_{i=1}^{M}\sum_{t=0}^{T}\left\{\frac{d^2C_i}{dx^2}\right\}dC_i(t)+0.5\sum_{i=1}^{M}\sum_{t=0}^{T}\left\{\frac{dC_i}{dx}\right\}\left\{\frac{d^2C_i}{dx^2}\right\}dt$, (7.4.10)

$$k_1=\sum_{i=1}^{M}\sum_{t=0}^{T}\left\{\frac{d^2C_i}{dx^2}\right\}^2dt\quad, \tag{7.4.11}$$

$$l_1=k_2=\sum_{i=1}^{M}\sum_{t=0}^{T}\left\{\frac{d^2C_i}{dx^2}\right\}\left\{\frac{d^2C_i}{dy^2}\right\}dt\quad, \tag{7.4.12}$$

$$m_2=\sum_{i=1}^{M}\sum_{t=0}^{T}\left\{\frac{d^2C_i}{dy^2}\right\}dC_i(t)+0.5\sum_{i=1}^{M}\sum_{t=0}^{T}\left\{\frac{dC_i}{dx}\right\}\left\{\frac{d^2C_i}{dy^2}\right\}dt,\ \text{and} \tag{7.4.13}$$

$$l_2 = \sum_{i=1}^{M} \sum_{t=0}^{T} \left\{ \frac{d^2 C_i}{dy^2} \right\}^2 dt \quad . \tag{7.4.14}$$

The two simultaneous equations in (7.4.9) can be solved to obtain the estimates of the unknown parameters, D_L and D_T, for a two-dimensional groundwater system. The solutions of equations (7.4.9) are,

$$D_L = \frac{m_1 l_2 - m_2 l_1}{k_1 l_2 - l_1^2},$$

and (7.4.15)

$$D_T = \frac{m_1 l_1 - m_2 k_1}{l_1^2 - k_1 l_2}.$$

We have estimated the longitudinal and lateral dispersion coefficients for 100 realisations for each of σ^2 value chosen, and their mean values are given in Table 7.1 .

The transverse dispersion coefficient is significantly less than the longitudinal dispersion coefficient for the flow length [0,1] when σ^2 is very small but approaches approximately 0.5 of longitudinal dispersion coefficient when σ^2 increases (Figure 7.12). Comparing Table 7.1 with Table 4.9, we see that the dispersion coefficient, therefore, the dispersivity, is smaller in 2 dimensions especially when $\sigma^2 > 0.01$. This needs to be expected as the lateral dispersion provides another mechanism of energy dissipation, thwarting the dispersion in the longitudinal direction.

σ^2	D_L	D_T
0.001	0.0251	0.0003
0.005	0.0258	0.0012
0.01	0.0264	0.0017
0.02	0.0273	0.0027
0.04	0.0293	0.0053
0.05	0.0304	0.0072
0.06	0.0314	0.0089
0.08	0.0332	0.012
0.1	0.0354	0.0145
0.15	0.04	0.0197

Table 7.1. Estimated mean longitudinal and transverse dispersion coefficients using 100 concentration realisations from SSTM2d for each of σ^2 value.

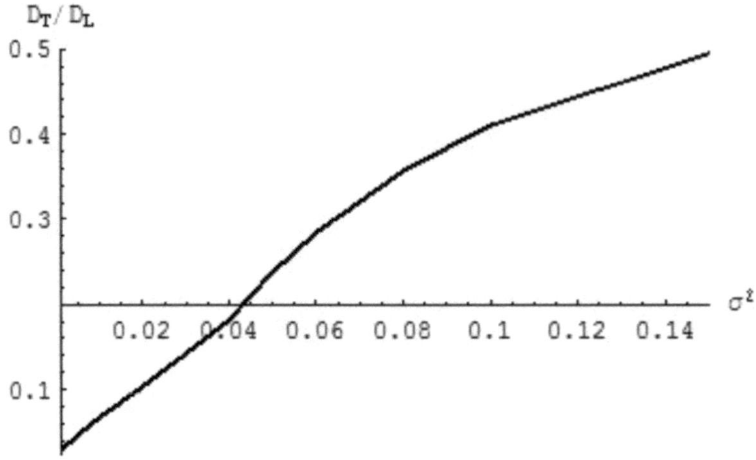

Figure 7.14. The ratio of the transverse dispersivity to the longitudinal dispersivity vs σ^2.

7.5 Summary

In this chapter, we developed the 2 dimensional version of SSTM for the flow length of [0,1], and estimated the transverse dispersivity using the Stochastic Inverse Method (SIM) adopted for the purpose. The SSTM2d has mathematically similar form to SSTM but computationally more involved. However, the numerical routines developed are robust. We will extend SSTM2d in a dimensionless form to understand multi-scale behaviours of SSTM2d in the next chapter.

8

Multiscale Dispersion in 2 Dimensions

8.1 Introduction

In Chapter 7, we have developed the 2 dimensional solute transport model and estimated the dispersion coefficients in both longitudinal and transverse directions using the stochastic inverse method (SIM), which is based on the maximum likelihood method. We have seen that transverse dispersion coefficient relative to longitudinal dispersion coefficient increases as σ^2 increases when the flow length is confined to 1.0. In this chapter, we extend the SSTM2d into a partially dimensional form as we did for 1 dimension, so that we can explore the larger scale behaviours of the model. However, the experimental data on transverse dispersion is scarce in laboratory and field scales limiting our ability to validate the multiscale dispersion model. In this chapter, we briefly outline the dimensionless form of SSTM2d and illustrate the numerical solution for a particular value of flow length. We also estimate the dispersion coefficients using the SIM for the same flow length.

8.2 Basic Equations

As in the one dimensional case, we define dimensionless distances to start with:

$$z_x = \frac{x}{L_x}, \qquad 0 \le z_x \le 1,$$

and

$$z_y = \frac{y}{L_y}, \qquad 0 \le z_y \le 1.$$

We also define dimensionless concentration with respect to the maximum concentration, C_0 :

$$\Gamma(x,y,t) = \frac{C(x,y,t)}{C_0}, \qquad 0 \le \Gamma \le 1.$$

As in Chapter 6, we derive the following partial derivatives:

$$\frac{\partial C}{\partial x} = \frac{C_0}{L_x}\frac{\partial \Gamma}{\partial z_x}; \quad \frac{\partial^2 C}{\partial x^2} = \frac{C_0}{L_x^2}\frac{\partial^2 \Gamma}{\partial z_x^2}; \quad \frac{\partial C}{\partial y} = \frac{C_0}{L_y}\frac{\partial \Gamma}{\partial z_y}; \text{ and } \quad \frac{\partial^2 C}{\partial y^2} = \frac{C_0}{L_y^2}\frac{\partial^2 \Gamma}{\partial z_y^2}.$$

As we have developed the SSTM2d for [0,1] domains in both x and y directions (see Chapter 6), we define the cosine and sine of the angle as follows,

$$\cos\theta = \frac{z_x}{\sqrt{z_x^2 + z_y^2}}, \text{and}$$

$$\sin\theta = \frac{z_y}{\sqrt{z_x^2 + z_y^2}}.$$

We can also express the partial derivatives of the mean velocities in both x and y directions in terms of dimensionless space variables:

$$\frac{\partial \bar{v}_x}{\partial x} = \frac{\partial \bar{v}_x}{\partial z_x}\frac{\partial z_x}{\partial x} = \frac{1}{L_x}\frac{\partial \bar{v}_x}{\partial z_x};$$

$$\frac{\partial^2 \bar{v}_x}{\partial x^2} = \frac{\partial}{\partial z_x}\left(\frac{\partial \bar{v}_x}{\partial x}\right)\frac{\partial z_x}{\partial x} = \frac{1}{L_x}\frac{\partial}{\partial z_x}\left(\frac{1}{L_x}\frac{\partial \bar{v}_x}{\partial z_x}\right) = \frac{1}{L_x^2}\frac{\partial^2 \bar{v}_x}{\partial z_x^2};$$

$$\frac{\partial \bar{v}_y}{\partial y} = \frac{1}{L_y}\frac{\partial \bar{v}_y}{\partial z_y}; \text{and,}$$

$$\frac{\partial^2 \bar{v}_y}{\partial y^2} = \frac{1}{L_y^2}\frac{\partial^2 \bar{v}_y}{\partial z_y^2}.$$

Similarly, we can express the derivatives related to solute concentration in terms of dimensionless variables:

$$\frac{\partial C}{\partial t} = C_0\frac{\partial \Gamma}{\partial t};$$

$$\frac{\partial^2 C}{\partial x^2} = \frac{C_0}{L_x^2}\frac{\partial^2 \Gamma}{\partial z_x^2}; \text{ and,}$$

$$\frac{\partial^2 C}{\partial y^2} = \frac{C_0}{L_y^2}\frac{\partial^2 \Gamma}{\partial z_y^2}.$$

We recall the SSTM2d in x and y co-ordinates,

$$dC = -C dI_{0,x} - \frac{\partial C}{\partial x} dI_{1,x} - \frac{\partial^2 C}{\partial x^2} dI_{2,x} - C dI_{0,y} - \frac{\partial C}{\partial y} dI_{1,y} - \frac{\partial^2 C}{\partial y^2} dI_{2,y};$$

$$\text{where } dI_{0,x} = \left(\frac{\partial \bar{v}_x}{\partial x} + \frac{h_x}{2}\frac{\partial^2 \bar{v}_x}{\partial x^2}\right)dt + \sigma\sum_{j=1}^{m}\sqrt{\lambda_{xj}\lambda_{yj}}P_{0j}db_j(t);$$

$$dI_{1,x} = \left(\bar{v}_x + h_x\frac{\partial \bar{v}_x}{\partial x}\right)dt + \sigma\sum_{j=1}^{m}\sqrt{\lambda_{xj}\lambda_{yj}}P_{1j}db_j(t);$$

$$dI_{2,x}=\left(\frac{h_x}{2}\bar{v}_x\right)dt+\sigma\sum_{j=1}^{m}\sqrt{\lambda_{xj}\lambda_{yj}}P_{2j}db_j(t);$$

$$dI_{0,y}=\left(\frac{\partial\bar{v}_y}{\partial y}+\frac{h_y}{2}\frac{\partial^2\bar{v}_y}{\partial y^2}\right)dt+\sigma\sum_{j=1}^{m}\sqrt{\lambda_{xj}\lambda_{yj}}Q_{0j}db_j(t);$$

$$dI_{1,y}=\left(\bar{v}_y+h_y\frac{\partial\bar{v}_y}{\partial y}\right)dt+\sigma\sum_{j=1}^{m}\sqrt{\lambda_{xj}\lambda_{yj}}Q_{1j}db_j(t);\text{and,}$$

$$dI_{2,y}=\left(\frac{h_y}{2}\bar{v}_y\right)dt+\sigma\sum_{j=1}^{m}\sqrt{\lambda_{xj}\lambda_{yj}}Q_{2j}db_j(t).$$

Because $\lambda_{xj}, \lambda_{yj}, h_x, h_y, P_{0j}, P_{1j}, P_{2j}, Q_{0j}, Q_{1j}$, and Q_{2j} are calculated for the domain [0, 1], we use the same values and functions but we use the following symbols: $\lambda_{z_x j}, \lambda_{z_y j}, h_{z_x}, h_{z_y}, P_{0j}, P_{1j}, P_{2j}, Q_{0j}, Q_{1j}$, and Q_{2j}. Now we calculate $d\Gamma$ based on the transformed partially dimensional governing equation:

$$d\Gamma=-\Gamma dI_{0,z_x}-\frac{1}{L_x}\frac{\partial\Gamma}{\partial z_x}dI_{1,z_x}-\frac{1}{L_x^2}\frac{\partial^2\Gamma}{\partial z_x^2}dI_{2,z_x}-\Gamma dI_{0,z_y}-\frac{1}{L_y}\frac{\partial\Gamma}{\partial z_y}dI_{1,z_y}-\frac{1}{L_y^2}\frac{\partial^2\Gamma}{\partial z_y^2}dI_{2,z_y};\qquad(8.2.1)$$

where $dI_{0,z_x}=\left(\frac{1}{L_x}\frac{\partial\bar{v}_x}{\partial z_x}+\frac{h_{z_x}}{2}\frac{1}{L_x^2}\frac{\partial^2\bar{v}_x}{\partial z_x^2}\right)dt+\sigma\sum_{j=1}^{m}\sqrt{\lambda_{z_x j}\lambda_{z_y j}}P_{0j}db_j(t);$

$$dI_{1,z_x}=\left(\bar{v}_x+h_{z_x}\frac{1}{L_x}\frac{\partial\bar{v}_x}{\partial z_x}\right)dt+\sigma\sum_{j=1}^{m}\sqrt{\lambda_{z_x j}\lambda_{z_y j}}P_{1j}db_j(t);$$

$$dI_{2,z_x}=\left(\frac{h_{z_x}}{2}\bar{v}_x\right)dt+\sigma\sum_{j=1}^{m}\sqrt{\lambda_{z_x j}\lambda_{z_y j}}P_{2j}db_j(t);$$

$$dI_{0,z_y}=\left(\frac{1}{L_y}\frac{\partial\bar{v}_y}{\partial z_y}+\frac{h_{z_y}}{2}\frac{1}{L_y^2}\frac{\partial^2\bar{v}_y}{\partial z_y^2}\right)dt+\sigma\sum_{j=1}^{m}\sqrt{\lambda_{z_x j}\lambda_{z_y j}}Q_{0j}db_j(t);$$

$$\partial I_{1,z_y}=\left(\bar{v}_y+h_{z_y}\frac{1}{L_y}\frac{\partial\bar{v}_y}{\partial z_y}\right)\partial t+\sigma\sum_{j=1}^{m}\sqrt{\lambda_{z_x j}\lambda_{z_y j}}Q_{1j}db_j(t);\text{ and,}$$

$$dI_{2,z_y}=\left(\frac{h_{z_y}}{2}\bar{v}_y\right)dt+\sigma\sum_{j=1}^{m}\sqrt{\lambda_{z_x j}\lambda_{z_y j}}Q_{2j}db_j(t).$$

The above equations constitute the multiscale SSTM2d and we developed the numerical solutions when the flow length along the main flow direction is 100 m and the flow length in the direction perpendicular to the main direction is 25 m.

8.3 A Sample of Realisations of Multiscale SSTM2d

For the illustrative purposes, we plot three realisations of concentration when C_0 =1.0 at (x=0; and y=0) when time is 20 days for two different σ^2 values, 0.01 and 0.1. These are shown in Figures 8.1 and 8.2.

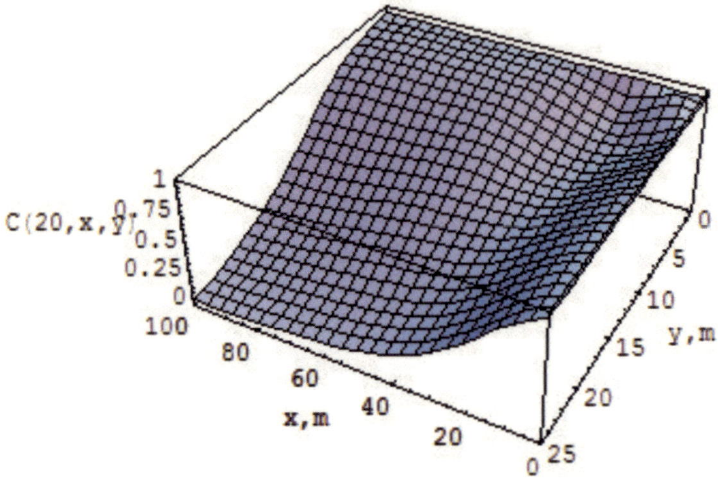

Figure 8.1. A concentration realisation when time is 20 days for σ^2 =0.01. Mean velocity in x direction is 0.5 m/day and, in y direction is 0.0.

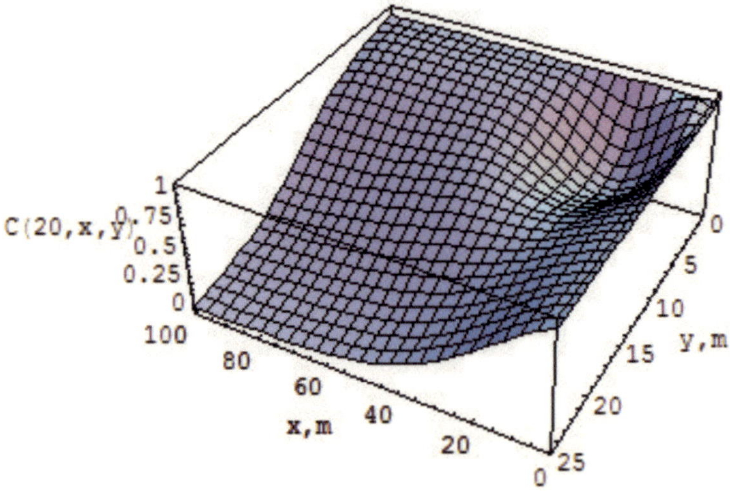

Figure 8.2. A concentration realisation when time is 20 days for σ^2 =0.1. (Same conditions as in Figure 8.1.)

8.4 Estimation of Dispersion Coefficients

We use the same methodology as in Chapter 7 with a slight modification to the advection-dispersion stochastic partial differential equation (SPDE) to make it dimensionless.

The SPDE becomes,

$$\frac{\partial \Gamma}{\partial t} = \left\{ \frac{D_L}{L_x^2} \frac{\partial^2 \Gamma}{\partial z_x^2} + \frac{D_T}{L_y^2} \frac{\partial^2 \Gamma}{\partial z_y^2} \right\} - \frac{\overline{v}_x}{L_x} \frac{\partial \Gamma}{\partial z_x} + \xi(z,t). \tag{8.4.1}$$

We can use the SIM to estimate the parameters but to obtain the dispersion coefficients, we note the following relations:

$$D_L = \left[\text{estimated}\left(\frac{D_L}{L_x^2} \right) \right] \times L_x^2 \text{;and}$$

$$D_T = \left[\text{estimated}\left(\frac{D_T}{L_y^2} \right) \right] \times L_y^2 .$$

Based on 60 realisations for each value of σ^2, Table 8.1 shows the estimated mean dispersion coefficients for the same boundary and initial conditions.

σ^2	D_L	D_T
0.01	5.445969667	0.259079583
0.1	6.853118	1.043493717

Table 8.1. The estimated mean dispersion coefficients for two different σ^2 values (b=0.1).

8.5 Summary

In this brief chapter, we have given sufficient details of development of the multiscale SSTM2d and a sample of its realisations. We also have adopted SIM to estimate dispersion coefficients in both longitudinal and lateral directions. The computational experiments we have done with the SSTM2d show realistic solutions under variety of boundary and initial conditions, even for larger scales such 10000 m. However, it is not important to illustrate the results, as we have discussed the one dimensional SSTM in detail in Chapter 6. If there are reliable dispersivity data in different scales, both in longitudinal and transverse directions, then one can develop much more meaningful relations between longitudinal and lateral dispersivities based on a properly validated model.

References

Abrahart, R.J., Linda, S., & Pauline, E.K., (1999). Using pruning algorithms and genetic algorithms to optimise network architectures and forecasting inputs in a neural network rainfall-runoff model. *Journal of Hydroinformatics*, 1 (2), pp.103-114.

Aly, A.H., & Peralta, R.C., (1999). Optimal design of aquifer cleanup systems under uncertainty using a neural network and a genetic algorithm. *Water Resources Research*, 35 (8), pp.2523-2532.

Anderson, M.P., & Woessner, W.W., (1992). *Applied groundwater modelling - simulation of flow and advective transport*. New York: Academic Press.

ASCE Task Committee on Application of Artificial Neural Networks in Hydrology, Artificial neural networks in hydrology. I: Preliminary concepts. 2000a. *Journal of Hydrologic Engineering*, ASCE, 5 (2), pp.115-123.

ASCE Task Committee on Application of Artificial Neural Networks in Hydrology, Artificial neural networks in hydrology. II: Hydrologic applications. 2000b. *Journal of Hydrologic Engineering*, ASCE, 5 (2), pp.124-137.

Accurate Automation Corporation. 2002. Retrieved October 17, 2002 from http://www.accurate-automation.com/products/nnets.htm

Azzalini, A., (1996). *Statistical inference: based on the likelihood*, Chapman & Hall/CRC, Boca Raton ; New York.

Balkhair, K.S., (2002). Aquifer parameters determination for large diameter wells using neural network approach. *Journal of Hydrology*, 265 (1- 4), pp.118-128.

Basawa, I.V.; & Prakasa Rao, B.L.S., (1980). *Statistical inference for stochastic processes*. New York: Academic Press.

Batu, Vedat., (2006). *Applied Flow and Solute Transport Modelling in Aquifers*. Taylor & Francis Group, Boca Raton.

Bear. J., (1972). *Dynamics of fluids in porous media*. New York: American Elsevier Publishing Company.

Bear, J., (1979). *Hydraulics of Groundwater*. Israel: McGraw-Hill Inc.

Bear. J., Zaslavsky, D., & Irmay, S., (1968). *Physical principles of water percolation and seepage*. France : Unesco Press.

Beaudeau, P. , Leboulanger, T., Lacroix, M., Hanneton, S., & Wang, H.Q., (2001). Forecasting of turbid floods in a coastal, chalk karstic drain using an artificial neural network. *Ground Water*, 39 (1), pp.109-118.

Bebis, G., & Georgiopoulos, M., (1994). Feed-forward neural networks: Why network size is so important. *IEEE Potentials*, October/November, pp.27-31.

Bennett, A.F., (1992). *Inverse methods in Physical Oceanography*. New York: Cambridge University Press.

Bibby, B.M., & Sorensen, M., (1995). Bernoulli, 17.

Bibby, R., & Sunada, D.K., (1971). Statistical error analysis of a numerical model of confined groundwater flow, in stochastic hydraulics. In C.L. Chiu (Eds.). *Proceedings first international symposium on stochastic hydraulics*, pp.591-612.

Bishop, C.M., (1995). *Neural networks for pattern recognition*. Clarendon Press; Oxford University Press, New York.

Carrera, J., (1987). State of the art of the inverse problem applied to the flow and solute transport problems. *In Groundwater Flow and Quality Modelling*, NATO ASI Series, pp.549-585.

Carrera. J., (1988). State of the art of the inverse problem applied to the flow and solute transport equations. *In Groundwater Flow and Quality Modelling*, NATO ASI serial, volume 224, pp. 549-585. Norwell, Mass: Kulwer.

Carrera, J., & Glorioso, L., (1991). On geostatistical formulation of the groundwater inverse problem. *Advances in Water Resources*, 14 (5), pp.273-283.

Carrera, J., & Neuman, S.P., (1986a). Estimation of aquifer parameters under transient and steady state conditions, 1, Maximum likelihood method incorporating prior information. *Water Resources Research*, 22 (2), pp.199-210.

Carrera, J., & Neuman, S.P., (1986b). Estimation of aquifer parameters under transient and steady state conditions, 2, Uniqueness, stability and solution algorithms. *Water Resources Research*, 22 (2), pp.211-227.

Caruana, R.L., & Giles, S. L., (2001). Advances in neural information processing systems, 402.

Castellano, G., Fanelli, A.M., & Pelillo, M., (1997). An iterative pruning algorithm for feed-forward neural networks. *IEEE Transactions on Neural Networks*, 5, pp.961-970.

Chakilam, V.M., (1998). Forecasting the Future: Experimenting with Time Series data. Unpublished master's thesis, Birla Institute of Technology and Science, India. Retrieved September 8, 2001 from http://www.ucs.louisiana.edu/~vmc0583/Thesis_report%5B1%5D.rtf.pdf

Chandrasekhra, B.C., Rudrajah, N., & Nagaraj, S.T., (1980). Velocity and dispersion in porous media, *Int. J. Engng. Sci.*, 18, pp.921-929.

Chapman, B.M., (1979). Dispersion of soluble pollutions in nonuniform rivers, I, Theory. *Journal of Hydrology*, 40 (1/2), pp.139-152.

Cooley, R.L., (1977). A method of estimating parameters and assessing reliability for models of steady state groundwater flow, 1, Theory and numerical properties. *Water Resources Research*, 13 (2), pp.318-324.

Cooley, R.L., (1979). A method of estimating parameters and assessing reliability for models of steady state groundwater flow, 2, Application of statistical analysis. *Water Resources Research*, 15 (3), pp.603-617.

Cooley, R.L.,(1982). Incorporation of prior information on parameters into nonlinear regrassion groundwater flow models, 1, Theory. *Water Resources Research*, 18 (4), pp.965-976.

Cooley, R.L.,(1983). Incorporation of prior information on parameters into nonlinear regrassion groundwater flow models, 2, Applications. *Water Resources Research*, 19 (3), pp.662-676.

Coulibaly, P., Anctil, F. Aravena, R. & Bobee, B., (2001). Artificial neural network modeling of water table depth fluctuations. *Water Resources Research*, 37 (4), pp.885-896.

Cressie, N., (1993). *Geostatistics: A tool for environmental modelers*. In M.F. Goodchild, B. O. Parks, and L. T. Stegert (Eds) Environmenatal modelling with GIS. N.Y.: Oxford Press.

Cvetkovic, V., Shapiro, A., and Dagan, G., (1992). A solute flux approach to transport in heterogeneous formations 2. Uncertainty analysis. *Water Resources Research*, 28 (5), pp.1377-1388.

Cybenko, G., (1989). Approximation by superpositions of a sigmoidal function. *Mathematics of Control Signals and Systems*, 2, pp.203-314.

Dagan, G., (1984). Solute transport in heterogeneous porous formations. *Journal of fluid mechanics*, 145, pp.151-177.

Dagan, G., (1985). Stochastic modeling of groundwater flow by unconditional and conditional probabilities: the inverse problem. *Water Resources Research*, 21(1), pp.65-72.

Dagan, G., (1986). Statistical theory of groundwater flow and transport: pore to laboratory, laboratory to formation, and formation to regional scale. *Water Resources Research* , 22 (9), pp.120S-134S.

Dagan, G., (1988). Time dependent macrodispersion for solute transport in anisotropic heterogeneous aquifers. *Water Resources Research*, 24 (9), pp.1491-1500.

Dagan, G., & Rubin, Y., (1988). Stochastic identification of recharge, transmissivity, and storativity in aquifer transient flow: A quasi-steady approach. *Water Resources Research*, 24 (10), pp.1698-1710.

Dagan, G., Cvetkovic, V., & Shapiro, A., (1992). A solute flux approach to transport in heterogeneous formations 1. The general framework. *Water Resources Research*, 28 (5), pp.1369-1376.

Daley, R., (1991). *Atmospheric data analysis*. New York: Cambridge University Press.

Dietrich, C.R., & Newsam, G.N., (1989). A stability analysis of the geostatistical approach to aquifer transmissivity identification. *Stochastic Hydrology and Hydraulics*, 3(4), pp.293-316.

Farrell, B.F., (1999). Perturbation growth and structure in time-dependent flows. *Journal of the Atmospheric Sciences*, 56 (21), pp.3622-3639.

Farrell, B.F., (2002a). Perturbation growth and structure in uncertain flows. Part I. *Journal of the Atmospheric Sciences*, 59 (18), pp.2629-2646.

Farrell, B.F., (2002b). Perturbation growth and structure in uncertain flows. Part II. *Journal of the Atmospheric Sciences*, Boston, 59 (18), pp.2647-2664.

Fetter, C.W., (1999). *Contaminant hydrogeology*. New Jersey: Prentice-Hall.

Fetter, C.W., (2001). *Applied hydrogeology*. New Jersey: Prentice-Hall.

Flood, I., & Kartam, N., (1994). Neural network in civil engineering. I: Principles and understanding. *Journal of Computing in Civil Engineering*, 8 (2), pp.131-148.

Foussereau, X., Graham, W.D., Akpoji, G.A., Destouni, G., & Rao, P.S.C., (2001). Solute transport through a heterogeneous coupled vadose zone system with temporal random rainfall. *Water Resources Research*, 37 (6), pp.1577-1588.

Foussereau, X., Graham, W.D., & Rao, P.S.C., (2000). Stochastic analysis of transient flow in unsaturated heterogeneous soils. *Water Resources Research*, 36 (4), pp.891-910.

Freeze, R.A., (1972). *Regionalization of hydrologic parameters for use in mathematical models of groundwater flow*. In J.E. Gill (Eds), Hydrogeology, Gardenvale, Quebec: Harpell.

Freeze, R.A., (1975). A stochastic-conceptual analysis of one dimensional groundwater flow in a non-uniform homogeneous media. *Water Resources Research*, 11 (5), pp.725-741.

Freeze, R. A., & Cherry, J.A., (1979). *Groundwater*. Englewood Cliffs, NJ: Prentice Hall.

Freeze, R.A., & S.M., Gorelick, (2000). Convergence of stochastic optimization and decision analysis in the engineering design of aquifer remediation. *Ground Water*, 38 (3), pp.328-339.

Fried, J.J., (1972). Miscible pollution of ground water: A study of methodology. In A. K Biswas (Eds.). *Proceedings of the international symposium on modelling techniques in water resources systems*, vol 2, pp.362-371. Ottawa, Canada.

Fried, J.J., (1975). *Groundwater pollution.* Amsterdam: Elsevier Scientific Publishing Company.

Frind, E.O., & Pinder, S.F., (1973). Galerkin solution to the inverse problem for aquifer transmissivity. *Water Resources Research*, 9 (4), pp.1397-1410.

Gaines, J.G., & Lyons, T.J., (1997). Variable step size control in the numerical solution of stochastic differential equations. *SIAM Journal on Applied Mathematics*, 57, pp.1455-1484.

Gelhar, L.W., (1986). Stochastic subsurface hydrology from theory to applications. *Water Resources Research*, 22 (9), pp.135S-145S.

Gelhar, L.W., & Axness, C.L., (1983). Three dimensional stochastic of macro dispersion aquifers. *Water Resources Research*, 19 (1), pp.161-180.

Gelhar, L.W., Gutjahr,A.L., & Naff, R. L., (1979). Stochastic analysis of microdispersion in a stratified aquifer. *Water Resources Research*, 15 (6), pp.1387-1391.

Gelhar, L.W., (1986). Stochastic subsurface hydrology from theory to applications. *Water Resources Research*, 22, (9), pp.135S-145S.

Ghanem, R.G., & Spanos, P.D., (1991). *Stochastic finite elements: a spectral approach.* New York: Springer-Verlag.

Gill W.N., & Sankarasubramanian, R.,(1970). Exact analysis of unsteady convective diffusion. *Proc. Roy. Soc. Lond.* A. 316, pp.341-350.

Gillespie, D.T., (1992). *Markov Processes: An Introduction for Physical Scientists.* Academic Press, San Diego.

Ginn, T.R., & Cushman., J.H., (1990). Inverse methods for subsurface flow: A critical review of stochastic techniques. *Stochastic Hydrology and Hydraulics*, 4: pp.1-26.

Gomez-Hernandez, J.J., Sahuquillo, A., & Capilla, J.E.,(1997). Stochastic simulation of transmissivity fields conditional to both transmissivity and piezometric data, 1, *Theory. Journal of Hydrology*, 203, pp.162-174.

Grindord, P., & Impey, M.D., (1991). *Fractal field simulations of tracer migration within the WIPP Culebra Dolamite.* Intera Inf. Technology, UK.

Groundwater Foundation. 2001. Retrieved on 22 May 2001 from http://www.groundwater.org/Group, W.S. 2005. Frederick, MD.

Gutjahr, A.L., & Wilson, J.R., (1989). Co-kriging for stochastic flow models. *Transport in Porous Media*, 4 (6), pp.585-598.

Hall, A.R., (2005). *Generalized method of moments.* Oxford University Press, Oxford; New York.

Harleman, D.R.F., & Rumer, R.R., (1963). The analytical solution for injection of a tracer slug in a plane. *Fluid Mechanics*, 16.

Harter, T., & Yeh, T.C.J., (1996). Stochastic analysis of solute transport in heterogeneous, variably saturated soils. *Water Resources Research*, 32 (6), pp.1585-1596.

Hassan, A.E., & Hamed, K.H., (2001). Prediction of plume migration in heterogeneous media using artificial neural networks. *Water Resources Research*, 37 (3), pp.605-625.

Hassoun, M.H., (1995). *Fundamentals of artificial neural networks.* Cambridge: MIT Press.

Haykin, S., (1994). *Neural networks : a comprehensive foundation.* New York: McMillan.

Hecht-Nielsen, R., (1987). Kolmogorov's mapping neural network existence theorem. *In 1st IEEE International Joint Conference on Neural Networks.* Institute of Electrical and Electronic Engineering, San Diego, 21-24 June 1987. San Diego, pp.11-14.

Hegazy, T., Fazio, P., & Moselhi, O., (1994). Developing practical neural network applications using back-propagation. *Microcomputers in Civil Engineering*, 9, pp.145-459.

Herlet, I., (1998). Ground Water Contamination in the Heathcote / Woolston area, Christchurch, New Zealand. Unpublished master thesis, Canterbury University, New Zealand.

Hernandez, D.B., (1995). *Lectures on Probability and Second Order Random Fields*, World Scientific, Singapore.

Hertz, J.A., Krogh, A., & Palmer, R.G., (1991). *Introduction to the theory of neural computation. Redwood City*, California: Addison-Wesley Publishing.

Hoeksema, R., & Kitanidis, P.K., (1984). An application of the geostatistical approach to the inverse problem in two-dimensional groundwater modeling. *Water Resources Research*, 20 (7): pp.1003-1020.

Holden, H., Øksendal, B., Uboe,J., & Zhang, T., (1996). *Stochastic partial differential equations*, Birkhauser, Boston.

Hong, Y-S. , & Rosen, M.R., (2001). Intelligent characterisation and diagnosis of the groundwater quality in an urban fractured-rock aquifer using an artificial neural network. *Urban Water*, 3 (3), pp.193-204.

Huang, K., Van Genuchten, M.T., & Zhang, R., (1996a). Exact solution for one-dimensional transport with asymptotic scale dependent dispersion. *Applied Mathematical Modelling*, 20 (4), pp.298-308.

Huang, K., Toride, N., & Van Genuchten, M.T., (1996b). Experimental investigation of solute transport in large, homogeneous heterogeneous, saturated soil columns. *International Journal of Rock Mechanics and Mining Sciences*, 33 (6), 249A.

Islam, S., & Kothari, R., (2000). Artificial neural networks in remote sensing of hydrologic processes. *Journal of Hydrologic Engineering*, 5 (2), pp.138-144.

Jazwinski, A.H., (1970). *Stochastic processes and filtering theory*. New York: Academic Press.

Johnson, V.M., & Rogers, L.L., (2000). Accuracy of neural network approximators in simulation-optimization. *Journal of Water Resources Planning and Management*, 126 (2), pp.48-56.

Kaski, S., Kangas, J., & Kohonen, T., (1998). Bibliography of Self-Organizing Map (SOM) Papers: 1981-1997. *Neural Computing Surveys*, 1, pp.102-350.

Keidser, A., & Rosbjerg, D.,(1991). A comparison of four inverse approaches to groundwater flow and transport parameter identification. *Water Resources Research*, 27 (9), pp.2219-2232.

Keizer, J., (1987). *Statistical thermodynamics of nonequilibrium processes*. Springer-Verlag, New York.

Kerns, W.R., (1977). Public policy on ground water protection, in *Proceedings of a National Conference*, Virginia Polytechnic Institute and State University, 13-16 April 1977. Blacksburg, Virginia: USA.

Kitanidis, P., & Vomvoris, E.G., (1983). A geostatistical approach to the problem of groundwater modelling (steady state) and one-dimensional simulation. *Water Resources Research*, 19 (3), pp.677-690.

Kitanidis, P.K., (1985). Prior information in the geostatistical approach. In C. T. Harry (Eds) *proceedings of the special conference on Computer Application in Water Resources*, Buffalo, N.J., June 10-12, 1985. N.J: ASCE.

Kitanidis, P.K., (1997). *Introduction to Geostatistics – application in hydrogeology*. Cambridge : University press.

Klebaner, F.C., (1998). *Introduction to stochastic calculus with applications*. Springer-Verlag, New York.

Kleinecke, D.S., (1971). Use of linear programming for estimating geohydrologic parameters of groundwater basins. *Water Resources Research*, 7 (2), pp.367-375.

Klenk, I.D., & Grathwohl, P., (2002). Transverse vertical dispersion in groundwater and the capillary fringe. *Journal of Contaminant Hydrology*, 58 (1-2), pp. 111-128.

Klotz, D., Seiler, K.-P., Moser, H., & Neumaier, F., (1980). Dispersivity and velocity relationship from laboratory and field experiments. *Journal of Hydrology*, 45 (1/2), pp.169-184.

Kloeden, P.E., Platen, E., & Schurz, Z., (1997). *Numerical solution of SDE through computer experiments*. Springer, Berlin; New York.

Kohonen, T., (1982). Self-organized formation of topologically correct feature maps. *Biological Cybernetics*, 43, pp. 59-69.

Kohonen, T., (1990). The Self-Organizing Map. In Proceeding of the IEEE, 78(9), pp.1464-1480.

Koutsoyiannis, D., (1999). Optimal decomposition of covariance matrices for multivariate stochastic models in hydrology. *Water Resources Research*, 35 (4), pp.1219-1229.

Koutsoyiannis, D., (2000). A generalized mathematical framework for stochastic simulation and forecast of hydrologic time series. *Water Resources Research*, 36 (6), pp.1519-1533.

Kruseman, G.P. , & De. Ridder, N.A., (1970). *Analysis and evaluation of pumping test data*. International Institute Land Reclamation Improvement Bulletin, 200(11).

Kubrusly, C.S., (1977). Distributed parameter system identification a survey. *International journal of control*, 26 (4), pp.509-535.

Kuiper, L.K., (1986). A comparison of several methods for the solution of the inverse problem in two-dimensional steady state groundwater flow modelling. *Water Resources Research*, 22 (5), pp.705-714.

Kulasiri, D., (1997). *Computational modelling of solute transport using stochastic partial differential equations – A report to Lincoln Environment Ltd*. Centre for Computing and Biometrics, Lincoln University, New Zealand.

Kulasiri, D., & Richards, S., (2008). Investigation of a stochastic model for multiscale dispersion in porous media. *Journal of Porous Media. 11*(6), pp.507-524.

Kulasiri, D., & Verwoerd, W., (2002). *Stochastic Dynamics: Modeling Solute Transport in Porous Media*, North-Holland Series in Applied Mathematics and Mechanics, vol 44. Amsterdam: Elsevier Science Ltd.

Kulasiri, D., & Verwoerd, W., (1999). A stochastic model for solute transport in porous media: mathematical basis and computational solution, *Proc. MODSIM 1999 Inter. Congress on Modelling and Simulation*, 1, pp.31-36.

Kutoyants, Yu. A., (1984). *Parameter estimation for stochastic processes*. Berlin : Herderman Verlag.

Lee, D.R., Cherry, J.A., & Pickens, J.F., (1980). Groundwater transport of a salt tracer through a sandy lakebed. *Limonology and Oceanograpgy*, 25 (1), 45-61.

Leeuwen, M.V., Butler, A.P., Te Stroet, B.M., & Tompkins, J.A., (2000). Stochastic determination of well capture zones conditioned on regular grids of transmissivity. *Water Resources Research*, 36 (4), pp.949-958.

Lipster, R.S., & Shirayev, A.N., (1977). *Statistics of random processes: Part I. General theory.* N.Y.: Springer.

Lindsay, J. B., Shang, J.Q., & Rowe, R.K., (2002). Using Complex Permittivity and Artificial Neural Networks for Contaminant Prediction. *Journal of Environmental Engineering*, 128 (8), pp.740-747.

Lischeid, G., (2001). Investigating short-term dynamics and long-term trends of SO4 in the runoff of a forested catchment using artificial neural networks. *Journal of Hydrology*, 243 (1-2), pp.31-42.

Loll, P., & Moldrup, P., (2000). Stochastic analysis of field-scale pesticide leaching risk as influenced by spatial variability in physical and biochemical parameters. *Water Resources Research*, 36 (4), pp.959-970.

Lorenc, A.C., (1986). Analysis methods for numerical weather prediction. *Quarterly journal of the Royal Meteorological Society*, 112, pp.1177-1194.

Maier, H.R., & Dandy, G.C., (1998). The effect of internal parameters and geometry on the performance of back-propagation neural networks: an empirical study. *Environmental Modelling & Software*, 13, pp.193-209.

Maier, H.R., & Dandy, G.C., (2000). Neural networks for the prediction and forecasting of water resources variables: a review of modelling issues and applications. *Environmental Modelling & Software*, 15, pp.101-124.

Maren, A., C Harston,., & Pap, R., (1990). *Handbook of neural computing applications.* California: Academic Press.

McLaughlin, D., (1975). *Investigation of alternative procedures for estimating ground-water basin parameters,* Water Resources Engineering. California: Walnut Creek.

McLaughlin, D., & Townley, L.R., (1996). A reassessment of the groundwater inverse problem. *Water Resources Research*, 32 (5), pp.1311-1161.

McMillan, W.D., (1966). *Theoretical analysis of groundwater basin operations.* Water Resour. Center Contrib., 114: University of California, Berkerly, 167.

Merritt, W.F., Pickens, J.F., & Allison,G.B., (1979). Study of transport in unsaturated sands using radioactive tracers. In P. J. Barry (Eds.). *Second report on Hydrological and geo-chemical studies in the Perch Lake Basin*, pp. 155-164.

Minns, A.W., & Hall, M.J., (1996). Artificial neural networks as rainfall-runoff models. *Hydrological Sciences Journal*, 41 (3), pp.399-417.

Miralles-Wilhelm, F., & Gelhar, L.W., (1996). Stochastic analysis of sorption macrokinetics in heterogeneous aquifers. *Water Resources Research*, 32 (6), pp. 1541-1550.

Morshed, J., & Kaluarachchi, J.J., (1998). Application of artificial neural network and generic algorithm in flow and transport simulations. *Advances in Water Resources*, 22 (2),pp.145-158.

Morton, K.W., & D.F. Mayers., (1994). *Numerical Solution of Partial Differential Equations.* Cambridge: Cambridge University Press.

Mukhopadhyay, A., (1999). Spatial estimation of transmissivity using artificial neural network. *Ground Water*, 37 (3), pp.458-464.

Nielsen, J.N., Madsen, H., & Young, P.C., (2000). Annual Reviews in Control **24**, 83.

Neuman, S.P., Winter, C.L., & Neuman, C.N., (1987). Stochastic theory of field scale Fickian dispersion in anisotropic porous media. *Water Resources Research*, 23 (3), pp.453-466.

Neuman, S.P., (1973). Calibration of distributed parameter groundwater flow models viewed as a multiple-objective decision process under uncertainty. *Water Resources Research*, 9 (4), pp.1006-1021.

Neural Ware., (1998). *Neural Computing: A Technology Handbook for NeuralWorks Professional II/PLUS and NeuralWorks Explorer* (324 pp). USA: Aspen Technology Inc.

Oakes, D.B., & Edworthy, D.J., (1977). Field measurements of dispersion coefficients in the United Kingdom. In groundwater quality, measurement, prediction and protection, *Water Research Centre*, England, pp.327-340.

Ogata, A., (1970). Theory of dispersion in granular medium. *U. S. Geological survey professional paper*, No.411-I.

Ogata, A., & Bank, R.B., (1961). A solution of the differential equation of longitudinal dispersion in porous media. *USGS, Professional paper*, No. 411-A.

Øksendal, B., (1998). *Stochastic Differential Equations*. Berlin: Springer Verlag.

Ottinger, H.C., (1996). *Stochastic processes in polymeric fluids: tools and examples for developing simulation algorithms*. Springer, Berlin; New York.

Painter, S., (1996). Stochastic interpolation of aquifer properties using fractional Levy motion. *Water Resources Research*, 32 (5), pp.1323-1332.

Painter, S., & Cvetkovic, V., (2001). Stochastic analysis of early tracer arrival in a segmented fracture pathway. *Water Resources Research*, 37 (6), pp. 1669-1680.

Peaudecef, P., & Sauty, J.P., (1978). Application of a mathematical model to the characterization of dispersion effects of groundwater quality. *Progress of Water Technology*, 10 (5/6), pp.443-454.

Pickens, J.F., & Grisak, G.E., (1981). Scale-dependent dispersion in a stratified granular aquifer. *Water Resources Research*, 17 (4), pp.1191-1211.

Polis, M.P., (1982). The distributed system parameter identification problem: A survey of recent results. *In 3rd Symposium of Control of Distributed Systems*, Toulouse: France, pp.45-58.

Press, W.H., Teukolsky, S.A., Vetterling, W.T., & Flannery, B.P., (1992). *Numerical recipes in C, The art of scientific computing - second edition*. Cambridge: University Press.

RamaRao, B.S, LaVenue, A.M., De Marsily, G., & Marietta, M.G., (1995). Pilot point methodology for automated calibration of an ensemble of conditionally simulated transmissivity fields, 1, Theory and computational experiments. *Water Resources Research*, 31(3), pp.475-493.

Ranjithan, S., Eheart, J.W., & Garrett Jr, J.H., (1993). Neural network-based screening for groundwater reclamation under uncertainty. *Water Resources Research*, 29 (3), pp.563-574.

Rashidi, M., Peurrung, L., Thompson, A.F.B., & Kulp, T.J., (1996). Experimental analysis of pore-scale flow and transport in porous media. *Advances in Water Resources*, 19 (3), pp.163 - 180.

Rogers, L.L., & Dowla, F.U., (1994). Optimization of groundwater remdiation using artificial neural networks with parallel solute transport modeling. *Water Resources Research*, 30 (2), pp.457-481.

Rogers, L.L., Dowla, F.U., & Johnson, V.M., (1995). Optimal field-scale groundwater remediation using neural networks and the genetic algorithm. *Environmental Science and Technology*, 29 (5), pp.1145-1155.

Rojas, R., (1996). *Neural Networks: A Systematic Introduction*. Berlin: Springer-Verlag.

Rajanayaka, C., & Kulasiri, D., (2001). Investigation of a parameter estimation method for contaminant transport in aquifers. *Journal of Hydroinformatics*, 3(4), pp.203-213.

Rumelhart, D.E., McClelland, J.L., & University of California San Diego PDP Research Group, (1986). *Parallel distributed processing : explorations in the microstructure of cognition* . MIT Press, Cambridge, Mass..

Ronald Gallant, A, & Tauchen, G., (1999). *Journal of Econometrics*, 92, pp.149.

Rashidi, M., Peurrung, L., Thompson, A.F.B., & Kulp, T.L., (1996). Experimental analysis of pore-scale flow and transport in porous media. *Adv. Water Resour.*, 19, pp.163-180.

Ripley, B.D., (1996). *Pattern recognition and neural networks*. Cambridge University Press, Cambridge ; New York.

Rubin, Y., & Dagan, G., (1992). A note on head and velocity covariances in three-dimensioanl flow through heterogeneous anisotropic porous media. *Water Resources Research*, 28 (5), pp.1463-1470.

Rudnitskaya, A., Ehlert, A., Legin, A., Vlasov, Y., & Büttgenbach, S., (2001). Multisensor system on the basis of an array of non-specific chemical sensors and artificial neural networks for determination of inorganic pollutants in a model groundwater. *Talanta*, 55 (2), pp.425-431.

Rudraiah, N., Siddheshwar, P.G., Pal, D., & Vortmeyer, D., (1988). Non-Darcian Effects on Transient Dispersion in Porous Media. *Proc. ASME Int. Symp.* HTD 96, pp.623-628.

Rumelhart, D.E., McClelland, J.L., & PDP Research Group. (1986). *Parallel distributed processing: Explorations in the microstructure of cognition.* Vol. 1. Cambridge: MIT Press.

Sagar, B., & Kisiel, C.C., (1972). Limits of deterministic predictability of saturated flow equations. In Proceedings of the second symposium on fundamentals of transport phenomena in porous media, vol 1, *international association of hydraulic research*, 1972. Guelph: Canada, pp.194-205.

Samarasinghe, S., (2006). *Neural Networks for Applied Sciences and Engineering: From fundamentals to Complex Pattern Recognition*. Taylor and Franscis Group, USA.

Sarle, W.S., (1994). Neural networks and statistical models. *In Proc. 19th Annual SAS Users Group International Conference*, April 1994, pp. 1538-1550.

Sarma, P.B.S., ; & Immaraj, A.,(1990). Estimation of aquifer parameters through identification problem. *Hydrology Journal*, 113 (1).

Scarlatos, P.D. (2001). Computer modeling of fecal coliform contamination of an urban estuarine system. *Water Science and Technology: a Journal of the International Association on Water Pollution Research*, 44 (7), pp.9-16.

Scheibe, T., & Yabusaki, S., (1998). Scaling of flow and transport behavior in heterogeneous groundwater systems. *Advances in Water Resources*, 22 (3), pp.223-238.

Spitz, K., & Moreno, J., (1996). *A practical guide to groundwater and solute transport modelling.* New Jersey: Wiley-Interscienc.

Sudicky, E.A., & Cherry, J.A., (1979). Field observations of tracer dispersion under natural flow conditions in an unconfined sandy aquifer. *Water Quality Research Journal of Canada*, 14, pp.1-17.

Sun, N.Z., (1994). *Inverse Problems in Groundwater Modelling*. London: Kluwer Academic Publishers.

Sun, N.Z., & Yeh, W.W.G., (1992). A stochastic inverse solution for transient groundwater flow: Parameter identification and reliability analysis. *Water Resources Research*, 28 (12), pp.3269-3280.

Taylor, G., (1953). Dispersion of soluble matter in solvent flowing through a tube. *Proc. Roy. Soc. Lond*, A. 219, pp.186-203.

Theis, C.V., (1962). *Notes on dispersion I fluid flow by geologic features*. In J. M Morgan, D. K Kamison and J. D. Stevenson (Eds.). Proceedings of conference on ground disposal of radioactive wastes. Chalk River, Ont., Canada.

Theis, C.V., (1963). Hydrologic phenomena affecting the use of tracers in timing ground water flow. *Radioisotopes in Hydrology*, pp.193-206.

Thompson, A.F.B., & Gray, W.G., (1986). A second-order approach for the modelling of dispersive transport in porous media, 1. Theoretical development. *Water Resource Res.*, 22(5), pp. 591-600.

Timmer, J., (2001). *Chaos*. Solitons & Fractals 11, 2571.

Timothy, W.E.H., Krumbein, W.C., Irma, W., & Beckman, W.A. (Jr)., (1965). *A surface fitting program for areally distributed data from the earth sciences and remote sensing*. Contractor report. NASA.

Towell, G.G., Craven, M.K., & Shavlik, J.W., (1991). Constructive induction in knowledge-based neural networks. *In proceedings of the 8th International Workshop on Machine Learning*, Morgan Kaufman, San Mateo, pp.213-217.

Triola, M.F., (2004). *Elementary statistics*. Pearson/Addison-Wesley, Boston.

Unny. T.E., (1989). Stochastic Partial Differential Equations in Ground Water Hydrology – Part 1. *Journal Hydrology and Hydraulics*; 3, pp.135-153.

Unny, T.E., (1985). Stochastic partial differential equations in groundwater hydrology. Part 1. Stochastic Hydrol. *Hydraul.*, 3, pp.135 – 153.

Vanderborght, J., & Vereecken, H., (2002). Estimation of local scale dispersion from local breakthrough curves during a tracer test in a heterogeneous aquifer: the Lagrangian approach. *Journal of Contaminant Hydrology*, 54 (1-2), pp.141-171.

Walton, W.C., (1979). Progress in analytical groundwater modelling. *Journal of hydrology*, 43, pp.149-159.

Wang, H.F., & Anderson, M.P., (1982). *Introduction to groundwater modelling*. USA: W.H. Freeman.

Warren, J.E., & Price, H.S., (1961). Flow in heterogeneous porous media. *Society of Petrol Engineering Journal*, 1, pp.153-169.

Watts, D.G., (1994). *The Canadian Journal of Chemical Engineering* **72**, 701.

Welty, C., & Gelhar, L.W. ,(1992). Simulation of large-scale transport of variable density and viscosity fluids using a stochastic mean model. *Water Resources Research*, 28 (3), pp.815-827.

Yang, J., Zhang , R., Wu, J., & Allen, M.B., (1996). Stochastic analysis of adsorbing solute transport in two dimensional unsaturated soils. *Water Resources Research*, 32 (9), pp.2747-2756.

Yeh, W.W-G., (1986). Review of parameter identification procedures in groundwater hydrology: The inverse problem. *Water Resources Research*, 22 (2), pp.95-108.

Young. N., (1988). *An introduction to Hilbert space*. Cambridge: Cambridge University Press.

Zhang, D., & Sun, A.Y., (2000). Stochastic analysis of transient saturated flow through heterogeneous fractured porous media: A double-permeability approach. *Water Resources Research*, 36 (4), pp.865-874.

Zheng, C., & Bennett, G.D., (1995). *Applied contaminant transport modelling*. New York: Van Nostrand Reinhold.

Zhu, A.X., (2000). Mapping soil landscape as spatial continua: The neural network approach. *Water Resources Research*, 36 (3), pp.663-677.

Zimmerman, D.A., Marsily, G. de., Gotway, C.A., Marietta, M.G., Axness, C.L., & Beauheim, R.L., (1998). A comparison of seven geostatistical based inverse approaches to estimate transmissivities for modelling advective transport by groundwater flow. *Water Resources Research*, 34 (6), pp.1373-1413.

Index